D1560450

Principles of Comparative Psychology

Gary Greenberg
Wichita State University

Maury M. Haraway
University of Louisiana, Monroe

Allyn and Bacon

Boston ■ London ■ Toronto ■ Sydney ■ Tokyo ■ Singapore

To our teachers, N. H. Pronko and John B. Wolfe

Executive Editor: *Carolyn Merrill*
Series Editorial Assistant: *Lara Zeises*
Senior Marketing Manager: *Caroline Croley*
Editorial-Production Service: *Omegatype Typography, Inc.*
Composition and Prepress Buyer: *Linda Cox*
Manufacturing Buyer: *Joanne Sweeney*
Cover Administrator: *Kristina Mose-Libon*
Electronic Composition: *Omegatype Typography, Inc.*

Library of Congress Cataloging-in-Publication Data

Greenberg, Gary.
    Principles of comparative psychology / Gary Greenberg, Maury M. Haraway.
    p. cm.
    Includes bibliographical references and index.
    ISBN 0-205-28014-5
    1. Pyschology, Comparative.   I. Haraway, Maury M.   II. Title.
BF671 .G74 2002
156—dc21

                2001022697

CONTENTS

FOREWORD

DUANE M. RUMBAUGH
Regents' Professor of Psychology and Biology (Emeritus)
Georgia State University

The field of comparative psychology is basic to all fields of general psychology. Whether one is interested in genetics, maturation, the emergence of cognition and intelligence, social behavior, organizational psychology, or, perhaps most encompassing of all, the arena of social psychology, government, and international relations, the field of comparative psychology has a great deal to offer. Comparative psychology has generated a great mass of studies and perspectives. It has a long affirmed relationship with the field of animal behavior.

Sadly, humans have been taught across generations that somehow they are different from animals, that they are not animals. That perspective is without foundation, without fact to defend it. We might want to believe that we are superior to animals in every manner, that we alone have language, that we alone suffer pain, have a sense of time, can count, and have a sense of aesthetics. Not so! We are very much an animal form, one that is probably no more distinctive in attributes and potentials than is any other animal form, and specifically a primate form, except for the obvious that we are more powerful in environmental effect than any other and, so to speak, rule the world.

That said, comparative psychology offers psychology and the world of science and politics a framework and a set of constructive principles of fundamental value to each of us. As a field, it has been subject to extreme attack and controversy. All of that reflects the fact that it is the crucible of human thought and politics. Yet, comparative psychology not only survives but also is beginning, once again, to thrive. It has its own imperative as a science: Animal/human forms compel comparison and contrast in every dimension.

It is timely that we have new scholarly efforts, new texts brought to the field of comparative psychology in response to its resurgence. In this book by Greenberg and Haraway, we find a logical organization of topics that are presented with the strength of current empirical research. The text very ably carries forward the traditions and traditional principles of the field. It also incorporates the authors' sustaining interest in how we can best account for the seeming trend in evolution toward complexity of structure and function. Research and theory from the life sciences are drawn on throughout the text. The text is well referenced and remarkably current. Perhaps the defining feature of the book is its adherence to a uniform theoretical framework throughout, a framework characterized by the newly emerging sciences of dynamic systems and complexity and the important organizing principle of integrative levels.

From the perspective of the professor, the text will prove to be a good choice for challenging the intellects of both upper-division and graduate students. The text will provide students with information that they need to know and also will provide for the professor provocative ideas to explore with them in the unceasing attempt to get students to read and to think critically, yet constructively.

As stated earlier, comparative psychology has its own imperative that will sustain its life. Although the name of the field is subject to modification, its basic tenets will never die. Thanks to the authors of this book, the field has a new champion in their scholarship and this text.

PREFACE

As psychology enters the twenty-first century, our young scientific discipline finds itself at a watershed. Over the last several decades, developments in molecular genetics, developmental and comparative embryology, and neuroscience have greatly enhanced our understanding of how biology is related to behavior. Moreover, significant advances in conceptual and theoretical frameworks have allowed the beginning of a synthesis of biological factors with interpersonal factors and social ecology. Coupling these theoretical advances with increased computing power and powerful analytic methodologies ranging from structural equations to nonlinear dynamics and complex systems theory has resulted in a psychology at the precipice of a major paradigm shift.

Our discipline is among the oldest in psychology—Romanes, a founder of the discipline, was a contemporary of Wundt's. Yet we continue to face great odds in the effort to preserve our identity. Obituaries for comparative psychology began appearing in 1969 with the charge by some that the discipline was unfocused, was not truly comparative, and was misguided in its adherence to old notions such as the evolutionary scale. We hope this book will provide answers to each of these challenges in the process of achieving its main goal of portraying the full range and rich detail of our field. This book looks to the future of comparative psychology in the twenty-first century. We differ from some others in being optimistic about the future success and development of our discipline as we enter the new millennium.

We understand comparative psychology to be the study of the evolution and development of behavior in all organisms. We conceive the field broadly, as the study of origins of *all* behavior. Thus, we see it as a general psychology that certainly includes—but is by no means confined to—the study of intelligence and cognitive processes. These latter issues remain an important part of comparative psychology but need not be seen as its major focus.

This book is different from other recent textbooks in the field in that it attempts to present a unified theoretical perspective throughout—a single perspective from which we attempt to understand the origins of all behaviors of all animal species. The theoretical ideas that form the foundation of the position we present here are drawn from the work of two great comparative psychologists of the early to mid-twentieth century: Zing-Yang Kuo and T. C. Schneirla, both of whom were devoted to the development of a unified theoretical position for comparative psychology. Kuo and Schneirla, and the many researchers they influenced, worked from a perspective that denied single-factor hereditary control of behavior in favor of a developmental and contextual perspective that is only now receiving widespread appreciation within the discipline.

Three themes are central to the theoretical position developed in this book. These are (1) the organizing principle of integrative levels, (2) the idea that there is a tendency toward increased biological and behavioral complexity with recency of species appearance in evolutionary advance, and (3) the contextual nature of determination of behavioral events. We have adopted a developmental perspective in which behavior is understood to be the result of a fusion of biological and psychosocial factors. Development is seen as a probabilistic outcome of a myriad of influences rather than as a product of preprogrammed genetic and biochemical causes. Nonlinear dynamic systems theory provides a theoretical language that is consistent with the description of behavioral development we wish to achieve here.

Three additional features throughout the book distinguish it to a greater or lesser degree from recent treatments of the same subject. First, we give particular recognition to some of the unique problems of our discipline in carrying out a careful application of scientific method to its chosen subject matter of mind and behavior. Second, we provide a large amount of detailed description of behavior patterns that we hope will be sufficient to evoke appreciation of the subtlety and intricacy of responses by which various species confront universal requirements for survival and reproductive success. Third, we undertake explicit articulation of major processes by which species-typical behavior patterns become flexible and adjustable to the often variable environmental conditions affecting their functional success at any given time.

We prepared this book primarily as a text for use in advanced undergraduate courses in comparative psychology and animal behavior, but we recommend it as well for use in graduate courses and by professionals who wish to pursue a psychobiological understanding of behavior from a perspective other than those currently popular in the disciplines of evolutionary psychology and sociobiology.

Acknowledgments

Writing a book such as this is never solely the work of the authors. The book we completed reflects the thoughtful input and help of several people. We acknowledge the critical reading of early chapters of the book by two former doctoral students, Emily Weiss and Ty Partridge, now pursuing successful careers of their own. The secretarial support provided by Marci Nelson was exceedingly helpful to us. Wichita State University provided one of the authors (GG) a summer research grant to allow him to devote himself full time to working on the manuscript. The administrations of Wichita State University and the University of Louisiana, Monroe, provided crucial support to us during our careers at those institutions. We are especially appreciative of the critical input provided by Duane Rumbaugh. The book was greatly improved by his many helpful suggestions. Our work on an earlier project, *Comparatve Psychology: A Handbook* (Greenberg & Haraway, 1998), introduced us to the current research in many areas of the field we were ourselves somewhat unfamiliar with. We are appreciative of the over one hundred authors we worked with on that book for fully revealing to us the breadth and scope of contemporary comparative psychology. Carolyn Merrill, our editor at Allyn and Bacon, helped us chart a successful course through the writing process. The book was greatly improved by her suggestions as well as those of the reviewers of our manuscript: Charles I. Abramson, Oklahoma State University;

Elaine Baker, Marshall University; Douglas Candland, Bucknell University; Jay E. Gould, University of West Florida; Raymond Kesner, University of Utah; Adrienne Lee, New Mexico State University; Celia L. Moore, University of Massachusetts, Boston; German Torres, State University of New York at Buffalo; Jeannette P. Ward, University of Memphis; and David A. Washburn, Georgia State University.

Finally we acknowledge the important moral and social support provided by our wives Cathy Haraway and Patty Cavan Greenberg.

CHAPTER

1

Introduction to the Field

What Is Comparative Psychology?

Comparative psychology often has been identified as the study of animal behavior. It is that, but it is also much more. In many respects the discipline is a general psychology, because comparative psychologists are searching for principles that apply to the behavior of all animals, including humans. We define **comparative psychology** as the study of the evolution and development of animal behavior. Its goal is to develop general principles that apply to the origins of all behavior in all animals.

Comparative psychology also speaks to a further interest that conveys both esthetic and philosophical, as well as scientific, benefits. In one of the most famous remarks attributed to him, Socrates advised: "Know thyself." We find this to be worthy advice. We do desire to know ourselves, as individuals and as a species, but can we define ourselves fully by considering our own species in isolation? Or must we also see ourselves as a part of the great natural process of this universe, and of this planet, our home? Comparative psychology provokes comparison of ourselves—our human characteristics of behavior—to other species across the broad array of the animal series. Such comparisons can reveal both the similarities we share with other life forms and the characteristics that distinguish us particularly and make us unique among the entire system of life.

Some may recognize that the focus of our definition of the field makes our discipline sound very similar to those of **ethology, sociobiology,** and **evolutionary psychology.** Indeed, we do share similarities with those fields of study. However, it is worth pointing out that the first two of these sciences are biological disciplines and that all three are based on attempts to *reduce* the determination of animal and human behavior characteristics to features of biological and physiological makeup deriving from genetics. **Reductionistic thinking** has a long history in science, but we believe it has now become clear that holistic, rather than reductionistic, thinking provides for more accurate and complete understanding, especially in the behavioral sciences (Peele, 1985; Sheldrake, 1995). In any case, we see a clear distinction between comparative psychology and other related disciplines that are similar to it. For us, psychology is qualitatively different from biology, although descended from it. This is to be a book about principles, and among the most important organizing principles for us is that the universe is hierarchically ordered (Rollo, 1994). In keeping with this principle, we can organize all the sciences along levels of increasing complexity, placing mathematics, physics, and chemistry at the bottom of this hierarchy; the biological sciences in the middle; and psychology, sociology, and anthropology at the top (Feibleman, 1954; Greenberg, 1988). Although each of these sciences follows, or emerges, from preceding disciplines, all have their own unique explanatory principles, laws, and theories. This approach is fundamental in science and is labeled the principle of **integrative levels,** or levels of organization (Feibleman, 1954; Novikoff, 1945). We introduce this principle here because it will play a crucial role in the chapters that follow. It is a cornerstone of the theoretical perspective on which this book is based.

The study of animal behavior already was a part of psychological tradition when Wundt founded psychology as an independent scientific discipline in 1879. Following Wundt's initial success, psychology was established as a science largely by the observational study of behavior in both human and nonhuman subjects. The study of animal behavior has been of critical importance in establishing general principles of behavior as well as in providing models of human behavior. Many principles of behavior presented in current textbooks of general psychology were demonstrated first in animal experiments (Domjan & Purdy, 1996). As comparative psychologists, however, our interests go beyond the use of animals as models of human behavior. They extend to the full range of evolutionary development of behavior, the full variety of behavior principles, the full range of behavioral complexity, and the full array of processes and systems by which behavior achieves organization.

No one is capable of envisioning in detail the evolution of behavior characteristics from simple to more and more complex species across the entire range of the animal series. Even so, we may be certain that the more complex species, including ourselves, proceeded from the biological and behavioral bases established by their ancestors and retained many similar characteristics to those of the species from which they arose. This relationship means that the characteristics of earlier established species are relevant to the understanding of behavior in all species that evolved later and establishes the basis of Romanes's proposal of a **continuum of mind** across the animal series. As we shall see shortly, Romanes's proposal forms an important part of the foundation for the study of comparative psychology.

A Dynamic Systems Approach

We readily acknowledge the major role of biology in behavior, but we intend to introduce principles here that are fundamentally different from those of biology, principles that are psychological in nature. In this book, we will not allude to genetic determinism, nor to other biological ideas, as explanatory principles. Rather, a fundamental organizing theme of the book will be **dynamic systems theory** (Lewin, 1992; Michel & Moore, 1995), an organizing paradigm that emphasizes the importance of *relations* between events. From a dynamic systems perspective, organisms are not simply collections of organs and other parts, but rather their parts are interdependent, regulating one another (Sherrington, 1906). Furthermore, organisms are not separate from or independent of their environments, but rather are *fused* with them. In this view, an organism and its environment are seen as being two parts of an "organismic whole." This important way of looking at organisms has a long history in modern psychology (Bertalanffy, 1933; Kantor, 1959; Lerner, 1998), and we will adopt a similar position in this book.

Factors Involved in the Genesis of Behavior Characteristics

The dynamic systems approach taken here views psychology not so much as a biological science but as a **biosocial science.** This approach resolves the nature–nurture controversy by recognizing that we are psychosocial as well as biological beings and that both nature and nurture play crucial roles in our behavior. Accordingly, we understand behavior to be a result of a dynamic interplay among the following five sets of factors (Seay & Gottfried, 1978).

Phylogenetic Set

Here we refer to an organism's evolutionary status—that is to say, what the organism is as a species. The role of the **phylogenetic set** of factors that we wish to develop in this book is embodied in Kuo's (1967) principle of **behavioral potentials,** which suggests that each species is endowed with the potential to behave in species-typical ways (Haraway & Maples, 1998a). One might say that "fish gotta swim, birds gotta fly...." Of course, there is no guarantee that those potentials will be actualized. As Montagu (1952/1962) said, "The wonderful thing about a baby...is its promise" (p. 17), suggesting that we are born *Homo sapiens,* but we have to develop into fully formed human beings, and there may be important variations in the degree to which different individuals accomplish this development. Another way of addressing this idea is to say that our human nature is not a direct product of our biology, but rather is a set of characteristics we acquire, or develop, during the course of our growth. The same can be said of other species.

Individual Set

The **individual set** of factors refers to the uniqueness of each individual organism and how that uniqueness influences its behavioral outcomes. A major factor involved here is the particular version of its species genetics that a given individual animal possesses. One animal may be more or less sensitive to sounds or may have a developmental abnormality that limits its interactions with its world. It may be larger or smaller than most other members of its species, or it may be faster or slower, and so on. This set of factors recognizes the contribution of the individual's unique genotype and how that genotype, in dynamic interaction with contextual influences, may render it a different-behaving creature from all others.

Ontogenetic Set

The **ontogenetic set** of factors addresses the developmental history of an organism, from the moment of its conception to its death. Included here is biological maturation, or the process of growth that brings the various tissues, organs, and other parts of the organism to full functional development. We underscore the *probabilistic* nature of this ontogeny. Development is always a matter of probability. Nothing in development, whether physiological or behavioral development, is guaranteed by the genes; nothing is preformed or preordained (Gottlieb, 1992; Nieuwkoop, Johnen, & Albers, 1985). In considering the developmental process, it is crucial to note that an organism's developmental status at any given time profoundly affects the forms of behavior it exhibits and the ways in which it reacts to stimuli.

Experiential Set

The multitude of experiences an organism accrues throughout its life does much to direct the future course of its development (Lerner & Busch-Rossnagel, 1981). We adopt Schneirla's (1972/1957) understanding of *experience* to mean "all stimulative effects upon the organism through its life history..." (p. 269). Kantor (1959) referred to this **experiential set** as the "reactional biography" (RB), literally a description of the organism in terms of its behavioral history. The reactional biography begins at conception and continues to be built up until the organism's death. Every stimulus affects the organism and changes it, although some stimulation has much more profound and obvious effects than others. Learning, for example, is an important force in changing behavior, but it is nothing more than the product of a special set of experiences.

Cultural Set

Every organism exists, or indeed is embedded, in an environment that exerts a considerable influence on its biological and behavioral development. This influence, or **cultural set,** is most obvious in humans, who have developed outstanding contextual influences such as religion, morality, social institutions, and dietary practices, all of which significantly affect the behavioral repertoire. The situation is similar, although less elaborate and complex, for other animals. Among many species, different populations may inhabit somewhat different environments, eat different foods, and live in different types of social groups. The importance of the cultural, or contextual, basis of development was recognized early along by the ethologist Jacob von Uexkull (1864–1944), who termed the behavioral environment of an animal its *Umwelt*, or its sensory-perceptual world.

Historical Context of Comparative Psychology

With the publication of Darwin's *On the Origin of Species* in 1859 and *The Expression of the Emotions in Man and Animals* in 1872, the study of animal behavior was catapulted into a prominence it had never before occupied in the history of academic thought. It now became a key to understanding the creative processes shaping the life of our planet and endowing our own species with its particular characteristics. The British naturalist George John Romanes (1882/1970), a close friend and informal student of

Darwin's, proposed the existence of a gradient of mental processes and intelligence from the simplest animals to man. He strengthened his proposal by a vast collection of anecdotal accounts, or informal stories of clever behavior in dozens of animal species. Although perhaps best known today for the fallacies inherent in his anecdotal method and for his easy assignment of human mental faculties to animals—a practice known as ***anthropomorphism***—Romanes nevertheless succeeded in establishing his idea of a gradient of mental processes across the animal kingdom as a basic premise of early comparative psychology. A quantum improvement in the theoretical analysis of behavior occurred with the 1900 formulation of **Morgan's canon** (Morgan, 1896; Thomas, 1998), a rule prohibiting invocation of higher mental processes to explain behaviors that could be accounted for by processes standing lower in the psychological scale (see Box 1.1).

The successful movement begun by Wundt in 1879 to change psychology from a philosophic into a scientific study took a decisive turn toward the study of animal behavior with the work of Pavlov (1906) and Thorndike (1898) on conditioning and learning, Yerkes's work with the behavior of various species (e.g., 1905, 1928), and Watson's (1913) call for **behaviorism,** which was to be an experimental psychology founded entirely on the study of observable behavior. Over the next several decades, the study of animal behavior in the United States became dominated by the use of animals primarily as models to illustrate general principles of learning and related motivational processes. This study retained fundamental characteristics of comparative psychology in its emphasis on learning as an adaptive process (e.g., Thorndike, 1911; Hull, 1943) and its efforts to establish principles that would apply across a wide variety of species.

Criticisms of comparative psychology came from both within (Beach, 1950; Lockard, 1971) and without (Lorenz, 1950; Tinbergen, 1951) for its restrictions to a narrow range of topics within the experimental study of learning and to the observation of a small number of species, most prominently the single species of the laboratory rat (see Box 1.2). Even during this time, however, quite a number of comparative psychologists with more wide-ranging interests pressed forward with important work. Included in this group were Frank Beach, C. R. Carpenter, Harry Harlow, Z. Y. Kuo, Karl Lashley, Daniel Lehrman, N. R. F. Maier, Henry Nissen, Jay Rosenblatt, T. C. Schneirla, John Paul Scott, Ethel Tobach, J. B. Wolfe, and many others (see Box 1.3).

The discipline of ethology emerged from European zoology in the 1930s, coalescing around the work of Karl von Frisch, Konrad Lorenz, and Niko Tinbergen, together awarded the Nobel Prize for Medicine in 1973 for their pioneering research. In its classical development, ethology centered on the study of instinct and displayed strong preferences for naturalistic field studies and biological explanations of behavior. Comparative psychology, by contrast, was skeptical of the concept of instinct, emphasized the process of behavior development, and leaned much more heavily upon laboratory experimentation. By the mid-1960s, the two disciplines had interacted with and adjusted sufficiently to each other that the sharp differences that had separated them were largely resolved in cooperative and intermingled work. This peacemaking process was furthered greatly by Robert Hinde's important 1966 publication, *Animal Behaviour: A Synthesis of Ethology and Comparative Psychology*. Much mutual respect between the

BOX **1.1**
Clever Hans

One of the most famous animal minds of history was that of Clever Hans, the horse of Herr von Osten of Germany, in the early 1900s. Having been systematically tutored in mathematics and language by his master, Hans solved complex problems of addition and subtraction, multiplication and division, even fractions and square roots, indicating his answers by tapping out the proper numbers with a forefoot. Hans also was able to demonstrate understanding of the German language, either written or spoken, as well as knowledge of the calendar year, by means of foot-tapping techniques devised by his master. His feats of knowledge were truly amazing.

Herr von Osten was convinced that his equine genius was entirely genuine, and he welcomed a suggestion to have Hans evaluated by a committee of experts led by the eminent psychologist Carl Stumpf and including fellow psychologist Oskar Pfungst, a well-known zoologist, a magician, and a circus manager, among others. The investigating committee determined initially that there was no evidence of obvious cues being provided or of any other tricks being used to support Hans's accomplishments. The committee then undertook a systematic study of Hans in search of the sources of his success.

Many of the experiments that followed were carried out by Oskar Pfungst, who also was active in devising many of the tests. Pfungst was praised by Professor Stumpf for his courage in carrying out this work, because Hans was far from a gentle animal. Pfungst had to endure frequent jostling and several painful bites in the course of his duty.

Pfungst discovered that Hans was unable to perform successfully while wearing blinders that prevented him from seeing his master, and that Hans was successful only on occasions when his master knew the answer to the question Hans was asked. Questions written on a small blackboard and presented to Hans were answered correctly if von Osten had read them first but incorrectly if he had not. Consideration was given to the possibility that Hans's answering capabilities might depend less upon his own power of reasoning than upon some sort of telepathy by which von Osten's brain might communicate answers to Hans, perhaps operating through the visual sense.

Then Pfungst began to notice very subtle movements by von Osten that seemed reliably associated with Hans's answering behavior. Eventually it became clear that a slight forward movement of von Osten's head was sufficient to start Hans's tapping and that a slight backward movement of the head or a slight lifting of the eyebrows was sufficient to stop the tapping. These cues were being supplied unintentionally and unawares by von Osten, and they enabled Hans to answer correctly any question to which von Osten knew the answer.

Pfungst found that he himself could control Hans's answering behavior by providing these same subtle cues. To his great surprise, he found he often was unable to keep himself from providing Hans with such cues even on trials when he had determined to provide none. Small wonder that von Osten had been unintentionally providing cues to guide a performance in which he had heavily invested.

Pfungst then undertook the ingenious tactic of placing himself in the horse's place. He had people quiz him with a series of questions to which he tapped out his answers with a foot, as Hans did. He was amazed to find that twenty-three of twenty-five people who tested him supplied unintentional cues sufficient for him to give correct answers even when he didn't know the questions that had been asked.

In the end, Pfungst was able to show that Hans's cleverness could be accounted for by his intensive training in responding appropriately to subtle cues of when to begin tapping and when to stop. His training had included the use of carrots as rewards and was an approximation of what we now call instrumental conditioning. Instrumental conditioning is quite a widespread phenomenon; its understanding does not require the assumption of extraordinary mental powers on the part of animal learners.

Hans, indeed, was quite a clever horse, but his skill rested not upon possession of humanlike intelligence, but upon the comparatively simple principles of instrumental conditioning. Our acceptance of Pfungst's explanation over von Osten's is a fitting application of Morgan's canon: That in the attribution of mental capabilities we must accept the simplest explanation that is available for a given example of behavior. Ironically, von Osten was unable to accept the committee's findings. He remained convinced that Hans possessed internal speech and humanlike intelligence and understanding. When he learned of the direction being taken by the committee's conclusions, von Osten withdrew his cooperation with the investigation and forbade any further experimentation with his famous horse.

Source: Pfungst, 1911/1965.

BOX 1.2

Mutual Criticisms Exchanged between Early Comparative Psychology and Early Ethology

Ethologists found that early comparative psychologists were

- Too focused on a small number of "model" species, most notably, the white Norway rat
- Overly restricted to a small range of study issues centering on the process of learning and motivational processes involved in learning and the performance of learned behavior
- Too restricted to studies done in artificial, experimentally controlled conditions, with too little focus on behavior in natural field conditions

Psychologists found that early ethologists were

- Too easily accepting of concepts such as instinct and fixed-action-pattern, which often carried connotations of animistic explanation, biologically built-in behavior, and single-factor genetic determination
- Too free in the assignment of causal roles to selected independent variables without benefit of sufficiently controlled experimental demonstration

BOX **1.3**
Biographical Sketches of Some Major Figures in the History of CP

Early Europeans
- **George John Romanes (1848–1894),** one of Darwin's young colleagues and friends, made the first important application of Darwinian theory to the study of animal behavior. Romanes believed that the comparison of mental structures by comparative psychologists could be just as scientific as the comparison of bodily structures by comparative anatomists. His reference work for comparing species on levels of intelligence expanded into three volumes: *Animal Intelligence* (1882), *Mental Evolution in Animals* (1885), and *Mental Evolution in Man: Origin of Human Faculty* (1887).

  Romanes was criticized for his use of **anecdotal evidence** to make inferences about the mental life of animals. His harshest critic was also his close friend and the executor of his estate, C. Lloyd Morgan.
- **Conway Lloyd Morgan (1852–1936)** was interested in mental evolution, but critical of the anecdotal method. He emphasized that one must observe animal behavior with an objective, "detached" perspective over long periods of time. His advice for making inferences about behavior based on these observations, known now as *Morgan's canon of interpretation* (discussed fully in the text), is still followed by present-day scientists of animal behavior.

American Beginnings
- **Margaret Floyd Washburn (1871–1939)** published *The Animal Mind: A Textbook of Comparative Psychology* in 1908. In its several editions over the next thirty years, the book became the predominant textbook used in comparative psychology courses in American universities. Washburn was the first woman to receive a doctorate in psychology in the United States. Her book made available in one place the experimental—as opposed to the anecdotal—data on animal intelligence from psychology and physiology on which inferences could be based.
- **Zing-Yang Kuo (1898–1970)** was the first person to complete a Ph.D. with Tolman when his thesis was approved in 1923; however, Kuo had returned to China before the degree was granted, and it was not officially awarded until 1936 when he returned to America. An arch-behaviorist, greatly influenced by John Watson, Kuo entirely rejected the concept of instinct.
- **Robert Mearns Yerkes (1876–1956),** one of William James's most influential students, always thought of himself as a psychobiologist. Yerkes's earliest papers were on the physiology of the nervous system. He then turned to studies of habit formation and problems of instinct. Yerkes worked with a wide variety of species. One of his most important publications was *The Great Apes: A Study of Anthropoid Life* (1929), co-authored, as was much of his work, by his wife, Ada Yerkes. Yerkes led the first major primate research faculty in the United States in Orange Park, Florida. It later became known as the Yerkes Regional Primate Center.
- **Frank Ambrose Beach's (1911–1988)** work on animal reproduction, well represented by his book *Hormones and Behavior* (1948), marked the beginning of the field of behavioral endocrinology. Beach was very concerned with comparative psychology as a discipline and, as Dewsbury (1984) reports, he was considered "the conscience of comparative psychology" (p. 297). Beach's (1950) paper "The Snark Was a Boojum" documented the

decline of a truly comparative psychology in North America as the learning theorists took control. He urged psychologists to adopt a broader perspective in their choice of research topics as well as the species studied. Beach was the first head of the Department of Animal Behavior at the American Museum of Natural History in New York.

- **Calvin Perry Stone (1892–1954)** was one of Karl Lashley's first graduate students. He was interested in development, instinctive behavior, and ecology and urged psychologists "to study instincts as they are related to the subject of behavioral ecology." Stone was editor of the third edition of the well-used book *Comparative Psychology* (1951) and was a productive researcher and teacher whose students included C. Ray Carpenter (1905–1975) and Harry Harlow.
- **Harry Harlow (1905–1981)** is best known for studies of mother–infant interactions in primates. This work was started by chance when pregnant wild-caught rhesus monkey mothers gave birth in the laboratory. Harlow removed the infants to prevent them from catching parasites carried by their mothers. He noticed that these infants displayed abnormal behavior, and he became interested in "the mechanisms through which the love of the infant for the mother develops into the multi-faceted response patterns characterizing love or affection in the adult" (1958, p. 673). His work showed the importance of "contact comfort" for the healthy psychological development of the young animals.

The Michigan Tradition
- **John Frederick Shepard (1881–1965)** was not widely known, even when he was an active researcher, but he is an important figure in the history of comparative psychology. Shepard influenced many students to continue to work in comparative psychology; among those who became well known for their contributions to comparative psychology were Norman Maier and Theodore Schneirla (see the following), and Ray Denny (1918–   ), whose textbooks of comparative psychology were used widely from the 1960s through the 1980s (e.g., Denny & Ratner, 1970; Denny, 1980).
- **Norman Raymond Frederick Maier (1900–1977)** held an NRC Fellowship at Chicago (1929–1931) working with Lashley. With an emphasis on evolution and development, his comparative psychology textbook *Principles of Animal Psychology* (1935), written in collaboration with T. C. Schneirla, who had been a fellow graduate student at Michigan, presented a very different approach to the field than the other texts of the time. Their book is now considered a classic. Maier's own animal research involved studies of problem solving and reasoning in rats.
- **Theodore Christian (Ted) Schneirla (1902–1968)** was Maier's co-author of *Principles of Animal Psychology*. Schneirla taught at New York University (NYU) (1928–1930) and then, following Maier, held an NRC Fellowship at Chicago with Lashley from 1930 to 1931. He returned to teach comparative psychology at NYU and later became associate curator in the Department of Animal Behavior at the American Museum of Natural History. Starting in 1932, Schneirla made numerous field trips to Barro Colorado Island in Gatun Lake, Panama, to work on army ants. There he observed that periods of migration in ant colonies were not innate, but rather related to "changes in morphology and in physiological processes" (Tobach & Aronson, 1970, pp. xiii–iv).

Throughout his career, Schneirla was critical of the concept of instinct, emphasizing instead a close interaction between development and experience at all stages of life. He "viewed the concept of levels as fundamental in all comparative and ontogenetic studies" (Tobach & Aronson, p. xvii). His criticisms of European ethology and its underlying genetic determinism were continued by his many devoted students including Daniel Lehrman and Ethel Tobach.

(continued)

BOX **1.3**   **Continued**

- **Daniel S. Lehrman's (1919–1972)** research involved studies of many species of mammals and birds, particularly the reproductive and social behavior of ring doves. Lehrman's (1953) critique of Konrad Lorenz's instinct theory started an initially rancorous debate between American comparative psychology and European ethology. However, in the long run, this debate did much to resolve the issues separating the two groups and marked the beginning of what would become a cooperative effort in the study of animal behavior.
- **Ethel Tobach (1921–)**, another of Schneirla's adherents, has been a long-time promoter of comparative psychology in the Schneirla tradition. Her important research interests have included susceptibility to TB in relation to behavioral stress; the role of the olfactory system in the behavior of newborn rats; the basis for inking behavior in *Aplysia;* and the relation of serotonin deficiency to taste in fawn-hooded rats. As well as writing and editing many books on comparative psychology, Tobach has attempted to promote comparative psychology around the world through the International Society for Comparative Psychology, which she was instrumental in establishing in 1983.

The Ethologists
- **Konrad Zacharias Lorenz (1903–1989)** was concerned with making careful observations of the motor patterns of various species, in an attempt to find homologies that would permit species classification. This approach is the basis for the field known as ethology, which, in collaboration with his colleague, Niko Tinbergen, Lorenz is credited with founding.

    Lorenz was a theoretician as well as an observer, and it was his theory of instinct that stimulated the harsh criticism of American comparative psychologists such as Lehrman (1953). Lorenz's initial reaction was strong and, to some extent, missed the point. However, as indicated earlier, the debate eventually led to mutual understanding. Lorenz also created considerable controversy with his ideas concerning the innate determination of human aggressive behavior (see, for example, Lorenz, 1966).
- **Nikolaas (Niko) Tinbergen (1907–1988)** spent several months in Altenberg collaborating with Konrad Lorenz in 1937. Dewsbury (1990) has said that if it were necessary to document the birth of the field of ethology, this would be the date. Although Tinbergen was a "curious naturalist," he was also a master experimenter. After making observations in the wild he would develop simple, but elegant, studies to identify both the causal factors and the adaptive function of the behavior patterns observed. His books *The Study of Instinct* (1951) and *Curious Naturalists* (1958) have had wide popular, as well as academic, appeal.

    More conciliatory and tactful than Lorenz, Tinbergen attended international meetings and was able to forge ties with American comparative psychologists, such as Lehrman and Beach, helping to establish a mutual respect between the two groups. When he arrived at Oxford, Tinbergen met the young graduate student, Robert Hinde.
- **Robert A. Hinde (1923–)** would become an effective advocate for ethology. Hinde's (1966) textbook, *Animal Behaviour: A Synthesis of Ethology and Comparative Psychology,* played an important role in bringing about the rapprochement between comparative psychology and ethology.

Source: Adapted from Innis, 1998. Some of the author's original phrasing is included here. A complete listing of publications cited here can be found in Innis, 1998.

(a)

(b)

(c)

FIGURE 1.1 Clockwise from upper left: (a) Zing-Yang Kuo (1898–1970), (b) T. C. Schneirla (1902–1968), and (c) Daniel S. Lehrman (1919–1972), principal champions of the interactionist viewpoint in psychological and behavior development.

two disciplines has taken root and flourished in recent years (e.g., Barnett, 1981). We are gratified by the present spirit of cooperation between these fields and trust they will continue to work closely with each other. At the same time, however, we find that meaningful differences between the two disciplines remain. In this book, we intend to emphasize characteristics of comparative psychology that make it unique among a number of disciplines currently concerned with the study of animal behavior, including ethology, sociobiology, **behavioral ecology,** and evolutionary psychology.

Science and the Study of Animal Behavior

Galileo studied the movement of spheres along inclined planes as a natural phenomenon. Psychology now views the behavior of animals to be just as natural a phenomenon as was the movement of the spheres studied by Galileo; our study of behavior must be as solidly based in observation as was that of the famous Italian physicist. **Observation** is the exclusive basis of fact in science (Chalmers, 1976). Nothing is held to be true except that which is empirically demonstrated. This axiom applies equally to all sciences beyond mathematics. All are founded on observed fact and the study of observable events. The sciences differ in the types of phenomena they focus upon and in the methods they use to make observations, but they are alike in basing their studies on observations.

You may think that observation is a simple task. All one has to do is look. But look at what? When we see an event, what part or parts of it should we attend to, what part should we observe? Every event consists of two essential components: objects and the fields within which those objects exist. It is not even that simple to determine which is object and which is field. This determination usually depends on the question one is asking. One of the founders of ethology, Niko Tinbergen, discussed elsewhere in this chapter, referred to this as the "four whys."

> Consider the question, "Why do birds sit on eggs?" The type of answer you want depends on where you put the emphasis in the question.
>
> > Why do birds sit on *eggs?*—that is, how do they recognize that eggs differ from stones?
> >
> > Why do birds *sit* on eggs?—that is, why do they respond to an egg in this rather than in any other way?
> >
> > Why do *birds* sit on eggs?—that is, birds as opposed to say, mammals?
> >
> > And finally *Why* do birds sit on eggs?—that is, what is the function of this type of behaviour for the bird? (Rose, 1997, pp. 25–26)

When scientists wish to make statements about events that cannot be directly observed, such as mental processes or internal experiences of nonverbal animals, the statements must be considered **hypothetical interpretations.** As such, they must be held accountable to all of the requirements we place upon scientific theory. Statements about mental processes must be framed carefully and used with deliberation.

Theories are the results of our efforts to make the best possible sense of the observed facts of an area of study. They are always rational interpretations of facts and, as such, are never accepted with the same confidence as facts are accepted. We can never know for certain when we may have achieved the best possible interpretation of the facts currently at hand, and we can never be sure when new facts may appear that do not fit the present interpretation. Accountability to the facts is the first test of a scientific theory. A theory must be stated so clearly and must be so accurate in its statements that its application to a set of actual circumstances permits deduction, or prediction, of the results that must be observed in those circumstances. As it predicts accurately, a theory succeeds; as its predictions fail, or as events occur that cannot be predicted, a theory fails and must be revised or rejected (Chalmers, 1976).

Theory building proceeds from facts to hypotheses to laws and finally to theories. **Facts** are the observable truths of the world, and the pool of facts changes as knowledge increases. **Hypotheses** are educated guesses about the relationships between facts. **Laws** are well-verified relationships, or principles. **Theories** are all-encompassing statements that subsume large numbers of laws and facts. Accordingly, theories are not merely speculative statements but, rather, logical organizations of proven principles. Thus, we cannot dismiss theories such as the theory of evolution by natural selection with the casual statement, that "after all, it is just a theory." Theory allows us to land spaceships on distant planets years after we launch them. Speculation belongs much lower in the theory-building hierarchy, at the level of hypotheses.

A major function of theory is to summarize and organize a great number of separate facts. This summary is achieved by the construction of a limited number of principles designed to state the general sense illustrated by those facts, and any additional facts of a similar nature that may someday appear. Of two or more competing theories that appear equally successful at accounting for the same set of facts, the one that succeeds by use of the fewest number of principles is judged the winner, because it has achieved the greatest degree of summarization. The evaluation of theory, then, follows the principle of **parsimony** that guides contemporary science (Epstein, 1984) (see Box 1.4).

Earlier we said that when psychologists wish to make statements about the mental processes of animals, these statements must take the form of hypothetical interpretations. Such interpretations can have real explanatory value, but only if the mental processes invoked are carefully tied to observable events both on the causal side and on the effect side. In that case the scientific requirement for an observable cause to be associated with an observed effect will be satisfied.

We may say, by way of example, that water deprivation made a horse thirsty, or willing to drink, and so it drank. The water deprivation and the drinking are observable events. The mental processes that intervene between the observed cause and effect are not observed and are useful only in a theoretical interpretation of the horse's behavior (see Box 1.5). Even if such mental processes could be observed, we still might not know whether they were critically important as determiners of the horse's actions or, if important, whether the interpretation that makes use of these processes is the best one that will ever be made. For these reasons, such statements remain theoretical; they never become the equivalent of fact. Theoretical structures that invoke unobserved

BOX **1.4**

Explanation in Science

In science, events are considered to have been explained when rules have been stated that allow control or prediction of those events (e.g., Guthrie, 1935; Hull, 1943). **Explanations** that permit control are stronger than those that permit only prediction, because control also permits prediction, but prediction does not always permit control. We are interested in both prediction and control because both allow us to prove our understanding by observable demonstration, as demanded by science. Not only do both prediction and control permit observable demonstrations of understanding, they also are the only means that do permit such demonstrations. Real explanations in science must allow us to control, or at least to predict, the events being explained. In the science of animal behavior, we must guard against several types of **pseudo-explanations,** which appear to explain things but always do so without telling us how to control the things explained.

Simple **circular explanations** label the behavior requiring explanation and then consider the label to be the cause of the behavior, for example: "A dog ate because it was hungry." This statement does not really tell us anything except that the dog ate. Animals that do this are labeled as hungry. This type of explanation depends upon knowledge of the effect as the only evidence of the existence of the cause. That is why it is called a circular explanation.

Let us consider a scientific explanation of this same event and note the difference: "A dog ate because it had been deprived of food for twenty-two hours." How do we know it was deprived? We could have observed this deprivation ourselves or could have had it filmed. This explanation tells us directly how to make dogs eat, information that could be useful if we ever need to film a dog food commercial.

Another type of pseudo-explanation is called **animistic explanation.** This type of explanation assumes that an action is caused by an animal spirit within the acting object. People once explained the rapid movement of clouds on days when the wind appeared calm by assuming that the clouds had their own internal power of movement and will. Now that we are able to observe the winds at different altitudes, however, we no longer need to instill the clouds with animal spirits. Animal spirits can never provide an observable explanation of behavior in any case, but the acceptance of animistic explanations can do real harm by preventing us from looking for observable explanations, even when they may be readily available.

Consider the following statement: "You can lead a horse to water, but you can't make it drink." This says we needn't bother to look for observable causes of a horse's behavior because the horse simply will do as it pleases. Nevertheless, it happens to be the case that we *can* make the horse drink. In fact, we can do it in several ways. Water deprivation for a suitable period of time would do the trick. Or we could feed the horse a good deal of dry food, the digestion of which would use bodily supplies of water and make the horse ready to drink. Or we could turn up the heat and sweat the horse heavily. A little experimentation would tell us how much heat to use and for how long a time. Or, if we were in more of a hurry, we could open a vein in the horse's leg and bleed out a sufficient quantity of blood; blood loss induces drinking rather quickly. Now, let us consider again the claim that we can't influence the behavior of a horse. What a surprise to thousands of successful horse trainers!

A further type of pseudo-explanation is the **teleological explanation,** or the explanation by purpose. "The chicken crossed the road in order to get to the other side." Some of us, however, have seen chickens struck down and killed by automobiles in the very midst of their road-crossing behavior. Were these chickens then actually intent on suicide? If we are merely guessing at the mental processes of chickens, we are in the same predicament as we were with the will of the horse in the preceding paragraph. We need observable causes for an explanation. The chicken's arrival at the far side of the road cannot be taken as the cause of her starting the run because the two events are in the wrong order. First, the chicken starts her run; second, the cause of her running occurs as she arrives on the other side of the road. If we really believe that causes can act backward in time, why don't we use that capability to stop the occurrence of many tragic accidents immediately after they occur? Of course, we realize such things are impossible.

processes to mediate or intervene between observable causes and effects are called **intervening variables.**

A complete explanation of any behavioral event is necessarily quite complicated. It must take into account not only the immediate or proximal cause of the event but also the question of why it is that such causes affect behavior as they do, or ultimate causes of the event. The complete explanation requires attention to all of the sets of factors discussed earlier as being involved in behavioral origins—the phylogenetic, individual, ontogenetic, experiential, and cultural sets.

Before proceeding to a full discussion of the substantive issues that form the subject matter of this book, it will be helpful to our readers to consider the following abbreviated introductions to six concepts that are fundamental to the study of comparative psychology: evolution, species-typical behavior, behavioral levels, development, learning,

BOX 1.5

Illustration of an Intervening Variable: Thirst

Observable Causes	Intervening Variable	Observable Effects
Deprivation of water…		…Increased vigor of approach to water
Loss of water through overheating…	THIRST	…Increase in amount of drinking behavior
Loss of water through the digestion of dry food…	(In this case, an Increase in Thirst)	…Increase in performance of water-rewarded responses
Appropriate manipulation of the hypothalamus…		…Increased vigor of approach to water-related conditioned stimuli

The statement of this intervening variable asserts that any one of the observable causes listed above is capable of producing any and all of the listed observable effects.

and motivation. These concepts figure prominently throughout the remainder of the book, and their introduction here supplies a convenient vocabulary of terms that will make later discussions more readily understandable.

Evolution

> The most consequential change in man's view of the world, of living nature, and of himself came with the introduction, over a period of some one hundred years beginning in the eighteenth century, of the idea of change itself, of gradual change over long periods of time, in a word, of **evolution.** Man's worldview today is dominated by the knowledge that the universe, the stars, the earth, and all living things have evolved through a long history of continual, gradual change shaped by more or less directional processes consistent with the laws of physics. (Mayr, 1979, p. 47)

The modern theory of evolution dates from a joint presentation by Charles Darwin and Alfred Wallace to the London Zoological Society in 1856. One of the basic ideas of evolution—that present forms of plant and animal life have changed over vast periods of time to become as they now are—is at least as old as the Greek philosopher Anaxamander, who believed that all life began in the sea and gradually evolved to take advantage of land as well as ocean environments. What was missing in older ideas of evolution was a mechanism or guiding principle by which evolution would be given order and direction. That principle was supplied by the idea of **natural selection.**

Darwin formed his idea of natural selection while on a mapping expedition over much of the world with the British Navy in the late 1830s. One of the most impressive experiences Darwin had was his realization, while exploring the tropical rain forest of South America, that each square meter of the open forest contained the seedlings of dozens of plants, some of which, if successful, would grow to fill the entire space of that square meter. Obviously, only a very few of the many young plants striving to grow in that space would be able to survive long enough to bear seed and pass their characteristics on to another generation of offspring. Those best equipped to take advantage of the circumstances surrounding them would have the best chance to reproduce themselves; most, however, were doomed to fail. The surviving individuals would emerge only after a process of natural selection. Darwin realized that all of life could be represented by the example of survival in that one square meter of rain forest floor. All species and all individuals must survive a natural selection. Here was a principle to give guidance and direction to the process of evolution. Evolution must flow always in the direction of functional effectiveness, in the direction of survivability. Of course, there is no guarantee that evolution will continue for any given species; extinction is always an alternative.

Darwin's theory of evolution involves three basic principles:

1. Species produce many more eggs and young than can survive and reproduce themselves.

2. Sexual reproduction permits a wide variety of genetically different offspring to be produced by each breeding pair, male and female.
3. Nature selects from among this variability individuals whose characteristics result in survival and breeding capability.

Darwin knew those characteristics that permit the organisms possessing them to survive were likely to be passed on through the successful reproduction of those organisms. He knew nothing, however, about the mechanism of such inheritance. Our current understanding of genetics, which began with the work of the monk Gregor Mendel, provides this mechanism. The present theory of evolution, called the "Modern Synthesis," actually is a combination of Darwin's ideas of natural selection and Mendel's ideas of genetics (e.g., Mayr & Provine, 1980).

Darwin had formed the basic ideas of his theory of evolution by the end of the 1830s, but came forth to publish those ideas only when Alfred Wallace independently conceived his own similar ideas in the mid-1850s. Following the joint publication with Wallace in 1856, Darwin made use of his twenty-year head start in working with his own theory of evolution. In 1859 he published his basic book on the subject. *On the Origin of Species* became an international sensation, and the theory of evolution soon became known as "Darwin's theory." It has become one of the most influential ideas in the history of thought. Mayr (1979) has said that the synthetic theory of evolution is "*the* organizing principle of biology" (p. 47) [emphasis added]. Dobzhansky (1973), another important contributor to the development of modern evolutionary theory, titled an article "Nothing in Biology Makes Sense Except in the Light of Evolution." Evolution is the process by which life has continued and thrived on this planet; it is the great source of the world's biological diversity and the originator of phylogenetic variation across millions of species. Indeed, our understanding of life, the world in which we live, and the universe that surrounds us is an evolutionary understanding.

Species-Typical Behavior

The idea of **species-typical behavior** was introduced by Maier and Schneirla (1935/1964) in their classic text *Principles of Animal Psychology*. The concept is at the heart of comparative psychology, because it expresses the idea that behavior is similar within species but varies between species. Species-typical behavior simply refers to behavior that occurs in a similar form in nearly all members of a species (Haraway & Maples, 1998a). It is important to realize that here we are speaking of similarity, not identity. We expect at least as much individual variation in species-typical behavior as occurs in species-typical physical features. Furthermore, much species-typical behavior is quite flexible, or situationally variable, so that it differs from one situation to another even in the same individual. Regardless of individual differences and situational variations, however, species-typical behaviors are easily recognizable and identifiable with a particular species.

Species-typical behaviors usually make their appearance according to a predictable schedule in the *ontogeny*, or individual development, of each species member.

Some features of species-typical behavior may also be gender specific, just as some physical features are. Some behaviors are obviously exclusive to a single species and serve to separate that species from all others. Birdsong is a good example of such species-distinctive or species-specific behaviors. Other species-typical behaviors occur in a similar manner among families of closely related species, such as flycatching behavior among the related families of birds known as flycatchers. It is likely, however, that sufficiently detailed description would reveal important species distinctions among even very similar behavior patterns such as flycatching (Haraway & Maples, 1998a).

Patterns of vocalization, particularly those occurring in the context of territorial behavior, are species-typical in most species. We mentioned birdsong above. A similar example is afforded by the vocalization patterns, also called songs, of the nine species of small, territorial apes of the gibbon family, genus *Hylobates* (Haraway & Maples, 1998b). Feeding behaviors are species-typical in nearly all species. That is why many examples of feeding behavior are described in field guides to birds as aids to species identification. Many species, such as the flycatchers, are actually named for their feeding behavior (Haraway & Maples, 1998a). Locomotor behavior also is a good example of species-typical behavior. The human pattern of heel-to-toe, bipedal walking is species-typical and has been shared by no species other than our own ancestors of the genus *Homo* and perhaps relatives such as the australopithicines.

The concept of species-typical behavior is different from the ethological concepts of **instinct** and **fixed-action-pattern** (Tinbergen, 1951), although it includes the behaviors addressed by these concepts, as well as behaviors addressed by more restrictive terms such as *reflex* and *tropism*. As mentioned previously, the concept specifically recognizes the existence of individual and situational variability in much species-typical behavior. Indeed, many behavior patterns, such as feeding and locomotor behaviors, could hardly be functional if they were not flexible (Haraway & Maples, 1998a). The flexibility of species-typical behavior distinguishes this concept from the concepts of instinct and fixed-action-pattern, in which behavior is regarded as being fixed in the genome and thus unmodifiable and inflexible. Species-typical behaviors, unlike instincts and fixed-action-patterns, are not considered to be genetically determined, but to result from **epigenetic processes** (Kuo, 1967; Miller, 1998; Moltz, 1965), as described in the later section on development. The identifying characteristic of species-typical behavior is its similar occurrence in nearly all species members, not the degree of genetic influence that may be involved in its development.

It is neither necessary nor helpful to establish a rigid dichotomy between the species-typical and the non-species-typical in behavior, despite the apparent attractiveness of dichotomous sorting in human formal thinking (Haraway & Maples, 1998a). With respect to a dichotomy involving species-typical behavior, we should recognize that all behaviors are species-typical to some degree. In instances in which the element of species-typicality is outstanding, we recognize it. In the absence of outstanding typicality, we simply refrain from applying the term. Where we do apply it, we should be ready to point out behavioral features that illustrate impressive typicality, and we should be prepared to invest our energy in the construction of detailed descriptions of those features.

Behavioral Levels

In this book we are attempting to present a unified view of comparative psychology organized around an important evolutionary concept called **anagenesis.** This concept proposes a discernible progression and direction in the evolution of new forms of life across vast periods of time (Aronson, 1984; Greenberg, 1995). "The cardinal defining features of behavioral and psychological anagenesis [are] increases in ontogenetic plasticity and improvements in behavioral versatility, the latter through enhanced perceptual, cognitive, learning, social, and/or motor skills" (Gottlieb, 1984, p. 454).

The idea of evolutionary progress has been troublesome to scientists since Darwin's time (Nitecki, 1988). The problem lies in finding a reasonable and objective basis on which to judge one species as representing an improvement, or an advance, over another. We will avoid such problems here by limiting our idea of progressive change to that of a sustained or continuing change in a particular direction. The direction of this change happens to be toward increasing complexity of newly emerging species as evolution continues across time. Maier and Schneirla (1935/1964) first described evolutionary progress in terms of increases in behavioral complexity and plasticity as one ascends through a hierarchy of behavioral levels of organization. Associated with that hierarchy are increases in nervous system complexity, organization, and integrative functions (Bonner, 1988; Jerison, 1994).

The idea of complexity is no longer the poorly defined construct it once was. By wide agreement, complexity in biological systems can be assessed by the number of different components—cell types, structures—possessed by organisms. Saunders and Ho (1976) have gone so far as to identify a positive relationship between progressive complexity and evolutionary advancement as a second law of evolution, along with the survival of the fittest. Increasing complexity is closely related to improved organization and increased plasticity of behavior, which accompany evolutionary elaboration of the nervous system.

Schneirla's concept of behavioral levels, described systematically in a paper written with his colleague and student Ethel Tobach (Tobach & Schneirla, 1968), is derived from the concept of integrative levels discussed earlier (Feibleman, 1954; Novikoff, 1945). The **behavioral levels** are separated into two major groups, one at which biological factors dominate behavior and one at which psychological principles become important. The levels originally proposed were the following:

1. Taxis. At this level behavior is under immediate stimulus control, such as in the case of a moth flying toward a light source.

2. Biotaxis. At this next, higher, level, behavior is differentially influenced by biochemical concomitants of other organisms, that is, by stimulus sources resulting directly from the presence of other organisms. An example is the sexual attraction of male moths to pheromones secreted by females.

3. Biosocial. At this level the social interaction of groups of animals plays an important role in organizing and regulating behavior. Among Schneirla's research contributions was his analysis of the behavior of army ants (1940), whose cyclic activity was seen to be a result of reciprocal social stimulation provided by the enormous number of individuals in an ant colony. One might study the behavior of individual ants fruitlessly to discern the source of their cyclical behavior pattern, which is displayed only when ants are together in large numbers.

4. Psychotaxis. At this level mediation by past experience enters into the behavioral equation, and behavior is no longer tied only to stimulation currently present in the immediate environment. Thus, an animal's current behavior may be affected by an earlier history of experiential effects. In their analysis of cat and kitten behavior, Rosenblatt and Schneirla (1962) showed that the relationship between infant and mother is founded in biotactic responses—the kitten orients to the mother by means of tactile and olfactory stimuli—but higher-order phenomena such as learning and reinforcement play an important role in later stages of that relationship.

5. Psychosocial. Behavior organized at this level is represented by the complex social bonds and social behaviors that are characteristic of advanced vertebrates. For example, among primates, lasting social bonds result from complex biosocial and biotactic interactions between an infant and a mother, such as those involved in rocking, providing of contact comfort, and nursing.

The conception of behavior across the animal kingdom as a series of increasing levels of complexity solves a serious problem in comparative psychology by providing a meaningful and objective framework within which to make behavioral comparisons between and among species. Comparisons may be made in a variety of ways within this framework. No matter what comparisons are chosen, they are informed by the relations, within the levels framework, of the species being compared. We agree with Tobach (1976) that the questions being asked should direct the choice of species selected for comparison. One might wish to ask how species at the same level, but subjected to different ecological pressures, may have evolved different solutions to particular ecological problems such as how to orient themselves within their environments, how to procure food, or how to attract and maintain possession of a mate.

For example, Greenberg, McCarthy, and Bergamo (1989) found that the gerbil (*Meriones unguiculatus*), a species that evolved spending much of its time in burrows and tunnels beneath the earth's surface, excels at making distance judgments on a flat plane and readily learns to distinguish between a long and a short arm in an enclosed T-maze. By comparison, a closely related species, the spiny mouse (*Acomys cahirinus*), which lives above ground among rocks, performs poorly in the T-maze task, but excels in a task requiring descent from platforms of differing heights above a surface. On the other hand, one might wish to compare species at different levels that had been subjected to similar ecological pressures; how similar or different are their evolved solutions to the same sorts of problems?

Tobach and Schneirla (1968) ended their analysis with a description of the psychosocial level. We see merit in developing the system somewhat further in an attempt to differentiate among several levels of primate behavior. Whereas all primates are represented at the pychosocial level, we now understand that there are differential levels of primate communication. All primates communicate, but a few individuals of several species have developed true language capabilities, though at a level far less sophisticated than human language (Savage-Rumbaugh et al., 1993). To accommodate these differences, we propose elaborating the psychosocial level into three categories: **psychosocial I,** represented by many nonprimates and by non-language-using primates, such as lemurs and vervets; **psychosocial II,** represented by language-using apes; and **psychosocial III,** represented by humans. We discuss this in greater detail in a later chapter.

Development

We have defined comparative psychology as the study of the evolution and development of behavior. Evolution is the great determiner of genetic makeup, which is a major influence of all behavior. All characteristics, however, whether biological or behavioral, must be viewed as joint products of genetics and development within some particular environment. Behavior is not built into organisms—is not, strictly speaking, a part of their biology; rather, behavior is a set of processes shaped by maturational and developmental forces that organisms experience during their growth. Kuo's (1967) definition of **development,** or **behavioral epigenesis,** is still the clearest.

> We shall define behavioral epigenesis as a continuous developmental process from fertilization through birth to death, involving proliferation, diversification, and modification of behavior patterns both in space and in time, as a result of the continuous dynamic exchange of energy between the developing organism and its environment, endogenous and exogenous. The ontogenesis of behavior is a continuous stream of activities whose patterns vary or are modified in response to changes in the effective stimulation by the environment. (p. 11)

Stated another way, as the organism matures, or grows biologically, it is exposed to a myriad of experiences that shape its behavior. These crucial factors include often overlooked prenatal and postnatal behavioral conditions such as incubation temperature; the organism's own physical interaction with itself, such as muscle twitching; the duration and timing of initial exposure to the normal day–night cycle; and diet.

To the extent that various species have different sensory systems, their experiential histories are necessarily different. This is one reason for behavioral diversity among them. The organism's status as a member of its particular species—that is to say, its phylogeny—endows it with a set of behavioral potentials that may or may not be actualized, depending on the experiences encountered during growth and development. "By behavior potentials we mean the enormous possibilities or potentialities of behavior patterns that each neonate possesses within the limits or range of normal morphological structure of its species" (Kuo, 1967, p. 125).

To change an organism's experiences, then, is to change its resulting behaviors. Kuo (1967) once asked the following question: Are cats rat killers or rat lovers? It turned out that the answer depends upon the cats' experiences. Many kittens raised with rats and away from cats that kill and eat rats themselves never eat rats, even when hungry. Having never seen a rat eaten, these cats simply do not treat rats as food. But that is precisely the point. In the context of the continuing nature–nurture debate, biological wisdom would have us believe that an animal's nature is a direct result of its genotype—something it inherits. Thus, it is asserted, many animals are aggressive and are killers because of their genetic makeups; cats kill rats because of their genes; even we humans can never escape our genes. But, on the other hand, research such as Kuo's shows that aggressiveness requires a component of learning in many animals; it is not only a product of the genes but also one of environment or experiential history. Consider the case of Elsa, the lioness of *Born Free* fame (Adamson, 1960). In this instance, the lion had to be taught by humans to hunt and kill when she grew too large to maintain as a pet.

A lion's aggressiveness and hunting skills are no more inescapable products of biology than are our human qualities of **nurturance,** affection, and love. As we have seen earlier, Montagu (1952/1962) pointed out that human beings are born only with a complex of potentialities whose realization depends upon development with experience. We will see that Montagu's statement applies not only to human characteristics but also to behavior characteristics across a wide range of species.

Learning

Learning is a primary process by which behavior is modified by experience. It is defined by lasting changes in behavior that accompany experience and is identified primarily with the procedures and effects of classical and instrumental conditioning, and naturally occurring experiences that approximate classical and instrumental conditioning. These procedures turn on the association of two or more separate events in experience. The learning that follows from these procedures is often known as associative learning. Forms of proto-learning known as habituation and sensitization involve lasting decreases and increases in an organism's responsiveness to a single stimulus, when that stimulus is frequently repeated.

In the classic learning theories of the first half of this century, as illustrated particularly by the work of Thorndike (1911) and Hull (1943), learning was considered as an important adaptive process, making behavior more functional and enhancing survival capability. Indeed, the apparent great survival value of learning is often cited as a major reason why learning became such a popular subject of study in the early days of experimental psychology, during which Darwin's theory of evolution was such a major influence on scientific thought.

Classical conditioning, often called Pavlovian conditioning after I. P. Pavlov, who first demonstrated it, is defined by the occurrence together of two stimulus events, neither of which is under the control of the subject's, or learner's, behavior (Papini, 1998). Actually, the two events do not occur exactly together, but rather one of the events shortly precedes the other in the manner of a signal. The signal event was called the conditional, or **conditioned stimulus,** by Pavlov, and the second event—the event being signaled—was called the **unconditioned stimulus.** Pavlov discovered early along that conditioning works best when the unconditioned stimulus is a strong or dominant event, perhaps one having great importance in the life of the learner. The signal event, however, need only be readily noticeable. The animal's original response to the unconditioned stimulus was termed an **unconditioned response;** the anticipatory response the animal acquires as a result of conditioning was termed a **conditioned response.**

During the course of conditioning, the signal event, or conditioned stimulus, comes to elicit behavior that appears to anticipate the occurrence of the unconditioned stimulus. In an animal's natural environment, conditioned anticipatory behavior can prepare the learner to deal effectively with a dominant event, and this can be a matter of life or death. Therein lies the potential adaptive value of learning in the mode of classical conditioning. In most cases, the conditioned response is noticeably similar in form to the unconditioned response.

The procedure that became known as **instrumental,** or **operant, conditioning** was first studied by E. L. Thorndike at about the same time Pavlov began his study of classical conditioning, in the late 1890s (Malott, 1998). The instrumental procedure differs sharply from classical conditioning in that here the important stimulus event of the procedure is under the direct control of the subject's behavior. Thorndike distinguished two important classes of stimulus events that were influential when they occurred as consequences of behavior. Today, these two classes of stimuli are known as appetitive stimuli, or **positive reinforcers,** and aversive stimuli, or **negative reinforcers.** The procedure in which a subject's response leads to the occurrence of an appetitive stimulus is called reinforcement. Reinforcement strengthens behavior, in that it causes the rewarded response to occur more frequently. Reinforcement can take two forms: positive reinforcement, as when a selected response leads to the *onset* of an appetitive stimulus, and negative reinforcement, as when a selected response leads to the *offset* of an aversive stimulus.

Alternative procedures, in which the subject's response leads either to the onset of an aversive stimulus or to the offset of an appetitive stimulus, are called **positive punishment** and **negative punishment.** Punishment weakens behavior or causes the punished response to occur less frequently.

Thorndike recognized quickly that learning through reward and punishment had great adaptive potential. In their natural environments, animals would be rewarded for behaving in ways that procured the things they needed in order to succeed in life: food, water, a safe nest or den, or a mate. The strength of these effective behaviors would be built up and maintained through the natural occurrence of rewards. Ineffective behaviors, however, would *not* be rewarded and so would be weakened or would remain weak, leaving the way clear for their replacement by more effective behavior. Behaviors that led directly to harm or trouble would be weakened by punishment. Thus, successful forms of behavior would be strengthened by an animal's experiences in its natural environment, whereas unsuccessful and dangerous responses would be weakened.

Motivation

The concern of **motivation** is how to get animals into motion—how to get them moving and acting. If animals always behaved the same way under similar stimulus conditions, the answer would be easy. We could say that animals go into motion simply as a function of the stimuli they receive. Stimulation certainly is intimately associated with the occurrence of behavior. However, the matter is somewhat more complicated; animals do not always behave the same way in the same stimulus conditions. Instead, responses to the same stimulus can vary widely according to other conditions. For example, an animal's response to food depends upon its degree of food deprivation. If highly deprived, the animal is highly responsive to food; if well fed, however, it is relatively unresponsive to food. Furthermore, certain stimuli, such as food, are much more likely that others to serve as the focus of an animal's behavior. The study of motivation deals with such variations.

Elizabeth Duffy (1962), an outstanding student of the subject, conceived of motivation as concerning the arousal and direction of behavior. By **arousal,** she referred to the degree of activation displayed in behavior, from the low-level activation of deep sleep to the high-level activation of emotional behavior. By **direction,** she referred, as had the important learning psychologist Tolman (1932), to the frequently observed tendency of behavior to lead toward or away from some particular point of reference. Schneirla (1959) also recognized the importance of these *toward* and *away from* orientations. He viewed **approach** and **withdrawal** as basic categories of behavior. His approach/withdrawal principle provided for all animals a dynamic of early behavior development and, for species at the lower behavioral levels, a motivational dynamic throughout the life span. Weak stimuli elicit approach responses and strong stimuli elicit withdrawal responses; this is true for neonates of species at the higher behavioral levels and throughout the lives of animals at the lower behavioral levels.

For example, in accounting for the initial pecking responses of newly hatched chicks, Kuo (1967) noted that the chicks were visually attracted to small visual stimuli, such as grains of food. These visual stimuli, of only moderate brightness, and impacting only small areas of the retina, are of low stimulus intensity. Successful pecks also result in positive consequences (ingestion of food), which further strengthen approach tendencies toward those stimuli through the operation of conditioning principles (Balsam & Silver, 1994). At first, chicks also peck at their own feces, which, because of their moderate brightness and small size, also are low-intensity visual stimuli. But in this case, successful pecks do not result in positive consequences; instead, they result in strong withdrawal responses occasioned by the high intensity of chemical stimulation from these ammonia-laden by-products of the organism's own metabolism. Anticipatory withdrawal responses then become conditioned to the specific stimulus features that have signaled encounter with ammonia. Following this conditioning, anticipatory rejection can prevent future pecking responses toward feces. For animals at the higher behavioral levels, such processes of experience importantly modify initial approach/withdrawal tendencies as development progresses. "Increasingly, meaningful aspects of stimulation replace stimulus intensity in eliciting approach and withdrawal responses. With development, approach responses become seeking, and withdrawal processes, avoiding stimulation" (Rosenblatt, 1995, p. 93).

We believe it is possible to frame a useful definition of motivation based on the simple approach and withdrawal tendencies of attraction and aversion, as follows: Motivation consists of the attractions and aversions that typify a species or an individual.

Having defined motivation in this manner, we may go on to predict, generally, that manipulations that alter the attractiveness or aversiveness of a stimulus as a focus of approach or withdrawal will cause similar variations in the effectiveness of that stimulus as an appetitive stimulus in instrumental conditioning. Further, the same manipulations also will cause similar variations in the performance of previously learned responses involving that reinforcer. For example, the attractiveness of food as an object of approach is increased in proportion to the degree of an animal's food deprivation. To a similar degree, food deprivation also enhances the effectiveness of food as a rewarding stimulus as well as the performance of previously learned responses that were rewarded by food attainment.

A Guide to the Book with Recommendations for Student Use

Following this introduction, we proceed to a discussion of important bases of behavior couched in biological structure and function and in fundamental characteristics of orientation and locomotion. Then we consider a number of important functional categories of behavior and the critical processes of learning and cognition. Throughout these discussions we cite numerous examples illustrating the issues being addressed. These examples have been chosen from the behavior of a wide diversity of species in an attempt to represent the status of behavior characteristics across the entire animal series. Generally, these examples are ordered in a progression from more anciently established species with relatively simple behavior characteristics toward more recently established species illustrating increasingly more complex behavior characteristics.

At the end of all chapters of the book but the last, we have included a section entitled Summary: Principles Introduced in this Chapter. We intend this section not only to emphasize the new principles encountered in the chapter but also to serve as a chapter summary. We recommend that you go through these summary sections carefully. It is a good study exercise for students to see whether you can (1) restate these principles in your own words, (2) remember examples from the chapter that illustrate each principle, and (3) think of examples of your own that also illustrate each principle.

Following the summary and principles section of each of the first ten chapters is a listing of key terms introduced in each chapter, together with a brief definition of each term. Terms in this list are in bold print at or near the point of their first appearance in the text. If, at any point in your reading, you find yourself confused about the definition of a key term, you can turn to the end of the chapter and find a brief definition of the term in question. The list of key terms should also be useful as a resource in reviewing your understanding of each chapter. You should be able to articulate the meaning and importance of each key term and, as well, should be able to make up your own example or construct your own sentence to illustrate an appropriate usage of the term. Finally, each chapter ends with a number of review questions. These questions provide a number of specific points around which you may elaborate on major features of the chapter as a further learning exercise, and they also provide means of checking on the adequacy of your understanding of the chapter.

The final chapter of the book presents a summarized statement of all of the principles encountered throughout the entire book. These statements are organized formally into the framework of a comprehensive theory of comparative psychology. You may want to look ahead to peruse this final chapter before beginning your study of the nine chapters that intervene between here and there. Doing so should enable you to discern the overall structure of comparative psychology in advance of your consideration, one at a time, of each of the separate elements that contributes to that structure. Looking ahead also should prepare you to appreciate the central importance of key principles upon the first occasion that you encounter them in Chapters 1 through 10. For your convenience, we next include an abbreviated statement of the theory presented in Chapter 11. We refer you to Chapter 11 itself for a complete treatment of any point on which a fuller account is desired. The latter section of Chapter 11, for example, traces the theoretical explanation, or deduction, of numerous specific principles of behavior as they are illustrated on a chapter-by-chapter basis throughout the book.

Major Principles of Comparative Psychology

First Principles or Postulates

   I. The Principle of Evolution
Genetic characteristics of all animal species are products of evolution by natural selection, or selection on the basis of differential success at survival and reproduction of past members of those species.
   II. Correspondence of Biological and Psychological Variation
Behavioral variation corresponds closely with biological variation.
   III. The Principle of Multiple Causation
The development of behavioral characteristics is the result of a dynamic interaction of multiple causal factors that, depending upon the level of behavioral complexity illustrated, include the following.
   A. The Phylogenetic Factor, species genetics, and evolutionary history
   B. The Individual Factor, individual genetics
   C. The Ontogenetic Factor, maturational status
   D. The Experiential Factor, history of experience
   E. The Cultural Factor, history of social experience in relation to group membership
   IV. The Principle of Hierarchical Levels
Behavioral characteristics across the animal kingdom describe a hierarchy of levels of complexity illustrating a progression of increasing complexity with recency of species origin. This hierarchical arrangement may be viewed as comprising five major levels of behavioral complexity.
   A. Taxis, direct stimulus control of behavior
   B. Biotaxis, behavioral distinction of biologic agents
   C. Biosocial, influences of the social group

    D. Psychotaxis, behavioral influences of past experience
    E. Psychosocial I, behavioral influences of past social experiences with recognized individuals; II, use of proto-language by certain great apes; and III, complex and wide-ranging use of language among humans

General Principles That Are Derivable from the Postulates

    I. Species-Typical Behavior
    All species possess numerous forms of behavior that occur in a similar form and under similar circumstances in nearly all members of the species. Differences in species-typical behavior distinguish each species from all others.
    II. Functionality of Behavior Characteristics
    Behavior characteristics shared in common by most members of a species have clear functional value to facilitate survival and reproductive success.
    III. Selective Orientation
    Behavior is focused on selective aspects of the environment that tend to be more relevant to survival and reproductive success than would be a random selection of all potential stimulus sources in the environment.
    IV. Motor and Locomotor Capacities
    The evolution of species-typical motor and locomotor capacities has been universal across the animal kingdom. The evolution of much locomotor movement has taken advantage of physical properties addressed by Newton's Third Law.
    Locomotor sequences that are frequently repeated within a species are subject to direct control by corresponding changes in sensory input.
    V. Approach and Withdrawal
    Approach and withdrawal are comprised of the combination of orientation and locomotion and are universal features of animal life. Stimuli for approach generally are beneficial to survival and/or reproductive success; stimuli for withdrawal generally are harmful or dangerous.
    Stimuli within the lower portion of the intensity range of differential responsiveness are likely to evoke approach whereas those in the higher portion of the intensity range are likely to evoke withdrawal. These tendencies are seen throughout life in organisms at lower levels of behavioral complexity but are increasingly modified by individual developmental experience in organisms at higher levels of behavioral complexity.
    VI. Motivation
    A. Motivational variation is practically universal in animal life. It combines persistent tendencies for approach and withdrawal with systematic variation in the strengths of these tendencies—and in the degree of behavioral arousal associated with them—with variations in physiological conditions and other behaviors in progress.

B. Motivation provides an important basis of reinforcement, or of reward and punishment, as described in treatments of instrumental learning.

VII. Learning and Cognition

Learning ability, or an ability of behavior characteristics to be modified by experience, is an important factor in behavior development across a wide range of species. Observations inviting interpretation in terms of the acquisition and use of information—that is, of cognition—occur increasingly among the more recent vertebrates.

Summary: Principles Introduced in This Chapter

Comparative psychology is concerned with the evolution and development of behavior in the animal kingdom. Animal behavior can be conceptualized, analyzed, and understood from a dynamic systems perspective. In this approach, behavior is understood to be a set of processes that emerge from the dynamic interplay of biological and experiential events falling into five crucial sets of factors: phylogenetic, individual, ontogenetic, experiential, and cultural.

Our understanding of all events in the universe is organized around the concept of change over long periods, of evolution. Although the occurrence of change, or evolution, is a fact, the mechanism of evolution is not. The most successful theory of evolution is that proposed by Charles Darwin, evolution by natural selection. The three fundamental principles of this theory are (1) species produce offspring in abundance; (2) sexual reproduction results in enormous genotypic and phenotypic variations among individuals of a species; and (3) nature selects the most fit individuals from among this variability (survival of the fittest).

Species can be identified by their morphology or structure, and also by their behavior. All species display characteristic sets of behaviors we call species-typical behavior. These behaviors are not under genetic control, nor are they instincts; rather, a set of probabilistic developmental events leads to the appearance of these behaviors. This probabilistic process is referred to as epigenesis.

Species can be hierarchically ordered according to a novel application of the principle of integrative levels. This ordering is similar, though not identical, to the typical structural taxonomy we are used to. In this system, behavioral complexity and nervous system development are the critical organizing concepts. The behavioral levels are, from lowest to highest, taxis, biotaxis, biosocial, psychotaxis, psychosocial I, II, and III.

Development is a crucial organizing principle for behavior, because all behavior is the result not of biology alone but of the dynamic interplay of the five sets of factors referred to earlier. In the course of this development, critical experiences, such as learning, shape the organism's behavior. The arousal and directional aspects of behavior, motivation, are addressed by a fundamental organizing principle: approach/withdrawal, which is seen to be an alternative to more traditional self-actional thinking.

KEY TERMS

Anagenesis   the idea that there is a directional progression over time in evolution; this directional progression is seen most clearly in the evolutionary appearance of new species out of the base provided by the existence of older, or more anciently established, species.

Anecdotal evidence   in psychology, evidence drawn from casual and uncritical observations without concern for whether the observations have any generality or whether they are repeatable.

Animistic explanation   a type of false or pseudo-explanation in which we endow an animal or other active agent with an unobserved spirit or feelings and then take the spirit or feelings as the causes of its observed actions (for example, that wasp stung me because it was mad, instinct causes birds to fly south before winter).

Anthropomorphism   the practice of ascribing human qualities and abilities to nonhuman animals.

Approach   locomotor movement toward a particular stimulus agent within the environment or, in some instances, actions that lead toward the occurrence of a particular outcome familiar to past experience.

Arousal   the feature of behavior identified with an animal's level of activation, usually ranging from high activation and excitement to deep sleep.

Behavioral ecology   a subfield of the biological science of ecology, emphasizing the matching of evolutionary adaptations to complex environmental or ecological systems; behavioral ecology focuses on the evolutionary adaptation of behavior to the complex of ecological conditions within which the evolution of particular species occurred.

Behavioral levels   the idea that behavior across the animal series illustrates a succession of levels, within each of which behavior is organized somewhat differently than at other levels and across which behavior varies in complexity.

Behavioral potentials   characteristics of behavior that are likely to develop in an individual as a normal representative of its species; *behavioral potential* was a term introduced by the comparative psychologist Kuo as a way of addressing species-typical behavior.

Behaviorism   the perspective on psychology urged by John B. Watson, in the early 1900s, that psychology should confine its study to *observable* behavior alone; Watson's attempt to establish psychology as a *science* based on the study of observable events had a great influence on the development of comparative psychology.

Biosocial level   biosocial organization represents the third behavioral level envisioned by Schneirla and Tobach, in which behavior is differentially influenced by groups of other organisms as social agents; the major behavioral levels include *taxis, biotaxis, biosocial, psychotaxis,* and *psychosocial.*

Biosocial science   by saying that psychology is a *biosocial science,* we mean to distinguish it from being merely a biological science, governed solely by *biological* laws; instead, we view psychology as not only subject to biological law but also influenced by factors at the higher organizational levels of psychological and sociological law.

Biotaxis   biotaxis represents the second level of behavioral organization, in which behavior is differentially influenced by the presence of biological agents outside the body of the behaving individual; across the major behavioral levels envisioned by Schneirla and Tobach, behavior is organized by *taxic, biotaxic, biosocial, psychotaxic,* and *psychosocial* influences.

Circular explanations   a form of false or pseudo-explanation in which an event to be explained is given a label, then the label is said to have caused the event (for example, the dog ate because it was hungry, and we know it was hungry because it ate).

Classical conditioning   a model type of learning experience in which, in typical cases, a dominant stimulus event occurs in series with a signal event that precedes it; the learning that often results from this type of experience is demonstrated when the learner responds to the signal event in ways that appear to anticipate occurrence of the dominant stimulus with which it has been associated; in strict classical conditioning procedure, the learner's behavior has no effect either to bring about or to prevent the occurrence of the dominant stimulus in question; the study of classical conditioning was pioneered by Pavlov, and the procedure is often called *Pavlovian* conditioning.

Comparative psychology   a branch of psychology that studies the evolution and development of animal behavior, taking particular interest in species-typical behavior.

Conditioned response   the name given by Pavlov to the response that an animal learns to make to the conditioned stimulus during the course of conditioning experience, so named because conditioning experience is required to ensure occurrence of this response to the conditioned stimulus.

Conditioned stimulus   the name given by Pavlov to the signal stimulus presented in classical conditioning procedure, so named because the response selected for study by the experimenter can be elicited by the conditioned stimulus only as a result of an animal's conditioning experience.

Continuum of mind   Romanes's idea—and a cornerstone of comparative psychology—that there is a more or less continuous progression of mental capability and complexity as one looks across the animal series from the simplest animals toward the most complex.

Cultural set   one of five sets of factors viewed as joint determiners of behavior; the cultural factors may be seen as a particular class of experiential factors; they are experiential influences deriving from an individual's membership in its particular social, or cultural, group.

Development   in the context of behavior, development refers to a process of emergence and adjustment of behavior patterns that accompanies physical maturation, physical growth, and experience.

Direction   the aspect of an animal's behavior that is identified with its orientation toward or away from particular stimulus agents within its environment.

Dynamic systems theory   a theoretical perspective that views its subject matter, such as behavior, for example, as being the product of an interaction of a number of different causal factors; alteration in any one of the causal factors usually present may change the mix sufficiently to produce quite a different outcome from that usually expected.

Epigenetic processes, epigenesis   a process envisioned as an interaction of numerous active influences in the determination of behavior; epigenesis stands in opposition to ideas of behavior determination that emphasize genetic causes to the near exclusion of other influential factors.

Ethology   a branch of biology that focuses upon animal behavior.

Evolution   a process of change over time; the process of change envisioned in the theory of evolution is guided by the natural selection of plants and animals whose characteristics enable them to survive and reproduce themselves in a hazardous world, passing on versions of their own genetics to future generations.

Evolutionary psychology   a branch of psychology that focuses upon genetic bases of human social behavior.

Experiential set   one of the group of five sets of factors viewed as joint determiners of behavior; the experiential factors are influences deriving from an individual's unique history of experience; they include *all* stimulative effects on the organism, throughout its life history.

Explanations, scientific explanations   scientific explanations state the general rule of which the occurrence being explained is an instance; in doing so, they must state a relationship between two separate observable events; only if they do this can they be tested by observation, that is, by science.

Facts   in science, facts are matters of observation—events that are known to us by way of sensory experience.

Fixed-action-pattern   a term that is rapidly becoming obsolete, along with the concept it sought to replace—*instinct;* like instinct, fixed-action-pattern referred to built-in, genetically determined, and fixed behavior patterns common throughout a species; an advantage of this term, as compared to instinct, was that it sought to avoid implication of animistic, internal causes that often seemed associated with the term *instinct.*

Hypotheses   hypotheses represent an early stage in the achievement of theoretical explanation; they are reasonable interpretations of observable events, but interpretations that have not yet been tested by application to a very large set of observations; hence, as interpretations that have not been widely tested, they are interpretations about which we must remain somewhat skeptical.

Hypothetical interpretations   a *reasonable* interpretation of a given set of observable events; the correctness and value of the hypothetical interpretation are judged by its agreement with the observed facts to which it is addressed and the degree of its simplicity as compared to competing interpretations of the same events.

Individual set   one of the group of five sets of factors viewed as joint determiners of behavior; the individual factors are the influences proceeding from the particular version of its species' genetic endowment that a particular individual happens to receive.

Integrative levels   the idea that the universe is well viewed as a progression of increasingly higher, or more complex, levels of organization; laws operating at higher levels may be different from—but not contradictory to—laws operating at lower levels.

Intervening variables   a form of theoretical statement in which it is supposed that an unobserved hypothetical process intervenes between observed causes and their observed effects *as though* the observed causes influence the intervening process that, in its turn, produces the observed effects; to remain within the realm of scientific interpretation, the intervening variable must be firmly tied to observed causes and observed effects in all cases.

Instinct   a term now largely outdated in psychology, instinct referred to built-in, innate, and fixed behavior patterns that were common throughout an entire species; old usages of the term often appeared to refer to unobserved and vaguely animistic internal causes of such fixed behavior.

Instrumental conditioning (operant conditioning)   a model type of learning experience in which a particular response by the learner controls the occurrence of an appetitive or an aversive stimulus (often known as positive and negative reinforcers); learning is demonstrated when the rate of the response in question is adjusted according to the consequences that the response has; the control of an important stimulus event by the learner's behavior in instrumental conditioning is in direct contrast to the situation presented by classical conditioning procedure, in which the learner's behavior has no such effects.

Laws   laws are statements that summarize and interpret a large number of observations; they are statements that have been verified many times in their application to observed facts and, therefore, are interpretations in which we have a higher degree of confidence than we have in hypotheses.

Learning   a process by which behavior changes according to the individual experience of the learner. Learning is defined by lasting changes in behavior such as those seen in conditioning.

Morgan's canon   a rule instituted by early comparative psychologist Lloyd Morgan that explanations should be based on the lowest degree of mental activity sufficient to account for the behavior observed; that is, it is improper to presume the presence of a high degree of mental functioning to explain instances of behavior that can be accounted for by simpler processes.

Motivation   the attractions and aversions that typify a species or an individual; closely associated with the arousal level and the directional orientation of behavior.

Natural selection   the differential representation of certain genetic variations across succeeding generations of plants and animals based on the differential reproductive success of individuals possessing those genetic variations; one requirement for reproductive success, of course, is survival to the age of reproductive maturity.

Negative punishment   a procedure of instrumental conditioning in which the learner's response causes removal or loss of an appetitive stimulus, with the usual effect of weakening (decreasing the occurrence of) the response in question.

Negative reinforcement   a procedure of instrumental conditioning in which the learner's response serves to terminate or remove an aversive stimulus, with the usual effect of strengthening (increasing the occurrence of) the response in question.

Negative reinforcer   an aversive stimulus; a stimulus whose termination or removal following a particular response serves to increase the frequency of occurrence of that response.

Nurturance (nurture)   these terms refer to environmental influences that impinge on an individual throughout its history.

Observation   one of the basic sources by which we human beings may obtain knowledge about the world and ourselves; other such sources recognized by early philosophers were reason and intuition; observation was chosen by science as its primary source of knowledge and its final arbiter of truth; observation relies on information deriving directly from sensory experiences such as seeing and hearing—information that is open to normal members of the public and can be attended to by several people at the same time, thus, *public* observation.

Ontogenetic set   one of the group of five sets of factors viewed as joint determiners of behavior; the ontogenetic factors are those deriving from an individual's age and its maturational status at its particular position in the life span normal to its species.

Parsimony   the quality of simplicity by which theoretical explanations are judged; one of the principal functions of a theoretical explanation is to summarize its subject matter, and the explanation that accomplishes this job by use of the least number of separate principles or laws is judged the simplest and the best.

Phylogenetic set   one of the group of five sets of factors viewed as joint determiners of behavior, the phylogenetic factors provide the potential characteristics of all members of an individual's species (e.g., birds fly, fish swim).

Positive punishment   a procedure of instrumental conditioning in which the learner's response causes presentation of an aversive stimulus, with the usual effect of weakening (decreasing the occurrence of) the response in question.

Positive reinforcement   a procedure of instrumental conditioning in which the learner's response causes presentation of an appetitive stimulus, with the usual effect of strengthening (increasing the occurrence of) the response in question.

Positive reinforcer   an appetitive stimulus; a stimulus whose presentation following a particular response serves to increase the frequency of performance of that response.

Pseudo-explanation   in science, explanations that name only one observable event rather than stating a relationship between at least two observable events are considered as false or pseudo-explanations.

Psychotaxis   psychotaxis represents the fourth level of behavioral organization envisioned by Schneirla and Tobach, in which behavior is influenced by stimulus agents according to the past experiences of the behaving individual with those stimulus agents; the major behavioral levels are *taxis, biotaxis, biosocial, psychotaxis,* and *psychosocial.*

Psychosocial   psychosocial organization represents the fifth behavioral level envisioned by Schneirla and Tobach, in which behavior is influenced by individual social agents according to past experiences of the behaving individual with those particular social agents; the major behavioral levels are *taxis, biotaxis, biosocial, psychotaxis,* and *psychosocial.*

Psychosocial I, II, and III   in the present book we have suggested dividing the psychosocial level to represent the additional behavioral complexities illustrated by the use of language by some individual apes, given a special history of experience (psychosocial II), and by nearly all humans (psychosocial III); psychosocial I is represented by the definition of *psychosocial* given in the entry immediately above.

Reductionistic thinking, reductionism   in psychology, an approach to the study of behavior that seeks to view behavior as a straightforward function of biological causes or factors; that is, an attempt to *reduce* psychology to a matter of biology.

Sociobiology   a branch of biology that focuses upon genetic bases of social behavior.

Species-typical behavior   behavior that is characteristic of an entire species and that develops at a predictable time in the life span in nearly all members of a species.

Taxis   taxis represents the first level of behavioral organization, in which behavior is controlled by the direct action of stimulus agents without behavioral distinction between biologic and nonbiologic agents and without influence of past experience with the stimulus; the major behavioral levels envisioned by Schneirla and Tobach are *taxis, biotaxis, biosocial, psychotaxis,* and *psychosocial.*

Teleological explanation   often called explanation by purpose, a type of false or pseudo-explanation in which the outcome of a series of events is taken as the cause of the series (for example, we developed large ears and noses in order to support eyeglasses).

Theories   a theory is a set of statements that, taken together, accounts for all observed facts within a given area of study or within the scope of the theory; theories essentially are statements of the laws that apply within an area and of the relationships that hold among those laws; a theory remains accountable for all of the facts that fall within its proper scope of application, both now and in the future, and remains open to competition from alternative theories that may provide a better account of the same facts.

Unconditioned response   the name given by Pavlov to the response elicited by an unconditioned stimulus, so named because the response could be elicited without prior benefit of conditioning experience.

Unconditioned stimulus   the name given by Pavlov to the dominant stimulus presented in classical conditioning procedure, so named because an animal required no conditioning experience to respond to this stimulus with the response selected for study by the experimenter (for example, salivation).

Withdrawal   locomotor movement away from a particular stimulus agent in the environment.

REVIEW QUESTIONS

1. Write one or two sentences to tell what is meant by the term *evolution*.

2. Do the same for the term *development*.

3. Describe the concept of species-typical behavior and give one or two examples to illustrate the idea.

4. Tell why the concept of species-typical behavior is an important one to the field of comparative psychology.

5. What did Romanes mean by his idea of a "continuum of mind"?

6. Relate Romanes's idea of continuum of mind to the idea of behavioral levels.

7. What is the chosen method of knowledge of science? Give an example to show what this means.

8. Is there a place for the use of reason in science? Briefly describe how reason is used.

9. An early comparative psychologist named Lloyd Morgan proposed a rule that came to be known as Morgan's canon. Write out your own description of what this rule means. Give an example to illustrate an application of Morgan's canon.

10. What aspects of behavior are addressed by the concept of motivation?

11. In the first half of the past century, comparative psychology and ethology had some mutual criticisms of each other. State at least one criticism in each direction.

12. Name another scientific field besides ethology that has very similar interests in common with comparative psychology.

13. Contrast the idea of multiple causation of behavior with an approach that would stress a single causal factor to the exclusion of others.

14. Name and describe two or more of the sets of causal factors involved in behavior determination according to this textbook.

15. How is the idea of multiple causation related to dynamic systems theory, and what do these ideas have to do with the idea of epigenesis?

16. State the idea of natural selection in your own words, or give an example of how natural selection might work.

17. Give an account of how natural selection is important to the theory of evolution.

18. State at least one important characteristic of scientific explanation.

19. Give at least one example of what is considered a pseudo-explanation.

20. Compare the scientific explanation to the pseudo-explanation and tell how they are different.

21. Choose one or two of the outstanding people involved in the founding of comparative psychology or ethology, and describe what contributions these individuals made.

22. What critical requirement must be met in order for an intervening variable to qualify as a scientific interpretation?

23. How did the work of the monk Gregor Mendel contribute to the modern theory of evolution?

24. Describe how the concept of learning is related to the level of behavioral organization known as psychotaxis.

25. Consider the idea of anagenesis. How is this idea related to the idea of behavioral levels advanced by psychologists Schneirla and Tobach?

REFERENCES

Adamson, J. (1960). *Born free.* New York: Bartholomew House.

Aronson, L. R. (1984). Levels of integration and organization: A reevaluation of the evolutionary scale. In G. Greenberg & E. Tobach (Eds.), *Behavioral evolution and integrative levels* (pp. 57–81). Hillsdale, NJ: Lawrence Erlbaum.

Balsam, P. D., & Silver, R. (1994). Behavioral change as a result of experience: Toward principles of learning and development. In J. A. Hogan & J. J. Bolhuis (Eds.), *Causal mechanisms of behavioural development* (pp. 327–357). Cambridge, England: Cambridge University Press.

Barnett, S. A. (1981). *Modern ethology.* New York: Oxford University Press.

Beach, F. (1950). The snark was a boojum. *The American Psychologist, 5,* 115–124.

Bertalanffy, L. von. (1933). *Modern theories of development.* London: Oxford University Press.

Bonner, J. T. (1988). *The evolution of complexity.* Princeton, NJ: Princeton University Press.

Chalmers, A. F. (1976). *What is this thing called science.* St. Lucia, Queensland, Australia: University of Queensland Press.

Darwin, C. (1859). *On the origin of species.* London: John Murray.

Darwin, C. (1872). *The expression of the emotions in man and animal.* New York: D. Appleton and Co.

Denny, M. R. (1980). *Comparative psychology: An evolutionary analysis of animal behavior.* New York: John Wiley.

Denny, M. R., & Ratner, S. C. (1970). *Comparative psychology: Research in animal behavior.* Homewood, IL: Dorsey Press.

Dobzhansky, T. (1973). Nothing in biology makes sense except in the light of evolution. *American Biology Teacher, 35,* 125–129.

Domjan, M., & Purdy, J. (1996). Teaching about animal research in psychology. *American Psychologist, 51,* 979–980.

Duffy, E. (1962). *Activation and behavior.* New York: John Wiley.

Epstein, R. (1984). The principle of parsimony and some explanations in psychology. *Journal of Mind and Behavior, 5,* 119–130.

Feibleman, J. K. (1954). Theory of integrative levels. *The British Journal for the Philosophy of Sciences, 5,* 59–66.

Gottlieb, G. (1984). Evolutionary trends and evolutionary origins: Relevance to theory in comparative psychology. *Psychological Review, 92,* 448–456.

Gottlieb, G. (1992). *Individual development and evolution: The genesis of novel behavior.* New York: Oxford University Press.

Greenberg, G. (1988). Levels of social behavior. In G. Greenberg & E. Tobach (Eds.), *Evolution of social behavior and integrative levels* (pp. 137–146). Hillsdale, NJ: Lawrence Erlbaum.

Greenberg, G. (1995). Anagenetic theory in comparative psychology. *International Journal of Comparative Psychology, 8,* 31–41.

Greenberg, G., McCarthy, T., & Bergamo, P. (1989). Depth/distance perception in gerbils and spiny mice: Ecological considerations. *International Journal of Comparative Psychology, 3,* 131–136.

Guthrie, E. R. (1935). *The psychology of learning.* New York: Harper.

Haraway, M. M., & Maples, E. G. (1998a). Species-typical behavior. In G. Greenberg & M. M. Haraway (Eds.), *Comparative psychology: A handbook* (pp. 191–197). New York: Garland.

Haraway, M. M., & Maples, E. G. (1998b). Gibbons, the singing apes. In G. Greenberg & M. M. Haraway (Eds.), *Comparative psychology: A handbook* (pp. 422–430). New York: Garland.

Harolow, H. (1958). The nature of love. *American Psychologist, 13,* 673–685.

Hinde, R. A. (1966). *Animal behaviour: A synthesis of ethology and comparative psychology.* New York: McGraw-Hill.

Hull, C. L. (1943). *Principles of behavior.* New York: Appleton-Century-Crofts.

Innis, N. (1998). History of comparative psychology in biographical sketches. In G. Greenberg & M. M. Haraway (Eds.), *Comparative psychology: A handbook* (pp. 3–24). New York: Garland.

Jerison, H. J. (1994). Evolution of the brain. In D. W. Zaidel (Ed.), *Neuropsychology: Handbook of perception and cognition,* 2nd ed. (pp. 53–82). San Diego: Academic Press.

Kantor, J. R. (1959). *Interbehavioral psychology.* Bloomington, IN: Principia Press.

Kuo, Z. Y. (1967). *The dynamics of behavior development.* New York: Random House.

Lehrman, D. S. (1953). A critique of Konrad Lorenz's theory of instinctive behavior. *Quarterly Review of Biology, 28,* 337–363.

Lerner, R. M. (1998). Developmental contextualism. In G. Greenberg & M. M. Haraway (Eds.). *Comparative psychology: A handbook* (pp. 88–97). New York: Garland.

Lerner, R. M., & Busch-Rossnagel, N. A. (Eds.). (1981). *Individuals as producers of their development: A life-span perspective.* New York: Academic Press.

Lewin, R. (1992). *Complexity: Life at the edge of chaos.* New York: Macmillan.

Lockard, R. B. (1971). Reflections on the fall of comparative psychology: Is there a message for us all? *American Psychologist, 26,* 168–179.

Lorenz, K. (1950). The comparative method in studying innate behavior patterns. *Symposium of the Society of Experimental Biology, 4,* 221–268.

Lorenz, K. (1966). *On aggression.* New York: Harcourt Brace Jovanovich.

Maier, N. R. F., & Schneirla, T. C. (1964). *Principles of animal psychology,* enlarged ed. New York: Dover. (Original work published 1935.)

Malott, R. W. (1998). Operant conditiong. In G. Greenberg & M. M. Haraway (Eds.), *Comparative psychology: A handbook* (pp. 576–585). New York: Garland.

Mayr, E. (1979). Evolution. *Scientific American, 239*(3), 46–55.

Mayr, E., & Provine, W. B. (1980). *The evolutionary synthesis: Perspectives on the unification of biology.* Cambridge, MA: Harvard University Press.

Michel, G. F., & Moore, C. L. (1995). *Developmental psychobiology: An interdisciplinary science.* Cambridge, MA: MIT Press.

Miller, D. B. (1998). Epigenesis. In G. Greenberg & M. M. Haraway (Eds.), *Comparative psychology: A handbook* (pp. 105–106). New York: Garland.

Moltz, H. (1965). Contemporary instinct theory and the fixed action pattern. *Psychological Review, 72,* 27–47.

Montagu, A. (1962). Our changing conception of human nature. In *The humanization of man* (pp. 15–34). New York: Grove Press. (Reprinted from *Impact [UNESCO],* 1952, *3,* 219–232).

Morgan, C. L. (1896). *Introduction to comparative psychology.* London: Scott.

Nieuwkoop, P. D., Johnen, A. G., & Albers, B. (1985). *The epigenetic nature of early chordate development: Inductive interaction and competence.* Cambridge, England: Cambridge University Press.

Nitecki, M. H. (1988). *Evolutionary progress.* Chicago: University of Chicago Press.

Novikoff, A. B. (1945). The concept of integrative levels and biology. *Science, 101,* 209–215.

Papini, M. R. (1998). Classical conditioning. In G. Greenberg & M. M. Haraway (Eds.), *Comparative psychology: A handbook* (pp. 523–530). New York: Garland.

Pavlov, I. P. (1906). The scientific investigation of the psychical faculties or processes in the higher animals. *Science, 24,* 613–619.

Peele, S. (1985). Reductionism in the psychology of the eighties. *American Psychologist, 36,* 807–818.

Pfungst, O. (1965). *Clever Hans.* New York: Holt, Rinehart and Winston. (Original work published 1911.)

Rollo, C. D. (1994). *Phenotypes.* London: Chapman & Hall.

Romanes, G. J. (1970). *Animal intelligence.* London: Kegan Paul, Trench. (Original work published 1882.)

Rose, S. (1997). *Lifelines: Biology beyond determinism.* Oxford, UK: Oxford University Press.

Rosenblatt, J. S. (1995). Schneirla's A/W biphasic processes theory. In K. E. Hood, G. Greenberg, & E. Tobach (Eds.), *Behavioral development: Concepts of approach/withdrawal and integrative levels* (pp. 89–96). New York: Garland.

Rosenblatt, J. S., & Schneirla, T. C. (1962). The behavior of cats. In E. S. E. Hafez (Ed.), *The behaviour of domestic animals* (pp. 453–488). London: Ballière, Tindall & Cox.

Saunders, P. T., & Ho, M. W. (1976). On the increase in complexity in evolution. *Journal of Theoretical Biology, 63,* 375–384.

Savage-Rumbaugh, E. S., Murphy, J., Sevcik, R. A., Brakke, K. E., Williams, S. L., & Rumbaugh, D. R. (1993). Language comprehension in ape and child. *Monographs of the Society for Research in Child Development* (serial no. 233), *58*(3–4).

Schneirla, T. C. (1940). Further studies on the army-ant behavior pattern: Mass organization in the swarm-raiders. *Journal of Comparative Psychology, 25,* 51–90.

Schneirla, T. C. (1959). Aspects of stimulation and organization in approach/withdrawal processes underlying vertebrate behavioral development. In D. S. Lehrman, R. A. Hinde, & E. Shaw (Eds.), *Advances in the study of behavior,* Vol. 1 (pp. 1–74). New York: Academic Press.

Schneirla, T. C. (1972). The concept of development in comparative psychology. In L. R. Aronson, E. Tobach, J. S. Rosenblatt, & D. S. Lehrman (Eds.), *Selected writings of T. C. Schneirla* (pp. 259–294). San Francisco: W. H. Freeman. (Reprinted from D. B. Harris [Ed.], [1957]. *The concept of development* [pp. 78–108]. Minneapolis: University of Minnesota Press.)

Seay, B., & Gottfried, N. (1978). *The development of behavior: A synthesis of developmental and comparative psychology.* Boston: Houghton Mifflin.

Sheldrake, R. (1995). *Seven experiments that could change the world.* New York: Riverhead Books.

Sherrington, C. S. (1906). *The integrative action of the nervous system.* New Haven, CT: Yale University Press.

Thomas, R. (1998). Lloyd Morgan's canon. In G. Greenberg & M. M. Haraway (Eds.), *Comparative psychology: A handbook* (pp. 156–163). New York: Garland.

Thorndike, E. L. (1898). Animal intelligence. An experimental study of the associative processes in animals. *Psychological Monographs, 2*(8).

Thorndike, E. L. (1911). *Animal intelligence.* New York: Macmillan.

Tinbergen, N. (1951). *The study of instinct.* Oxford, England: Clarendon Press.

Tinbergen, N. (1958). *Curious naturalists.* Garden City, NY: Doubleday & Co.

Tobach, E. (1976). Evolution of behavior and the comparative method. *International Journal of Psychology, 11,* 185–201.

Tobach, E., & Aronson, L. R. (1970). T. C Schneirla: A biographical note. In L. R. Aronson, E. Tobach, D. S. Lehrman, & J. S. Rosenblatt (Eds.). *Development and evolution of behavior: Essays in memory of T. C. Schneirla* (pp. xi–xviii). San Francisco: Freeman.

Tobach, E., & Schneirla, T. C. (1968). The biopsychology of social behavior of animals. In R. E. Cooke & S. Levin (Eds.), *The biologic basis of pediatric practice* (pp. 68–82). New York: McGraw-Hill.

Tolman, E. C. (1932). *Purposive behavior in animals and men.* New York: Appleton-Century.

Watson, J. B. (1913). Psychology as the behaviorist views it. *Psychological Review, 20,* 158–177.

Yerkes, R. M. (1905). The sense of hearing in frogs. *Journal of Comparative and Neurological Psychology, 15,* 279–304.

Yerkes, R. M., & Yerkes, D. N. (1928). Concerning memory in the chimpanzee. *Journal of Comparative Psychology, 8,* 237–271.

CHAPTER

2 Biological Foundations of Behavior

[A]ll living things are composed of nearly identical chemical constituents—specific sugars, amino acids, fats, lipids, and nucleic acids—and have basically similar metabolic processes. Most important, all organisms are linked to one another by a common genetic heritage. All of the millions of living species are the product of continuous evolutionary change since their origin from a common ancestry more than 3.5 billion years ago. (Carroll, 1997, p. 1)

For the writers of this book, this continuity of living species underscores the proposition that psychology is a biosocial science and behavior is the result of biosocial processes. That is to say that animals are both biological and psychosocial organisms. The word *organism* is closely related to the word *organization*. As the Nobel Prize–winning physiologist Sir Charles Sherrington put it in his important book of 1906, a healthy animal is a set of integrated organs that regulate one another, the whole making a self-regulating system. This is one way of defining the concept of **homeostasis** in physiology. Homeostasis refers to the ability of warm-blooded animals (**homoiotherms**) to regulate their internal environments. It represents an ability to maintain bodily functions at acceptable limits. For example, our own body temperature is maintained at near 98.6°F despite extreme variations in external temperature. We are made of many parts that are not separate but, instead, are interdependent. In the most complex animals, these organ systems and the crucial roles they play are as follows.

- The **integumental system,** or **skin,** which serves the purpose of protecting the organism from infection and confines it to a particular well-defined space
- The **skeletal system,** which is responsible for the structural support of the organism
- The **muscular system,** which provides the most important means by which organisms do things, by which they behave
- The **endocrine,** or **hormonal, system,** which provides crucial chemicals that regulate biological growth and development
- The **nervous system,** which allows sensory input and motor output to be integrated
- The **circulatory system,** through which blood services all parts of the body
- The **digestive system,** which provides fuel to keep the organism running
- The **excretory system,** which removes waste products from the body

- The **respiratory system,** which takes in oxygen and removes carbon dioxide
- The **reproductive system,** which provides for the continuation and survival of the species

It is important to note that the life processes of the organism depend on the interdependent functioning of all of these systems. No one system may be considered more critical for life than another. This statement applies to an organism's psychology as well; it applies to all aspects of an organism's life.

Organisms make their way through life as integrated systems of highly evolved and specialized parts. This integration is achieved mechanically (e.g., skeletal and muscular systems), chemically (circulatory and endocrine systems), and neurally (nervous system). We consider it the major function of the nervous system to integrate activity of all the systems rather than to control or determine specific behaviors (Greenberg, 1983). Biological processes are seen not as single determining or causal factors in behavior, but rather as important participating factors.

The first three of the five sets of factors we identified in Chapter 1 as contributing to behavioral origins are primarily biological: The phylogenetic set includes the organism's evolutionary history, the individual set includes the organism's unique genotype, and the ontogenetic set includes essential maturational processes and events. However, environmental events and experience also have a major effect on ontogenetic progress; and consideration of the remaining two sets of factors, the experiential set and the cultural set, is largely a consideration of events of experience. The dynamic interactions among all these sets of factors are fundamental to understanding behavioral origins—no one set of factors acts alone or is more important than any other. Next, let us examine several critical biological factors and see how they relate to behavior.

Evolution of Nervous Systems

The evolution of nervous systems and their corresponding increases in complexity are key to the concept of behavioral levels. Behavioral plasticity increases from the lower to the higher levels of complexity, as explained in Chapter 1. This plasticity is made possible by the increasingly complex nervous systems found in animals at each advancing level. Behavioral diversity, plasticity, and flexibility are related to the size of the nervous system: The larger the number of **neurons** and **synapses,** the greater the variety of responses available to the organism. As we pointed out in our earlier discussion, increase in complexity is seen by some to be a second law of evolution, after Darwin's principle of natural selection.

There is agreement among biologists that all existing life forms are related to a single ancestral form. Evidence for this agreement lies in the facts that all cellular life forms share the same genetic mechanism, **DNA,** and all cells are surrounded by the same type of membrane. This **cell membrane** is characterized by an internal negative electrical charge resulting in a state of polarity. When this polarity is disturbed, the disturbance travels as a wave across the membrane's surface. It is this characteristic of cell membranes that made nervous systems possible.

In single-cell organisms, information about the environment is conveyed chemically. In multicellular organisms, chemical communication between and among cells can likewise be achieved, for example, by hormones. But this is an inefficient and slow method of distributing important information to all parts of the organism. As soon as multicellular organisms reached a critical size, cells appeared that were specialized in membrane responsiveness. These became the first nerve cells. Nerve cells were a means by which the functions of large colonies of cells could be integrated. Activity in one part of a system of nerve cells could affect activity in other parts of the system, by either increasing or inhibiting activation at various locations. Nervous systems, then, are integrating systems. They move information into the organism and direct it out to the proper effectors. **Effectors,** the muscles and the glands, are the tissues and organs that allow us to behave. These are the only tissues that enable an animal to *do* something, to make a *response.*

The first nervous systems were primitive nerve nets (see Figure 2.1), found in existing coelenterates such as the hydra. In nerve net systems, neurons are not separate, but are linked together as are the separate strands of a fish net. Accordingly, they conduct their membrane impulses along their fibers in either direction depending on the predominant source of stimulation. Neural conduction consists of a wave of excitation that may pass through the entire organism. Locomotion and orientation remained somewhat limited with the advent of these nervous systems. "The nerve net was not like a maze with only one correct path through, but like a forest in which many tracks converge and diverge but all eventually lead to the other side" (Rose, 1989, p. 150). Animals with such a nervous system can make no specialized movements or distinguish between different types of stimuli. Neural propagation, the spread of sensory arousal, and the instigation of movement are diffuse. This type of nervous system persisted for hundreds of millions of years.

The next advance in nervous system evolution was the appearance of a new type of nerve cell that transmitted its impulse in one direction only. Accompanying this development was the addition of a chemical transmission system at the terminal end of the nerve cell. This transmission system accomplishes the transfer of neural activation from one cell to another. When nerve cells are stimulated, they generate an impulse that travels the length of the cell, along its **axon.** When the impulse reaches the end of the axon, it causes chemicals stored in pockets, or *vesicles,* to be released and fill the synapse into which extend the receiving parts (**dendrites**) of the next neuron. These chemicals, called **neurotransmitters,** contain information that tells the nerve cell either to act or to inhibit its action.

One-way conduction of neural information across chains of successive nerve cells enabled great advances over the organization and integration afforded by nerve nets. In the evolutionary development of nervous systems of this type, groups of neurons became clustered into close packed assemblies and well-defined nerve paths were developed leading from these assemblies and different sensory and effector areas. One of these clusters of closely packed neural cells is called a **ganglion.**

The increased neural organization permitted by these nervous systems resulted in improved locomotion and orientation, as demonstrated by the flatworm, planaria (order Tricladia). The worm achieves a sort of undulating and rhythmic gliding

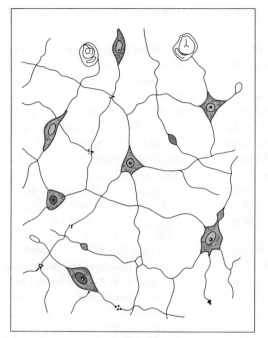

(a) The nervous system of the hydra. The neurons, which are of different shapes, form a nerve net.

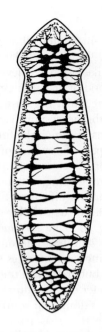

(b) The ladder-like nervous system of the flatworm. Note the concentration of nerve cells at the head end, forming a brain.

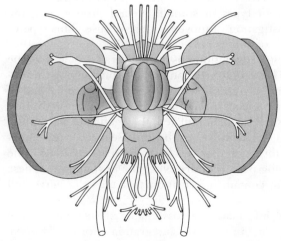

(c) The brain of the octopus. Nerves enter a variety of lobes, each of which is anatomically distinct and involved in different behavioral functions. The central lobes surround the gut.

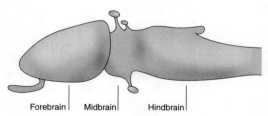

Forebrain | Midbrain | Hindbrain

(d) The primitive vertebrate brain, showing the three swellings of forebrain (cerebral hemispheres), midbrain (diencephalon), and hindbrain. The cerebellum appears as a tiny projection above the hindbrain, the pituitary as a projection below the midbrain.

FIGURE 2.1   Evolution of Nervous Systems

through the water because its nervous system permits coordination of the two sides of the animal and of different sections of the worm's body. The worm has a head end and a tail end. A loose form of coordination between the front and back is provided by a front end grouping of neural cells, the first, very primitive, brain. The appearance of this improvement in nervous system design was accompanied by the appearance of specialized receptors for light, touch, and chemical receptivity. These specialized **sensory receptors** made it possible, for the first time, for organisms to make differential responses to different types of stimuli. Neural evolution and sensory evolution went hand in hand. In annelids such as the earthworms, the head-end, or *cephalic*, ganglia assume even more central control than in planaria. Removing their "heads" interferes noticeably with their behavior. The behavior of burrowing, for example, is slowed down considerably (Maier & Maier, 1970).

The next major advance in nervous systems involved the elaboration of cephalic ganglia, or primitive brains, into more complex brains that coordinated relationships between other groups of ganglia distributed throughout the body. These more sophisticated brains, found in advanced invertebrates, loosely coordinate behavior throughout the animal. Such simple brains are found today in insects, spiders, lobsters, shrimp, and crabs, and are most highly developed in the octopuses and squids (Osorio, Bacon, & Whittington, 1997). In the octopuses, cephalic ganglia are fused into a brain that surrounds the esophagus. In arthropods, there is a cephalic brain, and the entire nervous system is bilaterally symmetrical.

More specialized and sensitive receptor systems appeared as well. The genius of this systematic ganglionic coordination by brains is that it ensures organization while permitting relative autonomy of different functional groups of neurons, allowing various parts of an organism to function with a limited degree of independence from what other parts of the organism are doing. Such coordination permits the growth of specialization. When a hydra reacts, the whole organism responds in a wave, but animals with more centralized nervous systems can move limbs independently of mouths, for example. The implications for improved orientation and locomotion are obvious.

Nevertheless, it is still possible for organisms with centrally organized nervous systems to function without their brains. Spieth (1966) reported that headless fruit flies preened and cleaned themselves normally and could walk and fly normally for brief periods. Headless males could even court females, if stimulated appropriately. Similarly, Horridge (1962) showed that headless cockroaches and locusts could acquire a conditioned (i.e., a learned) leg-position response. Findings such as these show that, in these simple animals, some important functions can be coordinated by nervous tissue outside the brain.

The final stage in nervous system evolution involved two major structural changes. First, there was greater differentiation and separation of specialized nerves. Second, there was greater central concentration of neural integration in a sophisticated brain. These changes were accompanied by the first steps toward bony skeletons, seen first in the form of a crude spinal column (notochord) found in a small seafloor fish, amphioxus, among the very first of the vertebrates. Amphioxus is representative of a group of species with a new organization of the nervous system. Whereas in the octopus the major nervous pathways circle the animal's gut, in amphioxus there is a neural tube embedded in the body running along its full length. Specialized incoming (**afferent impulse**) and outgoing (**efferent impulse**) pathways are present for the first time, representing still another evolutionary advance from the more primitive ganglionic nervous systems. This new arrangement immediately preceded the development of the spinal cord and brain.

The primitive vertebrate brain consists of three swellings: forebrain, midbrain, and hindbrain. Various functions are associated with each of these specialized parts: smell with the forebrain; vision with the midbrain; and equilibrium, vibration, and balance with the hindbrain. All subsequent evolutionary advances preserve this arrangement and involve simply increasing the number and size of these swellings. Advanced vertebrate brains have become larger, but retain the same pattern of division into forebrain, midbrain, and hindbrain. Larger brains mean more neurons, and more neurons, in turn, mean more pathways, circuits, and tracks in the nervous system (Deacon, 1990). More of neural processes resulted in greater and more refined organization permitting greater integration of neural functioning. The increase in neural integration that accompanied increased brain size allowed for greater behavioral plasticity and diversity. Indeed, we find impressive correspondence between increases in brain size and increases in behavioral plasticity and complexity (Jerison, 1994). Increases in body size and complexity require increases in brain size to permit the coordination of more cell and muscle types. As we discuss in a later chapter, these developments eventually made possible the appearance of language and complex culture.

However, the important factor is not mere brain size. Larger animals, even among individuals within the same species, have larger brains than do smaller animals. It is also obvious that many large species are not as behaviorally advanced as many smaller ones. No, the critical dimension is that of the relationship between brain and body size. In vertebrates, there is a trend toward **encephalization.** A relationship called the **encephalization quotient** provides an objective measure of the degree to which encephalization is illustrated in different species, providing "a true dimension based upon objectively measured structural attributes" (Plotkin, 1983, p. 128). Olson (1976) showed that progressive encephalization, particularly an increased amount of cerebral cortex, represents a greater capacity to process information. Killackey (1990) presented a corresponding argument, showing that neocortical expansion and improved information processing follow along phylogenetic lines. The idea of a consistent progression of changes that accompany phylogeny is known as **anagenesis** and is a principal feature of the theoretical orientation we are developing in this book. Improved information processing has been long recognized as a crucial indicator of evolutionary advance (Pantin, 1951).

The scaling of features such as brain size and body size against one another is called **allometry** (Thiessen & Villarreal, 1998), a topic we will discuss later. It is of interest here to point out that the allometric relationship between these two features— brain size and body size—among most mammals is negative, whereas among primates it is positive. That is, primate brains increase in size faster than do primate bodies. This resulted in a ballooning in the brain size of primates relative to their body size. Figure 2.2 illustrates this relationship by showing how large and convoluted the cerebral cortices of primates are compared to other species. As the brain increased so rap-

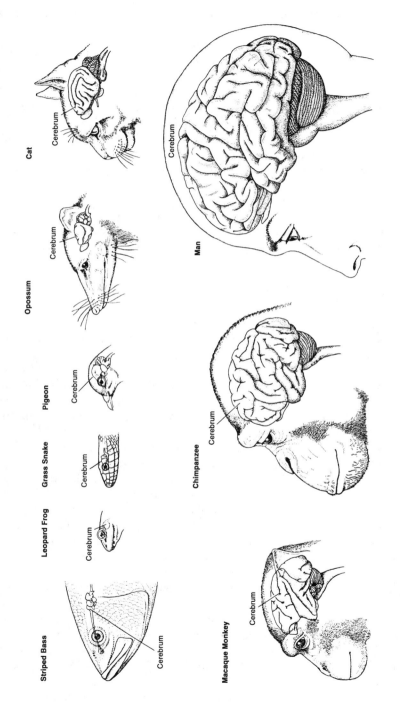

Striped Bass   **Leopard Frog**   **Grass Snake**   **Pigeon**   **Opossum**   **Cat**

Cerebrum

Cerebrum

Cerebrum

Cerebrum

Cerebrum

Cerebrum

Macaque Monkey

Cerebrum

Chimpanzee

Cerebrum

Man

Cerebrum

FIGURE 2.2   **Vertebrate Brains**

idly in size, it had to become squashed and folded like a raisin if it were to fit into the relatively small primate skull. Large animals have numerous and large muscles; complex animals have quite refined sensory/motor systems. Both of these features require great coordination and integration and this, in turn, requires bigger and more integrated brains.

In the primitive fishes such as Agnatha and Chondrichthyes, the forebrain is small and largely olfactory in function. In bony fishes, the forebrain, while still functioning as an olfactory center, is more highly differentiated. Amphibian and reptilian brains are noticeably advanced over those of fishes. The thalamus is larger, reflecting the need and the ability to integrate more advanced and refined sensory information; and the cortex displays the beginnings of a six-layer pattern of arrangement seen in the higher vertebrates. In birds, the cerebellum is more highly developed than in reptiles, reflecting their great facility of balance and motor control. The midbrain optic area is large, as are the cerebral hemispheres and the hypothalamus. In mammals, major advances seen are in forebrain structure and size, especially in respect to the hypothalamus, the limbic system, and the cerebral cortex (Maier & Maier, 1970).

How the Nervous System Works

The functioning of the nervous system displays both basic simplicity and extreme complexity. The basic structural unit of the nervous system is the neuron. Although neurons have the same genes, general organization, and biochemical apparatus as other cells of the body, neurons also have unique features that make the brain function in a very different way from, say, the liver. Important neural specializations include a distinctive cell shape, an outer membrane capable of generating nerve impulses, and a unique structural feature—the synapse, for transferring information from one nerve cell to another (see Figure 2.3).

The nervous systems of human beings contain about one hundred billion (10^{11}) neurons and over one trillion (10^{12}) other cells. Although no two neurons are identical, the forms they take fall into a limited number of categories and share similar structures: a cell body containing the nucleus and the biochemical cellular machinery necessary for life; dendrites, delicate tubelike extensions that branch repeatedly forming a bushy tree around the cell body and providing the main physical surface on which incoming signals are received; and axons, processes that extend away from each cell body and provide the pathways over which signals travel from one cell body to another throughout the nervous system.

When the nerve cell is disturbed, or stimulated, it generates an electrochemical discharge—a **neural impulse**—that is propagated along the axon toward the synapse, where it causes the nerve cell to release chemicals that flood the synapse, bathing the dendrites of the next neuron in the line of progression. These chemicals transmit the impulse to the receiving nerve cell and are known as neurotransmitters. Neurotransmitters can carry either stimulative or inhibitory information, and because as many as a thousand or more cells may come together at a single synapse, what the receiving cell does results from an algebraic summation of excitatory and inhibitory information

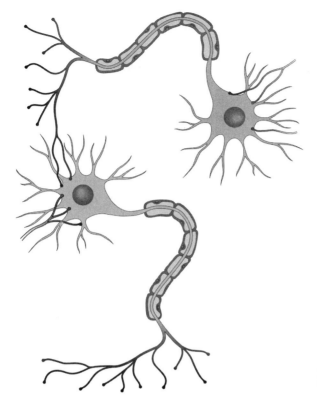

FIGURE 2.3   Illustration of Two Myelinated Nerve Cells

carried by the discharges of numerous axons together. We have known since the 1940s that neurons work in groups, or circuits, and that the constituent membership of these circuits is not predetermined, but rather is formed as a result of patterns of sensory input   (Hebb,   1949;   Petit,   1995).

In simpler organisms, nerve cells are uninsulated, whereas complex organisms tend to have a layer of insulation, or **myelin,** that covers the nerve cells and speeds up neural transmission, making the much larger nervous systems of these organisms function more efficiently. "Myelin is probably the primary factor that made possible the greatly increased complexity of the vertebrate brain" (Thompson, 1993, p. 71).

The Brain and Behavior

We wish to get away from the common description of the brain as being parceled into a number of separate regions, each of which exercises control over its own list of separate functions. Rather, we understand the brain to serve a great integrating function, channeling incoming sensory information to appropriate outgoing motor-control systems and circuits.

During the development of the embryo, animal brains grow an enormously complex web of neurons. Each of these establishes connections with many other neurons by means of the hundreds and thousands of filaments called dendrites. The arrangement of circuits among this tangle of neurons and dendrites—that is, the fine tuning of a brain—is the result of experiential input. In experiments in which kittens were raised in an environment painted with vertical stripes, it was shown that the kittens were unresponsive to horizontal stripes; their visual systems had become programmed to be sensitive to vertical stripes (Crair, Gillespie, & Stryker, 1998; Tieman & Hirsch, 1982). Indeed, **neuroanatomical plasticity** in response to environmental input is so widespread and integral to the functioning of so many brains that they might be considered bio-environmental or biosocial organs (Gibson, 1996). Thus, nervous systems are not prewired into controlling circuits. Rather, trophic processes, directed by incoming information, structure the nervous system into useful circuits. Experience, then, plays a major role in establishing connections and pathways in the nervous system (Benno, 1990; Purves, 1994). In simpler organisms, with far fewer neurons, the extent of variation in circuitry is necessarily limited. More complex organisms, by contrast, have many more neurons that experience can program, and reprogram, in many more ways. This view of neural development is essentially an epigenetic perspective; the young brain indiscriminately proliferates new connections and new routes of development, but only a few of these will survive the results of *neural Darwinism*, or the selective effects of experience (Edelman, 1992). An arrangement such as this is crucial to the development of highly plastic and malleable behavior in higher organisms. We believe it may be considered a major vehicle for the evolutionary emergence of *psychological* events as increasingly prominent factors among what had earlier been largely the *biological* determinants of behavior.

Evolution and Behavior

We suggested in Chapter 1 that an organism's status as a species endows it with the potential to behave in ways unique to that species. As we said, "fish gotta swim, birds gotta fly...." As species evolve, their behavioral potentials change. Unstated until now is the surprising nature of the close tie between behavior and evolution. The surprise is that the chain of influence in this relationship seems to run as much in the direction from evolution to behavior as from behavior to evolution. In a very important and real sense, it is what an organism *does* that allows it to survive and pass on its genes to future generations. Said another way, it is the **phenotype**—actual characteristics of a particular individual animal—in this case the animal's behavior, and not the **genotype** that drives evolution. The Nobel Prize–winning biologist Waddington (1969) put it this way:

> Now natural selection obviously acts on the phenotype. If for instance, natural selection demands that a horse can run fast enough to escape from a predatory wolf, what matters is not what genes the horse has got, but how fast it can run. It is irrelevant whether it can run fast because it has been trained by a good race horse trainer, or because it has got a nice lot of genes. (p. 360)

For almost fifty years Japanese primatologists (Nishida, 1986) have been studying the social behavior and emergent traditions of Japanese macaque monkeys. Provi-
sioned with novel foods—potatoes and rice—the monkeys soon began to toss handfuls
of rice gathered from the sandy beach into the water, where the rice would float and
the sand would sink. The monkeys thus discovered a way to wash sand from their
food. These practices spread throughout the colony and are now part of the animals'
normal behavioral repertoire. The practices are handed down from generation to generation. The case may be considered a primitive form of cultural transmission, although alternative explanations of this behavior have been proposed (Heyes, 1998).
Once they began spending more time near and in the water, young macaques began
playing in it. This play led to the development of new behavioral skills, such as swimming. The animals also incorporated new foods into their diets, such as fish. These
macaques may now be capable of swimming to distant islands. Behavior such as this
would subject them to new ecological pressures and, potentially, could affect the
course of their future evolution. The history of these Japanese macaques provides an
example of how behavior drives evolution. Of course, as organisms change over time
and new species evolve, the new biologies of these species endow them with new behavioral potentials. Thus we see a dual relationship between evolution and behavior:
Behavior drives evolution, but evolution drives behavior as well.

Genetics: The Mechanism of Evolution

When Darwin first put forth his theory of evolution by natural selection, he knew that
traits were passed on from one generation to the next but knew nothing of how that
was accomplished. It was only in the early part of this century that a group of biologists, including Ernst Mayr, Theodoseous Dobzhansy, and George Gaylord Simpson,
incorporated the Mendelian system of genetics into evolutionary theory. The result
produced what is now referred to as the **Modern Synthesis,** or the Synthetic Theory
of evolution, a synthesis of natural selection and genetics (Futuyma, 1986).

Evolution is now understood to involve the formation of new species by changes
in the gene pool that characterizes a parent species (Mayr, 1970). These changes arise
in several ways, most dramatically when a natural barrier arises and separates groups
of animals into two or more different breeding populations. The flow of genes between them is halted and each species, or isolated **gene pool,** now becomes subject to
different ecological pressures. Because the flow of genes is the result of reproduction,
the successful attraction of mates becomes a crucial event in evolution. Mate attraction, for the most part, is accomplished by behavioral means—birdsong, courtship displays, flash rates by fireflies, and so on. Again, we see the important links between
behavior and evolution.

Genes

We pointed out earlier that although Darwin was aware of inheritance of characters,
he knew nothing of the mechanisms of that inheritance. That knowledge would come

from the experiments of an Austrian monk, Gregor Mendel. His experiments, published originally in 1866 and ignored during his lifetime, were rediscovered in 1900. His findings about the inheritance of characteristics in garden peas form the foundation of the modern science of genetics. The important research of Maurice Wilkins, Rosalind Franklin, Francis Crick, and James Watson in the 1950s revealed that one important molecule underlies all life (Watson, 1968). That molecule is DNA (deoxyribonucleic acid), and it forms the genetic material of almost all living organisms.

The simple molecular structure of DNA is that of twin strands spiraling around each other like a staircase (Figure 2.4). The strands are made from four types of molecules, called "bases," held together by other chemicals. This structure permits DNA to encode information and to replicate itself. The coding of information is achieved by the sequence of the four bases and is frequently referred to as the **genetic code.** Replication of DNA is accomplished by the separation of the two strands and the re-creating of a matching strand for each. This process is so complex that it rarely occurs without errors. In sexual reproduction, in which the genes from a male and female join and mix, the room for replicative error provides for enormous flexibility and serves an important role in evolution. This flexibility helps to account, for example, for how a new species can evolve from an older one.

Genes do little more than code for the many different proteins that go into making up living things; the proteins are themselves incorporated into the ever-changing molecular and cellular structure and physiology that is an individual organism. One way of looking at an organism is as a chemical soup. Garrett Hardin (1956), the biologist, said that humans and other animals are not so much *things* as they are *places* where very interesting things are occurring. From this view, the DNA part of this chemical soup ensures that certain chemical reactions take place at certain times. Genes turn reactions on or off; they function as catalysts. They really operate by controlling the timing of important chemical events. When the default schedule is followed, certain interactions inevitably occur. This is the significance of the idea of self-organization we introduced earlier. It isn't necessary for genes directly to encode particular functional or structural features. Rather, important biochemical, and then biological, events will follow automatically from the laws of physics, chemistry, geometry, topology, and so on (Elman, 1996).

In this context it is again useful to distinguish between the *genotype* and the *phenotype*. The genotype is the actual genetic code, the genetic blueprint that influences every cell of our bodies. Because all of an individual's cells trace their beginnings to a single daughter cell, the genotype of each cell must be identical. The result of how those genes express themselves is the phenotype. So, although all of an individual's cells have the same genotype, some become bone cells, some blood cells, some skin cells. Human beings possess some 256 different types of cells. These different cells arise as a result of epigenetic forces acting upon the genes and causing them to express themselves in different ways. Appreciation of this fact provides a major accomplishment of the dynamic systems approach taken in this book. Genes express themselves in the context of a field of internal and external forces that impinge upon them (Stoltenberg & Hirsch, 1998).

Molecular biology has learned a great deal about the functioning of genes in the past few decades, exploding a number of ideas we now see to be myths (Keller, 2000).

Adenine

Thymine

Guanine

Cytosine

Hydrogen
bond

Gene

Amino acids

Proteins and enzymes

FIGURE 2.4   DNA—the Double Helix

These include the notion that single genes affect single traits—eye color, for example. Although some single gene–single traits are known to exist, the common mode is for genes to act in concert with others. What a gene does, then, is very much influenced by which other genes are being turned on or off at any particular time during development. In other words, genes always do their work in combination with other genes rather than individually. The developmental process, then, is not a predetermined one, but rather, a probabilistic one. Stated another way, "Since it has become evident that genes interact with their environment at all levels, including the molecular, there is virtually no interesting aspect of development that is strictly 'genetic,' at least in the sense that it is exclusively a product of information contained within the genes" (Elman, 1996, p. 21).

Genes and Behavior

The most important phenotype for us is the behavior of an organism. The behavior of the organism contributes to its survival, providing abilities to solve numerous problems in life that it cannot help but encounter. Because genes are only chemicals and behavior is the activity of an organism, the contribution of genes to behavior must necessarily be indirect; and it is. Genes are largely responsible for organisms having such things as wings, color vision, or upright walking. But using these processes in particular ways is always probabilistic or, as we said in Chapter 1, a result of an epigenetic process. This arrangement is addressed by the principle of behavioral potentials we introduced in Chapter 1. Each organism inherits the potential to behave in species-typical ways, but the experiences of organisms shape their behavior almost from the moment of conception. In the simplest organisms, the range of experiential possibilities is rather limited. We expect all ants to have a fairly homogenized array of experiences and a correspondingly homogenized array of behaviors. Primate experiences, on the other hand, are quite varied, as is individual primate behavior (Moltz, 1965).

Hormones and Behavior

The endocrine system is the second most important communication system of the body, after the nervous system (Saldahna & Silver, 1998). This form of communication is achieved through distribution by the bloodstream of hormones produced by the endocrine glands. Hormones serve two important roles: They organize tissue growth and development, and in some instances they activate behavior. *Organizing* effects are achieved by means of the influence of hormones on the characteristics of cell membrane potentials (a nongenomic influence) or on the genetic expression of target cells (a genomic influence). Activating effects are achieved by raising or lowering behavioral thresholds for stimulation and action.

An example of what we mean by the organizing effects of hormones would be the influence of estrogen and testosterone (female and male sex hormones) on the development of the genital organs. Although we simplistically label humans with XX and XY chromosomes as female and male, respectively, the development of appropriate female and male genitalia involves much more than the genes possessed by these X and Y chromosomes. As chemicals themselves, hormones serve as catalysts that affect the nature of chemical reactions. They activate some genes and inhibit the activation of others. Genes play an important role in the production of estrogen and testosterone, and the development of genitalia is greatly influenced by when, and in what amounts, these hormones are produced during embryogenesis. Recent research has shown that female mouse embryos (XX chromosomes) can be masculinized by being located downstream on the placenta from their sibling male mouse embryos (XY chromosomes) (Meisel & Ward, 1981). That is, being bathed in the male hormone testosterone, the female embryos develop masculine characteristics. This observation affords an excellent example of the dynamic systems model we have adopted in this book. Even the sex of an organism is determined not by genes or hormones alone, but rather by a dynamic interaction of these and other events and processes.

The *activating* effects of hormones are illustrated by the classic but still-important research of Lehrman (1964) that showed the way in which hormones influence the expression of sexual behavior of ring doves (*Streptopelia risoria*). The reproductive cycle in these birds lasts from six to seven weeks and includes one or more sequences of male courtship, nest building, copulation, egg laying and incubation, and feeding of the squabs until fifteen to twenty-five days of age. This behavior occurs reliably in experienced birds and only when they are together. Isolated experienced birds will not behave this way; indeed, isolated experienced females will not even lay eggs. There are, then, psychosocial underpinnings of this behavior.

Internal factors are at work also. The birds do not build nests simply in the presence of nest-building material, but do so only at one stage in the cycle. Egg incubation occurs only after the male and female have been together for a period of time and is not induced simply in the presence of eggs. The injection of the hormones progesterone, estrogen, and prolactin will induce these various behaviors, but only if administered in the proper succession of hormone secretions, as they occur during a normal reproductive cycle. The important conclusions drawn from this work are not only that hormones induce behaviors but also that they do so only in a dynamic relationship with other, psychological, factors, such as the presence of a mate, nesting materials, or eggs.

Other Biological Factors

Allometry

Allometry is the statistical comparison of biological and behavioral characteristics (Thiessen & Villarreal, 1998). It is the search for meaningful correlations between such variables, as in the brain–body weight relationship discussed earlier. An example is the relationship between locomotor speed and stamina in lizards. Sinervo and Huey (1990) were able to demonstrate that the small form of the lizard *Sceloponous occidentalis* shows low burst speed and has little cruising stamina. On the other hand, the larger form of this lizard shows high burst speed and better cruising stamina. Allometric analysis thus reveals a high correlation between body size and locomotor behavior. We tend to ignore the effects of body size on behavior, even though they are significant, because body size affects metabolic rates, sensory/motor capacities, and foraging strategies. Small animals have proportionally higher energy expenditures than do large animals and so tend to rush through life (Thiessen & Villarreal, 1998); they hear and produce higher sound frequencies than larger animals (Heffner & Heffner, 1998); and they have smaller home territories (Thiessen, 1990). Many other such relationships can be illustrated. The important point is that, together with anagenetic analysis, allometry provides a major way of relating evolutionary advance and behavioral plasticity and complexity.

Biological Rhythms

Much animal behavior shows a regular pattern of alternating activity and inactivity regulated by both internal and external stimuli or cues. These alternating activity patterns are called **biological rhythms** and occur in a great many living organisms, both plants and animals (Turek, 1994). Internal regulation, termed *endogenous*, is said to constitute a "biological clock"; it often involves hormonal and neural processes. External influences of biological rhythms are termed *exogenous* and are sometimes called **zeitgebers,** or time givers. These include such events as day length and temperature. Biological rhythms can vary greatly in the time intervals they encompass. Those shorter than a day are termed **ultradian,** twenty-four-hour rhythms are referred to as **circadian,** and those longer than a day are **infradian.** Ultradian rhythms include cardiac and respiratory rhythms, feeding cycles, and sleep, which we will treat in detail in the next section. Many ultradian rhythms are controlled by hormones, themselves released in an ultradian fashion. Circadian rhythms include the activity cycles of animals that are **diurnal** (active during daylight), such as most primates; **nocturnal** (active at night), such as many rodents and some birds such as owls; or **crepuscular** (active at sunset and at sundown), such as the Mongolian gerbil, a rodent kept frequently as a pet in the United States. For the most part, circadian rhythms are under endogenous control, although environmental changes frequently do alter these behaviors. Infradian rhythms include estrous cycles, the human menstrual cycle, hibernation, and annual migratory behaviors. These longest rhythmic behaviors are frequently under exogenous control. For example, migratory behavior is frequently begun in response to systematic changes in day lengths as seasons change.

It is of interest that many circadian rhythms are usually longer or shorter than a twenty-four-hour day. If uninfluenced by exogenous factors, the "free-running" sleep-activity cycles of the human and the mouse are, respectively, twenty-five and twenty-three hours. That is, when isolated from any cues about day or night (as in a submarine or a deep cave), the human cycle is not twenty-four hours, but rather twenty-five hours.

Can you recall how disturbed your behavior was when your regular sleep cycle was disrupted by an overseas trip, for example, by jet lag? Imagine that you are an astronaut aboard the space shuttle preparing to make repairs to the Hubble Orbiting Telescope. This work will involve an eight-hour EVA (extravehicular activity), during which time you will experience night every forty-five minutes and daylight every forty-five minutes as the shuttle completes each ninety-minute orbit. If jet lag is disruptive, what sorts of behavioral effects will this unusual day–night cycle produce (McEachron & Schull, 1993)? Because there is an acute need for astronauts to remain in peak condition at all times, additional research into this effect is needed as a practical consideration.

Although we know little about the clocks that regulate rhythmic alterations in activity, we do know that they may be set by external cues. Thus, the diurnal circadian activity cycle of the blow fly does not develop normally unless the developing fly larva is exposed to at least one twenty-four-hour light–dark cycle (Moltz, 1965). In nature, of course, such exposure is inevitable. At least one neural structure has been identified, the pineal gland, that is sensitive to light and acts something like a third eye in many birds in the regulation of activity cycles. This sensitivity appears to provide a mechanism that monitors day length and acts as a trigger to migratory and other infradian activity.

Sleep

An important aspect of biological rhythm is **sleep,** a behavior that occurs throughout the animal kingdom (Webb, 1998). We may not think of them as doing so, but even cockroaches sleep, as much as 14 hours per day! Among primates, humans sleep about 7 to 8 hours a day, less than do chimpanzees (8.3 hours), baboons (9.8 hours), or rhesus monkeys (11.8 hours). The sleep cycle is itself divided into still smaller cycles, identified by EEG records as *high-voltage, slow-wave sleep* and *low voltage, high-wave sleep.* The latter cycle is known as active, paradoxical sleep, and it is the period in which humans appear most often to dream. Of course, although many animals also display this type of EEG record and sleep stage (including preverbal humans), it is impossible to know whether they are dreaming because only humans can report that fact to us (see Table 2.1).

Why do animals sleep? The earliest idea in explanation of this problem stems from Aristotle, who recognized that all animals must stop moving for a time in order to restore their strength. This idea is the basis of the *restorative model* of sleep, and it is still an important explanatory principle today. But this idea is incomplete. For example, it follows from the restorative model that the longer an animal has been kept awake, the longer it should sleep when again given the chance. Observations simply do not bear out this expectation. A second explanation holds sleep to be an *adaptive behavior* in which an animal's sleep periods match its inactivity with the active periods of its natural predators. Thus, animals sleep while their predators are most active and are awake when their predators are least active. Sleep keeps animals relatively safe and quiet during the most dangerous times of day. The idea of "instinct" has sometimes been invoked to account for such observations as these. We are not tempted by such invocations, however, and much prefer the approach of Webb (1998), who developed an

evolutionary theory that assumes that sleep evolved as an adaptive process in the survival of each species in its ecological niche. Periods of non-responding are necessary for survival and sleep serves as a necessary condition to aid and maintain these periods of non-responding. (p. 344)

TABLE 2.1   Sleep Durations, PS within Sleep, and Dark–Light Placement of Sleep

Class/Species	Total Sleep/Rest (hours)	PS (hours)	Dark/Light (placement)	
Invertebrates				
cockroach	14.0		+	+++
Fish				
guppy	>6–7<		+	+++
Amphibians				
bullfrog	>0<			
lake frog	2.4			
Reptiles				
caiman	3.0		+++	+
alligator	12.5			
desert iguana	>16–18<			
python	>16–20<			
Birds				
chicken	17.6	1.2		
duck	8.8	1.4	++	++
penguin	10.5	1.4	++	++
pigeon	10.6	0.7	+++	+
swan	>3–4<	>?<		++++
herring gull	5.0	>?<	+++	+
Mammals				
Monotremes:				
echidna	8.6	>0<	+	+++
Marsupials:				
opossum	13.8	5.6	+	+++
Insectivores:				
hedgehog	10.7	4.1	+	+++
mole	8.4	2.1		
shrew	12.8	2.0	+	+++
brown bat	19.9	7.0		
Primates:				
rhesus	11.8	1.2	+++	+
baboon	9.8	7	++++	
chimpanzee	8.3	1.3	####	
human	>7–8<	1.7	####	
Endentates:				
sloth	16	>?<	##	##
armadillo	17.4	3.1	##	##
Rodents:				
squirrel	13.9	3.4	##	##
hamster	14.4	3.4	#	###
rat	10.6	2.6	#	###
Cetaceans:				
dolphin	10.4			

TABLE 2.1   Continued

Class/Species	Total Sleep/ Rest (hours)	PS (hours)	Dark/Light (placement)	
Carnivores:				
dog	8.6	2.5	###	#
cat	12.4	3.4	###	#
fox	9.8	2.4	#	###
Proboscidea:				
Asian elephant	>4–6<	>?<	####	
Perissodactyla:				
horse	2.9	0.8	###	#
Artiodactyla:				
sheep	3.2	0.6	###	#
cow	3.9	0.7	###	#
pig	8.4	1.9	###	#

Source: Webb, W. (1998). Sleep. In G. Greenberg & M. M. Haraway (Eds.), *Comparative psychology: A handbook* (pp. 328–329). New York: Garland.

Sensory Processes

We begin this discussion with the basic idea that animals are continuously and dynamically interacting with their environments: They eat, dispose wastes, exchange energy. The environment, too, is a dynamic and ever-changing field. It was thus always relevant to survival for animals to be able to detect and respond to significant aspects of environmental change. As organisms became more complex, responsiveness to environmental change became progressively more critical to their success. It is in this context that the specialized organs of sensory reception evolved. Animals are surrounded by a pressing, vibrating, radiating, chemically reacting manifold of physical energies. Into this maelstrom of forces extends the nervous system, in the form of the sense organs. Of necessity, an organism observes and reacts to the world through various modalities of sensation, of which there are many more than the traditionally stated five. The human organism, for example, possesses thirteen separate and distinct sensory systems: vision, hearing, touch (pressure), pain, warmth, cold, smell, the four tastes (sweet, sour, bitter, salty), kinesthesis, and the vestibular sense. Different animals have different sensory needs and so have evolved different senses. Some animals apparently can detect the magnetic fields of the earth and may utilize this information in orientation, homing, and migrating, which we will discuss in detail in Chapter 3. Other species are equipped with sensory receptors enabling them to detect stimuli such as web vibration (spiders), water pressure and velocity (fish), and electrical fields (fish) (Tamar, 1972). Of course, within each sensory spectrum, each species responds to only a narrow range of possible stimulus values.

- The human ear responds to sounds between 16,000 and 20,000 cycles per second.

- Bats and dogs respond to much higher frequencies (150,000 and 50,000, respectively).
- Bees can "see" light within the ultraviolet range, and snakes can "see" within the infrared range.
- Bees respond differentially to only nine of thirty-four substances that humans consider to be sweet.
- Primates seldom rely on olfaction as a primary orienting sense, whereas bloodhounds frequently do (Tamar, 1972).

Thus, the world is encountered in very different ways for animals of different species, and their reactions are guided by the different arrays of stimuli they sense. Behavioral differences between species, then, result from these sensory differences as well as other differences in the array of morphological adaptations provided them by evolution.

A careful reading of Maier and Schneirla (1932/1964) allows us to discern a number of principles that apply to the evolution of sensory systems:

1. Receptor systems become more complex as we ascend through the behavioral levels, taxis to psychosocial. This trend is especially true for hearing and chemoreception and somewhat less true for vision. Cephalopods and insects, for example, have well-developed eyes. As with all trends in evolution, reversals are found.
2. Evolution has resulted in the appearance of more specialized receptors as we ascend through the behavioral levels. The single-cell amoeba (*Amoeba proteus*), with no nervous system or receptors, is generally and indiscriminately responsive to light, chemicals, and tactile stimulation. Lacking a nervous system, the amoeba can respond only with the overall constituents of its organismic cell. The hydra, which possesses a primitive nerve net nervous system, does have receptors, yet it responds generally and does not differentiate between stimulus types. There are, however, reversals to be found in this trend. The single-cell euglena does have a specialized eye spot, sensitive to light.
3. Receptors illustrate a trend from detecting proximal stimuli to distal stimuli as animal sensory systems have become more specialized and sensitive. Some species of moths, for example, can detect female pheromones as distant as a mile away. There has been a related shift from reliance on proximal to distal receptor systems as we ascend the behavioral levels. Thus, we find that senses of chemoreception are less important among primates, which depend more heavily on their visual and auditory systems. This is especially true in reproductive behavior (e.g., Goldfoot, Essock-Vitale, Asa, Thornton, & Leshner, 1978).
4. There is a trend toward a greater degree of sensory integration as we ascend through the behavioral levels. In the amoeba, for example, stimulation from different sources simply summates, so that weak light and weak touch, neither of which alone results in a reaction, do so when presented together. In the more complex mollusks, different phases of reactions are governed by different stimuli. Thus, the scallop *Pecten* extends its tentacles at the sight of an approaching starfish. As the starfish comes near, chemical stimuli from the starfish stimulates valve closing and swimming away by the scallop. In animals at this level, simultaneous stimulation in two modalities may inhibit action. A snail cannot eat its food if its foot is being touched at the same time. The higher mammals, on the other hand, are able to uti-

lize stimulus cues from several modalities at once to guide their responses. Learning in one modality even transfers to other modalities.

Summary: Principles Introduced in This Chapter

Animals are biosocial beings. Biological processes are as essential to the development of their behavior as are psychosocial processes. The important biological processes that affect behavioral development are evolution, genes, nervous systems, and hormones. None of these factors works in isolation. There is, rather, a dynamic interplay between them all. Behavior drives evolution, by providing animals with the means to survive and pass on their genes. As brains evolved they got larger and more complex, and this provided a basis for the development of increasing behavioral complexity with phylogenetic progression. This relationship is known as anagenesis. The circuitry and programming of the nervous system are the result of trophic processes; experience, in the form of sensory input, strongly influences the final circuitry of the nervous system. Sensory systems are different among animal species. Sensory systems and their complexity co-evolved with nervous systems. More advanced animals tend to have more highly developed sensory systems.

KEY TERMS

Afferent impulse a neural impulse traveling in an incoming direction from the bodily extremities toward the brain.

Allometry the statistical comparison of biological and behavioral characteristics, as in describing the relation between an animal's size or weight and its maximum running speed or its normal heart rate.

Anagenesis the idea that there is a directional progression over time in evolution; this directional progression is seen most clearly in the evolutionary appearance of new species out of these provided by the existence of older, more anciently established, species.

Axon the transmitting end of a neuron that, by the flow of neurotransmitter chemicals, transfers the excitation of a neural impulse across a synapse to the dendrite of another neuron.

Biological rhythms regular patterns of alternating activity and inactivity; these patterns are regulated by both internal conditions and external stimuli.

Cell membrane the outer covering of each cell; like the skin of an organism, the cell membrane forms a cell's boundary and separates it from other cells.

Circadian activity cycles that are about the duration of a single day.

Circulatory system the system that supplies the circulation of blood to all parts of the body.

Crespuscular active during the edges of the day, at twilight and at dawn.

Dendrite the receiving end of a neuron, sensitive to the flow of neurotransmitter chemicals such as acetylcholine and epinephrine.

Digestive system the system that processes food into usable forms of energy for distribution through the circulatory system to all parts of the body.

Diurnal active during times of daylight.

DNA (deoxyribonucleic acid) the extensive molecules, formed in the shape of a double helix, whose details of construction comprise the genetic code.

Effectors the muscles and the glands, the tissues and organs that allow us to behave.

Efferent impulse   a neural impulse traveling in an outgoing direction from the brain toward effectors.

Encephalization   a concentration of the body's neural tissues inside the head; that is, a concentration of neural tissues in a brain.

Encephalization quotient   the ratio of brain weight to body weight, used as a rough measure of the relative degree of encephalization illustrated by different species.

Endocrine, or hormonal, system   the system that supplies critical chemicals regulating physiological functioning, growth, and development.

Excretory system   the system that collects and removes waste products from the body.

Ganglion   a cluster of closely packed neural cells located outside the brain.

Gene pool   the genes represented by all the surviving members of a species, containing all existing gene variations.

Genetic code   the code built in to the details of construction of DNA molecules and considered the physical agent of inheritance.

Genotype   the actual genetic makeup of an individual, regardless of whether the potential represented by that genetic makeup is developed or how it is developed.

Homeostasis   in physiology, the ability of warm-blooded animals (homoiotherms) to regulate their internal environments such that bodily functions are maintained at acceptable limits.

Homoiotherms   warm-blooded animals.

Infradian   activity cycles that are of longer duration than a day.

Integumental system (skin)   the tissues covering the external surface of the body, providing a boundary between the body and the environment and functioning to protect the organism from infection.

Modern Synthesis   the synthesis of the ideas of *natural selection* and *genetics* to form the modern theory of evolution.

Muscular system   the primary system enabling an organism's movement and action.

Myelin   a sheath of material covering the axons of many neurons, serving to increase the speed of transmission of neural impulses down the length of the axons.

Nervous system   the system that receives sensory input and integrates it with motor output.

Neural impulse   a wave of chemical/electrical action that travels along the cell membrane of a neuron from the dendrite to the axon and is transmitted by the release of chemicals across the synapse from the axon of one neuron to the dendrite of another neuron.

Neurons   individual cells of the nervous system.

Neuroanatomical plasticity   the ability of the circuitry of the brain to change over the lifetime of an animal as a result of its experience.

Neurotransmitters   the chemical agents that carry neural messages across the synapse between one neuron and the next.

Nocturnal   active during times of darkness.

Phenotype   the actual characteristics developed in the interaction of an individual's genetic makeup and the environment in which the individual develops.

Receptors, sensory receptors   neural cells that receive and transmit information about immediate conditions around them by means of their sensitivity to particular sources of energy from the environment.

Reproductive system   the system that manufactures and delivers or receives the physiological elements that provide for continuation of the species beyond the life span of the individual organism.

Respiratory system   the system that absorbs oxygen from the environment and removes carbon dioxide from the body.

Skeletal system   an organism's internal system of structural support.

Sleep   a state of relative inactivity and decreased responsiveness to stimulation that recurs on a regular basis.

Synapses   a space between two neurons, across which neural impulses are transmitted by the flow of neurotransmitter chemicals such as acetylcholine and epinephrine.

Ultradian   activity cycles that are of shorter duration than a day.

Zeitgebers   external influences of biological rhythms, from the German construction meaning "time givers."

REVIEW QUESTIONS

1. Briefly tell what it means to view behavior as the product of a dynamic interaction of factors.

2. Of course, survival and reproductivity depend upon the functioning of all systems of the body. Nevertheless, if you had to pick only two bodily systems that are directly related to behavior, which two systems would you pick? Give a reason for your choice in each case. (There may be more than two correct choices, provided good reasons for them are given.)

3. What is the significance of the DNA molecule?

4. What importance is attached to the evolutionary appearance of cells that were specialized in membrane responsiveness?

5. Describe the role of neurotransmitters in the conduction of a neural impulse.

6. What is the role of the dendrite in neural transmission?

7. What is the role of the axon in neural transmission?

8. How are sensory receptors distinguished from other neurons?

9. Give an example of an allometric relationship.

10. What two ideas are combined in the Modern Synthesis?

11. What is meant by the *gene pool* of a species?

12. What is the distinction between genotype and phenotype?

13. Distinguish among diurnal, nocturnal, and crepuscular animals.

14. Tell two distinguishing features of the state known as sleep.

15. Briefly describe how the encephalization quotient is related to the complexity and plasticity of behavior.

16. Draw a rough sketch of a neuron, showing the dendrite, the axon, the synapses, and the direction taken in the transmission of neural impulses.

REFERENCES

Benno, R. H. (1990). Development of the nervous system: Genetics, epigenetics, and phylogenetics. In M. E. Hahn, J. K. Hewitt, N. D. Henderson, & R. Benno (Eds.), *Developmental behavior genetics: Neural, biometrical, and evolutionary approaches* (pp. 113–143). New York: Oxford University Press.

Carroll, R. L. (1997). *Patterns and processes of vertebrate evolution.* Cambridge, England: Cambridge University Press.

Crair, M. C., Gillespie, D. C., & Stryker, M. P. (1998). The role of visual experience in the development of columns in cat visual cortex. *Science, 279,* 566–569.

Deacon, T. (1990). Rethinking mammalian brain evolution. *American Zoologist, 30,* 629–705.

Edelman, G. A. (1992). *Bright air, brilliant fire: On the matter of mind.* New York: Basic Books.

Elman, J. L. (1996). *Rethinking innateness: A connectionist perspective on development.* Cambridge, MA: MIT Press.

Futuyma, D. J. (1986). *Evolutionary biology*, 2nd ed. New York: Sinauer Associates.

Gibson, K. R. (1996). The biocultural human brain, seasonal migrations, and the emergence of the upper paleolithic. In P. Mellars and K. Gibson (Eds.), *Modeling the early human mind* (pp. 33–46). Cambridge, England: McDonald Institute for Archeological Research.

Goldfoot, D. A., Essock-Vitale, S. M., Asa, C., Thornton, J. E., & Leshner, A. L. (1978). Anosmia in male rhesus monkeys does not alter copulatory activity with cycling females. *Science, 199*, 1095–1096.

Greenberg, G. (1983). Psychology without the brain. *Psychological Record, 33*, 49–58.

Hardin, G. (1956). Meaninglessness of the word protoplasm. *Scientific Monthly, 82*(3), 112–120.

Hebb, D. O. (1949). *The organization of behavior.* New York: John Wiley.

Heffner, H. E., & Heffner, R. S. (1998). Hearing. In G. Greenberg & M. M. Haraway (Eds.), *Comparative psychology: A handbook* (pp. 290–303). New York: Garland.

Heyes, C. M. (1998). Theory of mind in nonhuman primates. *Behavioral and Brain Sciences, 21*, 101–148.

Horridge, G. A. (1962). Learning of leg position by the ventral nerve cord in headless insects. *Proceedings of the Royal Society, 157*, 33–52.

Jerison, H. J. (1994). Evolution of the brain. In D. W. Zaidel (Ed.), *Neuropsychology. Handbook of perception and cognition*, 2nd ed. (pp. 53–82). San Diego: Academic Press.

Keller, E. F. (2000). *The century of the gene.* Cambridge, MA: Harvard University Press.

Killackey, H. P. (1990). Neocortical expansion: An attempt toward relating phylogeny and ontogeny. *Journal of Cognitive Neuroscience, 2*, 1–17.

Lehrman, D. S. (1964). The reproductive behavior of ring doves. *Scientific American, 211*(Nov.), 48–54.

Maier, N. R. F., & Schneirla, T. C. (1932/1964). *Principles of animal psychology.* New York: Dover.

Maier, R. A., & Maier, B. M. (1970). *Comparative animal behavior.* Belmont, CA: Brooks/Cole.

Mayr, E. (1970). *Populations, species and evolution.* Cambridge, MA: Harvard University Press.

McEachron, D. L., & Schull, J. (1993). Hormones, rhythms, and the blues. In J. Schulkin (Ed.), *Hormonally induced changes in mind and brain* (pp. 287–355). San Diego: Academic Press.

Meisel, R. L., & Ward, I. L. (1981). Fetal female rats are masculinized by male littermates located caudally in the uterus. *Science, 213*, 239–242.

Moltz, H. (1965). Contemporary instinct theory and the fixed action pattern. *Psychological Review, 72*, 27–47.

Nishida, T. (1986). Local traditions and cultural transmission. In B. B. Smuts, D. L. Cheney, R. M. Seyfarth, R. W. Wrangham, & T. T. Struhsaker (Eds.), *Primate societies* (pp. 462–274). Chicago: University of Chicago Press.

Olson, E. C. (1976). Rates of evolution of the nervous system and behavior. In R. B. Masterton, W. Hodos, & H. Jerison (Eds.), *Evolution, brain and behavior: Persistent problems* (pp. 47–77). Hillsdale, NJ: Lawrence Erlbaum.

Osorio, D., Bacon, J. P., & Whittington, P. M. (1997). The evolution of arthropod nervous systems. *American Scientist, 85*, 244–253.

Pantin, C. F. A. (1951). Organic design. *The Advancement of Science, 30*, 138–150.

Petit, T. L. (1995). Structure and plasticity of the Hebbian synapse: The cascading events for memory storage. In N. E. Spear, L. P. Spear, & M. L. Woodruff (Eds.), *Neurobehavioral plasticity: Learning, development, and response to brain insults* (pp. 185–203). Hillsdale, NJ: Lawrence Erlbaum.

Plotkin, H. C. (1983). The functions of learning and cross-species comparisons. In G. C. L. Davey (Ed.), *Animal models of human behavior* (pp. 117–134). New York: John Wiley.

Purves, D. (1994). *Neural activity and the growth of the brain.* Cambridge, England: Cambridge University Press.

Rose, S. (1989). *The conscious brain*, rev. ed. New York: Paragon House.

Saldahna, C. J., & Silver, R. (1998). Hormones and behavior. In G. Greenberg & M. M. Haraway (Eds.), *Comparative psychology: A handbook* (pp. 304–312). New York: Garland.

Sherrington, C. S. (1906). *The integrative action of the nervous system.* New Haven, CT: Yale University Press.

Sinervo, B., & Huey, R. B. (1990). Allometric engineering: An experimental test of the causes of interpopulational differences in performance. *Science, 248*, 1106–1109.

Spieth, H. T. (1966). Drosophilid mating behavior: The behavior of decapitated females. *Animal Behaviour, 14*, 226–235.

Stoltenberg, S. F., & Hirsch, J. (1998). Behavior-genetic analysis. In G. Greenberg & M. M. Haraway (Eds.), *Comparative psychology: A handbook* (pp. 226–235). New York: Garland.

Tamar, H. (1972). *Principles of sensory physiology.* Springfield, IL: Charles C. Thomas.

Thiessen, D. (1990). Body size, allometry, and comparative psychology: Locomotion and foraging. In D. Dewsbury (Ed.), *Contemporary issues in comparative psychology* (pp. 80–100). Sunderland, MA: Sinauer Associates.

Thiessen, D., & Villarreal, R. (1998). Allometry and comparative psychology: Technique and theory. In G. Greenberg & M. M. Haraway (Eds.), *Comparative psychology: A handbook* (pp. 51–65). New York: Garland.

Thompson, R. F. (1993). *The brain,* 2nd ed. New York: W. H. Freeman.

Tieman, S. B., & Hirsch, H. V. B. (1982). Exposure to lines of only one orientation modifies dendritic morphology of cells in the visual cortex of cats. *Journal of Comparative Neurology, 211,* 353–362.

Turek, F. W. (1994). Circadian rhythms. In C. W. Bardin (Ed.). *Recent progress in hormone research,* Vol. 49 (pp. 43–90).

Waddington, C. H. (1969). The theory of evolution today. In A. Koestler & J. R. Smythies (Eds.), *Beyond reductionism: New perspectives in the life sciences* (pp. 357–395). London: Hutchinson.

Watson, J. D. (1968). *The double helix.* New York: Atheneum.

Webb, W. (1998). Sleep. In G. Greenberg & M. M. Haraway (Eds.), *Comparative psychology: A handbook* (pp. 327–331). New York: Garland.

CHAPTER

3 Orientation and Locomotion

The Problem of Orientation

The world is far from being a rose garden devoid of problems. Just making it through a single day is a challenge for most animals and demands solutions to numerous problems. Behavior patterns are the ways animals have developed to solve these problems of life. Survival and reproduction require solutions to the problems of finding one's way over short and long distances; selecting suitable places to live and to reproduce; finding food for one's self and avoiding becoming the food of some other animal. Solutions to these problems revolve around the question of how to find one's way around in the environment. This is the question of orientation, a main theme of this chapter.

Orientation refers to the directional aspect of behavior. It concerns the manner in which organisms are able to focus their behavior on particular features among a sea of potential stimuli and how they are able to guide their behavior according to those particular stimuli. Orientation may be defined as the process by which animals direct their behavior in relation to some point of reference—perhaps in relation to some **goal-object** or event. Traditional accounts of orientation have included discussion of migration, or periodic movement from one location or climate to another; of navigation, or the process and the cues by which animals maintain their positions with respect to reference points in moving over long distances; and of homing, in which animals return to their home sites after traveling far afield or having been displaced. We will address these topics in the present discussion and also will describe a theoretical perspective on the concept of orientation.

Orientation and Motivation

Orientation is evident in all behavior that relates to the environment surrounding an organism, even behavior that addresses part of an organism's body such as its own feathers, skin, or appendages. Orientation is one element in the mix of behavioral qualities that together define the concept of motivation. You may remember from Chapter 1 that Duffy (1962) defined *motivation* as the *arousal* and *direction* of behavior. Another behavioral quality ascribed to motivation by the learning theorist E. C. Tolman (1932) was that of persistence—what Tolman described as **persistence until.**

Tolman meant that motivated behavior has a quality of persisting in its occurrence until a particular, predictable goal-object or event is attained. Indeed, it was this feature of behavior that enabled Tolman to speak of it as being **goal-directed behavior** (see Box 3.1). As we stated earlier in Chapter 1, in the context of instrumental conditioning, **approach stimuli** may be identified with rewarding stimuli, or positive reinforcers, whereas **withdrawal stimuli** may be identified with punishing stimuli, or negative reinforcers. Orientation is not always accompanied by the additional qualities that define motivation. Of itself, it concerns only the direction or focus of behavior.

Orientation and Approach/ Withdrawal Theory

Orientation often occurs in combination with locomotor behavior, enabling an organism to relocate itself within its world in reference to some particular environmental feature, such as a food object, a hiding place, or a predator. The combination of orientation and locomotor movement toward or away from a particular point of reference provides approach and withdrawal behavior, basic adjustments common to numerous

BOX **3.1**

Observable Events Related to a Concept of Goal-Directed Behavior

Defining Events, Each Separately Observable from the Others

1. Occurrence of a distinctive and recognizable pattern of behavior-in-progress (Behavior A)
2. Occurrence of a specifically predictable outcome of that behavior, involving behavioral correspondence with a specific stimulus object (Outcome B)
3. Repetition of sequences of that behavior and its outcome, until a predictable criterion event is accomplished, such as the ingestion of a predictable amount of food to induce cessation of foraging (Criterion C)
4. Variation of the occurrence of the designated behavior and of the set point of the criterion event that ends that behavior with specific motivational conditions, such as the variation of foraging and eating behavior with variations in the amount of food deprivation in force (Motivational Condition D)

Summary Statement
Behavior A leads to Outcome B until the achievement of Criterion C, subject to variation with Motivational Condition D. These statements are open to repeated testing by observations that either verify or fail to verify clear predictions.

Theoretical Value of the Concept
The theoretical value of this concept is grounded in the evocation of an entire complex of relationships by a single phrase: goal-directed behavior.

behavioral functions and to all forms of animal life. Schneirla (1959) proposed that bi-phasic processes underlying approach and withdrawal are important ingredients of all perceptual, motivational, and cognitive development. A central proposal of Schneirla's **approach/withdrawal theory** is that much orientation is based upon the dimension of stimulus intensity (Raines & Greenberg, 1998). The theory emphasizes a general tendency for organisms early in the life span to approach sources of relatively mild stimulation and to withdraw from sources of relatively strong stimulation. Further, the theory notes that this general rule of orientation serves well to bring organisms into contact with things in the environment that promote survival and reproductive fitness, such as parents, food, and mates, and to take them away from contact with things that threaten survival, such as predators or other sources of tissue destruction. Orientation among many of the simpler species may be based upon relative stimulus intensity throughout the life span, whereas orientation among more complex species is supplemented and overridden by developmental experiences with various particular stimulus types (Rosenblatt, 1995).

One outstanding exception to the rule of general withdrawal from intense stim-ulation was noted particularly by Schneirla (1959). Each year thousands of moths and other insects of a variety of species lose their lives by flying into campfires and outdoor lights burned by humans around the world. The moths fail to turn away as closure with these light sources brings about progressively massive increases in their effective stimulus intensities. High levels of heat attendant upon the light sources likewise fail to dissuade the moths' approaches, until they crisp and die in midpursuit. Schneirla considered this example an anomaly, an outstanding departure from typical orienting responses, brought about by the highly unusual stimulus of an intense light within a dark surround. Indeed, he noted that the phenomenon had been termed a "trapping effect" by the zoologist Verheijen (1958). Of course, prior to the recent explosion of human populations and the even more recent invention of electric lights, "naturally ignited" fires would have constituted a negligible threat to moth survival.

Operating within the generality that weak stimulation generates approach be-havior is the principle that there is an optimum value for approach and a gradient of values to either side that are progressively more capable of provoking approach as they come nearer to the optimum value (Schneirla, 1959). This arrangement enables an organism to follow along **stimulus gradients** from either side until it arrives at opti-mum approach intensity and then to remain in that position. The situation with re-spect to a gradient of withdrawal behavior is similar except that the gradient extends from the intensity for maximum withdrawal downward toward neutrality.

Also operating within the generality of approach to weak stimulation is the possi-bility that certain specific types of stimulation are particularly likely to provoke approach on a species-typical basis. Schneirla (1959) cited the apparent approach to moonlight re-flecting from the surf by newly hatched loggerhead turtles at night, the proneness of certain lizards to approach green as opposed to other spectral hues and to approach fig-ures with smooth outlines rather than others with broken outlines. He noted that hon-eybees show the opposite tendency, approaching broken outlines rather than smooth ones. Schneirla proposed that one way in which species-typical approach responses to specific stimuli might be brought about is by evolutionary adjustments of stimulus thresholds and accompanying changes in the **effective intensity** of certain specific stimuli. Barnett (1981), in addressing species-typical orientations of both approach and withdrawal, cited the *taxis*, or forced movement, of fly larvae away from light, effectively causing them to bury themselves in the nutritious decaying materials that provide their food, and that of the woodlouse or pillbug, *Armadillidium*, to move away from light, generally, but to move toward light under conditions when it has been without food for an extended time or when its immediate environment either dries or heats up.

A careful analysis of the development of home orientation in newborn domestic kittens by Schneirla and his colleagues (Rosenblatt, Turkewitz, & Schnierla, 1972) provides a good example of this process in a mammalian species. Kittens initially display approach orientations toward the mother, particularly toward the mammary area and nipples, and toward one another. These orientations are consistent with the general stimulation of approach by mild stimuli and attraction along a gradient of mild stimulation provided by the odor of secretions of the mother's nipples and by tactile stimuli encountered in contacting a nipple.

Orientation and homing toward the home area, located within a corner of a three-by-three-foot box, were tested periodically by experimenters over the first several weeks of life (Rosenblatt, Turkewitz, & Schneirla, 1972). The mother and the litter were removed from the home area during test periods. The kittens' behavior during orientation was consistent with the idea that they were following a gradient of olfactory stimuli provided by deposits left in the home area by the mother and the litter. Kittens appeared to move toward the stronger and away from the weaker olfactory stimuli of deposits left by the mother and the litter. It seemed that a kitten maintained its forward direction in crawling as long as olfactory stimulation was increasing and turned away if olfactory stimulation was decreasing or was remaining constant.

Approach orientation to olfactory stimuli associated with the mother and the litter appeared to have been gained by learning experiences. Olfactory stimulation alone was not sufficient to provoke orientation and homing responses by socially inexperienced kittens that had been isolated shortly after birth. In socially experienced kittens, however, these odors had been closely associated with interactions with the mother and with other members of the litter. These interactions included huddling and being warmed by bodily contact, being groomed by the mother, and nursing.

Home orienting, enabling a kitten to move into the home area after being placed at the outside edge of the home corner, developed between the second and fourth days of life. Orientation and movement homeward from a corner adjacent to the home corner developed between the fifth and seventh days, and from the corner diagonal to the home corner between the fourteenth and sixteenth days. Olfactory stimulation appeared to dominate the kittens' orienting behavior until after their eyes first opened during the period from the seventh to the ninth day. Thereafter, visual stimulation began to supplement olfactory stimulation and became progressively more important as physical and behavioral development continued.

Specific Stimuli for Approach and Withdrawal

A good question to ask about the development of approach and withdrawal behavior may already have occurred to many readers: Besides the quality of intensity, what other characteristics do approach stimuli have in common? And what other characteristics do withdrawal stimuli have in common? As Schneirla (1959) noted, widespread tendencies to approach mild stimulation and withdraw from strong stimulation generally are adaptive tendencies. Only brief consideration is needed to impress upon us the fact that a great majority of the examples of species-typical approach and withdrawal responses also are adaptive responses. Indeed, the theory of evolution requires this prediction. We may confirm by observation that common objects of approach include food, social companions, potential mates, appropriate habitat and shelter, water, and temperature ranges compatible with an organism's internal temperature. Stimuli associated with species-typical activities of parental behavior, courtship behavior, breeding behavior, territorial defense, exploration of potential habitat, social play, and nest building become effective as approach stimuli through the course of experience in many organisms. The necessary relation of these stimuli and activities to the survival and reproductive fitness of the animals in which they are observed is apparent. The same is true of stimuli and activities that are typically associated with withdrawal behavior. Most of them involve obvious threats to continued life or reproductive capability. We may find exceptions, of course, as in the moth's approach to a campfire. Fortunately, however, the exceptions are few.

Additional Perspectives on Motivation

An influential theory of motivation proposed by the learning theorist Clark Hull (1943) associated all motivation with biological need and its satisfaction, or reduction. Hull's theory aligned motivation with the physiological concept of **homeostasis,** the idea that bodily systems automatically react to physical imbalances in such a way as to restore the balance. In Hull's theory, physical imbalances, or needs, cause buildup of a **drive state** specific to the particular need in force. This drive state then engenders or facilitates bodily and behavioral reactions that, in the evolutionary history of the species, have had a high likelihood of meeting that particular need. According to this theory, all sources of **need reduction** should be stimuli for approach behavior. Hull's formulation of drive provides an excellent example of the *intervening variable* approach in theory construction, discussed earlier in Chapter 1. His theory obviously fits the expectations of evolutionary theory discussed earlier, and it applies elegantly to a great many instances of motivation and motivated behavior. There are numerous instances of motivation, however, to which Hull's theory does not easily apply (e.g., Sheffield & Campbell, 1954; Sheffield & Roby, 1950; White, 1959; Wolfe & Kaplon, 1941).

Animals appear strongly motivated to perform a variety of species-typical behaviors such as exploration, locomotor behavior, listening to species-typical vocalizations, vocalizing with species-typical accompaniment, interacting with social companions, engaging in territorial defense (Haraway & Maples, 1998), and practically any other behaviors whose performance may be considered as exercising an individual's basic competence (White, 1959). Such motivations are not easily aligned with specific instances of biological imbalance and homeostasis but are directly addressed by the theory of Glickman and Schiff (1967). In their view, the appropriate occurrence of species-typical behaviors was of such great historical importance to survival that it formed the basis for much of the evolutionary development of motivational systems. Accordingly, a primary consequence of evolution is that the performance of species-typical behaviors generally has become appetitive or attractive.

Locomotion and Physical Principles

We have mentioned that the combination of **locomotion** and orientation provides approach and withdrawal behavior—the capability of an organism to relocate itself within its environment. We turn now to a consideration of the second element of this critically important combination. As we have implied, locomotion is behavior that moves or propels an animal from one place to another. Much locomotion across the animal kingdom is based on the principle of physics described by **Newton's Third Law:** For every action there is an equal and opposite reaction. This principle, as a basic feature of the physical world, was available to the evolution of locomotor behavior from the beginning of animal life on the planet. Much about locomotor behavior, as about behavior in general, may be understood in direct relation to opportunities afforded and limitations imposed by the laws of physics (Vogel, 1998).

Each time we take a step forward, we push backward against the earth with the front part of our trailing foot, propelling our bodies forward and imparting a slight impetus in the opposite direction to the earth. We take advantage of the pendulum-like action of our legs, swinging from the hip joints, as we alternately move each foot forward to take a new purchase on the earth. The pendulous action of our rhythmically swinging legs is joined by a rhythmical, pendulous swinging of our arms, coordinated to enhance the momentum of our forward movement.

Numerous species accomplish forward movement by pulling or pushing against the resisting medium of the earth's surface, moving their bodies either through air, as we do, or through water, as do aquatic species such as the squid (see Figures 3.1 through 3.3). Like our own, their evolution has provided structural and behavioral characteristics that take impressive advantage of the physical prospects afforded by nature. Still other animals have no means of self-locomotion and are instead moved passively. This is true of animals such as mussels, clams, and related species that are carried by currents and eventually settle on the seafloor.

Fish move primarily by thrusting their tail fins against the water. Their streamlined bodies, duplicated to a degree in the bodies of aquatic mammals such as sea lions and dolphins, decrease drag, or resistance, to the forward passage through the water. Similar streamlining is seen in the bodies of birds, and particularly in bird wings, the inner portions of which are structured to slip smoothly through the airstream (see Figure 3.4). At the same time, the shape of the wing requires that air travel a greater distance, and thus travel faster, over the top of the wing than under the bottom of the wing, creating relatively high pressure beneath the wing to provide lift. Meanwhile, forward momentum can be maintained or increased by power strokes achieved chiefly by the outer portions of the wings. The primary wing feathers are swept downward and outward against the resistance of the air. During the downstroke, low-pressure areas of the primaries are directed forward, adding to forward thrust (Ehrlich,

(a)

(c)

(b)

**FIGURE 3.1   Animals on the Move:
(a) a Herd of Elephants, (b) a Flock of
Emus, and (c) a School of Squid**

**FIGURE 3.2
A Leaping Mountain Goat**

FIGURE 3.3   Locomotor Movement of an Adult Male Orangutan

FIGURE 3.4   The Streamlined Contours of a Bird's Body

Dobkin, & Wheye, 1988; Pennycuick, 1975). The tail feathers provide additional control surfaces for the fine-tuning of flight direction and speed.

Swimming ducks travel the interface of water and air as they propel their bodies forward by rhythmically pushing backward against the water with their webbed feet, which are extended full surface against the water on the power stroke and closed for smooth passage on the recovery stroke. The maximum speed of this mode of movement is a function of the length of the duck's body that is submerged in the water (Vogel, 1998). This length determines the forward speed of the wave produced by passage of the duck's body through the water and, in turn, establishes the maximum speed the duck can achieve without catching up with its own wave. In this mode of travel, the duck is unable to break free of its forward wave and must either hold its speed within the limit of the wave or struggle continuously against the back of the wave.

All four-legged land mammals move through a series of gaits as they increase their speed of movement (Heglund, McMahon, & Taylor, 1974; Thiessen & Villarreal, 1998). They progress from a slow walk to a faster walk, shift from a fast walk to a trot, then from a fast trot to a gallop. Energy expenditure increases with speed of movement, but a savings occurs each time an animal changes from a slower to a faster **gait.** Energy expended at the beginning point of the new, faster gait is less than it was at the highest point of the previous gait. The use of gaits, then, permits animals more efficient use of energy in their locomotor behavior (Hoyt & Taylor, 1981). The point of switch over in gaits scales closely with the size of the species. Switch overs occur faster for a mouse than for a rat, faster for a rat than for a dog, and faster for a dog than for a horse (Thiessen & Villarreal, 1998).

It is often said that penguins lost the ability to fly because there were no land predators present in their habitat capable of posing a threat to an adult bird. Thus, they had little need to fly. This is likely true enough, but it tells less than half the story. More pertinent to the issue is the fact that penguins today maintain the ability to fly quite swiftly and efficiently, but they do their flying through the water—not through the air (Vogel, 1998). It is in the water where they must pursue the rapidly swimming fish that make up their prey and where they must elude fierce and swift predators such as the killer whale and the leopard seal that penguins face their greatest need for fast locomotion. In that watery world, speed is their edge against starvation and against being caught by a predator. In the selections contributing to their evolution, locomotor developments that favored water flight must have diverged importantly from those that favored air flight, and it must have been water flight that more significantly impacted survival and reproductive success.

Perception-as-Action in Locomotor Control

Regulation of locomotor movement in coordination with often complex environmental features is a basic problem of animal life. Each time a hawk stoops upon a scurrying rodent, a running antelope leaps across a coulee, a flying bird sweeps smoothly to a perch, or any of a multitude of similar actions are performed, this basic problem is successfully mastered. One means of thinking about such problems and solutions that has shown great promise in the past several decades is the theoretical perspective known as **per-ception and action** (Gibson, 1979). This perspective may be illustrated by the following treatment of the diving behavior of northern gannets (see Figure 3.5).

Gannets are large seabirds with wingspans of almost six feet. In their typical feeding behavior, they dive headfirst into the sea from heights as great as ninety feet to catch their prey of fish. The success of a dive requires that a bird maintain steering control by leaving its wings extended for as long into the dive as possible, enabling it to make continual adjustments to the movement of its prey in the water below. At the same time, the bird's immediate survival depends upon sweeping its wings into position along its sides for smooth entrance into the water at the proper moment. A moment too late and the wings would be broken in violent collision with the sea. As a bird plummets toward the sea, a systematic flow of visual stimulation is made available to its visual receptors. Close study of gannet dives by video analysis (Lee & Reddish, 1981) has shown that the timing of critical wing movements is consistent with the bird's use of a simple feature of the visual flow—a reliable indicator of time to contact—as a direct guide to its actions. The entire sequence of diving, making midcourse adjustments, and sweeping back the wings

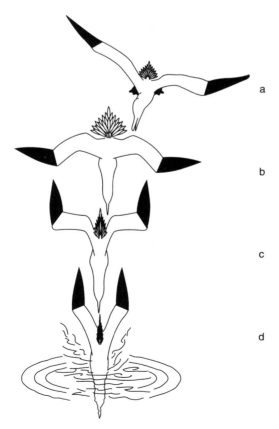

a

b

c

d

FIGURE 3.5   A Gannet's Dive

for entering the water may be viewed as a continuous flow of perception-as-action keyed directly to sensory input.

Locomotor Behavior and Individual Variation

Although certainly not absent of individual variation, the development of locomotor behavior is among the behavioral events most closely predictable on the basis of individual age. Further, locomotor development usually includes sequences or stages that occur almost on an invariable basis. Classic studies of locomotor development (Carmichael, 1926; Dennis & Dennis, 1940) have emphasized its stability in the face of moderate environmental alterations that have limited early opportunities for preliminary practice of locomotor advances. Indeed, there are instances in which locomotor development can be spectacularly rapid, as in the walking and running of newborn wildebeests or in the flying of any new-fledged member of the swallow family. Even so, locomotor development occurs only in the process of interaction with the environment over time. Anyone who has observed the early flights of blue jays, Carolina wrens, or American kestrels, or the early walking of young horses, dogs, or cattle, cannot have failed to appreciate the improvement in capability that is forged in experience, whether rapidly or at greater leisure. Later, in Chapter 9, we will consider how many locomotor skills are acquired by organisms on the basis of their individual learning experiences.

Habitat Selection

Few features of animal behavior are more predictable than the location of individuals within a **habitat** that is distinctively associated with their species. The habitat within which an individual is found contributes important cues to species identification in the field, so much so that habitat information has long been included in many field guides to bird identification (e.g., Peterson, 1947). Numerous birds are named partially for their habitats, such as the marsh wren, sedge wren, cactus wren, rock wren, and canyon wren. Birds are seldom seen outside their normal habitats. Even in migration, they are to be found in the closest available approximation of their preferred surroundings. Indeed, we may reflect that the active location and choice of appropriate habitat should have been a constant selective factor in the evolution of most species (Montevecchi, 1998). Appropriate habitat supplies the basic needs for successful life in the particular species concerned, from feeding needs to needs for predator protection (see Figure 3.6).

The strong tendency of individuals to locate themselves within habitats appropriate to their species is nicely illustrated by two unusual bird sightings in the state of Louisiana, the home state of one of the authors. One of the more unusual birds to be spotted in the state over the past few years was a rock wren, which turned up at least 700 miles east of its usual home in the dry, rocky areas of the western United States. It was found near the Gulf coast in a rock-covered parking lot that had been artificially provided with decorative boulders and that was surrounded by arid-resistant coastal

**FIGURE 3.6
Habitats and Songs
of Small Eastern
Flycatchers of the
United States**

shrubs. For south Louisiana, the area was a reasonable approximation of the rock wren's normal habitat. Another out-of-range bird recently observed in Louisiana was a Clark's nutcracker, a species that normally inhabits pine forests of the Rocky Mountains, where it feeds on nuts found in the cones of coniferous trees such as the ponderosa pine. In Louisiana, the bird was found in the Kisatchee Hills, an area of rocky, pine-covered bluffs that is Louisiana's nearest approximation of mountainous country. When found, the bird was feeding on the cones of longleaf pines, Louisiana's nearest approximation of the ponderosa pines of the Rocky Mountains.

Montevecchi (1998) points out that habitat selection may be well conceived as a series of hierarchical choices (Hutto, 1985) by which individuals locate themselves in progressively more finely tuned surroundings, or microhabitats. For example, a Hammond's flycatcher on its spring migration northward into the Rocky Mountains might select and follow a particular range of mountains, effectively separating itself from rangeland, brushland, and riverine habitats available in the plains nearby. It might then select a particular canyon system and begin to work its way upward into the mountains, making various selections at numerous forks of the canyon along its way. It might then focus upon a particular area of a canyon fork at a particular elevation of, say, 9,000 feet, then narrow its focus to a particular grove of Douglas fir trees on the south side of the canyon, and finally select a particular area and height in a single Douglas fir as the center of its breeding territory for the coming season. Its activities throughout the season would then be centered upon that spot and would spread only to a limited section of surrounding space and terrain.

Study of the development of habitat selection among deer mice (Wecker, 1963) has shown discernible influences of both genetic and environmental determination (Montevecchi, 1998). It appears that young animals in many species acquire long-term preferences for features of environment encountered in their earliest experiences (Hasler, 1960; Noseworthy & Lien, 1976). The apparently rapid and permanent attachments that form have been placed in comparison with similarly rapid and lasting social attachments acquired by young animals for social agents encountered in early experience; the former process has been termed **habitat imprinting** (Montevecchi, 1998), an allusion to the process of social attachment long known as imprinting. Attachment of young animals to features of habitat in which their own parents have achieved reproductive success has obvious functional utility.

Homing and Migration

All animals who establish home areas encounter a particular type of orientation problem each time they range any distance away from home—how can they find their way back at the end of the foray? As animals range greater distances from home and stay away for longer periods of time, the **homing** problem becomes more formidable. If they stay away for an entire season and need to return again later, then the problem becomes one of **migration,** perhaps requiring orientation skills that are complicated enough to be called **navigation.** Because it is likely to be a distinct advantage for animals to identify particular places where they can feed, rest, and reproduce successfully, and to be able to return to those places at appropriate seasons again and again, it seems that orientation abilities permitting reliable returns to such places would have been an important focus of natural selection for species displaying any degree of site fidelity (Papi, 1998).

Papi (1998) discussed a number of homing mechanisms illustrated by a variety of species. **Direct orientation** involves merely heading for a target that is affecting sensory activity at the time. **Indirect orientation,** or heading for a target that is outside the current range of sensory reception, is accomplished in a variety of ways. Outward-bound experience is the basis of much **route-based orientation,** but this type of orientation also includes use of trails laid down on the outward journey, as seen in some mollusks. **Course reversal,** based on the adoption of a homeward course that is opposite to the compass direction taken on the outward journey, is seen in many species of bees and wasps. Different animal species use a variety of compass mechanisms, relying on the sun, the stars, or the magnetic field of the earth. Some instances of course reversal appear to involve **path integration,** or a consolidation of information about the outward path to derive a straight path homeward. Many species appear to acquire **cognitive maps,** or internal representations of territorial features and arrangements, based on experiences individuals have gleaned during travels about the home area. These maps are considered to provide a basis of orientation throughout a familiar territory. In instances in which individuals appear to switch from one landmark to another in their homeward progress, they are said to be using the process known as **pilotage.** The most advanced mechanisms of orientation are those in which an individual seems to locate its position according to a cognitive map and then to select and follow a compass course to a target location. This type of orientation is called **true navigation.** It may be illustrated by the homing of pigeons and by migrations of fish, sea turtles, and birds. Box 3.2 presents a summary of the various forms of long-range orientation just discussed.

As we have already defined it, migration refers to periodic movements from one place and climate to another. These movements sometimes may be only one-way movements, especially in short-lived species, but for most species, they are round trips. Although we tend to think of such trips as being largely horizontal, for some animals they are primarily vertical. American elk, for example, move up and down mountain ranges in response to changing seasons and food supplies. The locomotor patterns of animals influence their migratory movements in that flying and swimming species are likely to move much greater distances than are crawling, walking, or burrowing species (see Figure 3.7). The golden plover (*Pluvialis dominica*), a well-known shorebird, for example, makes an annual round trip of 16,000 miles, from northern Canada to southern South America and back.

Understanding the phenomenon of migration will be furthered by identifying answers to the following set of questions:

1. Which species migrate and which do not? This question is addressed by using techniques that allow us to follow animals, marking them in some way by banding, the use of telemetry, and, more recently, by satellite imaging. Migration is indeed a species-typical phenomenon. Among some closely related species of birds, for example, some do it and others do not. Catbirds (*Dumetella carolinensis*) do and mockingbirds (*Mimus polyglottos*) do not; rose-breasted grosbeaks (*Pheucticus ludovicianus*) do but cardinals (*Richmondena cardinalis*) do not. Some members of migratory species may not carry out a full migration in some years. This phenomenon has become obvious recently among Canada geese that have taken to wintering over in mild winters in areas where plentiful food has become available, such as near feeding stations in wildlife refuges and at golf courses, parks, and zoos. (In many of the latter locations, the unwanted presence of large numbers of geese is becoming an increasing problem. Comparative psychologists have been called to the rescue in some cases! Golf courses

BOX **3.2**

Some Phenomena of Long-Range Orientation

Readers may note that most or all of these phenomena appeal to unobserved, hypothetical processes; theoretical interpretation would benefit from the formal conception of each of these hypothetical processes as an intervening variable.

Route-Based Orientation. Return movement to a previous location that appears to involve orientation to stimuli either encountered or laid down by an individual itself on an outward journey. Some instances of route-based orientation may also be examples of pilotage, described below.

Indirect Orientation. Any long-range movement that appears to involve orientation toward a stimulus agent that is outside an individual's sensory range. The phenomena that follow may be considered as different classes of indirect orientation.

Course Reversal. Return movement to a previous location that appears to involve the adoption of a course that reverses the compass heading it held on its outward journey.

Navigation, or True Navigation. The pursuit of a course of travel that appears to require some map-like representation of an extended area of environment and the following of a compass course in moving from one place to another within the area of the map.

Path Integration. Return movement to a previous location that appears to require an active combination of experiences acquired on the outward journey to achieve a more direct return than the path followed on the outward leg.

Pilotage. Return movement to a previous location that appears to require orientation to a succession of different landmarks encountered on an outward journey.

---

have hired animal behavior specialists to train dogs to patrol the fairways and greens, driving troublesome geese into other areas.)

2. Why does migration start? What are the proximal causes and predisposing factors? Are they exogenous, endogenous, or some combination of the two? Most often seasonal changes are involved. Systematic change in the length of days often is a major causal factor. In many species, accompanying changes in physiology provide additional mediating factors in the migratory process.

3. What routes are followed by migrating animals? And how can we know that an animal identified in Monroe, Louisiana, is the same one that started a journey from Kalamazoo, Michigan?

4. How do animals orient themselves during their migrations and what navigational cues do they use? Some animals travel at night; some invertebrates move under-

Major Migration Routes of Birds in North America

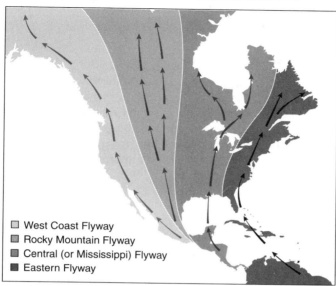

□ West Coast Flyway
□ Rocky Mountain Flyway
□ Central (or Mississippi) Flyway
■ Eastern Flyway

FIGURE 3.7 Major Migration Routes of Birds in North America: West Coast Flyway, Rocky Mountain Flyway, Central (or Mississippi) Flyway, and Eastern Flyway

ground; many fish travel through nearly featureless oceans. Remarkably, we have learned that animals use a variety of cues including the positions of the sun and stars. Some species use visual landmarks and follow coastlines. Some may utilize auditory cues from the ground below them, winds in the forest, sounds of surf, breeding congresses of frogs. And we now suspect that some bees and birds can utilize the magnetic field of the earth as a navigational cue.

5. As a repeating participant in migration, does an animal return to the same place year after year? This is the question of site fidelity or site tenacity.

6. What do animals do once they reach their final travel goals? Frequently, one end of the journey in migration is followed by reproductive behavior.

7. Finally, why did migration evolve in the first place?

The Evolution of Migration

Spawning Migrations of Salmon

Returns of several salmon species from large distances out in the ocean to their natal streams to spawn is interpreted as requiring at least compass orientation and as probably involving map-and-compass navigation (Papi, 1998). Once salmon arrive at a river system, further orientation has been shown to depend upon olfactory discrimination in following odor gradients of chemical constituents of the natal stream. Selective preference for the odor of the natal stream has been shown to be based on the early experiences of young salmon, although the learning processes involved have not been subjected to detailed study (Papi, 1998).

Nesting Migration of Sea Turtles

Adult females of many species of sea turtles return to the same nesting beach every few years to lay their eggs (Meylan et al., 1990), often after having earlier migrated to distant feeding grounds. Satellite tracking has shown that nesting migrations involve long journeys made at stable orientations and speeds over many days and that the final destination is closely associated with straight-line projections of the migratory direction (Papi & Luschi, 1996). These migrations are interpreted as instances of true navigation of the map-and-compass variety (Papi, 1998).

Homing of Pigeons

Homing success of inexperienced pigeons over distances as great as forty miles is only moderate, but success increases dramatically with experience. Experienced pigeons usually assume a proper homing orientation before disappearing on their homeward journeys when released at a strange site, and they usually return successfully from release points of more than one hundred miles distance (Papi, 1998). Experimental results indicate that pigeons orient to the sun, are sensitive to shifts in the biological clock, and depend upon prehoming experiences of odors and wind directions in the area of the home loft (Papi & Wallraff, 1992). They appear to use a combination of these factors, particularly odor cues, in orienting homeward from great distances and to depend more upon visual landmarks as they reach more familiar territory near the home.

Bird Migrations

Many migratory bird species show an ability to return to the general area of their upbringing in their breeding migrations. Many species also display a high degree of site tenacity, in which individuals return year after year to the same nesting area, often even to the same nest site. Evolution of site tenacity has depended to some degree on the durability of detailed features of nesting habitat. Cliff-dwelling species such as black-legged kittiwakes show strong development of site tenacity whereas species that nest in the highly changeable habitats of sandbars and sand beaches, such as least terns and royal terns, show little site tenacity (Erlich, Dobkin, & Wheye, 1988).

As described earlier, the ability to return to a specific site may rest upon a series of hierarchical decisions. In this instance, the decisions must be informed by an individual's experiences on its previous encounters with particular landmarks, landforms, wind currents, and other features. With respect to orientation decisions at great distances from the destination area, birds appear sensitive to a variety of cues, including the position of the sun, the stars, the magnetic field of the earth, wind directions, and odors (Ehrlich, Dobkin, & Wheye, 1988). Emlen (1975) carried out a series of experiments with caged indigo buntings, a neotropical species migrating between North

America and South America each year. Results showed that young birds acquire orientation preferences based on the rotation of star backgrounds encountered in early life. During early experiences, they pick out whatever star groups are made to remain in relatively constant position throughout the nightly rotation, as circumpolar constellations do, and they maintain stable orientations toward these constellations later when they become restless for the spring migration. The orientation maintained during these times is consistent with a course of travel that would guide them northward. When released at such times, the birds flew away in a northward direction for as long as they could be kept under observation.

Cognitive Behavior as a Factor in Orientation

Throughout discussions in the latter parts of this chapter, we have spoken of animals making decisions, making use of cognitive maps, compass mechanisms, navigational techniques, and so on. Obviously, it is not possible for us to gain direct observations of internal behavioral processes or mental activities in animals other than ourselves, and we are able to gain direct reports of such activities only in the case of other verbal organisms. Therefore, when we speak of such matters, it is important to remember we are speaking of *theoretical interpretations* that scientists have placed on animal behavior. These interpretations are ideas of the scientists—not necessarily of the animals whose behavior is being interpreted. The ideas represent the scientists' best efforts to make reasonable sense of facts that they have been able to establish by direct observation. The topic of **cognitive behavior** is addressed in some detail later as part of Chapter 10.

Summary: Principles Introduced in This Chapter

Orientation refers to the directional aspect of behavior, or to the question of what stimulus components are being addressed by behavior. Orientation often is combined with locomotor behavior, providing movement toward a point of reference, approach, or away from a point of reference, withdrawal. Approach and withdrawal are basic adaptive activities common to all animal species and important to many aspects of behavioral development. Together, orientation and approach/withdrawal make up two key elements of the concept of motivation.

In his approach/withdrawal theory, T. C. Schneirla proposed that young organisms have a general tendency to approach mild stimulation and to withdraw from strong stimulation. These tendencies are seen to serve organisms well in leading them toward sources of beneficial stimulation and away from sources of harm. Approach and withdrawal behavior becomes modified by individual experience in species that are capable of associative learning; in species whose behavior is less complex, the early approach and withdrawal tendencies provide an adaptive directional guide for behavior throughout the life span.

There are optimal points of stimulus intensity providing maximum evocation of approach and withdrawal. Gradients of approach run downward with departures from the optimal point in either direction. A gradient of withdrawal runs downward with departures toward lesser intensity from the optimal point. For many different species, there are also specific types of stimuli that are particularly effective in evoking approach and withdrawal responses. With few exceptions, stimuli that evoke approach behavior are beneficial in their effects upon an organism and those that evoke withdrawal are harmful in their effects. As the learning theorist Clark Hull emphasized, stimuli for approach often are associated closely with drive reduction. Other theorists—White, Glickman and Schiff—also pointed out that stimuli associated with the demonstration of competence and with the performance of species-typical behavior usually are also effective stimuli for approach. Approach and withdrawal also are of critical importance in the context of instrumental conditioning: Approach stimuli may be identified with rewarding stimuli, or positive reinforcers, whereas withdrawal stimuli may be identified with punishing stimuli, or negative reinforcers.

Much animal locomotion is based on Newton's Third Law, and consideration of physical law, generally, is particularly applicable to the understanding of locomotor behavior and associated bodily features and structures.

The theoretical perspective known as perception and action is helpful in understanding the control of locomotor movements. In this perspective, locomotor control flows directly from the incoming flow of sensory information, providing perception and action at once, or perception-as-action.

Animals are nearly always found within the limits of a specific range of habitat conditions. In the more complex species, location within the preferred habitat is seen as the result of a series of hierarchical choices in orientation. Homing and orientation during migration are seen in a similar way. Orientation cues implicated in the homing and migration of complex species such as fish, turtles, and birds have been local landmarks, chemical gradients within a water system, the sun's direction and movement over time, wind currents and odors, the earth's magnetic field, and circumpolar star constellations.

KEY TERMS

Approach stimulus a stimulus that elicits approach; an appetitive stimulus, one likely to be effective in the role of positive reinforcer.

Approach/withdrawal theory the theory of T. C. Schneirla that animals at the lower behavioral levels, throughout the life span, and all animals, during the early portion of the life span, tend to approach stimuli of mild intensity and to withdraw from stimuli of strong intensity.

Arousal the feature of behavior identified with an animal's level of activation, usually ranging from high activation and excitement to deep sleep.

Cognitive behavior behavior that is well understood by relating it to hypothetical mental, or cognitive, events that may be thought of as involving conscious awareness and active use of information; cognitive behaviors are usually associated with theoretical interpretations conceived as intervening variables.

Cognitive map an intervening variable that envisions cognitive, mental, or informational representation of the environment as a map, or a representation of the sort of information that is available on a map.

Course reversal a hypothetical process whereby animals return to a previous location by reversing the compass heading they held on the outward journey from that place; ideally, such hypothetical processes should be given formal statement as intervening variables.

Direct orientation   orientation involving heading for a target that affects sensory activity.

Drive state   a state of behavioral tension induced by a deficit or deprivation of some substance or activity needed to maintain the physical health or well-being of an organism; this concept is closely associated with Hull's treatment of motivation.

Effective intensity   an idea associated with Schneirla's approach/withdrawal theory, that the relative intensity of a stimulus must be judged within the context of a species' sensitivity to that type of stimulus and that variations in sensitivity to particular stimuli may have resulted from selective forces in the evolution of each species.

Gait   a particular pattern of locomotor behavior; animals often progress through several different patterns of locomotor behavior, or gaits, as their speed of travel increases.

Goal-directed behavior   behavior that appears to be organized around the attainment of a particular outcome; the behavior in question must be recognizable independently of its usual outcome, and the outcome must be clearly specified in each case to which the term *goal-directed behavior* is applied.

Goal-object   the stimulus agent identified with the outcome of an instance of goal-directed behavior.

Habitat   a complex of environmental surroundings within which a particular species is usually found.

Habitat imprinting   an experiential effect in which young animals acquire an attraction to or affiliation with features of the environment present during their early development; this term makes allusion to a similar process known as social imprinting or, simply, imprinting.

Homeostasis   the idea that the physiological conditions characteristic of normal life within each species will be maintained within specifiable limits of variation; imbalances in these conditions usually induce reactions that tend to reestablish the normal balance.

Homing   the locomotor movement of an animal back to its home area from some distance away.

Indirect orientation   a hypothetical process whereby animals orient themselves with respect to places or locations that are outside their current range of sensory reception; ideally, such hypothetical processes should be given formal statement as intervening variables.

Locomotion   behavior that moves or propels animals from one location to another within the environment.

Migration   movement of animals over distances much greater than those traveled on a frequent or daily basis within the home environment, particularly seasonal movements that may recur several times in the life of a single individual.

Navigation, true navigation   a hypothetical process of complex orientation that envisions animals using a cognitive map of large portions of the environment and following compass courses in moving from one place to another within the area of the map; ideally, such hypothetical processes should be given formal statement as intervening variables.

Need reduction (also, **drive reduction)**   the reduction or satisfaction of a physical need and of the state of behavioral tension that accompanies such need, according to the treatment of motivation provided by psychologist Clark Hull.

Newton's Third Law   a basic law of physics—that for every action there is an equal and opposite reaction; this law established an important condition of the environment in respect to the evolution of locomotor behavior in various species.

Orientation   the directional focus of an animal's behavior on particular stimulus agents in its environment.

Path integration   a hypothetical process whereby animals appear to combine outward-bound experiences to achieve a more direct return to a place than that offered by the path followed in the outward journey; ideally, such hypothetical processes should be given formal statement as intervening variables.

Perception and action   the theoretical perspective that perception consists of an animal's responses to information that is directly available within the environment it encounters.

Persistence until   a phrase used by psychologist E. C. Tolman to indicate a defining quality of *goal-directed* behavior—that such behavior may be expected to continue in progress until it achieves a predictable outcome.

Pilotage   a hypothetical process whereby animals appear to orient, in turn, on a succession of different landmarks in returning to a given location; ideally, such hypothetical processes should be given formal statement as intervening variables.

Route-based orientation a hypothetical process whereby animals return to a place on the basis of stimuli laid down themselves, or on the basis of learning experiences along the route of their outward journey from that place; ideally, such hypothetical processes should be given formal statement as intervening variables.

Stimulus gradients the distribution within the environment of graded intensities of a particular stimulus such that an animal's locomotor movement may result in its encountering progressively stronger intensities of that stimulus, if approaching it, or progressively weaker intensities of the stimulus, if withdrawing from it.

Withdrawal stimulus a stimulus that elicits withdrawal, or movement away from the stimulus; often an aversive stimulus, one likely to be effective in the role of negative reinforcer.

REVIEW QUESTIONS

1. How may we identify whether a particular stimulus qualifies as an approach stimulus for a particular species?

2. Make up your own example of a problem of orientation faced by an animal, or describe an example of the same from this chapter.

3. What is the main idea of T. C. Schneirla's approach/withdrawal theory?

4. What is meant by the direction of behavior?

5. What quality of behavior is addressed by the term *arousal?* Make up your own example to illustrate a variation in arousal.

6. Name and identify one of the defining characteristics of goal-directed behavior.

7. Select any one of the hypothetical processes invoked in the discussion of complex orientation, and see if you can set it up formally in the guise of an intervening variable.

8. What is meant by identifying something as a physical need? Describe how a physical need can be related to the state of an animal's motivation.

9. Describe an example or two in which physical law can be applied to the evolution of locomotor behavior.

10. What sort of information is the basis of animal perception according to the perspective of *perception and action?*

11. Considering our ideas about how animals evolved, what sort of a stimulus would we expect the current members of a species to approach on a species-typical basis? How about a withdrawal stimulus?

12. What is the source of the information considered to be used in hypothetical processes associated with the terms *cognitive map* and *path integration?*

13. Describe one or two of the causal factors considered to be involved in the homing migration of salmon.

14. Suggest a reproductive advantage likely to have been involved in the evolution of migratory behavior.

15. Tell in your own words how the concept of motivation is related to approach behavior and withdrawal behavior.

16. How are animals well served by the selection of habitat that is typical of their species?

17. Describe a mainstay of species-typical locomotor behavior for one or two species or groups of species.

18. Briefly tell how these locomotor behaviors involve specific examples of the application of Newton's Third Law.

19. How may the concept of goal object be related to the ideas of approach stimulus and withdrawal stimulus?

20. Show how complex examples of habitat selection can be represented as a series of choices or decisions, as in the spring migration of Hammond's flycatchers. Try to recall at least two such decisions in the series leading to the arrival of a flycatcher at its breeding habitat.

REFERENCES

Barnett, S. A. (1981). *Modern ethology.* New York: Oxford University Press.

Carmichael, L. (1926). The development of behavior in vertebrates experimentally removed from the influence of external stimulation. *Psychological Review, 33,* 51–58.

Dennis, W., & Dennis, M. G. (1940). The effect of cradling practices upon the onset of walking in Hopi children. *Journal of Genetic Psychology, 56,* 77–86.

Duffy, E. (1962). *Activation and behavior.* New York: John Wiley.

Ehrlich, P. R., Dobkin, D. S., & Wheye, D. (1988). *The birder's handbook.* New York: Simon & Schuster.

Emlen, S. T. (1975). The stellar-orientation system of a migratory bird. *Scientific American, 233,* 102–111.

Gibson, J. J. (1979). *The ecological approach to visual perception.* Hillsdale, NJ: Lawrence Erlbaum.

Glickman, S. E., & Schiff, B. B. (1967). A biological theory of reinforcement. *Psychological Review, 74,* 81–109.

Haraway, M., & Maples, E. (1998). Species-typical behavior. In G. Greenberg & M. M. Haraway (Eds.), *Comparative psychology: A handbook* (pp. 191–197). New York: Garland.

Hasler, A. D. (1960). Guideposts of migrating fishes. *Science, 131,* 785–792.

Heglund, N. C., Taylor, C. R., & McMahon, T. A. (1974). Scaling stride frequency and gait to animal size: Mice to horses. *Science, 186,* pp. 1112–1113.

Hoyt, D. F., & Taylor, C. R. (1981). Gait and the energetics of locomotion in horses. *Nature, 292,* 239–240.

Hull, C. (1943). *Principles of behavior.* New York: Appleton-Century-Crofts.

Hutto, R. L. (1985). Habitat selection by nonbreeding migrating land birds. In M. L. Cody (Ed.), *Habitat selection in birds* (pp. 455–476). Orlando, FL: Academic Press.

Lee, D. N., & Reddish, P. E. (1981). Plummeting gannets: A paradigm of ecological optics. *Nature, 293,* 293–294.

Meylan, A., Bowen, R. W., & Avise, J. C. (1990). A genetic test for the natal homing versus social facilitated models for green turtle migration. *Science, 248,* 724–727.

Montevecchi, W. A. (1998). Habitat selection. In G. Greenberg & M. M. Haraway (Eds.), *Comparative psychology: A handbook* (pp. 679–681). New York: Garland.

Noseworthy, C. M., & Lien, J. (1976). Ontogeny of nesting habitat recognition in neonatal herring gull chicks, *Larus argentatus* Pontoppidan. *Animal Behaviour, 24,* 637–651.

Papi, F. (1998). Homing and related phenomena. In G. Greenberg & M. M. Haraway (Eds.), *Comparative psychology: A handbook* (pp. 687–695). New York: Garland.

Papi, F., & Luschi, P. (1996). Pinpointing "Isla Meta": The case of sea turtles and albatrosses. *Journal of Experimental Biology, 199,* 65–71.

Papi, F., & Wallraff, H. G. (1992). Birds. In F. Papi (Ed.), *Animal homing* (pp. 263–319). London: Chapman & Hall.

Pennycuick, C. J. (1975). Mechanics of flight. In D. S. Farner & J. R. King (Eds.), *Avian biology,* Vol. 5 (pp. 1–76). New York: Academic Press.

Peterson, R. T. (1947). *A fieldguide to the birds.* Boston: Houghton Mifflin.

Raines, S., & Greenberg, G. (1998). Approach/withdrawal theory. In G. Greenberg & M. M. Haraway (Eds.), *Comparative psychology: A handbook* (pp. 74–80). New York: Garland.

Rosenblatt, J. (1995). Schneirla's A/W biphasic processes theory. In K. F. Hood, G. Greenberg, & E. Toback (Eds.), *Behavioral development: Concepts of approach withdrawal and integrative levels* (pp. 89–96). New York: Garland.

Rosenblatt, J. S., Turkewitz G., & Schneirla, T. C. (1972). Development of home orientation in newly born kittens. In L. R. Aronson, E. Tobach, J. S. Rosenblatt, & D. S. Lehrman (Eds.), *Selected writings of T. C. Schneirla* (pp. 689–711). San Francisco: W. H. Freeman.

Schneirla, T. C. (1959). Aspects of stimulation and organization in approach/withdrawal process underlying vertebrate behavioral development. In D. S. Lehrman, R. A. Hinde, & E. Shaw (Eds.), *Advances in the study of behavior,* Vol. 1 (pp. 1–74). New York: Academic Press.

Sheffield, F. D., & Campbell, B. A. (1954). The role of experience in the "spontaneous" activity of hungry rats. *Journal of Comparative and Physiological Psychology, 47,* 97–100.

Sheffield, F. D., & Roby, T. B. (1950). Reward value of a non-nutritive sweet taste. *Journal of Comparative and Physiological Psychology, 43,* 471–481.

Thiessen, D., & Villarreal, R. (1998). Allometry and comparative psychology. In G. Greenberg and M. M. Haraway (Eds.), *Comparative psychology: A handbook* (pp. 51–65). New York: Garland.

Tolman, E. C. (1932). *Purposive behavior in animals and men.* New York: Appleton-Century.

Verheijen, F. J. (1958). The mechanisms of the trapping effect of artificial light sources upon animals. *Archives of Neerl. Zoology, 13,* 1–107.

Vogel, S. (1998). Locomotor behavior and physical reality. In G. Greenberg & M. M. Haraway (Eds.), *Comparative psychology: A handbook* (pp. 713–719). New York: Garland.

Wecker, S. C. (1963). The role of early experience in habitat selection by the prairie deermouse, *Peromyscus maniculatus bairdi. Ecological Monographs, 33,* 307–325.

White, R. W. (1959). Motivation reconsidered: The concept of competence. *Psychological Review, 66,* 297–333.

Wolfe, J. B., & Kaplon, M. D. (1941). Effect of amount of reward and consummative activity on learning in chickens. *Journal of Comparative Psychology, 31,* 353–361.

CHAPTER

4 Feeding Behavior and Foraging

The central importance of **feeding behavior** is made obvious by considering two simple facts: Animals, unlike plants, must obtain food from the environment by their own active behavior; and food is the necessary energy source for metabolism, the basic physical process of life. An individual animal continues to live only as long as its feeding behavior remains effective.

Feeding behavior combines a persistent orientation toward food-related stimuli with **locomotor behavior** that brings an animal into contact with a food object. This pattern of behavior is typically referred to as **foraging**. The immediate proximity of food occasions **capturing behavior** that, if successful, is followed by **consummatory behavior** leading to ingestion of the food. Many of these orienting, locomotor, and consummatory behaviors are describable and predictable on a species-wide basis. Animals that seek out others for food are known as **predators;** the animals they eat are known as **prey.**

In the descriptions that follow, examples of the feeding behavior of a variety of phyla, classes, and species will be presented in chronological order, according to the time when representatives of those groups first appeared on earth. With one exception—the starfish, a representative of the phylum Echinodermata—we will begin with the oldest groups and proceed at each step toward more recently evolved groups. As we proceed, we will be able to notice a definite trend: As evolution has continued over vast amounts of time, it has produced animals that are progressively more complex in their behavior. The echinoderms are an outstanding exception to this rule; their origins are far more recent than those of many groups whose behavior is more complex.

Evolution of Feeding Behavior across the Animal Series

Subkingdom Protozoa

The class Amoeba contains thousands of species of one-celled organisms that live in freshwater and salt water worldwide (see Figure 4.1). Weak stimulation reaching the cell membrane of a reactive individual, of *Amoeba proteus*, for example, directly brings about an extension of the ectoplasm of the cell membrane in the area of stimulation and an accompanying flow of endoplasm in the direction of the stimulus source. Relatively

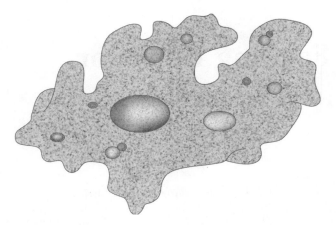

FIGURE 4.1   An Amoeba

strong stimulation, on the other hand, produces the opposite reaction of thickening or solidifying of protoplasm in the area of stimulation and a cessation of any movement that was in progress in the direction of the stimulus (Farmer, 1980).

In a moving amoeba, the extended, or bulging area of the cell body takes the lead. This area is called a **pseudopod,** or stimulated foot. When there is a continuing source of mild stimulation, the expansion of ectoplasm in the area of stimulation continues, and highly fluid endoplasm continually flows forward to the inner boundary of the pseudopod and is deflected back along the cell membrane toward the rear, thickening into a less fluid form as it proceeds. At the same time, there is a corresponding conversion of endoplasm from the more solid to the more fluid form at the central area of the cell, providing a continuing stream of endoplasm into the expanding pseudopod. The expanding tube of the pseudopod becomes anchored to the substratum at numerous places, affording points of purchase past which the organism advances in forward movement (Farmer, 1980).

Let's suppose that the stimulation we have been considering is provided by chemical substances exuding from an object that might be soluble within the amoeba's protoplasm—a potential food source. Continued movement directly stimulated by these chemical traces of food brings a portion of the amoeba's cell membrane into contact with the object itself, providing a marked increase in the local intensity of stimulation, which now includes tactual as well as chemical components. This intensity of stimulation causes rapid thickening of the protoplasm in the immediate area of contact. Forward movement is halted in the contact area but continues unabated in adjacent areas, which continue to receive mild chemical stimulation from the nearby, but not yet contacted, food object. As this process continues, the pseudopod soon flows completely around the food object, until the object is enclosed within the amoeba's body. Once the food object has been ingested, its soluble components begin to be assimilated, its insoluble components eventually will be ejected as *contractile vacuoles.*

The **reactivity** of an individual amoeba—its sensitivity to stimulation—is directly related to the recent assimilative processes of its protoplasm. An amoeba that presently is assimilating or recently has assimilated an ingested object is less reactive than is an amoeba that has gone for some time without such assimilation. In other words, a well-fed amoeba is less sensitive to food, and to other stimuli, than is a poorly fed, or "hungry," amoeba.

The feeding of amoebae, one of earth's simplest classes of organisms, is organized entirely at the taxic level—the simplest of the five levels of behavioral complexity suggested by Schneirla and Tobach (see Chapter 1). Nevertheless, it illustrates basic components of feeding that are seen in organisms throughout a broad range of behavioral complexity. Reception of stimulation from a potential food source results in the stimulated individual's approaching, capturing, and ingesting a food object. Moreover, reactivity to food-related stimulation and the occurrence of feeding behavior in amoebae illustrate the rudiments of **motivational variation,** in that a well-fed individual is relatively unreactive to stimulation and unlikely to engage in feeding behavior, whereas a food-deprived individual is more highly reactive, generally, and more likely to engage in feeding behavior.

Locomotor movement and feeding behavior of the more complex, yet still one-celled, organisms of the genus *Paramecia* show marked advances as compared to those of the amoeba. The paramecium has a permanent body shape with a definite head end and tail end. It has specialized structures such as an *oral groove*, through which substances are ingested, and **cilia,** small, hairlike structures that cover the outer surface of the cell membrane and provide for much more rapid locomotion than seen in the amoeba. The beating of these cilia toward the organism's tail end propels the organism rapidly forward along a spiraling course, whereas a reversal of the direction of the cilia's stroke quickly stops forward movement and sends the organism rapidly backward, perhaps away from a harmful situation.

The paramecium feeds on small organisms such as algae and bacteria. When a swimming paramecium encounters an area in which bacteria are concentrated, it often engages in a series of frequent changes of direction, in effect, circling back and forth through the food-rich site. It may also slow the frequency with which its cilia are beating, thereby slowing its rate of passage through the food site (Wichterman, 1953). As the paramecium passes among bacteria, cilia in the oral groove capture potential food particles, as well as other small objects in the vicinity, and sweep them into a structure called the *cytostome*, where an undulating membrane aids their passage through to the animal's gullet and into the interior endoplasm. There assimilation of food and ejection of insoluble materials eventually take place.

Surprising as it may seem, there are serious and still controversial claims that paramecia are able to modify their feeding behavior in a lasting fashion on the basis of feeding experiences (Gelber, 1952, 1965). If Gelber's observations could be repeated in experiments that incorporate more extensive experimental controls, the results would provide evidence of **associative learning** in paramecia. This outcome would be spectacular because of the total absence of a nervous system in paramecia and also because it would demonstrate a tremendous range of behavioral complexity among Protozoan species. For the present, however, it appears that Gelber's results have been successfully accounted for without accepting the involvement of associative learning (Dewsbury, 1978).

Phylum Porifera

Among adult sponges, locomotor behavior that is normally an integral component of feeding is replaced by actions that bring about a continuing flow of environmental materials into and through the bodies of these unmoving animals, which are permanently attached to the bottom in either salt water or freshwater. In moving water, the beating of cilia lining the body cavities of these organisms draws water through their pores, into their central cavities, and propels it outward through their **osculums**—openings at the tips of each of the animal's columns. Oxygen is absorbed from the flowing water and small food items passing through the pores are caught against the individual cell walls and digested (Berguist, 1978).

The osculum atop each column of the body usually is closed in still water. In moving water, the osculum can be made to close by the occurrence of a harsh tactual or chemical stimulus. Each cell of the osculum contracts individually in response to direct contact with the external stimulus or, indirectly, in response to the tug imposed by contraction of the adjacent cell. In that manner, a reaction is propagated slowly around the entire circumference of an osculum without the presence of a nervous system. Closing of the osculum shuts off the flow of water through the system, the cilia cease their beating, and the sponge enters a condition of quietude (Berguist, 1978). The range of adjustive behavior in the adult sponge, then, is reduced to the relative degree to which the animal is actively straining water through its body or is not doing so.

A number of species of sponges readily form large colonies in which many individuals live in social proximity to one another. There is no reason to think that the social condition in such colonies has any effect on the feeding behavior of the individuals living there, however; and the feeding behavior of sponges appears entirely organized at the taxic level of complexity.

Phylum Cnidaria

The name of this phylum means *nettle bearing*. It is a large and successful group of some 9,000 species. All of these species live in water—most in salt, or marine, conditions, but some also in freshwater. As a result of unusual reproductive processes occurring within this group, which we will consider in a later chapter, organisms of most species of this phylum exist in two distinct forms—the polyp, or hydroid, form and the medusa, or jellyfish, form. Both forms show **radial symmetry.** Cross sections taken from any portion of the body reveal structures that are symmetrically arranged on all sides. Although these two forms are greatly different in their appearance, they actually remain quite similar to one another in both structure and behavior. Although most species exist in both hydroid and medusa forms, there are some that exist only in hydroid form and others that exist only in medusa form (Hickman, Roberts, & Hickman, 1984).

We will focus primarily on the hydroid form for the remainder of this account. These animals have long, tubular bodies with a mouth at one end and a pedal disk at the other. The mouth is surrounded by muscular, individually movable tentacles, which are covered with nematocysts. The pedal disk usually is attached to some solid surface within the organism's watery environment. The attachment is a permanent one in some species but is changeable in others, in which individuals repeatedly move about from one site of attachment to another. This movement may be accomplished by a slow, crawling glide by the pedal disk, aided by a flow of mucus, and also by means of alternate contraction and extension of the tubular body, in the manner of movement employed by the familiar "measuring worm." Hydra possess a primitive nerve net, which permits neural transmission of excitement among the tentacles and among various bodily parts. Sensory cells are scattered over the body, being concentrated on the tentacles and about the mouth and the pedal disk. Each sensory cell has a projecting thread of tissue that is excited by chemical and tactual stimuli (Burnett, 1973).

A hydra in feeding mode may sit quietly with its tentacles extended or may extend its tentacles in response to chemical stimulation from a potential prey animal that comes nearby. If the prey comes close enough to contact one or more of the hydra's tentacles, it will be pierced and entangled by the harpoon-like points and filaments of numerous **nematocysts** on the tentacles and will be rendered helpless as the tentacles bend toward the mouth, which slowly opens wide enough to enfold most prey completely (Burnett, 1973). Feeding is accomplished essentially in the same manner in the medusa form of the animal, except that the medusa is floating freely in the water rather than being anchored to some underwater structure, and its tentacles are located on the underside of the animal when it is in its usual floating position.

The feeding of hydra appears organized at the taxic and biotaxic levels of complexity but in one respect, at least, it enters into the third, or biosocial, level in some species. When a hydra distinguishes between living, or recently living, material and nonbiological material as objects of ingestion, it exhibits biotaxic organization. Additionally, many hydroid species form large social colonies in which all of their life activities occur. In most cases, the location of an individual in one of these colonies may have little influence on its feeding behavior. In species such as *Hydractinia milleri*, however, individual hydra join colonies established on the shells of living animals such as the hermit crab. This social arrangement benefits members of the hydra colony, which often are able to share in stray bits of their host's meals (Hickman, Roberts, & Hickman, 1984). The hermit crab benefits from the added protection of having hundreds of hydra, with their thousands of nematocysts, blanketing the back of its shell. The arrangement also places the feeding behavior of some Cnidaria species at least partially within the biosocial level of organization.

Phylum Echinodermata

The echinoderms are a recently evolved group in comparison to the species just considered, as well as to several of the groups that follow them in this account. We turn to them now because this position in our series of descriptions is suited to the complexity of their behavior. The starfish, a creature familiar to most of us since childhood, is a good representative of its phylum, the spiny-skinned creatures.

Starfish have complex bodies that are arranged in radial symmetry. They possess a relatively well-developed nervous system, with a central nerve ring connected to radial nerves extending to the tip of each of the five rays of their star-shaped bodies. They are responsive to stimulation from sources at greater distances than those sensed by the animals previously considered. Starfish are particularly sensitive to chemical and tactual stimulation and have some sensitivity to light. Sensory cells are scattered over the surface of the body, and a primitive eyespot is found at the tip of each ray.

Many species of starfish are carnivorous and prey on mollusks, crustaceans, and a wide variety of creatures, including small fish. Chemical stimulation from a food source, perhaps at some distance away, reaches sense receptors near the end of one of the rays of the starfish (*Asterias forbesi*) and elicits a **step reflex** in the tube feet, which are hollow, muscular appendages lining the oral side of each ray from its tip to the animal's central disk. The tube feet contract toward the center of the ray upon activation of longitudinal muscles in the tube and extend toward the source of stimulation upon activation of muscles within the interior of the ray. Each step reflex includes a contraction of a tube foot toward the center of the ray followed by an extension of the foot back toward the source of stimulation (Hyman, 1955). Contact with the substratum, combined with continued stimulation from the original source, keeps the animal moving in a stable direction. In locomotion, the tube feet on all rays step in the same direction—toward the direction of travel—not toward the tip of each ray. This coordination may be aided by the animal's central nerve ring but seems mainly a result of simple stimulus effects imposed by contact between the substratum and the tube feet of all rays but the leading ray, as the tube feet of the leading ray start the animal moving in a given direction and thereafter, as this same pattern of stimulation continues.

Contact with a prey object causes the affected tube feet to begin "stepping" the prey toward the center of the starfish. As this occurs, the starfish wraps itself around the prey with two or more of its rays. As the prey is brought to the center of the oral disk, stimulation to the area of the mouth causes a portion of the stomach to evert, reach the prey, and begin digestion. In a starfish's attack upon a bivalve creature such as an oyster, a constant pull is exerted by the tube feet of two or more rays attached to opposite halves of the bivalve. These feet step, pull, release, step and pull again, and again until, eventually, the muscle holding the bivalve's shell closed begins to fatigue. The shell opens, perhaps only a fraction of an inch, the everted stomach of the starfish enters, and feeding begins (Burnett, 1960).

Despite its many advanced features of physical structure, including particularly its rather advanced nervous system, there is no convincing evidence that starfish are capable of associative learning, despite numerous attempts to provide such evidence. In most species, the feeding behavior of starfish appears well accounted for on the basis of direct stimulus effects at the taxic and biotaxic levels of complexity. However, in several species of Ophiuroids, brittle stars, numerous individuals live together in the water canals of large sponges, where they partake of a commensal feeding arrangement, obtaining food from the flow of water provided by the sponge. This is an example of biosocial organization in echinoderm feeding behavior.

Phylum Platyhelminthes

Planaria, of the phylum of flatworms, are small invertebrates with **bilateral symmetry** and an elongated body shape. In bilateral symmetry, an animal's body is arranged in two sides, with corresponding structures on each side, throughout. Flatworms live primarily as free-ranging individuals in either freshwater or salt water and are the first organisms in the animal series to possess a nervous system with an impressive degree of central organization. There is a central nerve ganglion in the head region connected to longitudinal nerve branches running down each side of the body. There are two eyespots on the dorsal sides of the head, and the animal shows sensitivity to light, tactual sensitivity, and acute sensitivity to chemical stimulation from sources that can be some distance away. Chemical and tactual stimulation are critical to the organism's predatory feeding behavior (Hyman, 1951).

The outer covering of the body is ciliated and contains structures that exude a protective mucus coating. There are also anterior glands that secrete a mucus trail along which the remainder of the animal's body travels in locomotor behavior. The planarian glides along surfaces within its watery environment, propelled forward along its own mucus track by the beating of its cilia as well as by muscular waves that pass from the anterior to the posterior of the body. Upon receiving chemical stimulation from a prey animal, such as a tiny crustacean or insect, the planarian glides toward the source of the stimulus. Making contact, the planarian entangles its prey in a flow of mucus and bends its body around the prey, starting at its own anterior end and wrapping its ventral surface against the prey. It extends the pharynx from its mouth, which is located ventrally near the middle of the body, and begins to suck bits of food into the mouth, intestine, and gastrovascular cavity. Its intestine also *exudes* an enzyme that flows outward upon the prey, beginning a digestive process on the tissues of the prey while it is still outside the planarian's body (Hyman, 1951).

There are numerous and persuasive demonstrations that the planarian (*Dugesia dorotocephala*) is capable of associative learning as a consequence of both classical and instrumental conditioning procedures (e.g., Block & McConnell, 1967; McConnell, Jacobson, & Kimble, 1959; Thompson & McConnell, 1955). Instrumental learning demonstrated by planaria included increases in the success with which individual planaria followed a path leading to food as they received food-reinforced practice at following the path. There have been no studies relating this learning directly to the natural lives of free planaria, but the demonstrated capability for such learning ensures at least the possibility of its functional importance to most planaria. If we suppose that the prey of planaria are not randomly scattered throughout the environment, but rather, are likely to be concentrated in certain limited locations having distinctive stimulus features, then it is easy to imagine how a planarian that has learned to approach those distinctive features would have an advantage over a planarian without such learning. The feeding behavior of the planarian, then, must be accepted as being organized, at least in small part, at the psychotaxic level of complexity.

Phylum Mollusca

Aplysia, a genus of this phylum, is a family of rather large sea snails ranging in size from 100 grams to 13 kilograms, or about 28 pounds (see Figure 4.2). Their bodies are arranged in bilateral symmetry, and they have well-developed central nervous systems. There are two eyes at the anterior portion of the head, but the visual sense seems poorly developed. Of much greater importance to feeding behavior in aplysia is their

FIGURE 4.2   An Aplysia

sensitivity to chemical stimulation via two pairs of tentacles located at the anterior and posterior limits of the head. Receptors in these tentacles allow aplysia to sense and approach their plant prey of seaweed from a distance. Locomotion occurs by crawling on a laterally extended foot that is both a holdfast and a locomotor organ (Kandel, 1979).

In forward movement, the anterior part of the foot extends forward, attaches to the substratum, and holds. This is followed by a similar action of the middle part of the foot and then the posterior part of the foot. These movements occur in repeated cycles, moving the animal steadily forward. Phase relationships within this sequential pattern remain constant across a wide range of forward speeds (Kandel, 1979).

Prominent in the feeding behavior of aplysia is an orienting behavior called the **appetitive response,** in which an individual lifts its head and waves the head and tentacles alternately to one side and then the other, enabling it to sample the gradient of chemical stimulation coming from each side of the head. Animals typically do not make their way directly toward food but proceed with much trial and error and numerous head-waving responses (Kandel, 1979). Aplysia are able to select the "baited" goal arm of a T-maze by chemoreception from seaweed at a distance of at least 15 centimeters from the choice point (Preston & Lee, 1973).

Upon reaching seaweed, an individual brings its mouth into contact with the food and makes a biting response, closing its lips on the food. It then opens the inner mouth and protrudes its tooth-supplied pharynx, or *ordontophore*, which opens to grasp the food and then retracts, bringing the food past the mouth and into the esophagus, where it is swallowed. Swallowing appears directly stimulated by contact of food with the inner mouth. A reversal of the swallowing reaction can be triggered by inedible objects, causing them to be rejected (Kandel, 1979).

Different species of aplysia have definite food preferences, and these can be manipulated, at least in young animals, by feeding experiences. Carefoot (1967) found that animals given many days of feeding exclusively on a normally nonpreferred species of seaweed later selected that species for several days in choice trials against a normally preferred species of seaweed. This learned reversal of food preference in favor of a recently familiar food source illustrates a capability for psychotaxic organization in the feeding behavior of these grazing animals, whose feeding behavior otherwise seems organized primarily at the taxic and biotaxic levels.

Development of feeding behavior has been traced from the larval, or *veliger*, form to the adult form of aplysia. Veligers swim about freely by means of beating long cilia located about the head region of their bodies. As the veligers swim about, algae cells are swept into their mouths by currents generated by their cilia. The foot of the veliger begins its development into the prominent structure seen in the adult aplysia at about thirty days after hatching, and the larvae acquire an ability to crawl along the substrate at this time. They continue to spend most of their time in swimming but, over the next several days, display a growing tendency to settle to the substrate and crawl. Soon they encounter a suitable substrate on which they settle for an extended time. Once they remain settled for three hours, they lose their former ability to swim and, in most species, depend exclusively upon crawling for the remainder of their lives. Their early crawling is aided by the action of pedal cilia, but the coordinated pedal contractions seen in adult locomotion grow progressively important with continued development (Kandel, 1979).

During the process of metamorphosis from larval to adult form, at about 34 days of age, veligers continue to feed by means of sweeping algal cells into their mouths through the action of anterior cilia. On day 35, however, they begin making appetitive orienting responses for the first time. Shortly after these responses make their appearance, the metamorphic animals begin to perform incomplete approximations of the adult consummatory response, lowering the pharynx down to the opening of the mouth, but without lowering the head and mouth to food and without projecting the odontophore from the mouth to take food. These precursor feeding responses are performed on days 35 and 36. During this time, veligers do not eat at all, having stopped their ingestion of algal cells. On day 37, they begin to perform the complete adult form of the consummatory response and to eat seaweed (Kandel, 1979).

Octopus is a genus of the class Cephalapoda, widely considered the most complex members of the phylum Mollusca. The familiar species, *O. vulgarius*, hatches from the egg as a tiny octopus two millimeters long and grows to an adult size of a meter or more, with a weight of several kilograms. As their name implies, octopuses have eight muscular arms extending from an upright mantel, or head. The arms are supplied on their ventral sides with muscular sucker disks that are both excellent grasping and holding organs as well as sensitive sensory organs of touch and chemoreception. The octopus nervous system is highly developed and includes a relatively large brain providing a brain–body weight ratio that compares favorably with those of many vertebrate animals. Octopuses eat crabs, bivalves, gastropods such as snails, other crustaceans, and perhaps some fish (Wells, 1978).

Newly hatched individuals of *O. vulgarius* immediately swim up into a plankton cloud at the surface of the sea and reside there for some time before descending to the bottom to make a home among rocks or other structures. Newly descended individuals undoubtedly have had considerable experience as predators while living among the plankton. In any case, they are observed to attack prey readily and with success from the beginning of their lives on the seafloor. Newly hatched young of cuttlefish—a genus very similar to the octopus—are somewhat larger at hatching and descend immediately to the bottom, where they have been observed attacking prey successfully on their first encounter with a prey object. It is suspected that the young octopus may possess a similar capability (Wells, 1978).

This is not to say that predatory attack behavior is not adjustable on the basis of learning experience, either in cuttlefish or the octopus. Maldonado (1964) found that octopuses that were experienced at attacking prey in their aquarium tanks made faster and more accurate attacks and initiated their jet-propelled leaps onto prey from greater distances than did inexperienced and slightly experienced individuals. It is known that young cuttlefish expand their range of acceptable attack stimuli as their experience at attacking prey grows. Thus, their originally limited food preference is overlaid and shaped by individual learning experience. Wells (1978) suggests that the same thing happens in young octopuses. He finds this arrangement reasonable for an animal that must alter its choice of prey objects many times in the course of a 500-fold growth in the size of its own body. The same growth requires that an octopus change the location of its home area numerous times in its life as the nooks and crannies that accommodated it earlier become too cramped. These individuals must learn to recognize new landmarks and homing cues many times over the course of their lifetimes, and they obviously are able to do so. Each octopus is possessive of its home place and the immediate surrounding area, defending them against intrusion by **conspecifics** (Wells, 1978). This behavior keeps octopuses dispersed across expanses of suitable habitat and illustrates an element of biosocial organization in their feeding behavior.

In the feeding behavior of aquarium-bound octopuses, an individual rests in its home cranny while visually observing the surrounding scene. The appearance of a crab in the area stimulates a rapid orientation of the octopus so that one of its two eyes is directly pointed toward the prey. Often the octopus raises and lowers its head several times in succession as if monitoring cues for depth perception. The octopus initiates its attack by walking forward smoothly on its arms, often stopping when its prey stops and moving when the prey moves. At a certain point of closure with the prey, the octopus blows water outward from a muscular funnel beneath the head and swims forward suddenly in a jet-propelled leap to fall upon the prey, covering the prey with the web of tissue connecting the anterior ends of its arms beneath the mouth and head (Figure 4.3). The octopus then clutches the prey with its sucking disks and moves the prey toward its mouth by bending its arms (Wells, 1978).

Crabs are held within the interbrachial pouch—the enclosure formed when the arms are held together tightly beneath the mouth—while saliva is injected into the area. The saliva contains a number of active agents, at least one of which is deadly to crabs. A crab held in this way dies quickly, and it is likely that soft tissues are decomposed sufficiently that their removal from skeletal attachments is made easier before the octopus actually begins ingesting its prey. Ingestion is aided by a parrot-like beak that can be rotated widely within the muscular mouth. The mouth is also served by a rake-like or saw-like structure called the *radula*. This structure is used when an octopus bores its way into the shell of a bivalve animal to gain access to the soft tissues within (Wells, 1978).

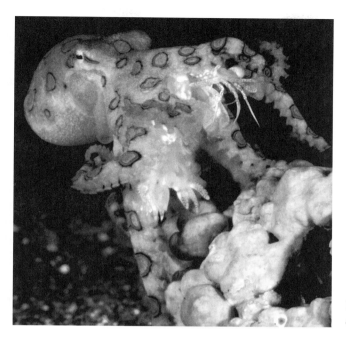

FIGURE 4.3   Octopus Attacking a Stomatopod

Octopuses in the natural environment probably do most of their ranging from the home area and much of their feeding at night. Undoubtedly, at these times, much of their prey is located by tactile senses rather than by sight. Octopuses often are observed probing with their arms into holes and crannies in rocks, rock faces, and coral reefs, making quick capture moves as they locate prey by touch and by chemoreception (Wells, 1978).

Numerous experimental observations testify to the octopus's great learning ability (Mather, 1998). The animals readily learn tactile discriminations based on surface texture and on chemical cues but are not responsive to tactile cues of shape, weight, or size. In visual discrimination tasks, they perform well on discriminations of shape, size, orientation of a figure, and brightness and polarization of light, but not of color (Wells, 1978).

In the octopus we find the first animal in the present series of accounts that establishes a home base from which it ranges widely and to which it returns repeatedly; we find as well the first animal for which learning must be accounted a major factor in the organization of both its feeding and its ranging behavior. These aspects of octopus behavior illustrate organization at the psychotaxic level of complexity. Moreover, the octopus is the first animal in our series to display clear examples of what is known as **goal-directed behavior** outside the immediate presence of a **goal-object** or goal-related stimulus. Goal-directed behavior is defined as a recognizable pattern of behavior that predictably ends in the attainment of a particular goal object or attractive outcome. As we have seen, octopuses frequently range far from their homes to engage in exploratory probing of locations where prey animals are likely to be hiding, and they predictably obtain food as a consequence of that behavior. When engaging in such probing behavior, it seems that the octopus is at first responding not to the presence of prey but to other stimuli similar to those that often have been associated with the presence of prey in the past. The behavior of the octopus alters dramatically upon its actual detection of prey in each instance of searching, detecting, and capturing behavior. Goal-directed behavior in the absence of immediate goal objects and goal-associated stimuli also occurs in all species to be covered later in this series.

Phylum Arthropoda

Members of this phylum populate the earth more densely and over a greater range of environments than do those of any other phylum (Hickman, Roberts, & Hickman, 1984). Members of the class Arachnida, the spiders, are familiar to all of us from early childhood. Spiders are supremely effective predators of almost any insects smaller than themselves and, in some cases, of other small creatures of various types. Spiders are served by an array of simple eyes—usually eight—spread about the head area. These are useful primarily in detecting movement in most species, although some species make running charges or leaps in attacking their prey, which suggest that those species, at least, are well able to detect specific visual forms. Spiders are liberally provided with *sensory setae*, hairlike receptors of vibrations of air, web, or other, more solid surfaces. They are also equipped with excellent receptors of chemical stimulation. Different groups of spider species capture their prey in various species-typical ways.

Huntsmen, or wolf spiders of the family Lycosidae, range through their environments as though in search of prey, often remaining stationary from time to time at a watching post. Once a prey object appears, the huntsman sprints forward on its eight long, powerful legs, to run down the prey and catch it between the *chelicarae*. These are a pair of small but powerful appendages serving the area of the mouth, as do another pair of appendages, the *pedipalps*. Although twice the size of the chelicarae, the pedipalps still are only one-fourth the size of the foremost pair of legs. Jumping spiders, such as *Misumenoides aleatorius*, are of a more compact body build, with short but powerful legs. They stalk near to their insect prey, then make a spectacular leap of up to ten times their own body length to come down upon the prey animal and catch it with their two front feet (Cloudsley-Thompson, 1958). Gardner (1966) observed that the probabilities of a spider's making hunting responses, making orientation responses toward prey, and pursuing prey were increased by food deprivation. The garden spider, *Miranda aurantia*, builds a species-typical web, spun of material from its spinnerets and silk glands, then awaits the arrival of prey from a location near the center of its web. As it waits, it is partially hidden behind a heavier silk screen it has woven in that area. This visual shield at the middle of the web slightly resembles a written message and is responsible for the common name of "writing spider" applied to these animals. They are among the strongest and most beautiful of spiders. Their attack upon the unfortunate moth or grasshopper that becomes entangled in the web is swift and of certain outcome. The spider dashes across the web to its prey, catches the prey in its legs and twirls the prey about rapidly, enclosing it within a cocoon of web. Within a few seconds the prey is completely helpless. The spider is then at leisure to inject its prey with digestive juices that render the internal tissues of the prey into a partially digested broth that the spider ingests by means of a powerful sucking action.

Numerous arthropods have demonstrated good ability for associative learning in a variety of situations, involving both classical and instrumental conditioning procedures. Spiders have been taught to associate sounds of different wave frequencies either with sugar-coated or quinine-coated flies and, thus, to show an appetitive reaction toward the sugar-associated cue but an aversive, avoidance reaction toward the quinine-associated cue (Walcott, 1969). It is to be expected that spiders in their natural environments can learn cues associated with productive areas to hunt, which creatures to attack and which to leave alone, routes back to a home area from various directions in the surrounding terrain, and so on. Thus, we consider spider feeding behavior as being organized to an important degree at the psychotaxic level of organization.

Honeybees (*Apis mellifera*) have fascinated students of animal behavior since at least the time of Aristotle. Their social living in communal groups of several tens of thousands of individuals is part of the reason for this interest, as is the honey produced and stored as a food supply by the bees. Our liking for honey led long ago to the keeping of bees domestically in hives designed to permit the beekeeper to make regular harvests of honey, and this practice led to the growth of an unusual degree of human familiarity with honeybee behavior.

Honeybees of three castes are found in most hives. First, there is the queen, who lays a continuing supply of eggs that provide for the future of the hive. Second, there are the workers, nonfertile female bees who carry out almost all the work of the hive. Workers care for the queen and direct her activities; they build and repair honeycomb; they feed and care for developing larvae and pupae; and they forage for the substances necessary to hive life: nectar, pollen, and water. Finally, there are the drones, males whose only function is to fertilize the queen at very infrequent intervals.

Honeybees begin their careers as foragers at the age of twenty-one days and continue as foragers for the rest of their lives, usually a period of from one to several weeks. As they begin their foraging careers, the substances for which they forage—honey, pollen, and water—are long familiar as objects of lifelong consumption, up to now having been provided to them directly by older worker bees. Foragers leave the hive and fly far afield. In their explorations, they are attracted to nectar and pollen by the bright colors and the strong scents of flowers, and to water by its bright reflection and perhaps by water-associated odors. Indeed, honeybees possess good odor and taste sensitivity, good color vision, especially for the blue end of the spectrum, and an ability to distinguish the polarity of light waves. These senses, along with excellent learning ability, enable them to find and return to good foraging sites and to navigate by the sun on inbound flights back to the hive. Honeybees are efficient at learning landmarks around the immediate neighborhood of the hive, but must depend on solar navigation to return to that vicinity from positions far afield.

Individual foragers function successfully from the beginning, but their efficiency improves greatly during their first week of foraging experience, presumably as a result of learning. From the beginning to the end of the first week of foraging, individuals demonstrated a doubling of their beginning levels of foraging efficiency, as measured by net rate of forage uptake (Dukas & Visscher, 1994). Learning also plays an important part in the most sensational of all honeybee characteristics: Their apparent ability to communicate information about the location of foraging sites by means of a language composed of dance movements! But the exact nature of the detailed communication involved in the famous **dance language** of honeybees was soundly questioned in a recent review of the subject by Wenner (1998; Wenner & Wells, 1990) as seen in Box 4.1.

What aspects of the honeybee dance phenomenon remain safe from the challenge of Wenner and his colleagues? Actually, several aspects of the phenomenon stand independently of this challenge. Honeybees often do perform dancing movements upon returning from a foraging site, and their dances often are effective in recruiting large numbers of foragers to depart the hive to forage themselves. Odor cues identified with the foraging site are available to observers of a forager's dance, and these cues may be effective in guiding dance observers to approach any site offering the same odor. This sort of guidance is readily afforded by classical conditioning, a process at which honeybees have been shown quite capable (Batson, Hoban, & Bitterman, 1992; Buchanan & Bitterman, 1989; Wenner, 1998). Frequent foragers making repeated straight, or beeline, flights to and from a particular site leave scent trails through calm air that may be used by first-time visitors as signposts to the popular site.

Thus, even if the language hypothesis must be weakened or partially abandoned, honeybee foraging will continue to be seen as being organized at quite a high level of complexity. It displays biosocial influences in the impact of social interactions upon foraging behavior. Moreover, it displays numerous instances of psychotaxic organization. Learned cues are established as guides of foraging behavior, and perhaps some of these are supplied in the course of dancing interactions. Individual foragers also display great improvements in their foraging capabilities as they gain experience at the task (Dukas & Visscher, 1994).

Phylum Chordata, Subphylum Vertebrata

At this point in the animal series, we come to the vertebrates, most recently evolved of all major groups of animals and, of course, the group to which our own species belongs. Impressive learning ability found in numerous species throughout the subphylum makes it likely that associative learning is a major factor in the feeding behavior of nearly all vertebrate species. Thus, we consider that the feeding behavior of all of the following groups is influenced by psychotaxic organization. We will note outstanding instances of learning, as well as outstanding instances of biosocial and psychosocial organization as we describe behavior in a variety of vertebrate groups and species.

Class Osteichthyes

Newly hatched largemouth bass (*Micropterus salmoidius*) feed passively at first by absorption of the yolk sac of the egg from which they emerged. Within a few days, they begin their lives as predators, feeding first on very small organisms such as mosquito larvae, or "wigglers," and expanding the size of prey proportionally as the bass increase in size toward a maximum weight of seven to twenty or more pounds. The

BOX **4.1**
The Honeybee Language Controversy

The hypothesis of a honeybee language was proposed by the classic ethologist and Nobel Prize–winner Karl von Frisch (1947). Impressed by the fact that numerous bees often visited a particular site shortly after it had been visited by the first bee of the day to have discovered it, von Frisch arranged actually to look inside a beehive as a forager returned from a newly discovered food source. What he saw amazed him. The returning forager performed a regular series of movements that were closely observed by other workers. The observers often drew near to touch the performing bee and to move along with her through several of her movements.

Von Frisch named this sort of performance a **figure eight dance.** In performing the dance, a bee made a straight run always in the same direction and at the end of it, veered off to one side and ran in a half circle back to the starting point of her previous straight run. On alternate runs she made her half circle first to one side, then to the other such that, if the straight run were made horizontally on the vertical surface of a honeycomb, the bee's movements would trace a rather squashed form of the numeral eight. Von Frisch noted that the dance seemed to recruit numerous foragers to leave the hive after watching a performance, and he was impressed by the large number of those watchers that turned up later at the very site visited by the dancing bee. The results of numerous experiments convinced him that the dance of a returned forager conveyed precise information of the location of a foraging site to workers that observed the dance.

After much study, von Frisch proposed that the straight run of the dance contained encoded information about both the direction of and the distance to a foraging site. Direction was conveyed by the direction of the straight run, indicated in relation to the position of the sun. (Because dances usually were made on vertical surfaces, straight runs directly toward the site could not be made.) The speed or duration of the straight run conveyed information about the distance to a site; slower runs indicated longer distances.

Honeybee dancing, von Frisch proclaimed, constituted a **language** in which precise and detailed information was symbolically encoded and by which information was reliably communicated from one bee to another. Von Frisch's proposal was sensational but was widely accepted by his fellow scientists for five decades, although it was seldom without individual critics (Wenner, 1998).

The results of numerous experiments by himself and colleagues over a period of several years converted Wenner (1998) from a supporter of the language hypothesis into perhaps its severest critic. Outstanding among these persuasive findings were the following:

- Experiments comparing numbers of foragers arriving at a site visited by a dancer to other sites in the neighborhood yielded random results. These experiments were similar to those used by von Frisch to garner support for his hypothesis but included sites distributed over a wider area than von Frisch had employed.
- Most recruited bees engaged in widespread wandering after watching a dance performance. Few acted as though they were in possession of language-provided information about a site location.
- Bees exposed to different dance information in two different hives turned up in equal numbers at four different sites, showing no indication that dance information affected site selection.

(continued)

B O X   **4.1**   **Continued**

- No successful recruitment was shown in experiments that denied the use of odor cues in identifying a foraging site.
- Experiments that pitted dance cues against odor cues yielded results supporting the use of odor cues alone.

These findings mount a serious challenge of the honeybee language hypothesis (Wenner, 1998), although recent supporters of the hypothesis continue to offer argument and evidence on its behalf (e.g., Gould, 1976; Michelsen, Anderson, Storm, Kirchner, & Lindauer, 1992; Kirchner & Towne, 1994).

small bass, attracted visually by the jerky movements of the wigglers, rushes to the attack, opening its mouth sharply as it overtakes a wiggler, producing a strong suction that draws the wiggler deep into the mouth, which the bass then closes sharply. Bass depend primarily on excellent vision but also sense sounds and other vibrations by means of their lateral line organs. They have effective taste and odor sensitivity as well, but these senses are not as heavily involved in their feeding behavior.

Locomotion is accomplished by sinuous undulations of the lower half of the body, particularly the tail region. The amplitude of such movements reaches maximum expression at the widespread tail fin that, thrusting against the resistant medium of water to one side and then the other, propels the body rapidly forward. The movement of bass, as we might expect from such a consummate predator, can be impressively sudden and quick, especially over the short distances usually involved in a bass's dash toward its prey.

As indicated by its name, largemouth, the bass's mouth and head are unusually large in proportion to the remainder of its body, enabling it to take a wide range of sizes of prey. The size of the head and mouth in this predator provides one instance of a defining physical feature of a species having been evolved in the service of feeding behavior. We will see several examples as we proceed to other species.

During most of the year, bass forage on an individual basis. At certain seasons however, numerous individuals school together in feeding groups (Lau, 1983). These "wolf packs" position themselves beneath schools of minnows and force them toward the surface, then drive them in confusion back and forth among the voraciously feeding pack members. The efficiency of an individual's participation in this group feeding behavior seems a certain prospect for improvement with learning experience. The overall behavior pattern affords an excellent example of biosocial organization of feeding.

Class Amphibia

The bullfrog, *Rana catesbeina*, and the toad, *Bufo americanus*, like most adult amphibians, are predators, feeding on insects, spiders, snails, worms, and almost anything else that is small enough for them to swallow. Their capturing behavior is triggered by the stimulus of visual movement. They often reach out to catch fairly distant prey with a tongue lash or flick of their tongues, which are attached at the front of the mouth and are free for their remaining length. The tip of the tongue is covered with a sticky secretion that is helpful in holding prey (Porter, 1967).

Bullfrogs living in a laboratory colony displayed anticipatory feeding responses in relation to an established feeding routine. Prior to the arrival of caretakers, the frogs approached the usual feeding site and aggregated there, but did this on workdays only, not on holidays, when they were not fed in the usual way. The cues for approach responses were contained within the milieu of events associated with the beginning of each workday at the lab. These responses could be changed in a matter of a few feedings by altering the time or the site of feeding (Van Bergeijk, 1967). These observations suggest the importance of psychotaxic organization in the feeding behavior of bullfrogs in their wild environment. The territorial dispersion of male bullfrogs across areas of prime breeding habitat, from which they also do much feeding, illustrates an element of biosocial organization in their feeding behavior, as well.

Class Reptilia

Green anole lizards (*Anolis carolinis*) patrol their home ranges on the alert for insects and other prey, which they discern by means of excellent color vision. Spotting prey, they creep near to it in a stalking fashion, then rush forward in several quick steps to catch it with their tongues and jaws. Anoles capture much of their prey in fairly close cover, often having to maneuver around angles of leaves or twigs or around the circumference of a limb to take a victim. Thus, a more far-reaching tongue lash, such as seen in frogs, as well as in lizards of the chameleon group, might often prove unsuitable. The dispersal of male anoles in their individual territories provides an instance of biosocial organization in their feeding behavior, which is very likely affected by psychotaxic organization as well.

Rattlesnakes (genus *Crotalis*) have excellent chemical sensitivity by way of the tongue and the organ of Jacobson, located in the roof of the mouth. Their predatory behavior is also enhanced by heat-sensitive pits located between the nasal opening and the eye on each side of the head. Vision often can be an important guide in striking prey. Hearing appears to have little effect on behavior, generally. Rattlesnakes are efficient followers of scent trails left by rodents and other prey at night. They can locate prey at close distances by means of the prey's body heat. Prey are struck and injected with venom, then left to wander and die. The snake is well capable of discerning the particular odor of an individual deer mouse it has injected and can follow its scent trail even when it has been crossed by the trails of other deer mice (Chiszar & Smith, 1998). Thus, the snake is able easily to locate the prey for consumption after it has died, even if it has managed to wander quite some distance after being struck. The ability to distinguish the individual odor of a particular prey animal very likely depends upon learning, or psychotaxic organization.

Class Aves

The birds are a fascinating group of species whose behavior is organized at very high levels of complexity. Thanks to their obvious presence in many environments that we occupy every day, and to the fact that most birds are active in the daylight hours when we can see them, birds are the wild animals most familiar to most of us. The herons and egrets (family Ardeidae) are a group of predatory birds whose distinctive and identifying physical features obviously evolved in the service of feeding behavior. Their long legs, long necks, and long bills enable them to wade into the watery habitat of the fish, frogs, and other aquatic animals that make up their prey, to stretch forward to search areas of the habitat that are at some distance from the spot where their feet are located at a given moment, and to reach out and take prey from that distance by means of strikes that often are spectacular to observe. All of the eleven species of herons, egrets, and bitterns native to North America make use of the basic feeding techniques described by Meyerriecks (1960) as **stand and wait** and **walk slowly** (Kushlan, 1976). In these techniques herons stand quietly in or along the edge of water and watch for prey; or they wade slowly through the water watching for and stalking prey, which they capture by a rapid forward movement of the neck and head coordinated with a forward thrust of the entire body. These techniques are well demonstrated in the feeding of great blue herons, great egrets, and little blue herons.

Very active techniques apparently designed to flush prey from hiding are employed more by snowy egrets, reddish egrets, and tricolored, or Louisiana herons. One of these techniques, called **foot stirring**, benefits, in the snowy egret, from the bright gold coloration of the feet in this species. Located at the ends of the snowy egret's black legs, the golden feet must give the appearance of independent, living creatures as they flash along the subsurface among the hiding places of the egret's prey. Other very active techniques are termed *running, hopping,* and *wing-flicking* (see Figure 4.4).

FIGURE 4.4   A Tricolored Heron Catching Prey

Overall, herons are widely versatile in the variety of feeding techniques they employ. Kushlan's (1976) review includes twenty-eight different techniques used by North American herons. The snowy egret is the versatility champion, using seventeen different techniques as compared to thirteen for the little blue heron, eight for the great blue heron, and only two for the American bittern. Many of these techniques probably involve learning in their development (Kushlan, 1973; Meyerriecks, 1971), especially a behavior known as *baiting* (see Figure 4.5), in which green herons have been observed repeatedly positioning bait objects, to which small fish were attracted, in the areas where the herons were fishing (Lovell, 1958). Additionally, Recher and Recher (1969) found that little blue herons with at least eighteen months of foraging experience made fewer misses in their strike attempts and obtained more food per minute of foraging than did younger herons nine months or less in age.

The hawks (order Falconiformes) are another group of species with obvious physical attributes that support their **predatory behavior.** They are defined as a group by their powerful, clawed feet and their large, curved, and sharp-pointed bills. They are also known, quite accurately, for their spectacular vision. Not only are their eyes very densely packed with cones, they are very large, taking up a far greater proportion of head weight than do the eyes of humans. In addition, their structure, with rather flattened lenses located far from the retina, makes each eye function as a telescope (Snyder & Miller, 1978). Many North American hawks practice two modes of hunting behavior. They either **hunt while soaring** or **hunt from a watching post,** awaiting the appearance of prey. They close upon their prey either by a gliding dive or by a burst of powered flight and kill it with their powerful, clawed feet. Large **falcons**

FIGURE 4.5   Green Heron Using Bait

such as the peregrine and prairie falcons often hit the large birds upon which they prey high in the air, falling upon them from above and striking them with their talons, then releasing them to tumble head over heels to the ground. The falcon follows at leisure to claim its prey. **Accipiters** such as Cooper's hawk catch other birds in the cover of woods or brush, chasing them down by rapid, powered flight.

The zone-tailed hawk alters the pattern common to most **buteos,** or soaring hawks. Instead, its flight seems to mimic the distinctive, rocking glide of the turkey vulture, from which it may be distinguished by the zoned tail for which it is named. Many features of the hawk's coloration are closely similar to those of the turkey vulture. Small rodents in the habitat of the zone-tailed hawk may be subject to a very unpleasant surprise when a harmless vulture they may have ignored turns out to be a swiftly attacking hawk. Craighead and Craighead (1956) showed that red-tailed hawks, the most representative of North American buteos, establish **search images** through their learning experiences, leading them to take their favorite prey in significantly greater proportions than that prey's proportion of the total prey population being utilized at a given time.

The flycatchers are another group of birds identified closely with their common feeding behavior of catching flying insects out of the air by means of sometimes spectacular flights. The flycatcher sits at its watching post, moving its gaze about every few moments as it watches for the movement of its prey. It springs into flight, follows the evasive pattern of its escaping prey, closes upon it, and captures it with an audible snap of its bill, then returns again to the same watching post to continue its vigil. This description was written with the eastern pewee (*Contopus virens*) in mind, but similar descriptions would apply to many of the more than thirty species of flycatchers that breed in North America.

The **corvids** (family Corvidae) include jays, nutcrackers, and crows. Several members of this group engage in the behavior of **caching food** in summer and autumn and harvesting their **caches** in winter, a season that otherwise would be a time of food scarcity. Successful location of cached food supplies throughout a long winter places great demands on systems of learning and spatial memory in these birds. Undoubtedly, it is no coincidence that members of this group have developed outstanding capabilities of just that sort. Clark's nutcracker, a corvid species occupying habitats at high elevations in the Rocky Mountains of North America, hides stores of pine nuts in hundreds of locations and returns to harvest a large percentage of its stores each season. A study of nutcrackers' harvesting of caches (Tomback, 1980) found that marks left by attempts at probing for cached food were clustered around locations where a cache was found rather than being randomly scattered about a vicinity. Such evidence suggests that the nutcrackers relied on memory of where caches had been placed. Laboratory study has supplied abundant evidence of impressive spatial memory in this species (Balda & Kamil, 1989; Kamil et al., 1994). The bluejay, another corvid and a familiar inhabitant of suburban lawns and woodlots, has demonstrated an ability for mastering complex learning sets that is comparable to that seen in many mammals, including marmoset monkeys (Hunter & Kamil, 1971).

Several species of crows are regularly observed dropping captured shellfish onto rocks, breaking open the shells, then consuming the exposed meat (Ehrlich, Dobkin,

& Wheye, 1988). Northwestern crows often carry whelks a considerable distance from the water's edge where they are captured and drop them repeatedly onto rocks, until the shells break open. The crows show a decided preference for capturing large whelks, which break open more easily, rather than the more numerous but harder to break small whelks. A number of individual differences are observed in the particular shell-dropping styles developed by different crows (Zach, 1978, 1979).

Beyond the high levels of psychotaxic organization seen in the feeding behaviors just described, there are many instances in which the feeding of birds enters the highest level of behavioral organization. Psychosocial organization depends upon social interactions among individuals that are known to one another by experience. The feeding of fledgling birds by parents in the open habitat, as the fledglings explore the broader environment and begin to develop their own feeding capabilities, is importantly influenced by shared social experiences among the individuals involved. In many species of crows, offspring remain with the parental pair throughout almost their first two years of life, continuing to feed with the parents as members of a group in which the individuals are well known to one another through much experience together (Kilham, 1984). Extended group feeding among parents, offspring, and other familiar, or known, individuals also is seen among a number of other species groups, including cranes, turkeys, swans, and geese.

Class Mammalia

The mammals display the most complex behavioral organization of any group of animals. Squirrels and chipmunks (family Sciuridae) have encountered similar feeding problems to those of Clark's nutcracker and other corvids, and their evolutionary response to those problems has been similar. Both of these groups inhabit environments in which there are great seasonal differences in the availability of the food. Both groups evolved the behavioral strategy of caching food during times of plenty, and both groups evolved correspondingly great capacities of learning and spatial memory enabling them to find their food caches in times of need (Devenport & Devenport, 1998). Thirteen-lined ground squirrels were observed making numerous caches in a naturalistic experimental situation. After caches were made, experimenters dug similar artificial caches nearby. In about half the cases, a squirrel's real cache was robbed of seeds and these were placed instead in the artificial cache nearby. In the other cases, the seeds were left in the real cache and the artificial cache was simply a similar hole that had been dug, left empty, and refilled. Experimenters later observed that squirrels almost always dug first into the site of their real caches rather than the artificial caches nearby, whether the seeds that had filled the original caches had been relocated or not. Furthermore, squirrels overwhelmingly visited their own caches rather than those of other squirrels that were located in the same vicinity. These observations indicated that the squirrels remembered the locations of their own caches and that they found them from memory rather than by sniffing out buried seeds in the area.

Other observations by the Devenports (1998) showed that chipmunks vary their use of remembered or learned information according to the recency of the information. Free-ranging chipmunks were given feeding experiences at two different feeding stations. The first site was given a long history as the richer food source of the two, then the second site was made the richer station for the chipmunks' most recent experiences. Which one of the two sites would the chipmunks visit first when given their next access to the feeding stations? The answer depended on how soon they were given their next access. If allowed access again within a short time, while their last experience was still recent information, the chipmunks chose the second site, which, at last encounter, had been the richer of the two. But if more than a few hours had passed since their last access, the chipmunks chose the first site for their next visit, returning to the site that, over the majority of their experience, had been the richer of the two. The Devenports suggested that an ability to base foraging decisions on remembered information would be of great functional value to foragers such as chipmunks, whose food resources are subject to rapid depletion by competing foragers of their own and other species.

Bighorn sheep (genus *Ovis*) of the Rocky Mountains of North America display an interesting example of psychosocial organization in their feeding behavior. Young rams are attracted to large-horned older rams and often keep company with a particular older ram for several years as they grow and develop the large horns that may enable them one day to become dominant rams themselves (Geist, 1998). While keeping company with an older ram, young males accept his dominance and follow his lead as the group goes about its daily activities. This social behavior allows them to benefit from the skills of food location and predator avoidance possessed by the older ram, whose large horns, which grow cumulatively over many years, are visible evidence of his long-term use of rich pasturage and his successful avoidance of predators. Young female sheep, on the other hand, keep company with the same group of older females, usually including their own mothers, for many years, being guided in their activities by experienced females with which they are well familiar as individuals. Wild horses and many species of deer also feed and spend most of their time in long-term groups composed of the same individuals. The behavior of each individual in such groups is influenced by the social interaction among the group, whose more dominant and influential members are likely to be its most experienced individuals.

Social predators live in long-term groups of individuals whose great familiarity with one another enables them to achieve cooperative hunting behavior of impressive complexity. The gray wolf (*Canis lupus*) lives in groups that are organized around the family structure of a mated pair and a number of their offspring, which remain with their natal group for several years before departing to establish their own mateships and separate groups. Members of the wolf pack coordinate their activities and cooperate closely with one another in their feeding behavior. Mech (1966) made extensive observations of wolves hunting moose on Isle Royale in Lake Superior near the border between the United States and Canada. He observed that wolves initially challenged twelve moose for every one on which they pressed an attack for any length of time. When the wolves did make a prolonged attack, however, they nearly always made a kill on that individual. This observation, along with physical evidence of weakness such as heavy parasite infestation or excessive age in the wolf kills he examined, convinced Mech that the wolves were skillful at judging vulnerability or weakness in a prospective victim. This ability might be particularly important when attacking a prey animal of the size of a mature moose.

Mech observed that a number of wolves worked together in attacking prey and that kills were shared among pack members. He noted that wolves attacking a cow moose and her calf often arranged themselves on two sides and challenged the cow strongly on only one side at a time. Wolves on the other side remained watchful. If a calf failed to accompany its mother by remaining under her belly as she charged the attacking wolves, then those keeping watch on the other side moved in quickly to disable the calf. On the other hand, if a calf did remain beneath the protection of its mother as she put up a confident defense for a short time, the wolves would withdraw, leaving the pair in peace. Wolves might be capable of making a kill in such instances, but at what cost? One effective jab of a cow's forefoot might break bone in a wolf, imposing what would become a death sentence.

Another cooperative tactic Mech observed was the use of what might be called *relay running* when wolves made extended chases of a single moose. During these chases, several wolves kept in close pursuit of the running moose, matching it step-for-step, while others followed along at an easier pace, just keeping in touch with the chase. From time to time, individuals that had maintained close pursuit for a while dropped back to the easier pace of the followers and, in response, several of them moved forward to join the close pursuit.

Wolves made cooperative attacks in bringing down moose. Early in an attack, the wolves concentrated their efforts on the rump area, biting and holding until they tore loose, inflicting large, vascular wounds in the process. Late in an attack, a wolf would attempt to catch the moose by the front of the nose while others continued to attack the rump area. A moose might be thrown several times before it succumbed to blood loss and shock. Wolves may demonstrate a variety of effective cooperative tactics in their joint attack upon their prey (Figure 4.6). Eskimo hunters of the Nunamiut tribe report a tradition among the old-time Nunamiut of consciously imitating the behavior of hunting wolves in carrying out their own attacks upon large game animals

FIGURE 4.6   Wolves in Joint Attack on a Bison

(Lopez, 1978). This level of respect from human hunters is impressive recognition of the complexity and effectiveness of the gray wolf's ability as a social predator.

The lions (*Panthera leo*) of the Serengeti in Africa live in long-term social groups called prides. A female lion may live her entire life in the same pride she was born in, in company with the same females she has known all her life (Figure 4.7). Young females growing up in such a group have opportunities to hunt again and again with the same lionesses, including their own mothers and many other pride members possessing vast amounts of cooperative hunting experience. This appears an ideal situation for the cultural transmission of hunting traditions through learning processes. Schaller (1972) reported numerous examples in which groups of hunting lionesses halted their approach to a feeding herd while still at a considerable distance away. Several of the group then waited in place as four or five others moved off in several directions to reach positions on the flanks of the herd on both sides. Once the flankers were in place, all the lionesses began to creep stealthily forward, gradually closing the distance between themselves and the now partly surrounded herd. When the herd finally exploded into flight in every direction, some individuals usually passed near one or more lionesses, affording good chances for a lion kill (Figure 4.8).

The majority of feeding among most primate species occurs within a social context in which all members of the group are well known to one another. The young primate's earliest experiences at obtaining its own food from the environment occur as it maintains proximity with its mother, a location in which it has the opportunity to obtain some of the same food she is eating. Development of feeding behavior proceeds always in the context of proximity with social agents that are well experienced at finding and obtaining food within their familiar home range, in which they also are well experienced at avoiding predators and other hazards.

FIGURE 4.7   Lioness at a Zebra Kill

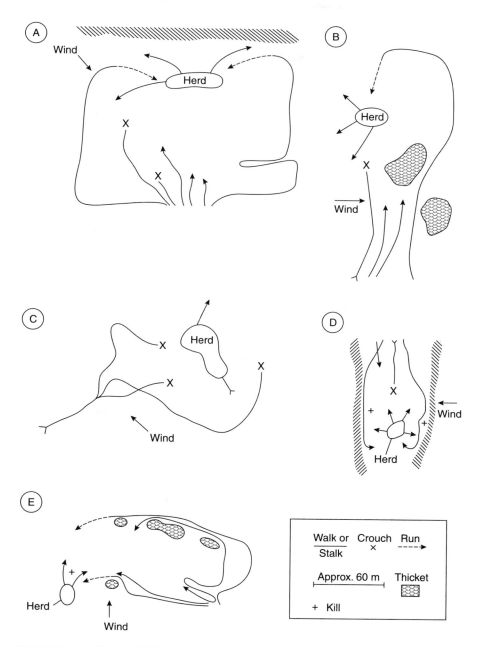

FIGURE 4.8   Routes Taken by Lionesses in Stalking Herds of Prey

Gibbons, for example (genus *Hylobates*), are nine species of small apes that, together, are the fourth nearest living relatives of the human species (Haraway & Maples, 1998). They live in small family groups composed of a **monogamous** mated pair of adults and their subadult offspring. They remain almost always within the confines of their own fixed territories, the features of which are thoroughly familiar from long experience and through which they travel as a group to obtain their food. Gibbons are arboreal animals, spending nearly all their time high in the trees of the climax forests of their homelands in Southeast Asia. Their basic form of locomotion, called **brachiation,** is to swing by their hands and arms beneath branches or other sources of support. This locomotor behavior is ideally suited to their feeding behavior of harvesting fruits and flower buds. As a gibbon moves out to the end of a branch where the fruit is located, the branch bends downward, bringing the fruit into close range of the gibbon's face as the animal hangs beneath the branch.

Similar to the cultural transmission of feeding behaviors among group members of Japanese macaques, discussed earlier in Chapter 2, is the apparent cultural transmission of stone **tool use** among chimpanzee (genus *Pan*) communities at various locations in West Africa (Matsuzawa, 1998). Stone tools are used as "hammer" and "anvil" to break open a variety of nuts by these animals, but the use of stone tools by chimpanzees is unknown in East Africa, such as at the Zombe Stream Reserve where Jane Goodall has studied chimpanzees for more than thirty years. Similarly, termite fishing with twig wands as tools at Gombe (Goodall, 1964) was observed as well in a group studied by Matsuzawa (1998) at Bossou but was not observed among a group he studied at Nimba.

The same species of leaf was used to obtain water from streams by both chimpanzees and the local human population in one area, but the leaves were simply folded by chimpanzees, whereas they were shaped into a cup by people. Wands were also used by chimpanzees in West Africa as tools for dipping up safari ants (Sugiyama, Koman, & Sow, 1988). Grass stems and twigs were stripped of leaves to form the wands. A unique example of tool use recently observed in West Africa was the use of palm leafstalks to pound holes in the crowns of oil palms, allowing access to the juicy pulp within, which was eaten (Sugiyama, 1994). This tool use was termed *pestle pounding.* The flexibility of chimpanzee tool use is impressively illustrated by two additional observations. Matsuzawa (1998) reported that when a stone anvil was broken by hard use, the broken pieces were shortly pressed into service as hammers. He also observed several chimpanzees attempting to use a stone anvil with a top surface that sloped so severely that nuts always rolled off onto the ground before they could be hit with a hammer. After being frustrated in these efforts for a short time, one of the animals picked up a nearby stone and wedged it under the anvil, leveling up the anvil's surface such that it could be used successfully.

Archeological evidence indicates that *Homo erectus,* our own immediate ancestor, had established a pattern of stone toolmaking, meat eating, and the use of home bases by about 1.5 million years ago. A pattern of **hunting and gathering** developed in which it is likely that males specialized in hunting and gathering meat while females, often encumbered by pregnancy or by young children, specialized in gathering plant foods (Lee, 1979). This same general pattern remained widely practiced around the world even by our more recent ancestors until it began to be replaced by animal and plant domestication, largely within the past 10,000 years. All food-gathering techniques within this pattern would have been subject to cultural transmission, and many would have involved close cooperation among numerous individuals who were well known to one another. The **home base** was a place where the very young, the ill, and the very old could be cared for and to which far-ranging foragers could return to rejoin their group, among which food could be shared by all.

Analysis of Feeding Behavior Based on Levels of Complexity

As we have proceeded through this section describing feeding behaviors in a broad array of animals, we have designated levels of behavioral organization illustrated by each group of species. We said at the beginning that a trend toward greater complexity of behavior would be noticeable as we made our way from the earliest toward the most recently evolved animals. Now that we have reached the end of our series, we are in a position to look back and evaluate progressive changes seen in complexity of feeding behavior. Such an evaluation is summarized in Table 4.1, which shows the higher levels of organization illustrated in the behavior of each major group of species considered in this chapter. The same relationship is depicted in Figure 4.9, in which degree of behavioral complexity is plotted against recency of species origin. Ratings of behavioral complexity were obtained by applying Schneirla's and Tobach's scale of complexity, as modified in this book, to the feeding behavior of various groups, and by assigning a value of one point to each upward step in stage of complexity. Recency of species origin was expressed in the figure as the reciprocal of species age on the logarithmic scale.

TABLE 4.1 Higher Levels of Behavioral Complexity Displayed by Major Groups Considered in This Chapter

Major Groups	Higher Levels of Complexity Illustrated
Protozoa	Taxis
Porifera	Taxis
Cnidaria	Biotaxis, Biosocial
Echinodermata	Biotaxis, Biosocial
Platyhelminthes	Biotaxis, Psychotaxis
Mollusca	Biosocial, Psychotaxis
Arthropoda	Biosocial, Psychotaxis
Osteichthyes	Biosocial, Psychotaxis
Amphibia	Biosocial, Psychotaxis
Reptilia	Biosocial, Psychotaxis
Aves	Psychotaxis, Psychosocial
Mammalia	Psychotaxis, Psychosocial

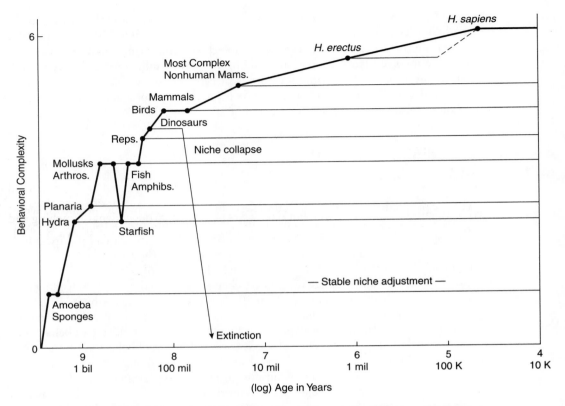

FIGURE 4.9 Behavioral Complexity Expressed as a Function of Recency of Origin

Formal Treatments and Simulations of Foraging Behavior

The central idea of a theoretical perspective known as **optimal foraging theory** is that, once an appreciable amount of evolution has occurred in a species, its members should have evolved into optimal foragers. That is, they should approach maximal efficiency in their foraging behavior given the constraints imposed by their environments. Because it is possible for theorists to make reasonably accurate estimates of what optimal behavior should be like under a variety of circumstances, we should be able to test propositions of optimal foraging by establishing circumstances of particular interest and observing animals' foraging behavior in those circumstances (see Mellgren, 1998).

Charnov's (1976) **Marginal Value Theorem** proposed that in an environment in which objects of foraging are distributed unevenly in clumps, or patches, there is an optimum time for a forager to leave a patch in which it is currently foraging and go in search of another patch. The time to leave is when the rate of capturing prey in a patch falls to the average value of capturing prey in the entire habitat as a whole. Charnov showed mathematically that an animal following this marginal value rule would capture a maximum number of prey per minute spent foraging. Findings have been partially supportive of Charnov's Marginal Value Theorem. Its greatest contribution thus far has been as a stimulus to research and to additional theory development in the area of foraging (Mellgren, 1998).

There is a large array of evidence to support the basic idea that foraging capabilities of animals approach the optimal in many instances. We learned earlier in this chapter of impressive feats of spatial memory by squirrels (Devenport & Devenport, 1998) and by corvids (Balda & Kamil, 1989). A particularly relevant finding of Balda and Kamil's was that Clark's nutcracker, which is heavily dependent upon recovering food caches for its survival, displays much greater capacity for spatial memory than does the scrub jay, another corvid species, but one that is not nearly so dependent on caching and recovering food. Other impressive feats of spatial memory have been shown by birds such as black-capped chickadees and marsh tits (e.g., Cowie, Krebs, & Sherry, 1981).

Additional support is drawn from studies demonstrating near optimal foraging of rats on **radial mazes.** These mazes are formed of eight arms radiating out from a central location, from which a rat begins foraging. The animal's foraging is considered optimal if it can obtain the small amount of food located at the end of each of the radial arms without repeating visits to arms from which it has already harvested the food. Most rats perform very efficiently at this task and seldom make mistaken reentries even after having been several hours removed from the maze midway through their harvesting of it (Brown & Mellgren, 1994). Another area of support for the idea of evolution of optimal foraging capabilities comes from demonstrations that animals are able to associate varying amounts of food value with various flavors, enabling the animals to choose foods that deliver high nutrition (e.g., Capaldi & Powley, 1990).

Theorists have modeled the behavior of small birds in risk of starvation in midwinter, when the food gathered during the day may not be sufficient for birds to maintain internal temperatures at survivable levels through a long, cold night. They have calculated that a bird faced with a choice between highly variable patches with occasional high payoff and very reliable but low payoff patches should choose to forage at reliable, low payoff patches on days when its expected energy budget for the day is positive. On days when its expected energy budget is below adequate, however, the bird should change its strategy and choose to forage at high-risk, potentially high-payoff patches. The observed behavior of dark-eyed juncos in winter appears to fit these predictions rather nicely (Caraco & Lima, 1987).

Theorists in optimal foraging often derive complex equations in the process of calculating how animals should behave under specified conditions. They calculate what sort of behavior natural selection, as an **ultimate cause,** should have produced as ideal solutions to foraging problems. Theorists make these determinations through the use of rigorous formal thinking. No one must suppose that the animals themselves are aware of these necessities or that they are acting consciously to meet them. Much additio7nal work like that mentioned earlier by the Devenports and by Kamil and his colleagues is needed to describe **proximal mechanisms** that contribute to optimal foraging. Further, we should remember that animals must perform many necessary tasks besides foraging in their conduct of a successful life. The necessities imposed by all of these tasks must be balanced in the overall behavior of successful animals.

Collier and his colleagues (Collier & Johnson, 1998) have made an extensive study of foraging behavior within experimental simulations of natural environments for a variety of mammals and birds. An important feature of their experimental environments was that they provided **closed economies** in which animals spent all of their time and earned all of their food or water. The amounts of food or water available were not limited by the experimenters, although both search–procurement costs and costs of consumption were varied. Their findings generally support basic ideas of optimal foraging theory, although the support is rather of a qualitative than a precise nature (Collier & Johnson, 1998). The following are among the most important findings thus far produced by these efforts:

- As the costs of procuring relevant resources increases, animals decrease the frequency of feeding and watering bouts and increase the time or size of each bout. Throughout these changes, total intakes of food and water are conserved.
- When the cost of procurement varies from one meal to another, cats and rats increase the size of each meal in relation to the *average* procurement cost per meal rather than in relation to the cost of the current meal at a given time, indicating that these animals establish their foraging strategies in relation to their experiences over a rather extended time window.
- Cost amounts in time used and in energy expended affect foraging decisions in the same manner.
- Rats also adjust meal sizes in relation to consumption costs, eating smaller meals in high-cost conditions and in patches that simulate rapid depletion of resources, but procurement cost is a greater influence of foraging behavior than is consumption cost.

An overall conclusion from this work is that a simple motivational system based on the idea of deprivation and restoration, or depletion and repletion of needed resources, is not adequate to describe variations in foraging behavior of animals inhabiting closed-economy environments that simulate nature. Rather, the situation is more complicated, suggesting that animals "can behave in anticipation of their requirements, using information about the economic structure of their habitat in a cost-reducing fashion" (Collier & Johnson, 1998, p. 1613).

Summary: Principles Introduced in This Chapter

A gradient from lower toward higher complexity in the organization of feeding behavior is seen as one moves across the animal series from the earliest to the most recently evolved groups of species. Furthermore, as one moves forward across the animal series, particularly from the mollusks onward, feeding behavior is seen to be increasingly a product of development, with developmental experience and learning becoming increasingly important at higher levels of behavioral organization.

Within limits, animals become increasingly more responsive to stimulation and more likely to engage in foraging behavior as their state of food deprivation increases. At the higher levels of behavioral organization, however, the situation is more complicated. At the level of birds and mammals, at least, animals are sensitive to the economic structure of their habitats, and their behavior anticipates requirements imposed by accustomed conditions.

Animals have evolved toward optimal efficiency in their foraging behavior such that their present behavior may be seen as an approximation of optimal foraging. Optimal evolution of foraging, however, must be seen as reflecting a balance among the variety of survival and reproductive tasks required of all successful individuals of a particular species.

KEY TERMS

Accipiters a group of species of hawks with short, broad wings and long tails that are adept at chasing down other birds on the wing, often while flying through heavy cover in woods or brush; members of this group are largely responsible for use of the name *chicken hawk* by country people and farmers.

Appetitive response generally, a response to an appetitive stimulus or approach stimulus; however, the term has specific application to a distinctive behavior pattern that occurs in the feeding behavior of aplysia.

Associative learning learning that is understood as involving associations of events that have occurred together or in sequence, as do the events in classical conditioning and instrumental conditioning procedures. (Definitions of the terms *learning, classical conditioning*, and *instrumental conditioning* appear in the Glossary at the end of this book.)

Bilateral symmetry a symmetrical design of the body in which each side of the body is closely similar or identical to the other.

Brachiation locomotor movement by means of swinging from hand to hand beneath a source of support such as a limb; an important locomotor behavior of all species of apes at some portion of the life span and the mainstay of locomotion in gibbons, the lesser apes, throughout the life span.

Buteos a group of species of hawks with long, broad wings and broad tails that are particularly adept at soaring and that do much of their hunting while soaring, so much so that they are often called the soaring hawks (although all hawks are capable of soaring).

Caches Supplies of some substances, usually food, that have been hidden away and that may be used at a later time by the animal that made the caches.

Caching food hiding of a supply of food, as in making a food cache.

Capturing behavior a basic component of feeding behavior, whereby an animal captures or takes hold of its food or prey.

Cilia movable, hair-like cells covering the skin surface or outer membrane surface of some animals; the movement of cilia aids in locomotion as well as in moving material along the length of the body and away from the animal.

Closed economies this term is usually applied to an experimental design in which subjects of an experiment must obtain all of their food by the means specified by experimental procedure and are given no food outside of that procedure; closed economies represent attempts to approximate the situation faced by animals in nature.

Conspecifics two or more animals of the same species.

Consummatory behavior a series of responses that culminates in bringing an animal into a state of adjustment.

Corvids members of a group of avian species that includes jays, crows, nutcrackers, and others.

Dance language as proposed by ethologist Karl von Frisch, the predictable movements made by returning foragers among honeybees can be represented as a dance whose movements encode information about the location of the last food source visited by the forager before its return to the hive; these movements are seen as a "language" that communicates food locations to other foragers in the hive.

Falcons   a group of species of hawks with long, pointed wings and swift and graceful flight; most species in the group prey upon other birds in open terrain.

Feeding behavior   the behavior by which an animal gains its food; feeding behavior is species-typical to a large degree in all species except our own; even so, we humans retain the behavioral capabilities to develop hunting-and-gathering skills that were mainstays of feeding behavior in the lives of our distant ancestors.

Figure eight dance   one of the types of dances proposed by von Frisch whereby honeybees communicate the location of food sources; the dance forms an approximation of a figure eight and includes a straight-line run that is repeated numerous times; characteristics of this straight run were thought by von Frisch to communicate specific information about the direction of and distance to a food location.

Foot stirring   a behavior pattern employed in the feeding behavior of some herons and egrets wherein the wading bird moves its feet rapidly back and forth across an area of the bottom of a pool; the behavior probably serves to drive small aquatic animals to the surface, and feeding birds often make a succession of rapid captures just after engaging in foot-stirring behavior.

Foraging   behavior that usually serves to obtain or gather some needed substance such as food or water.

Goal-directed behavior   behavior that appears to be organized around the attainment of a particular outcome; the behavior in question must be recognizable independently of its usual outcome and the outcome must be clearly specified in each case to which the term *goal-directed behavior* is applied.

Goal-object   the stimulus agent identified with the outcome of an instance of goal-directed behavior.

Home base   a location where an animal spends much of its time and to which it returns repeatedly after forays or journeys into the surrounding environment; specific to the hunter–gatherer society of early humans, the home base was a place where very young, very old, and ill or indisposed members of the social group could remain protected while other members of the group went out on hunting-and-gathering ventures.

Homo erectus   the species considered the direct ancestor of our own, *Homo sapiens.*

Hunting and gathering   the descriptive name applied to basic foraging behaviors that appear to have been important in early human society from the time of *Homo erectus;* hunting for meat and gathering of vegetable foods.

Hunt from a watching post   one of two basic styles of hunting employed by most species of hawks—to remain at a perch while keeping alert to the appearance of their prey; the other basic style of hunting is to hunt while soaring.

Hunt while soaring   one of two basic styles of hunting employed by most species of hawks—to hunt on the wing; the other basic style of hunting is to hunt from a watching post.

Language   a system of communication based in the use of symbols according to rules of grammar and syntax and displaying the capability to generate new words and phrases.

Locomotion, locomotor behavior   behavior that moves or propels animals from one location to another within the environment.

Marginal Value Theorem   an early proposition of optimal foraging theory, that in an environment containing food patches of varying richness, there is an optimal time for an animal to leave one food patch and go in search of another; that time is when the success rate in the patch being foraged falls to the success rate that holds for the environment as a whole.

Monogamous   a mating system in which a single male and a single female mate exclusively with each other.

Motivational variation   a variation in motivation, that is to say, in arousal, in the attractive value of an approach stimulus, or in the aversive value of a withdrawal stimulus.

Nematocysts   cells containing the barbed filaments that are the "weapons," or nettles, of members of the phylum Cnidaria, the nettle bearers.

Optimal foraging theory   a theoretical perspective proceeding from the proposition that evolution should have made animals into approximations of ideal foragers; thus, if we can calculate how an ideal forager must behave under particular sets of conditions, we can generate many testable predictions as to how real animals should behave.

Osculum the passageway to the interior of the body located at the tip of a sponge's ray or rays; opening and closing of this passageway coordinates the overall activity of the sponge.

Predator an animal that obtains its food by killing and eating other animals; an animal that preys upon others.

Predatory behavior the behavior whereby one animals preys upon another, as in killing and eating it.

Prey an animal eaten as food by other animals, known as predators.

Proximal cause an influence coming from the immediate internal condition or external environment of an animal.

Proximal mechanism a system of cause–effect relationships guiding an animal's behavior during a particular time frame.

Pseudopod the leading portion of an amoeba's body in locomotion; it often forms a rather narrow, extended pouch that can be likened to a "false foot," or pseudopod.

Radial maze a maze consisting of a central starting area from which numerous narrow pathways (usually eight of them) lead outward from the center as radials of a circle; these mazes are often used to test animals' foraging efficiency.

Radial symmetry an organization of the body in which cross sections of the body display structures that are symmetrically arranged on all sides.

Reactivity the relative degree to which an animal is responsive to stimulation from one time or one condition to another.

Search image a hypothetical process applied to the observation that certain "preferred" types of prey are taken at a greater proportion than would be expected on the basis of their relative presence within the overall population of potential prey within a given environment.

Social predators predators that hunt together as a social group; good examples are wolves, African lions, and killer whales.

Stand and wait one of two basic styles of feeding behavior employed by nearly all species of herons, egrets, and bitterns, in which an individual stands still within the habitat of its prey while remaining alert to feeding opportunities; the other basic style of feeding behavior is called *walk slowly*.

Step reflex the rays of an echinoderm, such as a starfish, are served on their undersides by numerous muscular appendages called tube feet; a step reflex is a single cycle of movement in which a tube foot reaches outward, toward a source of stimulation, then back toward the center of the ray; step reflexes are important in locomotion and in the capture and ingestion of prey.

Tool use using an object from the environment to enable the performance of goal-directed behavior.

Ultimate cause in evolutionary theory, characteristics that convey reproductive fitness are naturally selected to continue in future generations of a species; this process is regarded as the ultimate cause of species characteristics.

Walk slowly one of two basic styles of feeding behavior used by nearly all species of herons, egrets, and bitterns, in which an individual stalks slowly through the environment of its prey while remaining alert to feeding opportunities; the other basic style of feeding behavior is called *stand and wait*.

REVIEW QUESTIONS

1. Feeding behavior can be described as a combination of several basic behavioral components or elements. Sketch such a description yourself.

2. Describe feeding behavior in the amoeba or in the paramecium.

3. How is the step reflex related to feeding behavior in the starfish?

4. Describe an increase in the complexity of feeding behavior of the planarian as compared to that of the starfish.

5. Trace the development of feeding behavior across the early life span in one of the following groups of animals: aplysia, octopus, honeybee.

6. Describe the attack of an octopus upon its prey.

7. Tell how the feeding behavior of the octopus can be described as an illustration of goal-directed behavior.

8. What claims were made in von Frisch's hypothesis of a honeybee dance language?

9. State one of the findings by Wenner and his colleagues that suggests limitations on the dance language hypothesis.

10. Compare the hunting behavior of wolf spiders and jumping spiders.

11. Try to make up your own description of how feeding behavior depends upon accurate sensory perception in both the octopus and the jumping spider.

12. Briefly describe two basic feeding techniques seen among most species of hawks.

13. Briefly describe the behavior of herons and egrets that is called *stand and wait*, and comment on the importance of this behavior in the lives of these species.

14. Give an example of evidence that feeding behavior develops with age and experience among herons.

15. Describe the social circumstances under which feeding behavior develops among primates.

16. Give an example that illustrates social cooperation in the hunting behavior of wolves.

17. Give an example that illustratres social cooperation in the hunting behavior of African lions.

18. Tell how the complexity of feeding behavior varies across the animal series as one looks from the more ancient species to the more recently established species.

19. In your own words, give a statement of the basic idea of *optimal foraging theory*.

20. What behavioral change is the focus of the Marginal Value Theorem?

21. Describe one or two instances in which the feeding behavior of chipmunks and corvids (jays, crows, and others) might be analyzed in terms of the use of information.

22. Do the same with respect to the findings of Collier's experimental analysis of feeding behavior in rats.

REFERENCES

Balda, R. P., & Kamil, A. C. (1989). A comparative study of cache recovery by three corvid species. *Animal Behaviour, 38*, 486–495.

Batson, J. D., Hoban, J. S., & Bitterman, M. E. (1992). Simultaneous conditioning in honeybees (*Apis mellifera*). *Journal of Comparative Psychology, 106*, 114–119.

Berguist, P. R. (1978). *Sponges*. Berkeley: University of California Press.

Block, R. A., & McConnell, J. V. (1967). Classically conditioned discrimination in the planarian, *Dugesia dorotocephala*. *Nature, 215*, 1465–1466.

Brown, S. W., & Mellgren, R. L. (1994). Distinction between places and paths in rats' spatial representations. *Journal of Experimental Psychology: Animal Behavior Processes, 20*, 20–31.

Buchanan, G. M., & Bitterman, M. E. (1989). Learning in honeybees as a function of amount of reward: Tests of the equal-asymptote assumption. *Animal Learning and Behavior, 17*, 475–480.

Burnett, A. L. (1960). The mechanism employed by the starfish *Asterias forbesi* to gain access to the interior of the bivalve *Venus mercenaria*. *Ecology, 41*, 583–584.

Burnett, A. L. (1973). *Biology of* Hydra. New York: Academic Press.

Capaldi, E. D., & Powley, T. L. (1990). *Taste, experience, and feeding*. Washington, DC: American Psychological Association.

Caraco, T., & Lima, S. L. (1987). Survival, energy budgets, and foraging risk. In M. L. Commons, A. Kacelnik, & S. J. Shettleworth (Eds.), *Quantitative analyses of behavior, Vol. 6, Foraging* (pp. 1–21). Hillsdale, NJ: Lawrence Erlbaum.

Carefoot, T. H. (1967). Growth and nutrition of *Aplysia punctata* feeding on a variety of marine algae. *Journal of the Marine Biological Association, U.K., 47*, 335–350.

Charnov, E. L. (1976). Optimal foraging: The marginal value theorem. *Theoretical Population Biology, 9*, 129–136.

Chiszar, D., & Smith, H. (1998). Snakes. In G. Greenberg & M. M. Haraway (Eds.), *Comparative psychology: A handbook* (pp. 485–491). New York: Garland.

Cloudsley-Thompson, J. L. (1958). *Spiders, scorpions, centipedes and mites*. New York: Pergamon.

Collier, G., & Johnson, D. (1998). Laboratory simulations of foraging. In G. Greenberg & M. M. Haraway (Eds.), *Comparative psychology: A handbook* (pp. 696–712). New York: Garland.

Cowie, R. J., Krebs, F. R., & Sherry, D. F. (1981). Food storing in marsh tits. *Animal Behaviour, 29*, 1252–1259.

Craighead, J., & Craighead, F. (1956). *Hawks, owls, and wildlife*. Harrisburg, PA: Stackpole.

Devenport, J., & Devenport, L. (1998). Squirrel foraging behavior. In G. Greenberg & M. M. Haraway (Eds.), *Comparative psychology: A handbook* (pp. 492–498). New York: Garland.

Dewsbury, D. A. (1978). *Comparative animal behavior*. New York: McGraw-Hill.

Dukas, R., & Visscher, P. K. (1994). Lifetime learning by foraging honey bees. *Animal Behaviour, 48*, 1007–1012.

Ehrlich, P. R., Dobkin, D. S., & Wheye, D. (1988). *The birder's handbook*. New York: Simon & Schuster.

Farmer, J. N. (1980). *The protozoa: Introduction to protozoology*. St. Louis: Mosby.

Frisch, K. von. (1947). The dances of the honey bee. Annual Report of the Board of Regents of the Smithsonian Institution, Publication 3490 (pp. 423–431). Washington, DC: U.S. Government Printing Office. (Original work published 1946.)

Gardner, B. T. (1966). Hunger and characteristics of the prey in the hunting behavior of salticid spiders. *Journal of Comparative and Physiological Psychology, 62*, 475–478.

Geist, V. (1998). Mountain sheep. In G. Greenberg & M. M. Haraway (Eds.), *Comparative psychology: A handbook* (pp. 441–445). New York: Garland.

Gelber, B. (1952). Investigations of the behavior of *Paramecium aurelia*. I. Modification of behavior after training with reinforcement. *Journal of Comparative and Physiological Psychology, 45*, 58–65.

Gelber, B. (1965). Studies of the behavior of *Paramecium aurelia*. *Animal Behaviour Supplement, 1*, 21–29.

Goodall, J. (1964). Tool-using and aimed throwing in a community of free-living chimpanzees. *Nature, 201*, 1264–1266.

Gould, J. L. (1976). The dance–language controversy. *Quarterly Review of Biology, 51*, 211–244.

Haraway, M. M., & Maples, E. G. (1998). Gibbons: The singing apes. In G. Greenberg & M. M. Haraway (Eds.), *Comparative psychology: A handbook* (pp. 422–430). New York: Garland.

Hickman, C. P., Jr., Roberts, L. S., & Hickman, F. M. (1984). *Integrated principles of zoology*. St. Louis: Times Mirror/Mosby.

Hunter, M. W., & Kamil, A. C. (1971). Object-discrimination learning set and hypothesis in the northern bluejay (*Cynaocitta cristata*). *Psychonomic Science, 22*, 271–273.

Hyman, L. H. (1951). *The invertebrates: Platyhelminthes and Rhynchocoela*, Vol. 2. New York: McGraw-Hill.

Hyman, L. H. (1955). *The invertebrates*, Vol. 4, Echinodermata. New York: McGraw-Hill.

Kamil, A. C., Balda, R. P., & Olson, D. J. (1994). Performance of four seed-caching corvid species in the radial arm maze analog. *Journal of Comparative Psychology, 108*, 385–393.

Kandel, E. R. (1979). *Behavioral biology of Aplysia*. San Francisco: W. H. Freeman.

Kilham, L. (1984). Cooperative breeding of American crows. *Journal of Field Ornithology, 55,* 349–356.

Kirchner, W. H., & Towne, W. F. (1994). The sensory basis of the honey bee dance language. *Scientific American, 270,* 52–59.

Kushlan, J. A. (1973). Aerial feeding in the snowy egret. *Wilson Bulletin, 84,* 199–200.

Kushlan, J. A. (1976). Feeding behavior of North American herons. *The Auk, 93,* 86–94.

Lau, G. (1983). *Bigmouth*. St. Paul: A videofilm by Scientific Anglers/3M.

Lee, R. B. (1979). *The Kung San: Men, women, and work in a foraging society*. Cambridge: Cambridge University Press.

Lopez, B. H. (1978). *Of wolves and men*. New York: Scribner's.

Lovell, H. B. (1958). Baiting of fish by a green heron. *Wilson Bulletin, 70,* 280–281.

Maldonado, H. (1964). The control of attack by *Octopus. Zeitchrift fur Vergleichindephysiologie, 47,* 656–674.

Mather, J. (1998). Cephalopod behavior. In G. Greenberg & M. M. Hathaway (Eds.), *Comparative psychology: A handbook* (pp. 355–359). New York: Garland.

Matsuzawa, T. (1998). Chimpanzee behavior: A comparative cognitive perspective. In G. Greenberg & M. M. Haraway (Eds.), *Comparative psychology: A handbook* (pp. 360–375). New York: Garland.

McConnell, J. V., Jacobson, A. L., & Kimble, D. P. (1959). The effects of regeneration upon retention of a conditioned response in the planarian. *Physiological Psychology, 52,* 1–5.

Mech, L. D. (1966). *The wolves of Isle Royale*. Washington, DC: U.S. Government Printing Office.

Mellgren, R. L. (1998). Foraging. In G. Greenberg & M. M. Haraway (Eds.), *Comparative psychology: A handbook* (pp. 666–673). New York: Garland.

Meyerriecks, A. J. (1960). Comparative breeding behavior of four species of North American herons. *Nuttall Ornithology Club Publication* No. 2, 158 pp.

Meyerriecks, A. J. (1971). Further observations on use of the feet by foraging herons. *Wilson Bulletin, 83,* 434–438.

Michelsen, A., Andersen, B. B., Storm, J., Kirchner, W. H., & Lindauer, M. (1992). How honey bees perceive communication dances, studied by means of a mechanical model. *Behavioral Ecology and Sociobiology, 30,* 143–150.

Preston, R. J., & Lee, R. M. (1973). Feeding behavior in Aplysia California: Role of chemical tactile stimuli. *Journal of Comparative and Physiological Psychology, 82,* 368–381.

Porter, G. (1967). *The world of the frog and the toad*. New York: Van Nostrand.

Recher, H. F., & Recher, J. A. (1969). Comparative foraging efficiency of adult and immature little blue herons (*Florida caerulea*). *Animal Behaviour, 17,* 320–322.

Schaller, G. B. (1972). *The Serengeti lion*. Chicago: University of Chicago Press.

Snyder, A. W., & Miller, W. H. (1978). Telephoto lens system of falconiform eyes. *Nature, 275,* 127–129.

Sugiyama, Y. (1994). Tool use by wild chimpanzees. *Nature, 367,* 327.

Sugiyama, Y., Koman, J., & Sow, M. B. (1988). Ant-catching wands of wild chimpanzees at Bossou, Guinea. *Folia Primatologica, 51,* 56–60.

Thompson, R., & McConnell, J. (1955). Classical conditioning in the planarian *Dugesia dortocephalia. Journal of Comparative and Physiological Psychology, 48,* 65–68.

Tomback, D. L. (1980). How nutcrackers find their seed stores. *Condor, 82,* 10–19.

Van Bergeijk, W. A. (1967). Anticipatory feeding behaviour in the bullfrog (*Rana catesbeiana*). *Animal Behaviour, 15,* 231–238.

Walcott, C. (1969). A spider's vibration receptor: Its anatomy and physiology. *American Zoology, 9,* 133–144.

Wells, M. J. (1978). *Octopus*. London: Chapman & Hall.

Wenner, A. (1998). The honey bee "dance language" controversy. In G. Greenberg & M. M. Haraway (Eds.), *Comparative psychology: A handbook* (pp. 823–836). New York: Garland.

Wenner, A. M., & Wells, P. H. (1990). *Anatomy of a controversy: The question of a "language" among bees*. New York: Columbia University Press.

Wichterman, R. (1953). *The biology of Paramecium*. New York: McGraw-Hill.

Zach, R. (1978). Selection and dropping of whelks by northwestern crows. *Behaviour, 67,* 134–138.

Zach, R. (1979). Shell dropping: Decision making and optimal foraging in northwestern crows. *Behaviour, 68,* 106–117.

CHAPTER

5

Social Behavior I: Grouping Patterns, Dominance Relations, Kin Selection, and Territory

Human beings are highly social animals. Most of us have never spent as long as twelve hours alone, while awake, at a single stretch. Some elderly people, living alone and unable to get around easily outside their homes, may endure long periods without human companionship. Even with their telephones, televisions, radios, and pets, they often find themselves lonely in such circumstances. The imposition of **social** isolation has long been recognized as a severe deprivation for people, and solitary confinement has been widely used as a means of inflicting a harsher level of punishment upon individuals already incarcerated in prisons. Prisoners of war subjected to a variety of harsh treatments including poor feeding and various forms of physical abuse have reported that long periods of social isolation were the most difficult to endure of the forms of maltreatment they experienced. Throughout the history of our immediate ancestors, long-term separation from the social group meant death to any child and grave danger for most adults. Only within the social framework of a group did the individual have a decent chance of surviving, finding a mate, and reproducing successfully. For most of us, then, life means social life. It is hard to imagine it otherwise. We cannot be certain what a solitary life would be like, but it surely would be quite different from our common experience.

Advantages and Costs of Social Behavior

On a late winter's afternoon several years ago, one of the authors stood at the edge of a large open field along a river watching a number of hawks and eagles hunting across a vast expanse of terrain under view. As he watched, a flight of about 150 pintail ducks began to circle a spot on the open field before him. After numerous passes over the area, they began to descend and land in the field. Almost immediately a second flight of pintails began to circle and after only two passes, they began to settle beside the first group. Over the next 20 minutes, flight after flight of pintails poured into the spot. As the number of ducks already gathered in the area became larger and larger, arriving flights appeared quickly assured of the safety of the location as they came down to land directly, without making even one preliminary circle. Eventually the number of pintails on the spot had grown to about 2,000 birds.

These ducks were settling down for an extended rest—perhaps for the entire night ahead. It was immediately obvious that the group would be difficult to approach by a predator that might be desirous of a meal of duck's flesh. The ducks were located in an open area, with large distances separating them from the nearest cover on all sides. There were 2,000 sets of eyes and ears available to pick up early warnings of impending attack. Particularly favored in the arrangement were the 150 individuals of the first group to land, now located near the center of a living circle of watchers and listeners.

Protection from predators is a long-appreciated advantage of social grouping (Figure 5.1). The additional protection afforded by a group derives not only from increased likelihood of early detection of an impending attack but also from a *decreased* likelihood, for each individual, of becoming the focus of an attack. If there are 3 ducks in a group attacked by a predator, the probability of being the focus of attack is roughly 1 in 3 for each duck; if there are 2,000 ducks in the group being attacked, this probability drops to roughly 1 in 2,000 for each duck. Not only that, but the swirling escape flight of 2,000 individuals may make it more difficult for a predator to focus its attack effectively on any single individual (e.g., Pitcher, 1998). Of course, a large group may be more likely to attract a predator's attention than a small group or a single individual. Pitcher (1998) suggests that the increased probability of detection of

FIGURE 5.1 Impalas at a Water Hole

large groups may entirely balance the decreased likelihood of being targeted that derives from group membership—if other factors are not considered. However, he reports empirical evidence, at least with groups of fish, that predators are hesitant to attack large groups and that the success of attacks that are made decreases with increasing group size. These matters are dealt with in detail in a later chapter.

Being attracted to large gatherings of their species guides ducks not only to safe resting places but also, on many occasions, to good feeding places. It is the same with many other types of animals; the presence of many members of their own species feeding together in a large group is a reliable indicator of a good place to eat. Not only do other group members passively indicate the opportunity for feeding, but various individuals may join in combined feeding tactics that increase the likelihood of feeding success for **cooperative** group members. We have seen earlier that largemouth bass often hunt together in temporary packs, driving small fish to the surface and attacking them together en masse. Colonies of nesting cave swallows often maintain a flow of foragers back and forth between the nest colony and large insect swarms on which the swallows feed. Any swallow leaving the colony on its first foraging trip in a given period of time need merely follow along this flow of other foragers to find the insect swarm that is located at its outward limit (Brown & Brown, 1986). Wolves and African lions hunt cooperatively with other group members with which they have shared numerous hunting episodes in the past. The tactics developed by these social groups are impressively complex and well coordinated.

Balanced against these advantages of group feeding, of course, there are costs. In such situations, competition among group members for particular food items is likely to occur, and the greater the number of individuals feeding in the same way in a given location, the faster the available food in the immediate area will be used up. Group size, therefore, is limited by a combination of factors including the amount of food available in a given location and the ease of changing frequently from one location to another by the feeding group.

Social grouping that includes males and females in the same group affords each individual a ready opportunity to find a prospective mate when the breeding season approaches. Coordinated social behavior between reproducing partners is practically universal among sexually reproducing animals as the means of arranging for the transfer of sperm and fertilization of the egg. Courtship and breeding provide many instances of species-typical social behavior, some of which are described in Chapter 7. **Competition** among several potential suitors for a particular mate is an unavoidable hazard of group living at these times. In many species in which males provide little parental investment beyond the contribution of sperm, competitions among males at breeding time are among the most spectacular instances of social behavior to be observed on the planet.

Parental behavior, at least that which occurs after hatching or birth of offspring, is a further example of social behavior. Extended parental care following birth or hatching enables young organisms to grow physically and to acquire developmental experiences that will enhance their likelihood of surviving to sexual maturity. Again, there are costs involved for the parents, as well as benefits. Parental investment in any given set of offspring may greatly increase the parents' chances of achieving reproductive success with those particular offspring, but the hazards and hardships of making that investment may decrease the parents' chances of surviving long enough to become a father or mother again in later breeding seasons.

Examples of Social Grouping across the Animal Series

Volvox is a family of protozoan species whose members live together in globe-shaped colonies made up of thousands of genetically identical one-celled organisms formed from cellular divisions originating with a single parent cell (Koufopanou, 1994). Each of these organisms contains a nucleus and a pair of flagella, similar to organisms of the *Euglena* group (Figure 5.2). A single layer of these organisms forms the outer surface of a hollow globe. Coordinated beating of the flagella of the individual organisms provides colony locomotion—a slow rolling of the colonial globe through its environment of water. Locomotion enables the colony to keep itself within a limited range of variation in the water column, to approach light, maintain proximity to food, and withdraw from predators.

These control capabilities are a result of specialization along the taxic dimension, in which cells on the side away from light, for example, beat their flagella in an uneven stroke, while cells on the side facing the light source beat evenly in a balanced fashion (Bonner, 1955). The colonial living arrangement is importantly involved in the reproductive cycle of volvox. Colonies first reproduce asexually, primarily in the spring of the year. Special reproductive cells divide repeatedly to construct genetically identical daughter colonies that reside within the hollow globe of the parent colony until later in the season, when they mature and break free upon the rupture of the parent colony.

A particular colony and its offspring continue through several cycles of asexual reproduction, followed by a cycle of sexual reproduction (Hickman, Roberts, & Hickman, 1984). Numerous cells near the equator of the colony specialize as germ cells. Some of these become ova and some become sperm cells. Sperm, equipped with their own flagella, are released from their parent cell at maturity and move about the colony and other colonies in readiness to approach mature ova, which remain at the sites at which they matured. In some species, a given colony produces both sperm and egg

FIGURE 5.2   Colony of Volvox

cells whereas in others one colony produces only eggs and another only sperm. Once they are fertilized, egg cells form a hard protective covering around themselves and encyst. These zygotes continue to grow through cellular division while encysted and often survive the winter to start the reproductive cycle once again the following spring. These remarkable superorganisms, volvox, are made up of thousands of identical individual cells that are nevertheless able to function differently in response to the presence of other cells and different environmental stimuli. Their complex organization and differential reactions provide a perfect example of the influence of biotaxic factors.

Most species of spiders lead rather solitary lives, but a few species establish large social groups in which individual group members cooperate in web building, capturing prey, and the **communal behavior** of feeding of young offspring of the group (Krafft, 1979). There is evidence that large groups achieve captures on a higher percentage of prey opportunities (Pasquet & Krafft, 1992). Social spiders also capture larger prey than do solitary spiders using similar types of webs. Numerous spiders attack each large prey and subdue it cooperatively (Nentwig, 1985). Careful investigation of the social species, *Achaearanea wau*, revealed no evidence of the type of **caste** development seen in the social insects—an example of which follows in our discussion of honeybees. In respect to individual reproduction, the females of a group that reproduced within a given study period also spent an extra amount of time feeding on communal supplies but did not spend an extra amount of time hunting as compared to females that did not reproduce (Vollrath & Rohde-Arndt, 1983).

Honeybees live together in colonies, or hives, containing tens of thousands of members (Seeley, 1995; Wilson, 1971). Three castes of individuals are produced in each hive. Fertilized eggs become female bees. Nearly all of these become infertile workers, most of which live only for a few weeks. These workers accomplish almost all the work of the colony and die without reproducing. However, workers that are at their prime as winter approaches and the activity of the colony is greatly slowed may survive the winter and contribute to the accomplishment of colony activities in the early spring.

A very few fertilized eggs, housed as larvae in special, large-sized chambers and fed a special, rich diet as larvae by their nursery attendants, will develop into fertile queens. Usually, there is only one queen in a hive at a given time. New queens are produced when an old queen falls off in her egg production or dies, or when a colony has become overcrowded. Several new queens are usually started in their development at the same time by nursery attendants. If two of these emerge as adults at the same time, they will fight to the death. If either queen emerges as victor, she quickly moves to sting to death other developing queens in their larval cells, as a new queen also does if she is the first to mature and emerges alone as an adult. Two queens may remain in the same hive for a time if the old queen is laying few eggs or, in the case of an overcrowded hive, until the old queen and many of the older workers gather in a swarm and move out of the old home to start a new hive in other quarters.

Drones perform only one function in hive life—occasionally they form a competing group of suitors in courtship of a queen, either of their own hive or of another, as she engages in a *wedding flight.* When a drone succeeds in fertilizing queens from hives other than his own, he spreads the genetic heritage of his own hive to neighboring hives. Queens are able to retain large quantities of sperm in special repositories and do not have to make wedding flights very often. Because drones are the product of unfertilized eggs, they are certain to be produced when needed—whenever a queen has no more sperm stored in her repository.

As workers continue their maturation following emergence from the larval stage, they pass through a succession of different behavior patterns as they perform, in turn, a series of different tasks in the life of the hive (Lindauer, 1961). These tasks include cleaning; feeding and caring for larvae; attending the queen; and construction and repair of larval chambers, honeycomb, and other storage cells of the hive. In their later maturity, workers become more outwardly oriented, receiving and storing material from incoming foragers, then remaining near the doorway of the hive, where they serve as guards. In the last stage of their lives they become active foragers, ranging far from the hive to collect nectar and other storable material for a few weeks before their life spans come to an end.

These interesting changes in the behaviors of bees show a developmental history—much simpler, of course—analogous to that demonstrated in advanced vertebrate social species. Analysis of the processes involved in and the mechanisms responsible for this behavioral development shows a remarkable interaction among genetic, neurobiological, hormonal, and environmental factors (Robinson, 1998). Genes influence the production of proteins, which in turn are much involved in the production of hormones such as *juvenile hormone* and other biochemical processes such as *Queen mandibular pheromone*, both of which regulate the timing of the appearance of developmental behavioral changes among honeybees. Additionally, the age of colony members also influences the timing of behavioral changes in hive members. The rate of behavioral change among hive members is regulated by the proportion of older bees in a colony. This influence appears to be the result of direct tactual contact among older and younger colony members. Of more interest is the fact that these various factors all influence the size of several brain areas, some of which may be related to learning ability in these invertebrates. All told, this remarkable set of interconnected factors provides a clear illustration of the *biosocial regulation* of behavior development in social insects.

Whereas the behavioral roles of individuals of different castes of honeybees are somewhat dependent on the animal's genetic makeup, among some social insects the behavioral role is affected by environmental factors. In many social insects—as in honeybees—individuals perform one task for a particular portion of the life span and then become likely to perform other tasks. This phenomenon is known as *age polytheism* (Gordon, 1997). In harvester ants, when environmental conditions change, individuals switch tasks as well as their overall activity levels. In many instances, the number of ants performing one task influences the number performing another. Additionally, it has been suggested that a social insect colony functions much as a complex dynamic system and that, accordingly, task allocation, as well as other features of social organization, may be the result of self-organizing factors discussed in Chapters 1 and 2 (Stuart, 1997). Thus, genetics and developmental maturation are not the only factors affecting task allocation, but rather biosocial factors make an important contribution to this process.

Among most seabirds, herons, and many other groups of species, reproduction centers around a highly social activity called **colonial nesting.** Many dozens or hundreds of breeding pairs build their nests close together in large nesting colonies. Each breeding pair builds its nest on an individual territory that may be only a few feet across. These territories are defended against intrusion by neighboring conspecifics. Species-typical social displays warn offending birds off of an owner's territory while other displays help the resident pair to reconcile themselves to one another as joint occupants of the territory. In many colonial nesting species, as in the herring gull (*Larus argentatus*) (Tinbergen, 1953), birds from throughout a colony join in attacks on predators that threaten any part of the colony. The benefits of colonial nesting appear affordable only to species in which adults are able to range far afield in their foraging behavior and return to deliver food to their young in an efficient manner. Solitary nesting species, which often maintain territories large enough to encompass foraging as well as nesting activities, gain the advantage of having plentiful food supplies located nearby the nest but forego the predator protection afforded by colonial nesting.

In many avian species such as whooping cranes, sandhill cranes, and numerous species of geese, including the Canada goose (*Branta canadensis*), mates form a long-term **pair bond** and young remain with the parents throughout the entire first year of life or longer (Ehrlich, Dobkin, & Wheye, 1988). Young members of these species are guided through developmental experiences at the side of a parent from their earliest days until the time of their maturity. Under this parental tutelage they encounter nearly all facets of the environment they are to inhabit and nearly all tasks they are to accomplish as independent adults. The same extended introduction to species life under parental guidance is afforded a great many young mammals. Accordingly, much avian and mammalian social behavior is organized along psychotaxic and psychosocial dimensions.

Mountain sheep such as the North American bighorn (*Ovis canadensis*) live for most of the year in separate male and female groups (Geist, 1998). As they begin to mature, young males form an attachment to a mature, large-horned ram and accompany him as he feeds, rests, and avoids predators. The large horns of an older male are emblems both of his long avoidance of predators and the richness of the pastures he has frequented. Maturing females remain with the mother, her mature female associates, and their young offspring of both sexes.

In most solitary predators such as the cougar, the leopard, and most bears, young animals remain with the mother throughout their early maturation and separate from her only in the second or third year of life. Mature males in these species live solitary lives except for the social behavior involved in courtship and mating, and defending a territory. In **social predators,** some members of a long-term group remain together for many years, often for life. Offspring of the gray wolf (*Canis lupus*) remain with their natal groups for at least two to three years before some of them depart to find mates and start their own groups. The wolf pack, then, often includes the mated pair of parents and several generations of their offspring—brothers and sisters from a number of different years of parental reproduction. Prides of the African lion (*Panthera leo*), by contrast, are comprised somewhat differently (Schaller, 1972). Females born to a pride usually remain in that pride for life, in company with their mothers, sisters, aunts, nieces, and female cousins. Young males approaching maturity, however, are driven from the natal group by the pride males. Pride males are often two brothers deriving from a breeding group not closely related to the pride females. They may be able to maintain their positions in the breeding group for only a few years, during their physical prime, before being displaced by younger challengers (Figure 5.3).

Primates typically live in social groups of long-term, stable membership. Because we are primates ourselves, and our species emerged from a long primate heritage, we take a special interest in the variety of grouping patterns illustrated among today's primates. As you will see, the complexity of social interactions among primates places them solidly in the psychosocial category with respect to social behavior (Matsuzawa, 2001).

The howler monkeys of South America are divided into six species of the genus *Aloutta*. They are large, arboreal, or tree-dwelling, monkeys that advertise their group presence in an area by episodes of very loud and low-pitched growling, or howling, for which they are named. These growls may help to provide a space free of competitor howler groups around the vicinity of the calling group as well as to keep distant members of the calling group informed about the the group's location. Howlers were the first nonhuman primates to be described on the basis of field study in the natural environment, being an early focus of study by the great pioneer of field primatology, comparative psychologist C. R. Carpenter (1934). The reproducing group of howler monkeys is composed of perhaps three mature adult males, seven to nine adult females, and six or more immature offspring. Most groups are made up of eighteen or fewer individuals, suggesting that when groups reach more than that number, they are prone to divide. In addition to reproducing groups, there are groups of young males as well as numbers of older adult males that may move in and out of reproducing groups on an occasional basis. Howler monkeys are known for the easygoing and egalitarian nature of their social relations. They display numerous friendly or appetitive-appearing social interactions and few quarrelsome or competitive interactions.

FIGURE 5.3 Family Life for a Pride Male

As is the case with most primate groups, howlers devote a substantial amount of social behavior to the activity of **social grooming,** although they do not groom as extensively as do some other groups, such as rhesus monkeys (Bramblett, 1976). A social groomer uses its fingers, lips, tongue, and teeth to comb, arrange, and clean the pelage and skin of another in a rather systematic fashion. A bout of grooming may remain in progress for many minutes, and as a groomer completes its attentions to a companion, the groomer may exchange roles and receive grooming in its turn. Social grooming appears an appetitive activity for both parties involved, but receiving grooming clearly is more appetitive than providing it. Dominant individuals often receive a greater amount of grooming than they provide to others. Social grooming is widely considered an important source of social cohesion among primate groups (Boccia, 1998).

Rhesus monkeys (*Macca mulatta*) are members of a large family of Asian species known as macaques. They display many similarities to the grouping behavior of howler monkeys but also some outstanding differences in their social behavior. Whereas howlers are rather easygoing and display little evidence of individual variations in dominance, rhesus monkeys are quarrelsome and are distinctly ordered in dominance status. Lower-ranking members must clear the way for higher-ranking members and must give way whenever challenged by them. Even so, the rhesus social group is a turbulent one in which there are frequent aggressive interactions and displays. **Status** depends upon an individual's physical size and aggressiveness in challenging and in meeting the challenges of others and is influenced by the status of key individuals with which one keeps close company, such as a baby's mother or an adult female's male consort. Rhesus monkeys have many characteristics in common with those of other macaques, particularly the Japanese macaque (Bramblett, 1976; Smuts et al., 1987).

Guenons are members of a very large African genus known as the Cercopithicines. Ranging from five to thirty pounds in size, most species of this group are forest-dwelling monkeys possessing colorful pelage, especially about the face and buttocks. Rapid movements of these areas of the body provide flashes of color that probably are important sources of intragroup communication within the thick forest foliage in which these groups dwell. Most guenon species live in reproducing groups of one adult male, several adult females, and young, but there is some species to species variation. Among the species *Cercopithicus neglectus*, for example, groups of one adult male and one adult female predominate (Cords, 1987).

Patas monkeys (*Erythrocebus patus*) are often considered with the Cercopithicine group as another African species that is found in one-male reproductive groups. Unlike the Cercopithicines, however, patas monkeys are especially adapted to a terrestrial, rather than to an arboreal, existence. Important adaptations to terrestrial life afford patas monkeys protection from predators in the open grassland habitat. They are built for speed, along the lines of racing dogs such as the greyhound, and are long-limbed and slender. They run on their toes, as do many swift-running species. Adult males quickly reach speeds in excess of thirty miles per hour and are able to continue at that pace for long distances, enabling them to stay comfortably ahead of terrestrial predators (Bramblett, 1976). These monkeys also excel at remaining quiet and wary as they go about their daily rounds, and they are superb at hiding and remaining motionless and unnoticed. Indeed, once an observer spots a male in a tree and continues watching him for a while, soon she may notice another male, then still another—often as many as three or four in the same tree, usually about fifty meters apart. They exchange glances back and forth but display no other interaction with one another (Rowell, 1988).

Group males often perform showy escape maneuvers when a predator threatens the group, leading the predator away as the rest of the group fades into hiding. The group male also enters alone into open feeding areas and to the edges of water holes. In the absence of predatory threat, he begins feeding or drinking, and is then quickly joined by the remainder of his group (Hall, 1965). At thirty pounds, adult males are roughly twice the size of females, and they sometimes take the attack to a threatening predator of comparable or near-comparable size. They may be joined and aided in these defensive attacks by other patas males in the vicinity, even though the extra males are not members of the group under threat (Struhsaker & Gartlan, 1970).

Male patas monkeys remain as breeding partners to their group of several adult females only by their own ability to displace and repel other males. The group male receives little or no help from the females, which appear indifferent to intramale competition. Numerous free-ranging males may steal copulations with females of another male's group, and there are numerous occasions when several extra-group males infringe upon another male's group at one incursion. The tenacity of males in gaining and maintaining sole male membership in a group of females indicates a reproductive advantage in following that tactic, at least during portions of the life span, but the frequent opportunities for breeding achieved by free-ranging males indicate a strong likelihood of reproductive success couched in that pattern of action as well (Cords, 1987).

Species of the genus *Papio* (baboons) share such great similarity that taxonomists have considered classifying them together as subspecies under a single species designation (Bramblett, 1976). Members of this genus have succeeded in utilizing a terrestrial grassland habitat more widely than any nonhuman primate. Their success in a habitat affording such limited access to the safe haven of trees has depended in large part on the evolution of complex patterns of social behavior that provide protection from formidable grassland predators such as the leopard.

Like the largely terrestrial patas monkey, the genus *Papio* also provides excellent examples of **sexual dimorphism;** males are quite large and robust, weighing forty-five to sixty pounds, or about twice the weight of their female conspecifics. And males, particularly, are endowed with large canine teeth—impressive weapons for use in any sort of aggressive encounter. Baboon social groups are centered around one or more dominant males, which quickly come to the fore and defend the group when it is threatened by a predator.

The different species of baboons occupy somewhat different habitats, and the makeup of their social groups and salient characteristics of their social behavior appear to have been shaped by the demands of the particular habitats in which they reside. Savanna baboons (*Papio papio*), of central and southern Africa, forage through large expanses of open grassland characterized by moderately plentiful food sources in combination with heavy predator pressure (Figure 5.4). Their reproductive social group consists of three or more dominant males, several subdominant males, six or seven adult females, and young offspring of the group. Dominant males maintain long-term

FIGURE 5.4   Savannah Baboons, a Group of Females

alliances in which they cooperate with one another in mounting defenses against predators as well as in withstanding challenges from extra-group males. Most adult males within a group will have opportunities to mate with the group's estrous females, but dominant males are able to accomplish this activity with less social interference from other males and are able to monopolize a female's company during the high point of her **estrus,** when ovulation is most likely (Bramblett, 1976).

Hamadryas baboons (*Papio hamadryas*), by contrast, inhabit the desert steppes of Ethiopia, an environment that is sparse in food resources, yet imposes moderate predatory dangers. In this habitat, hamadryas baboons evolved basic social units consisting of a single dominant male, several adult females, and assorted young. Adult females of these groups maintain long-term, exclusive mating relationships with the group male. These basic social units are separated from other groups of conspecifics during foraging periods, insuring that only a few animals will be attempting to exploit meager food resources in the same places at the same times. In connection with nonforaging activities, however, such as nooning at a waterhole, several one-male bands may join together, increasing the social presence of the overall group and affording the extra predator protection of several dominant males together. Groups of several one-male units that often associate with one another in this manner are known as *clans*. The males of these groups often bear strong morphological resemblances to one another and are thought to be close kin individuals that have been brought up together in the same one-male group (Stammbach, 1987). Numerous clans draw together at the same sleeping cliff to spend the night—a time of particular activity for predators—forming large social groups known as *troops*. These associated clans, when joined together, have great social presence and formidable predator defenses.

The gibbons are a genus (*Hylobates*) of highly territorial and arboreal Asian apes whose social groups bear a striking resemblance to core family units established by their close relative, *Homo sapiens.* All nine species of gibbons live in family units composed of a mated pair of adults and their subadult offspring, which remain with the parental group until they leave as young adults to find mates and establish territories and families of their own. The similarity between gibbon and human family groups is impressive; as we consider this similarity, however, it is important to realize that gibbons and humans differ widely in the complexity of their cognitive and communicative capabilities.

Gibbons establish and maintain their territories by means of loud, complex, and species-typical vocalizations known as songs. These vocalizations are called songs in recognition both of their musical quality and of their functional resemblance to birdsongs, as primary means of territorial possession (Haraway & Maples, 1998a, b). Members of a gibbon group remain in close proximity to one another most of the time throughout the day and night. Males and females are approximately the same size, and social relations within the group display little evidence of dominance or of social tension. Whereas gibbon family groups remind us of our own core families, their social relations beyond the family unit are strikingly different from ours, as they remain on their own territories almost at all times and interact with neighbors mainly at a considerable distance. We will consider more about the songs and neighborhood relations of gibbons later in this chapter in our discussions of communication and of territoriality.

Chimpanzees (*Pan troglodytes*), with their cousins the bonobos (*P. paniscus*), are the species considered most closely related to our own. Indeed, genetic and DNA analyses are now able to show that chimpanzees and humans share more than 98 percent of their genetic material (Diamond, 1992). Chimpanzees display social relations that may be likened in many ways to those of a small human community, although there is no long-term presence of an adult male within the basic family unit of a mother and her dependent offspring (Goodall, 1968). Members of the overall group sharing the same home range are all known to one another as individuals but are divided most of the time into smaller groups of mothers and offspring, friends, and frequent close associates. Males are more prone to long-term friendships and alliances than are females. Males of the same group generally are quite tolerant of one another and often watch without disturbance while another male copulates with a female nearby. The most dominant males are likely to monopolize a receptive female as the time of ovulation arrives. This behavior probably assures these males a valuable reproductive advantage, although other males have good opportunity for reproductive success as well. Although there is some immigration into new groups by individual adults, particularly adult females, relations between neighboring groups of chimpanzees generally are hostile. Fights between the members of different groups often result in fatal injuries, particularly to males and inflicted largely by males of the competing group.

Conflicts between group members that reach the status of physical fights are often followed in the next few minutes by resolution behaviors that have been termed as **peacemaking** (Aureli & de Waal, 1998). In instances of this behavior, the parties involved in a recent fight remain in close proximity to each other and perform invitational hand gestures, followed by reassuring body contacts and often mouth-to-mouth kissing. Peacemaking may have widespread value as a method of preserving the cohesion of groups that are beneficial to all of their members, including, of course, the re-solving animals themselves. Since the initial description of peacemaking behaviors by de Waal and Yoshihara (1983), instances of similar behavior have been observed in many species of apes, monkeys, and lemurs—even among species with reputations for social intolerance, such as the rhesus macaque.

Bonobos have not been studied nearly as well as chimpanzees, but they seem to have many very similar behavior patterns (de Waal, 1988; Ingmanson, 1996). Among bonobos there appears to be some dissociation of sexual behavior from an entirely reproductive function. Sexual interactions occur between same-sex as well as opposite-sex individuals, both in males and females. One function of these interactions proba-bly is as a means of conflict resolution (de Waall, 1995). It also appears that females, whether related to one another or not, are prone to form close alliances and to act co-operatively in competition with males for the possession of preferred food objects (Parish, 1996). Bonobos inhabit a tropical rain forest environment that is quite differ-ent from the drier mixed forest–grassland habitat of chimpanzees. They forage in larger groups and often create trail signs at decision points along a route that enable other group members following later, as well as human field observers, to make the same turns and to reach the same foraging destination as the first group (Savage-Rumbaugh, Shanker, & Taylor, 1998). Creation and following of these signs indicate a very high level of cognitive behavior of these animals in their natural habitat.

Of the remaining apes comprising our closest living relatives, gorillas (*Gorilla go-rilla*) live in what are basically single-male reproductive groups. However, additional adult males—so long as they remain submissive to the leader—often are tolerated within these groups and allowed to copulate with females of the group (Figure 5.5). Fully adult silverback males that continue as long-term members in a leader's group may often be his brothers (Harcourt, 1979). Orangutans (*Pongo pygmaeus*), the great apes of Asia, are highly arboreal, rather than being largely terrestrial, as are the African apes we have just discussed. Orangutans do not form the sort of reproductive groups

FIGURE 5.5   Gorilla Group in Wild Habitat

seen in other apes, yet they engage in more social behavior than had long been thought to be the case (Rogers & Kaplan, 1998). Females of reproductive age are accompanied by one or two recent offspring in their seminomadic travels along individually predictable forest routes. Youngsters are weaned at two years but remain with the mother until the age of about six years. Adult males live largely solitary lives, except for male–male interactions involved in territorial behavior and male–female interactions involved in courtship and copulation. (See Figure 5.6 for a comparison among apes.)

Dominance and Submission

Dominance relations within animal groups offer an excellent opportunity for analysis according to the principles of instrumental learning, discussed briefly in Chapter 1. In any competition between two individuals for an attractive object such as a morsel of food, a prospective mate, a good territory, or a position at a watering place, the assertive behavior of the winner is rewarded, or reinforced, by his gaining possession of the contested object. By contrast, the loser receives no reward for his assertive behavior. However, he does receive a reward for turning aside from the competition; that behavior on his part terminates the aversive, combative actions of the dominant animal in the competition. This is a negative reinforcement—based on the removal of aversive stimulation—but it is a reinforcement, nevertheless. In these competitions, then, winners are rewarded for assertive behavior and losers are rewarded for turning away from competition. Through ordinary operation of the principles of positive and negative reinforcement, winners should become progressively more assertive with each win while losers should become progressively more submissive with each loss. One

FIGURE 5.6 **A Comparison among Apes**

general prediction deriving from this analysis is that early individual differences in assertiveness should become more pronounced as individuals acquire different learning experiences involving the consequences of assertive behavior.

Because animals in long-term groups live for extended periods in company with the same individuals, group members are likely to have many experiences that illustrate which other members of the group they can dominate and which others consistently dominate them. This sort of arrangement is ideal for **discrimination learning.** An environmental feature that reliably predicts reinforcement or nonreinforcement of a particular response is known as a **discriminative stimulus.** Depending on the discriminative stimulus provided by the identity of the individual being confronted, a challenger faces either predictable reinforcement of assertive behavior, if challenging a group member he can dominate, or predictable nonreinforcement of assertive behavior, if challenging a group member he cannot dominate. Established principles of discrimination learning predict that learners will acquire habits of performing assertively in the presence of stimuli predictive of reinforcement and omitting assertive behavior in the absence of such stimuli.

The circumstances of life in many long-term groups, then, when considered in combination with the principles of discrimination learning, prompt the prediction of dominance hierarchies, or orderings of individuals in relative degree of dominance or assertiveness. Development of dominance orders based on discrimination learning requires repetitive interaction of the same individuals; competition for limited resources; and learning capability, enabling organization of behavior at the psychotaxic level of complexity. Precise prediction of dominance relations in a given species is complicated by species differences in competitiveness, limitations of competition across genders or within family or kinship groups, group size, and probably a number of other factors. In human groups, for example, competitions between individuals usually are influenced by group recognition of standards of fairness and expectations with respect to individual rights and privileges.

An early description of dominance ordering was produced in 1922 by Schjelderup-Ebbe, who introduced the idea of the **pecking order** among domestic chickens. Schjelderup-Ebbe found that domestic flocks could be arranged in rank orders such that each bird's rank indicated its degree of dominance within the flock: It could dominate all individuals of lower rank than itself but was dominated by all individuals of higher rank. In social groups in which there are no exceptions to the dominance order, the order is described as **linear.** Exceptions to the dominance order, as when a bird of low overall rank may dominate one or two individuals of overall higher rank, are instances of nonlinearity.

Dominance orders that approach linearity have been described in numerous groups of species, including crayfish, lobsters, wasps, fish, lizards, birds, and many mammals (Brown, 1975; Collias, 1944; Yeh, Russell, & Edwards, 1996). Social experience appears to alter physiological responses related to dominant and submissive behavior in crayfish. The tail flip is an important locomotor response in crayfish. Administration of serotonin, a natural neurotransmitter substance, temporarily decreased the neural response to sensory stimuli of the command neuron for tail flipping in subjects with social experience as **submissive** animals. The same treatment had the opposite effect of increasing that response both in animals with dominant social experience and in animals that had been isolated from either type of social experience (Yeh, Russell, & Edwards, 1996). The fact that the serotonin treatment had similar effects on both dominant and socially inexperienced animals may indicate the presence of a species tendency toward asserting dominance that is adjustable by social experience.

The advantages of attaining high dominance status in a group are obvious. Dominant individuals have first choice of access to scarce resources such as food objects and potential mates. But what advantages could there be in an individual's acceptance of submissive status? Acceptance of submissive status allows a weak individual to avoid nonproductive and potentially injurious competition with stronger and more aggressive members of its group. At the same time, the weak individual is able to maintain its membership in the group despite being unable to compete successfully with most of the group members. Such an individual may have much greater chances of survival and reproductive success as a low-ranking group member than as an extragroup loner. As long as adequate resources exist, even a low-ranking group member will gain access to the materials it needs; it merely has to wait, sometimes, before gaining access. Tolerance of low-ranking group members also has potential benefits to high-ranking individuals. Their presence contributes to the social resources of the group at very little expense to members of higher rank.

Altruistic Behavior and Kin Selection

Altruistic behavior is behavior that benefits another at the expense of the individual performing the behavior. In other words, it is behavior that appears to help others more than it helps oneself. Earlier in this chapter we noted the very high degree of cooperation that exists in the behavior of social insects such as honeybees. Such behavior often appears self-sacrificing. Extremely cooperative behavior is seen also in the numerous species of volvox, in which individual members of a colony cooperate with one another almost as fully as do the individual cells of a single, multicelled organism. We have remarked that parental behavior, which often is critically important to the survival of offspring must, in many cases, be provided at considerable expense to the parent. How could behavior patterns of extreme cooperation—which, at first view, appear to *decrease* the reproductive fitness of the acting individual—possibly have evolved through the operation of a selective process based on the *enhancement* of reproductive fitness? This question expresses the challenge posed for evolutionary theory by the widespread existence of altruistic behavior.

An important clue to answering this question is available from a consideration of the full consequences of parental behavior. Although this behavior is expensive to provide, in many species it is the only means of assuring survival of the offspring and *representation of the parent's genetic makeup* in the next generation of its species. In most sexually reproducing species, each parent contributes one-half of the genetic material that will be possessed by each of its offspring. Through their reproduction in the offspring, these genes continue to exist independently of the survival of the parent. As long as an offspring remains alive, then, the portion of the parent's genes contained by that offspring also continues to live. Many genes may be passed on for generation after generation by a succession of offspring that go on to become successful parents in their turn. Once a successful parent has reared several surviving offspring—each possessing a randomly selected half of the parent's genes—it should have accomplished the transfer of all, or nearly all, of its genes to other individuals, which can live on after it is gone and can carry its genes forward to future generations. Parental behavior then, if viewed in its full consequences, is revealed as producing a gain in the reproductive fitness of the parent. These considerations explain the evolution of parental behavior so readily that it usually is excluded from formal definitions of altruistic behavior (e.g., Brown, 1975); far from being a complete sacrifice, this behavior is easily seen as providing a direct benefit to the behaving individual.

Other instances of cooperative and self-sacrificing behaviors are not so easily seen as benefiting the behaving individual, however, and these instances of altruistic behavior still remained, for a time, as a challenge to the theory of evolution by natural selection. Honeybees defending against intruders that threaten to invade the hive may sting an intruder, thereby losing their stingers, disemboweling themselves, and dying in the process. Now, these defenders are worker bees. They have no offspring and are physically incapable of having any. How, then, can this apparent sacrificial behavior be seen to benefit their own reproductive fitness? The widely accepted answer was supplied by Hamilton in 1964. That answer lies not in selection of the sacrificial individual itself, but rather in the reproduction of many of its genes through selection of its kin: **kin selection.**

Let us begin our discussion of kin selection by considering the example of identical human twins (see Table 5.1). These individuals have almost identical genetic makeup. The successful parenthood of one's identical twin reproduces about the same number of one's genes as would result from one's own reproductive success. Of course, the genes from one's twin are different physical particles than one's own genes, yet they are very nearly physically identical, or interchangeable, just as are the genes contained in the different cells of one's own body. Genetically, it doesn't matter much whether one reproduces in one's own right or if one's twin does instead. The same genetic messages are represented in the next generation in either case. Therefore, if a

TABLE 5.1   Comparative Genetic Identity among Relatives in the Human Species

Parent–child	50 percent identity
Grandparent–grandchild	25 percent identity
Full siblings	Average of 50 percent identity
Half-siblings	Average of 25 percent identity
Aunt/uncle–niece/nephew	Average of 25 percent identity
First cousins	Average of 12.5 percent identity
Second cousins	Average of 6.25 percent identity
Third cousins	Average of 3.125 percent identity
Fourth cousins	Average of 1.5625 percent identity

sacrificial act of yours enables your twin to survive and later to reproduce successfully, then your action has benefited your own reproductive fitness as much as your twin's.

Ordinary siblings, unlike twins, possess an average of only 50 percent genetic identity with each other. Because each has received a randomly selected one-half of each parent's genes, two siblings should have about half of these genes in common, although the actual amount of commonality is subject to variation with each pair of siblings. The arrangement is nicely illustrated by the following analysis. There are two forms of each of a parent's chromosomes, an A form and a B form. Now suppose that sibling I has received from its mother chromosomes 1A, 2A, 3B, 4B, and so on, through the twenty-three pairs of chromosomes that contain the human genetic complement. The chances that another ordinary sibling, sibling II, will also receive chromosome 1A from the mother are 50–50; it could just as well receive chromosome 1B. The chances that it will receive chromosome 2A also are 50–50, as are the chances it will receive chromosomes 3B, 4B, and so on. Therefore, the overall degree of genetic identity expected in ordinary siblings is 50 percent, with random variation around that central value. This fact means that if my sacrifice enables my brother or sister to survive and go on to reproduce successfully, then that outcome is approximately half as good, reproductively, as my surviving to reproduce in my own right.

The higher the degree of genetic identity that exists between me and my kin, the more it benefits me to aid their survival and reproductive success. Human beings have 50 percent genetic identity with their children, 25 percent genetic identity with their grandchildren and also with their nieces and nephews. First cousins have only 12.5 percent genetic identity and so on. Appreciation of the importance of kin selection to the evolution of altruistic behavior suggests that the greater the amount of genetic identity that exists between any two individuals, the more we must expect them to behave altruistically toward one another.

Now let's turn again to the problem of altruistic behavior among honeybees. In nearly all cases, the workers of a hive are full sisters to each other and to most of the progeny of the hive. Because queen bees can store large amounts of sperm from a single mating, all of the workers of a hive at any given time usually have both the same mother and the same father. Drones derive from unfertilized eggs and possess, in consequence, only one-half the amount of genetic material as do queens and workers. They contribute the entire amount of this genetic material with each sperm cell. Workers born of a union of the same drone and queen thus receive identical genetic contributions from the father and 50 percent identical contributions from the mother. Thus, the workers have 75 percent genetic identity with one another. This is a greater degree of genetic identity than a queen has with her own female offspring, which have received one-half their genetics from their father. If the progeny of a given beehive continue to succeed, eventually one of them will become a fertile queen, which, by her prodigious reproduction, will confer reproductive success on all her sisters of previous generations, each of which shares 75 percent genetic identity with her. According to the theory of kin selection, this high degree of genetic identity should have resulted in the evolution of extremely cooperative behavior among honeybee workers and this, of course, is exactly what we see.

With volvox, we have an opportunity to observe the degree of cooperative behavior obtained when the different members of a social group all have identical genetic makeup. In this case, reproductive success of one is the same, genetically, as reproductive success of any of the others. Under these circumstances, the total cooperation that exists among members of a volvox colony is readily understandable. Consideration of volvox also affords an opportunity to address a final important point about altruistic behavior. We have said that the evolution of altruistic behavior is based on the reproductive success that this type of behavior has conferred on altruistic individuals in past generations. The members of a volvox colony behave quite altruistically toward one another, but we do not for a minute believe they do so in any conscious appreciation of the benefits deriving from such behavior. Neither is it necessary, or even helpful, to suppose that any other animals—even ourselves—behave altruistically out of an awareness of benefits deriving to themselves. The idea of kin selection answers the question of how altruistic behavior evolved; that is quite a different matter from the question of what factors within a current situation provoke its occurrence. The first question involves ultimate causes, the second, proximal causes. We are interested in understanding the answers to both sorts of questions.

Territoriality

Many animals live for extended periods of time within the confines of a fixed area or location known as the **home range.** The entire home range, or any smaller area contained within it, may be defended against intrusion, particularly by other members of the same species, or conspecifics. Defended areas are known as **territories.** Often other members of the defender's family or immediate social group are permitted within the territory and may help to defend it. In the case of breeding territories, usually held by males, females may be welcomed within a territory that is vigorously defended against male intrusion. Once a female has joined a male in his territory, she often begins defending it herself. Her defense is likely to be particularly directed against intrusions into the territory by other females. Territory owners are very difficult to dislodge from their own territories, once they have successfully occupied a location for a time. At the expense of territorial defense, they enjoy the advantages of having sole use of a territory's resources, including food, water, shelter, and an available mate or mates (Stamps, 1998).

One of the most ancient groups of species to establish a home range and to defend a specific location within it is the octopus. *Octopus vulgarius* establishes a small home base in a recess or a hole protected by surrounding cover such as rocks. It defends this home base against occupancy by other octopuses (Maldonado, 1964). An individual must change its home base many times as its physical size expands greatly with growth. Observations of wild individuals of *O. dofleini* revealed free movements within a home range of 250 square meters. Overlapping ranges of numerous individuals along with the absence of a tendency for individuals to maintain a constant distance between themselves indicated that this species is basically solitary and that territorial defense must be limited to the immediate area of the home base (Mather, Resler, & Cosgrove, 1985).

Male carpenter bees such as *Xylocopa pubescens* defend territories at nesting sites, food plants, and outstanding landmarks. They hover for long periods within a tightly defined area and fly out to challenge and fight other males and to chase females that come within twenty meters of the hover point (Barrows, 1983). Mating occurs both in fall and in early spring. Patrolling bees not holding a territory in the area frequently chase females and attempt mating as interlopers within another male's territory. Alcock (1996) found that males of *Xylocopa varipuncta* advertise their presence on territory by releasing a pheromone that attracts females. He also found that male territorial behavior is highly correlated with female activity, suggesting males are able to allocate their territorial efforts to times when mating potential is high. An earlier study by Alcock (1993) showed that less than 10 percent of carpenter bee males that he marked for study were long-term territorial residents of any particular landmark site and that the territorial bees had mating frequencies similar to those of the male population in general. Site fidelity to a landmark territory thus appears only one of perhaps numerous male activities associated with successful mating.

In many species of fish, such as the stickleback (*Gasterosteus aculeatry*) and the largemouth bass (*Micropterus salmoides*), males construct nests or prepare nesting sites during breeding season and defend the surrounding area against intrusion by other males as well as by potential predators of eggs or young hatchlings. Anole lizards (*Anolis carolinensis*) patrol territories and court females by repeatedly extending a colorful throat fan and holding it extended while doing a series of quick leg-bending bows, or pushups, of the upper body (Crews & Wade, 1998). Females have smaller throat fans that are not displayed in the context of courtship. Neurons innervating the muscles used in extending the throat fan were shown to be larger in males than in females (Wade, 1998), providing an interesting parallel between structure and function.

Male bullfrogs maintain breeding territories along the edges of a pond or lake and call loudly with their familiar bull-like bellows as a means of attracting females. Much smaller males sometimes trespass unobtrusively in another male's territory, earning the advantage of encountering a breeding female at the risk of being attacked and perhaps eaten by the resident male (Howard, 1978).

Songbirds such as the familiar northern cardinal and the robin maintain breeding territories that are also large enough to serve as feeding territories throughout the breeding and parenting season. Males begin singing from prominent perches in early spring and defend their territories by vigorously chasing and displacing intruding males. Once a female establishes herself as a mate on a territory, she begins singing herself and joins the male in defending the territory, being particularly attentive to incursions by rival females. In colonial nesting groups such as gulls and herons, breeding territories are much smaller, often encompassing only enough space to accommodate the nest and a small amount of bordering edge (Tinbergen, 1953). One outstanding cost of the colonial nesting arrangement is that the large number of birds foraging in the vicinity of the colony quickly places great demand on the food supply. Birds in these colonies must be able to range far afield in their feeding activities and to carry large amounts back to their chicks at each return for effective foraging.

The red-capped cardinal of South America (*Paroaria gularis*) establishes its territory along the shores of rivers and narrow lakes. Rather than locating its territory along a single shoreline, it lays claim to adjacent areas on both sides of the water. This choice requires it to cross the open water numerous times each day to forage and to patrol its territory. Eason (1998) found that this noteworthy arrangement enables the cardinal to do a better job of protecting its territory from intrusion than would the arrangement of the entire territory along a single shoreline. She showed that a territory owner detects the presence of an intruder much more readily from across the water than from an equal distance away on the same shoreline as the territory owner himself.

Black-tailed prairie dogs (*Cynomys ludovicianus*) live in large communities called towns. These are formed of numerous smaller social units, or coteries, which are the reproducing units of prairie dog society (Brown, 1975). Each coterie contains one or more adult males and usually two or more adult females. Members of a coterie share the same territory and defend it as a group against intrusion by neighbors. Social interactions within the coterie are very friendly and include grooming, playing, and "kissing." Young prairie dogs perform territorial calls and greet other prairie dogs with a kiss at their earliest emergence from the burrow. In their early days youngsters are tolerated on adjacent territories when they wander there, but as they grow older they are rebuffed by their neighbors, at first rather gently, then with increasing severity as maturity increases. They soon learn to distinguish members of their own coterie from neighbors and to restrict their territorial calling and most of their wandering to their own territorial limits. Coterie groups increase greatly in number with the production of young, then decrease again as offspring mature and leave to establish their own territories and breeding groups.

Each of the nine species of gibbons, genus *Hylobates*, lives on distinct territories in reproducing groups of a single mated pair of adults and their subadult offspring (Haraway & Maples, 1998a; Marshall & Marshall, 1976). Gibbons live in climax forest on territories averaging about 100 acres, or 40 hectares, in size with variations depending partly on the density of fruiting trees. Territories are announced and maintained partly by the performance of extended episodes of complex vocal behavior called songs. Songs not only are clearly species-typical, as well as sex-specific, but also show individual variation, permitting individual identification of the singer. Individual distinctions may result partly from individual genetic variation but could also be impacted by individual developmental experiences of singing within the natal group over the first three or four years of life. A gibbon's reproductive success, at least into the second generation, should be enhanced by the location of its territory in fairly close proximity to those of several conspecifics, ensuring a ready supply of prospective mates for his own offspring, once they grow to adult maturity and leave the parental territory.

Summary: Principles Introduced in This Chapter

Numerous examples of social grouping are displayed by species at all levels across the animal series. Advantages for survival and reproduction provided by social grouping and social behavior may be considered under the following four headings.

1. Social grouping provides protection from predators. First, the grouping of numerous individuals in one area concentrates numerous sets of sensory systems and allows attention to be given to avenues of approach in numerous directions

at the same time. The likelihood of early detection of predator approach is increased.

Second, for numerous prey species, being a member of a large group decreases the overall likelihood of becoming the focus of predator attack for each individual. In addition, predators may be confused by the escape flight of the numerous individuals and have difficulty selecting and focusing on a single individual for attack.

Third, in many species, members of a threatened group may be able to make a group counterattack upon a predator. In these cases, the greater the number of counterattackers, the greater the defensive advantage. Examples are the behavior of honeybees, wasps, ants, and other social insects; the defensive strategies of baboons, in which a number of dominant males often band together as a unit in facing a predatory challenge; the group mobbing of predators by colonial nesting birds such as the herring gull.

2. Social grouping benefits the use of environmental resources both by facilitating the location of resources and by increasing the efficiency of exploiting these resources once they are located. Examples include the location of food by large groups of ducks, by cave swallows, by honeybees, and by young males among bighorn sheep; the efficiency of capturing prey by social spiders, by feeding "wolf packs" of largemouth bass, by gray wolves, and by African lions; the protection afforded young baboons and other young primates as they feed, rest, play, learn, and develop socially, always in the company of their elder group members.

3. Social grouping affords the opportunity of finding a mate for sexual reproduction. Regardless of what social arrangements obtain within the population of a given species, those arrangements must provide for the union of sperm and egg cells if sexual reproduction is to occur. In most species, this is accomplished by means of social interaction between a male and a female of the species.

4. Social grouping provides for the occurrence of active parental behavior. In some species this behavior involves a primary group made up only of a mother and her offspring or a father and his offspring. In others it involves both parents and their offspring. And in still others it involves a larger group of numerous individuals, only some of which may yet have become parents. In those larger groups, young animals benefit from the actions of other members of their overall group as well as from those of one or more of their parents.

With respect to any benefits of social grouping we can suggest, there will also be attendant expenses or costs. We must see the evolution of social behavior as a dynamic process that continually balances these related costs and benefits, tending toward the production of social behaviors that provide the greatest benefits at the lowest possible costs.

Animals that spend extended periods of time together with other members of a stable group often develop orderly dominance relations in which certain individuals are relatively dominant and others are relatively submissive. Often dominance hierarchies develop in which individuals may be ranked in dominance from most to least dominant, with very few breaks in rank order being observed. The development of dominance rank orders may be understood as a result of a process of discrimination learning, and such rank orders are observed only in species possessing advanced learning capabilities. Advantages of dominance ranking are derived by both dominant and submissive individuals in social circumstances in which there is competition for limited resources.

Among highly social species many instances of behavior are observed in which one individual appears to help another at the expense of a loss to itself. Instances of this sort are known as altruistic behavior. Their evolution was once considered a problem for a theory of natural selection that stresses the importance of characteristics that favor individual survival and reproductive success. This dilemma was solved by the realization that altruistic behavior often may contribute to the survival of close relatives of the altruistic actor. When a characteristic promotes survival of one's genes, that characteristic should be selected, even if the copies of one's genes that are saved are carried in a relative's body rather than in one's own. Thus, the evolution of altruistic behavior is now understood as a product of kin selection.

In a great many species individuals confine their activities to the same physical space or home range for extended periods of time, perhaps for life. Sometimes the entire home range or some portion of it may be defended against use by other conspecifics. Such defended areas are called territories. The particular conspecifics that may be permitted within one's territory are determined by the pattern of social grouping displayed by one's species. Males of solitary living species may admit unattached females into their territories during breeding season but defend the same areas against intrusion by a rival male. Once a female has established herself on a male's territory, she may defend the area against intrusion by other females. In some species all of the members of one's own large group are permitted within the territory, and many members of the group will join forces to defend against use of the territory by a rival group.

Through the practice of conducting all of one's activities within the same limited space, one has an opportunity to learn every feature of that space that relates to those activities. By defending that area against occupation by competitor members of one's species, one retains exclusive use of the area's resources for one's self and one's fellow group members.

KEY TERMS

Altruistic behavior   behavior that benefits another animal at the expense of the behaving individual.

Caste   a distinct class of individuals within a social group; members of a caste display certain characteristics that distinguish them from other members of the social group that are not members of the same caste.

Colonial nesting   the habit of many species of birds, particularly seabirds, of building their nests and rearing their young in close proximity to other nesting pairs of the same species in what are known as nesting colonies.

Communal behavior   actions undertaken together by several members of the same community of animals.

Competition   two or more animals competing against one another for an attractive or appetitive outcome that may be available to only one of them.

Cooperative, cooperation   two or more animals working together in a way that is likely to produce progress toward the attainment of an attractive or appetitive outcome.

Discrimination learning   learning to distinguish between closely similar stimuli, usually on the basis that one of two similar stimuli signals that a particular response will be reinforced while the other stimulus signals that the same response will *not* be reinforced and indeed, may even be punished.

Discriminative stimulus   the stimulus in discrimination learning that is associated with reinforcement.

Dominance   an individual's standing on the issue of "who defers to whom" among the members of a social group; the dominant individual often has first right of access to mates, food items, and other sources of attraction within the common environment of a social group.

Estrus   the physiological condition that is distinctly associated with sexual receptivity of females in many species; the term also may be applied to patterns of behavior that may be uniquely associated with this condition.

Home range   an area or location within which an individual remains and lives for an extended period of time.

Kin selection   the reproduction of an individual's genes by way of the selection of one of its relatives, who possesses some genes in common with the individual in question.

Linear   in respect to dominance orders, a dominance order is said to be *linear* when members of the order can be ranked in dominance such that no exceptions in ranking occur; that is, if an individual ranks fourth, for example, it dominates every individual of a lower rank and submits to every individual of a higher rank, without exceptions. In dominance ranking, number one is the highest, most dominant rank, number two is the second most dominant, and so on.

Pair bond   a lasting social bond of mutual attraction between mated individuals.

Parental behavior   behavior of a parent toward its offspring or in relation to its offspring.

Peacemaking   a term applied to certain recognizable behaviors that appear to function in resolving conflicts between individuals within a social group.

Pecking order   a term used to describe dominance order among chickens, referring to the issue of "who gets to peck whom" among the members of a flock; this term sometimes is used in a general way to refer to dominance orders among other animals besides chickens.

Sexual dimorphism   the possession of widely different bodily characteristics by the males and females of a species, particularly in regard to the relative size of males and females.

Social   having to do with groups of animals; that is, relations or interactions involving two or more individuals.

Social grooming   grooming refers to behavior that adjusts or cleans an animal's skin, hair, or feathers; in social grooming, one animal grooms the body of another member of its social group.

Social predators   animals that display social cooperation in their predatory behavior, as in hunting together and jointly attacking the same prey animal or group of prey animals.

Status   status refers to an individual's social standing within its group; individuals of high status usually are dominant over individuals of lower status.

Submissive, submission   to defer to another in respect to dominance.

Territories, territory   an area that is defended against intrusion by other members of one's own species, particularly others of the same sex as the defender.

REVIEW QUESTIONS

1. What is meant by the designation *social behavior*?

2. Name or cite at least two potential advantages of membership in a social group.

3. What is at least one potential cost of social membership?

4. Give an example to illustrate what can be considered as social cooperation in animal behavior.

5. Give an example of social behavior among spiders.

6. Very briefly compare the functional role of workers and queens in the life of honeybees.

7. Cite an example of how behavior development is related to hormonal factors in honeybees.

8. Tell briefly what is meant by the term *colonial nesting*.

9. Among what group of animals do we see the first pair bonds?

10. What high level of behavioral organization and complexity is illustrated by pair bonds?

11. Briefly describe the origin and composition of a wolf pack.

12. Tell how grooming behavior is related to social organization in many primates.

13. Give a rough description of the social organization of patas monkeys.

14. Tell how the phenomenon of sexual dimorphism is illustrated among baboons.

15. Briefly describe the social relations maintained among dominant males in baboon troops.

16. Describe the social circumstances that generally accompany the behavior development of young primates.

17. Tell how the family organization of gibbons resembles that widely seen among humans.

18. Describe the type of behavior by which gibbons defend the family territory.

19. Give an example to illustrate the idea of peacemaking among nonhuman primates.

20. Briefly describe the social organization of breeding groups of gorillas.

21. Cite an unusual characteristic of social organization among orangutans, as compared to most other primate species.

22. Give an example in which an animal receives reinforcement for submissive behavior in dominance competition. What type of reinforcement is illustrated here?

23. Tell at least one advantage that accrues to an individual of high dominance status.

24. Describe how the degree of genetic relationship between two animals predicts the likelihood that they will display altruistic behavior toward one another according to the idea of kin selection.

25. The ideas of home range and territory are similar but not identical. What is an important difference between the two?

REFERENCES

Alcock, J. (1993). Differences in site fidelity among territorial males of the carpenter bee *Xylocopa varipuncta* (Hymenoptera: Anthophoridae). *Behaviour, 125*, 199–217.

Alcock, J. (1996). Timing of mate-locating by males in relation to female activity in the carpenter bee *Xylocopa varipuncta* (Hymenoptera: Apidae). *Journal of Insect Behavior, 9*, 321–328.

Aureli, F., & de Waal, F. B. M. (1998). Peacemaking in primates. In G. Greenberg and M. M. Haraway (Eds.), *Comparative psychology: A handbook* (pp. 720–724). New York: Garland.

Barrows, E. M. (1983). Male territoriality in the carpenter bee *Xylocopa virginica virginica*. *Animal Behaviour, 31*, 806–813.

Boccia, M. L. (1998). Grooming behavior of primates. In G. Greenberg & M. M. Haraway (Eds.), *Comparative psychology: A handbook* (pp. 674–678). New York: Garland.

Bonner, J. T. (1955). *Cells and societies.* Princeton, NJ: Princeton University Press.

Bramblett, C. (1976). *Patterns of primate behavior.* Palo Alto, CA: Mayfield.

Brown, C. R., & Brown, M. B. (1986). Cliff swallow colonies as information centers. *Science, 234,* 83–85.

Brown, J. L. (1975). *The evolution of behavior.* New York: W. W. Norton.

Carpenter, C. R. (1934). A field study of the behavior and social relations of howler monkeys, *Alouatta palliata. Comparative Psychology Monographs, 10(2),* 1–168.

Collias, N. E. (1944). Aggressive behavior among vertebrates. *Physiological Zoology, 17,* 83–123.

Cords, M. (1987). Forest guenons and patas monkeys: Male–male competition in one-male groups. In B. B. Smuts et al. (Eds.), *Primate societies* (pp. 98–111). Chicago: University of Chicago Press.

Crews, D., & Wade, J. (1998). Biopsychology of lizard reproductive behavior. In G. Greenberg & M. M. Haraway (Eds.), *Comparative psychology: A handbook* (pp. 348–354). New York: Garland.

de Waal, F. (1988). The communicative repertoire of captive bonobos (*Pan paniscus*) compared to that of chimpanzees. *Behaviour, 106,* 183–251.

de Waal, F. (1995). Sex as an alternative to aggression in the bonobo. In P. R. Abramson & S. D. Pinkerton (Eds.), *Sexual nature, sexual culture. Chicago series on sexuality, history, and society* (pp. 37–56). Chicago: University of Chicago Press.

de Waal, F., & Yoshihara, D. (1983). Reconciliation and redirected affection in rhesus monkeys. *Behaviour, 85,* 224–241.

Diamond, J. (1992). *The third chimpanzee: The evolution and future of the human animal.* New York: HarperCollins.

Eason, P. (1998). Territorial defense. In G. Greenberg & M. M. Haraway (Eds.), *Comparative psychology: A handbook* (pp. 771–776). New York: Garland.

Ehrlich, P. R., Dobkin, D. S., & Wheye, D. (1988). *The birder's handbook.* New York: Simon & Schuster.

Geist, V. (1998). Mountain sheep. In G. Greenberg & M. M. Haraway (Eds.), *Comparative psychology: A handbook* (pp. 441–445). New York: Garland.

Goodall, J. (1968). The behavior of free-ranging chimpanzees in the Gombe Stream Reserve. *Animal Behavior Monographs, 1,* 165–311.

Gordon, D. M. (1997). Task allocation and interaction rates in social insect colonies. In G. Greenberg & E. Tobach (Eds.), *Comparative psychology of invertebrates: The field and laboratory study of insect behavior* (pp. 125–134). New York: Garland.

Hall, K. R. L. (1965). Behaviour and ecology of the wild patas monkeys, *Erythrocebus patas,* in Uganda. *Journal of Zoology, 148,* 15–87.

Hamilton, W. D. (1964). The genetical evolution of social behavior I, II. *Journal of Theoretical Biology, 7,* 1–52.

Haraway, M. M., & Maples, E. G. (1998a). Gibbons, the singing apes. In G. Greenberg & M. M. Haraway (Eds.), *Comparative psychology: A handbook* (pp. 422–430). New York: Garland.

Haraway, M. M., & Maples, E. G. (1998b). Flexibility in the species-typical songs of gibbons. *Primates, 39,* 1–12.

Harcourt, A. H. (1979). Contrasts between male relationships in wild gorilla groups. *Behavioral Ecology and Sociobiology, 5,* 39–49.

Hickman, C. P., Jr., Roberts, L. S., & Hickman, F. M. (1984). *Integrated principles of zoology.* St. Louis: Times Mirror/Mosby.

Howard, R. D. (1978). The evolution of mating strategies in bullfrogs, *Rana catesbiana. Evolution, 32,* 550–571.

Ingmanson, E. J. (1996). Tool-using behavior in wild *Pan paniscus:* Social and ecological considerations. In A. E. Russon & K. Bard (Eds.), *Reaching into thought: The minds of the great apes* (pp. 190–210). Cambridge, England: Cambridge University Press

Koufopanou, V. (1994). The evolution of soma in the volvocales. *The American Naturalist, 143,* 907–931.

Krafft, B. (1979). Organization and evolution of spider societies. *Journal de Psychologie Normale et Pathologique, 76,* 23–51.

Lindauer, M. (1961). *Communication among social bees.* Cambridge: Harvard University Press.

Maldonado, H. (1964). The control of attack by *Octopus*. *Zeitchrift fur Vergleichindephysiologie, 47,* 656–674.

Marshall, J., & Marshall, E. (1976). Gibbons and their territorial songs. *Science, 193,* 235–237.

Mather, J. A., Resler, S., & Cosgrove, J. (1985). Activity and movement patterns of *I Octopus defleini. Marine Behaviour and Physiology, 11,* 301–314.

Matsuzawa, T. (2001). (Ed.). *Primate origins of human cognition and behavior.* Tokyo: Springer-Verlag.

Nentwig, W. (1985). Social spiders catch larger prey: A study of *Anelosimus eximius (Araneae: Theridiidae). Behavioral Ecology and Sociobiology, 17,* 79–85.

Parish, A. R. (1996). Female relationships in bonobos (*Pan paniscus*). *Human Nature, 7,* 61–96.

Pasquet, A., & Krafft, B. (1992). Cooperation and prey capture efficiency in a social spider, *Anelosimus eximius (Araneae, Theridiidae). Ethology, 90,* 121–133.

Pitcher, T. J. (1998). Shoaling and schooling behavior of fishes. In G. Greenberg & M. M. Haraway (Eds.), *Comparative psychology: A handbook* (pp. 748–760). New York: Garland.

Robinson, G. E. (1998). From society to genes with the honey bee. *American Scientist, 86,* 456–462.

Rogers, L., & Kaplan, G. (1998). Orangutans. In G. Greenberg & M. M. Haraway (Eds.), *Comparative psychology: A handbook* (pp. 465–472). New York: Garland.

Rowell, T. E. (1988). What do male monkeys do besides competing? In G. Greenberg & E. Tobach (Eds.), *Evolution of social behavior and integrative levels* (pp. 205–212). Hillsdale, NJ: Lawrence Erlbaum.

Savage-Rumbaugh, E. S., Shanker, S. G., & Taylor, T. J. (1998). *Apes, language, and the human mind.* New York: Oxford University Press.

Schaller, G. B. (1972). *The Serengeti lion.* Chicago: University of Chicago Press.

Schjelderup-Ebbe, T. (1922). Beitrage zur sozialpsychologie des haushuhns. *Zeitschrift Psychologie, 88,* 225–252.

Seeley, T. D. (1995). *The wisdom of the hive: The social physiology of honeybee colonies.* Cambridge, MA: Harvard University Press.

Smuts, B. B., Cheney, D. L., Seyfarth, R. M., Wrangham, W. W., & Struhsaker, T. T. (1987). *Primate societies.* Chicago: University of Chicago Press.

Stammbach, E. (1987). Desert, forest and montane baboons: Multilevel societies. In B. B. Smuts et al. (Eds.), *Primate societies* (pp. 112–120). Chicago: University of Chicago Press.

Stamps, J. (1998). Territoriality. In G. Greenberg & M. M. Haraway (Eds.), *Comparative psychology: A handbook* (pp. 761–770). New York: Garland.

Struhsaker, T. T., & Gartlan, J. S. (1970). Observations on the behaviour and ecology of the patas monkey (*Erythrocebus patas*) in the Waza Reserve, Cameroon. *Journal of Zoology, 161,* 49–63.

Stuart, R. J. (1997). Division of labor in social insect colonies: Self-organization and recent revelations regarding age, size and genetic differences. In G. Greenberg & E. Tobach (Eds.), *Comparative psychology of invertebrates: The field and laboratory study of insect behavior* (pp. 135–155). New York: Garland.

Tinbergen, N. (1953). *The herring gull's world.* London: Collins.

Vollrath, F., & Rohde-Arndt, D. (1983). Prey capture and feeding in the social spider *Anelosimus eximius. Zeitschrift fuer Tierpsychologie, 61,* 334–340.

Wade, J. (1998). Sexual dimorphism in the brainstem of the green anole lizard. *Brain, Behavior and Evolution, 52,* 46–54.

Wilson, E. O. (1971). *The insect societies.* Cambridge, MA: Harvard University Press.

Yeh, S., Russell, A. F., & Edwards, D. H. (1996). The effect of social experience on serotonergic modulation of the escape circuit of crayfish. *Science, 271,* 366–369.

CHAPTER

6

Social Behavior II: Communication and Development

Communication

In nearly all of the cases of territorial behavior discussed in the preceding chapter, territories are established and maintained with the aid of communicative signals. These signals take many forms and make use of a full range of sensory possibilities. Territorial relations are one of many areas of animal life importantly impacted by communication. **Communication** is demonstrated whenever a particular response of one individual has a predictable effect on other individuals of the same species and, perhaps, on members of other species as well.

The releasing of **pheromones** by male carpenter bees has a predictable attractive influence on sexually receptive females that encounter them. Other examples of communication by chemical stimulation include scent marking, by urine, of territorial boundaries by the males of reproducing wolf packs during the breeding season and the preparation and urine scenting of scrapes within a breeding territory by male whitetail deer. Tactual stimulation is an important element of courtship behavior in a great many species as well as a coordinating factor in breeding or copulatory behavior.

Earlier in the book, in Chapter 4, we discussed the long-standing idea that foraging honeybees communicate specific information about the direction and distance of food sources they have visited by means of a series of dancing movements they perform before other workers upon returning from a successful foraging trip. The detail and specificity of the "messages" communicated through **honeybee dancing** has been severely challenged by recent work (Wenner, 1998). Nevertheless, at a minimum the dancing does appear to acquaint observers with the odor of the food source just visited by a dancer and to stimulate observers to go foraging and often to visit the same or similar food sources.

Visual communicative actions include the flashing of fireflies, in which flashing patterns are both species-typical and gender-specific (Figure 6.1). Male flashes provoke answering flashes by sexually receptive females, which can then be approached for courtship. The throat-fan extension and leg pumping of male anole lizards attracts ap-

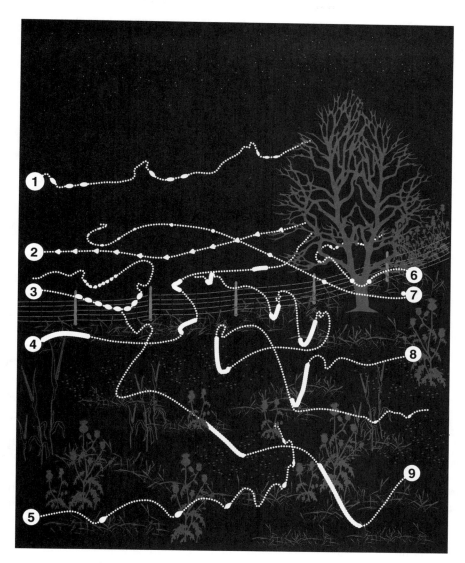

FIGURE 6.1   Flash Patterns of Several Firefly Species

proaches by receptive females, whose visual proximity stimulates a marked increase in the frequency of performing leg pumping and throat-fan extensions as a transition from territorial patrolling and sexual advertisement to active **courtship** of a particular individual (see Figure 6.2). The dance courtship of numerous fishes such as stickleback and largemouth bass are comprised largely of visual signals, as are the dances of numerous species of cranes and those of other avian groups such as grouse and peacocks.

FIGURE 6.2   A Male Anole Lizard with Throat Fan Extended

Auditory stimulation is the primary medium of a great deal of animal communication. The stridulations of male crickets are well known, as are the vocalizations of numerous species of cicadas, toads, frogs, and tree frogs. Mention of these familiar night sounds may spark memory of the vocalizations of well-known night birds such as the whippoorwill, the chuck-will's-widow, and the great-horned owl. All of these sounds are territorial signals as well as attractions to the approach of prospective mates.

Birdsong is among the most familiar varieties of animal auditory communication. Ornithologists distinguish between bird calls and songs on the basis of comparatively greater length and complexity of songs, although the distinction is not always clear or easy to make (Ehrlich, Dobkin, & Wheye, 1988). Birdsong serves the two functions just mentioned, territorial possession and mate attraction, as well as preservation of established pair bonds and perhaps coordination of the pair in copulatory behavior.

Birdsongs are outstanding examples of species-typical behavior, being similar enough within single species and different enough between species to serve as a major key to species identification of birds in the field. Songs are the primary means of field identification in the North American Breeding Bird Survey carried out each year by the U.S. Fish and Wildlife Service (Peterjohn, Sauer, & Link, 1994). Many guides to bird identification include verbal descriptions of birdsongs and calls as well as visual representations of the songs by means of sonograms.

Within the broad pattern of species-typical singing behavior, individual variations in singing have been described in many species of birds. In many instances, individuals holding a fixed territory come to recognize the individual songs sung by territorial neighbors and to respond differentially to the playback of a stranger's song in their vicinity (Ehrlich, Dobkin, & Wheye, 1988). Many birds develop large repertoires of individual song variations (Boughey & Thompson, 1981). The size of the individual repertoire appears to function as a factor in mate selection in some cases, with increased size providing an advantage in male attractiveness to females (Searcy, Search, & Marler, 1982; Yasukawa, 1981; Yasukawa, Blank, & Patterson, 1980).

In addition to the territorial and reproductive functions of birdsong, many bird vocalizations serve to coordinate behavior within a group. Calls made at roosting time in many species attract other conspecifics to roost in the same area as that in which the callers are roosting. This calling behavior benefits the survival of late arrivals who haven't yet located a good place to spend the night, and some of these late arrivals may be the offspring or siblings of the callers. In any event, the presence of extra eyes and ears increases the safety of all taking shelter in the vicinity for the night.

The calls of crows and of cranes undoubtedly play a role in coordinating the daily activities of these long-term groups of closely associated individuals. Anyone familiar with the common crow of North America (*Corvus brachyrhynchos*) can distinguish several distinctive calls. Alarm calls are given, for example, when a group of crows is suddenly confronted by a person near their feeding or resting place. These calls often are given only by the bird that was the first to spot the intruder but are responded to with precipitate flight by other members of the group. Mobbing calls are very loud and particularly raucous calls that are given when crows spot and harass a potential predator such as a hawk or an owl, and these calls appear to draw other groups of crows from the surrounding countryside. Crows also make a variety of contact-maintaining calls that are performed in a back-and-forth manner by group members at some distance from one another. These interchanges are often followed by a gathering together of several group members at the vicinity of one of the callers. (For additional information, see Chamberlain & Cornwell, 1971; Goodwin, 1976.)

A number of distinctive calls have been identified in several species of cranes, and these are used reliably in different specific contexts, as suggested by the names *food begging, contact, guard,* and *unison* calls (Grier & Burk, 1992; Johnsgard, 1983). The reliable association of particular calls with particular contexts makes it possible that young group members will learn appropriate anticipatory behaviors to the calls through the process of classical conditioning. (See Chapters 1 and 8.) Such learning may play an important part in the species-typical development of call recognition in these species.

Gibbon songs are another example of long-distance territorial communication similar to birdsong. The songs are distinctively different according to species and are useful in determining the identities of captive gibbons of several species whose physical features are very similar. In most of the nine gibbon species, mated pairs sing **duets** together that are consistently arranged as three separate movements, each of which is composed and performed differently from the others. Each performance of a duet begins with an **introductory sequence,** leads on to an **organizing sequence,** and moves to a climax in a **great-call sequence** (Haimoff, 1984). The pair then returns to the organizing sequence and performs alternating organizing and great-call sequences until the duet ends, usually after ten to thirty minutes of singing. Many of the calls of gibbons are gender-specific, and in the duet, certain parts are performed only by females and others only by males. In a number of gibbon species, the female's part in the duet greatly overshadows the male's part. In most of those species, males also regularly sing alone in **dawn solos.**

The complex coordination of behavior that is achieved between mates in the performance of duets is well illustrated by the great call of the siamang gibbon (*Hylobates syndactylus*), which Marshall and Sugardjito (1986) have called the most complex song performed by a land vertebrate other than man (Table 6.1). The male siamang brings the organizing sequence to a close by performing a series of massive ascending booms—deep "oom" sounds of ascending pitch. These calls serve as an invitation to the female to begin the great call by performing a distinctive series of high-pitched barks performed only by females. Once the female has made seven or eight high barks in series, the male performs a single ascending boom, whereupon the female immediately accelerates the pace of her high barks. The male then overlays her continuing high bark series with a mighty two-toned, or bitonal, scream. (This scream sounds a little like Tarzan's scream in the old Tarzan movies. The resemblance is close enough to make us suspect that the Tarzan scream was modeled on this call of the male siamang.) The female then continues with a new series of high barks, which the male overlays with a one-toned scream that ends in a chatter, or ululation. The pair then ends the great call with a joint display of vigorous locomotor behavior and barking. (More detailed descriptions are given by Haimoff, 1981.)

Gibbons display impressive flexibility in their song performance. If a male siamang's mate fails to respond to his first "invitation" to begin a great call, he repeats his ascending boom series, often several times in succession (Maples, Haraway, & Hutto, 1989). Females show similar flexibility. If a male fails to perform his bitonal scream at his usual place in the female's performance of her high-bark series, she will continue her series well past the usual point of male entry, allowing the pair an opportunity to complete the great call in their usual coordination with one another. Numerous additional examples of flexibility in the singing behavior of gibbons may be seen in Haraway and Maples (1998).

In addition to the loud calls, which broadcast a territorial message to neighbors as well as providing communication within the family group, there are other calls that

TABLE 6.1 Arrangement of Male and Female Vocal Phrases in the Performance of a Siamang Great Call

Male Vocalizations	Female Vocalizations
Double-boom invitation	Answering boom... Start of first high-bark series
Ascending boom	Acceleration of high-bark series
Bitonal scream	Continuation of high barks into second series, then acceleration of second series
Ululating scream	Completion of second series as male completes his ululating scream
Male locomotion call and display	Female locomotion call and display

communicate only within the gibbon family. These include distress calls; whimpers of appeasement; squeals of a fleeing animal; whistles paired with an aggressive posture; and startle, or alarm, calls (Carpenter, 1940; Gittens, 1984).

The gray wolf (*Canis lupus*) is a creature of ancient familiarity to humankind and the primary ancestor of our domestic dogs (Figure 6.3). For many people, the howl of the wolf is a powerful symbol of wild nature. Wolves also engage in a number of other vocalizations of potential value as signals (Klinghammer, 1998; Mech, 1966). Barks are given sometimes in greeting by a mother wolf returning to her pups, providing a means by which her pups can identify her at a distance. Barks may also be a means of challenging a predator such as a grizzly bear or of directing group attention to the presence of other animals of any sort. Growls are effective warnings of impending attack toward competitors outside the pack structure or toward other members of one's own pack—unless they desist from the behaviors that provoked the growl. The loud howls and chorus howling and barking of wolves may serve several communicative functions. These behaviors provide location markers for absent pack members and are a means of contact between separated pack units. Chorus howling may serve as a means of solidifying and maintaining social ties within the pack and may also be helpful in maintaining separation among different packs living within proximity of one other.

The precise usage of specific alarm calls, each of which designates a different type of predatory threat, has become a celebrated behavior characteristic of vervet monkeys (*Cercopithecus aethiops*) (Seyforth & Cheney, 1990). These monkeys face predatory threats from eagles, leopards, and snakes, such as pythons. Monkeys spotting these sources of threat give acoustically distinct alarm calls that are specific to each predator type. Individuals hearing these calls react to each in a different and appropriate way: They look up in response to eagle warnings, run toward trees in

FIGURE 6.3 Arctic Gray Wolf

response to leopard warnings, and look down in response to snake warnings (Bramblett, 1980; Owren & Bernacki, 1988; Seyforth & Cheney, 1980). The responses of infant and very young vervets to these different alarm calls are much more general. They have many opportunities to form specific associations of calls with predator types in their developmental experiences (Seyforth & Cheney, 1980). Adult vervets showed a tendency to generalize habituation experiences not only on the basis of acoustical similarity but also on the basis of semantic similarity. Individuals habituated to the alarm calls of starlings to the presence of a raptor such as an eagle subsequently showed distinctly decreased responsiveness to vervet eagle alarm calls as compared to vervet leopard alarms and snake alarms (Seyforth & Cheney, 1990).

Dolphins such as *Stenella frontalis* produce a wide variety of loud vocalizations, many of which probably serve to communicate with other dolphins. In long-term field studies of wild dolphins (Dudzinski, 1996; Herzing, 1996), numerous vocalizations were found to be specifically associated with particular conditions or social circumstances as well as with particular postures or gestures. It seems likely that many of these sounds and gestures had specific communicative value. Experimental studies of the complex learning and information processing skills of dolphin species (e.g., Herman, Kuczaj, & Holder, 1993) demonstrate the feasibility of complex communication occurring among dolphins. The whales, another group of cetacean species, also are well known for the wide variety of their long-distance vocalizations. Playback experiments with southern right whales (*Eubalaena australis*) (Clark & Clark, 1980) showed that the whales approached the source of playback and made answering vocalizations to recorded vocalizations of other southern right whales but made few vocalizations and swam away from recorded water noise of similar frequency, as they also did in response to recorded humpback whale vocalizations. Thus, these animals do differentiate the vocal sounds of their own species from other similar sounds.

Chimpanzees perform a wide variety of communicative gestures and numerous communicative vocalizations (Nishida & Hiraiwa-Hasegawa, 1987). Their gestures of kissing, touching, and embracing are used in situations that imply functions of greeting, reassuring, peacemaking, and comforting. Very light biting, or mock biting, by a dominant individual appears also to function as a sign of reassurance to a subordinate, particularly after an aggressive display by the dominant animal. Aggressive displays include charging vigorously toward or past another animal while shaking branches, dragging a branch, and slapping and stamping the ground (Goodall, 1968). Prominent vocalizations include the pant-grunt—often made by subordinates toward a displaying dominant animal and responded to by a reassuring gesture on its part—and the pant-hoot. The pant-hoot is made in a wide variety of situations; it seems indicative generally of increased excitement or arousal and provides widespread notice of the location of the vocalizing individual. Bonobos display similar communicative behaviors to those of chimpanzees but replace the chimpanzees' pant-grunt with soft "ku-ku-ku" sounds in similar circumstances. Bonobos also show more elaborate communications associated with courtship and copulation. These include mutual gazing prior to copulation and facial expressions and gestures indicating particular copulatory postures, of which a greater variety are used by bonobos than by chimpanzees (Savage-Rumbaugh & Wilkerson, 1978).

Development of Social Behavior

Honeybee workers exist within a social environment long before their emergence from the pupa state and remain within a social context throughout their continued development as adult bees. We have seen (Chapter 4) that the particular nature of their social interactions, as well as the particular types of tasks they perform in and around the hive, vary in a predictable manner with age from the time of their emergence (Lindauer, 1961). In the final stage of their development, the workers begin to forage and thus leave the immediate environment of the hive for perhaps the first time in their lives. Their foraging behavior remains in a social context, however, as they gather materials such as nectar and pollen and return with them to the hive, where they are shared with great numbers of their sisters. As we have seen earlier, foragers often perform predictable dancing movements upon arriving at the hive and these movements influence subsequent foraging activities of the observers. We have seen also that honeybee workers show progressive improvement in the efficiency of their foraging behavior over the period of their first week of foraging experience. Much of this improvement presumably is the result of learning (see Chapter 4).

Offspring of most species of fish hatch together in large groups and remain together through at least the first few weeks of life. Many are prone to form large groups under various circumstances throughout the life span. Pitcher (1998) distinguishes between two terms to which groups of fish may be referred: *shoal* and *school.* **Shoal** is the more general term and refers to groups of fish in a variety of behavioral modes, whereas **school** is restricted in its application to shoals that are engaged in coordinated locomotor movement. Schools display a number of distinctive characteristics such as uniform polarity of orientation and uniform density of distribution of individuals making up the school. Visual stimulation as well as stimulation of vibration or pressure waves received by the lateral line organs are important in achieving coordination of individuals with the movements of their fellow group members.

Pitcher (1998) characterizes shoals and schools as being products of moment-to-moment decisions of numerous individual fish whether to join, leave, or stay with a given group. Schools thus are seen as dynamic assemblages subject to constant variation in size and membership as the individual fish that form them encounter a stream of environmental and physiological demands relating to feeding, predators, currents, and so on. Pitcher and fellow researchers (Crowder, 1985; Fitzgerald & van Havre, 1985; Godin, 1986; Magurran, Oulton, & Pitcher, 1985; Pitcher, Magurran, & Winfield, 1982; Turner & Pitcher, 1986) have demonstrated numerous advantages of schooling that we may expect to hold true under a wide range of conditions. Demonstrated advantages have included the following: (1) more rapid location of hidden food resources by larger schools, (2) increased budgeting of time to foraging and increased boldness of foraging in larger groups, (3) more efficient switching of food patches by members of larger groups, (4) decreased overall likelihood of selection for predatory attack, (5) increased vigilance against predation, and (6) increased success of defensive reactions–decreased success of predatory attacks with larger groups. Schooling and shoaling behavior appear organized primarily at the biosocial level of complexity. Additionally, however, there also are numerous learning experiences available to most individuals whereby these behaviors may be shaped by psychotaxic organization.

Development of Social Attachment

Early social stimulation is critically important to the social development of **precocial** birds, as was made famous by one of the founders of ethology, Konrad Lorenz (1937). Precocial birds are those in which newly hatched offspring are able to leave the nest shortly after hatching, moving about and feeding for themselves as they accompany their mother. In such species, it is vital for the young animals to become attached to the mother very quickly. Once the brood leaves the nest, any young animal that becomes separated from its group is not likely to survive for long by itself. The rapid attachment to social stimuli encountered in the early environment was termed **imprinting** by Lorenz. The process has been widely observed in ducks, geese, and gallinacious, or chicken-like, birds such as chickens, quail, and turkeys.

It may seem to us that young animals should be hatched or born already possessing the ability to recognize other members of their own species, but Lorenz (1937) demonstrated that this is not the case. Rather, they will accept and become attached to any of a variety of arbitrary stimuli, such as a person, a large ball, or a duck decoy, as long as the object moves about the environment and can be approached by the young animal. Sounds emanating from an stimulus increase its effectiveness as an imprinting object, however, and imprinting to artificial objects requires greater exposure than needed for imprinting to the natural parent (Salzen, 1998). Early social experience has very long-lasting effects on later social behavior. Individuals remain socially attracted to the objects of early social experience throughout adult life whereas individuals that are denied contact with any sort of social stimulus in early life may continue forever as asocial loners.

Early social experience provides an excellent example of what is called a **critical experience**—one that is critically important to normal development in a species. Without the appropriate occurrence of a critical experience, then, development is likely to be abnormal in a specific and predictable way. Critical experiences have their greatest effects only within specific time limitations during development, often located in the early portion of the life span. These times are known as **sensitive periods.** Critical experiences may be relatively ineffective if they occur either too early or too late.

Sensitive periods for imprinting in the precocial birds we have just been considering occur much earlier in the life span than they do for *altricial* birds, which are relatively helpless at hatching and require numerous days of development to become competent enough in locomotor behavior to leave the nest. Individuals of these species have frequent and active social interactions with the parents in connection with feeding, and these experiences are sufficient to provide for imprinting well before the young are mature enough to fly away from the nest. Of course, normal imprinting can be prevented in these species, as well, by rearing individuals in isolation from all social stimulation or by exposing them only to an artificial imprinting object.

The facts of imprinting are now recognized in the conservation of endangered avian species. Great care is now taken to expose artificially reared young of species such as the California condor and the whooping crane to appropriate social objects early in life. Appropriate social experiences often are provided by use of hand puppets that mimic stimulation normally provided by contact of a young animal with adults of its species. Only if early social experiences are adequate will artificially reared animals have a chance to recognize their own species and reproduce normally when introduced to a prospective mate within a zoo or breeding compound or when released into a wild habitat.

As implied in the preceding paragraph, early social attachment plays a critical part in the development of normal sexual behavior. Sexual behavior is, after all, social behavior in most animal species. Such behavior must be properly directed toward another member of one's own species to have any chance of being successful. This requires appropriate social orientation and social attachment. Species orientation in sexual behavior generally corresponds to the orientation of social attachment. The focusing of sexual orientation on the basis of early social experience is often called **sexual imprinting.**

Lasting social attachment to social objects encountered in the early environment also occurs among mammals and often with impressive rapidity. This is particularly true among hoofed mammals such as horses, cattle, deer, and antelope. The wildebeest calf of Africa, for example, is able to rise to its feet in the first minute or so after birth and to run alongside its mother within a very few minutes after birth. In those first few minutes, it must interact socially with its mother and attach itself to her sufficiently to stay at her side as she mixes into a large group containing many wildebeest cows and their calves. Each calf's survival depends upon its ability to keep with its mother within the herd. Wildebeests inhabit an environment that contains many dangerous predators: lions, hyenas, leopards, cheetahs. How long would a lone, unattached wildebeest calf be expected to survive in this environment? How long would a lone cow and calf, separated from the herd, be expected to go unnoticed? Such an environment places a survival premium on rapid locomotor and social development of young animals born in the open and without formidable parental protection, as is the wildebeest.

Again, as we have seen with birds, mammals in which locomotor development occurs at a more leisurely pace also display a more leisurely development of social attachment. The early development of social behavior in domestic kittens occurs amid persistent mild stimulation provided by contact with the mother cat as well as with other littermates. This stimulation is encountered in combination with the warmth of bodily contact and the milk produced by suckling at the mother's breast. Separation from the mother and the litter provokes increased arousal and loud vocalization whereas reunion with the litter establishes relaxation and quiet. A study in T. C. Schneirla's laboratory (Rosenblatt, Turkewitz, & Schneirla, 1972) found that as kittens reach five to seven days of age, they become well able to return to the home area of the brood cage from an adjacent corner within three minutes. By the age of fourteen to sixteen days, they become able to return within three minutes from the diagonal corner of the home cage, ready to show active approach responses to stimuli associated with the litter and the mother and to learn to take an efficient route in making repeated returns to the rewarding social stimulation provided by the litter and the mother. Schneirla (Aronson, Tobach, Rosenblatt, & Lehrman, 1972) viewed all development as an interactive process involving current stimulation, already existing behavior patterns, and emerging behavior patterns. He found that removing a kitten from the social environment of the litter and keeping it in social isolation for a number of days during early social development resulted in marked deficits that were not readily recovered simply by placing the kitten back with its litter at a later age. Responses of social affiliation were no longer emerging in a kitten of that age. At the time when such responses had been ready to emerge, the current stimulation needed to support their occurrence and development was not present in the environment of the isolated kitten. The deficit represented a loss in developmental opportunity that was not easily overcome.

Harry Harlow (1971) raised a number of infant rhesus monkeys in social isolation in an effort to provide them uniform histories of experience and to separate them from parasites that plagued their wild-caught mothers. He provided the young animals with everything he thought young monkeys needed to do well in life but found that many of the infants failed to thrive and, instead, showed obvious developmental deficits and poor health. What were the young monkeys missing that they apparently needed so much? The answer that occurred to Harlow was that they were missing the social stimulation normally provided by an attentive mother. He decided to launch a series of studies on the development of social and affectional responses of young monkeys under carefully controlled conditions. The results of his studies were spectacular.

First, Harlow (1971) found that young monkeys separated from their real mothers benefited from the provision of a substitute or surrogate mother. The surrogates were made of wooden frames covered with heavy screen wire and covered with terry cloth. They had round faces with stylized eyes and other features. A lightbulb placed within the dummy's chest cavity was kept lighted to provide a source of heat to make the terry cloth skin warm to the touch. Thus, the surrogate mothers provided some of the same sort of social stimulation normally provided by a real mother. The breast area of the surrogate also possessed a nipple, attached to a baby bottle hidden within the body cavity, and young monkeys fed at this nipple as at a normal mother's breast. The young monkeys fared well with these surrogate mothers. They developed well physically and appeared to develop strong affectional responses toward the surrogate. They clung to the surrogate and rocked themselves to sleep on her breast using the same rocking tempo by which real mother monkeys rock their young. They showed separation anxiety when isolated from the surrogate and strong approach to her when she was brought back. They cowered in a far corner when a novel stimulus object was brought in her absence but moved boldly forward to investigate the new object if the mother were present. In sum, the young monkeys displayed strong social attachment to their surrogate mothers and appeared to behave toward them much as young monkeys behave toward their real mothers.

We mentioned earlier that social stimulation received by young kittens usually is encountered in association with warmth and food. At the time of Harlow's work there was a popular belief in psychology that much or perhaps all of the attractive appeal of social stimulation derived from its association with other good things that served real physical needs, as do food and warmth. From his observations of how poorly young monkeys get along without a mother or a mother substitute, Harlow suspected that social stimulation was important to a young monkey independently of its association with other sources of attraction such as food. In a particularly clever experiment,

Harlow (1971) pitted several sources of social stimulation—providing what he called **contact comfort**—against food as a basis for the development of affectional responses and social attachment. He raised a number of young monkeys with two surrogate mothers. One of these provided the sources of contact comfort described above but did not have the nipple at the breast or any other means of providing food. Instead, the young monkeys received all of their food from a nipple at the breast of the second surrogate, which had food to offer, but had no soft covering of warm terry cloth skin and also had less realistic facial features than the first surrogate. Which, if either, of these surrogates would the young monkeys come to love, the food provider or the provider of contact comfort? The answer was overwhelmingly in favor of the provider of contact comfort. The young monkeys developed the same attachment to her as described earlier, and they spent nearly all of their time with her, only visiting the food-delivering mother long enough to complete a meal, then returning to sleep on the provider of contact comfort. These observations are extremely important because they show that social stimulation is a powerful source of attraction on its own and a more powerful basis of social attachment than is food.

When Harlow introduced a number of young monkeys raised only with surrogate mothers to the social life of a normal semi-free-ranging laboratory colony of monkeys at the age of six months, he made another important discovery (1971). These formerly isolated monkeys remained loners. They formed no social attachments and made no normal adjustment to social life despite lengthy exposure to the group and numerous friendly approaches from other group members. The sensitive period for social attachment—or the time when social attachment normally emerges as a pattern of behavior—had passed sometime during the first six months of life, but the isolated infant had missed receiving social stimulation from other monkeys during that time. The only social agent present during the emergence of social attachment had been a surrogate mother.

Monkeys removed from social isolation at the age of two months, however, were able fairly quickly to adjust to social living and to develop normal social attachments. Thus, the sensitive period for social attachment was still in progress at that age, and normal social development occurred quickly once the appropriate current stimulation was made available. Harlow also raised some young monkeys with a mother alone as the only social agent and other young monkeys with only another young monkey, or peer, as a social agent. Monkeys raised in either of these ways for the first six months showed normal social development. The social stimulation they had received early in life was much less than that encountered by normally raised infants, yet it was sufficient to support normal development (see Figure 6.4).

A final set of observations that Harlow made in this series was to determine what sort of maternal behavior would be shown by mothers that had been raised as social isolates. He arranged for a number of formerly isolated females to be made pregnant when they reached sexual maturity. This was not easy to accomplish because the former isolates sought to have nothing to do with other monkeys, even when they were ovulating—a physiological condition normally associated with sexual receptivity. Even so, sufficient sexual behavior was arranged to produce several pregnancies among the former isolates. When they gave birth, they failed to make any of the normal maternal

FIGURE 6.4   A Young Japanese Macaque Plays with a Snowball She Has Made.

behaviors usually observed in new mothers of their species. Thus, it appeared that an important basis of maternal behavior lay in the prior social development of the mother, and these once-isolated females were seriously deficient in their social development.

Harlow's observations hold important implications for human social development. Early social stimulation undoubtedly has lifelong influences on social behavior in our own species as well, and normal social development requires at least some approximation of the normal social environment to support it. Harlow's findings suggest that development may occur normally under a variety of social arrangements, as long as some measure of normalcy in the occurrence of social stimulation is provided. Disturbances of social development may be expected to be associated later with abnormalities in sexual behavior and, if parenthood occurs, abnormalities in parental behavior. Studies of human children suggest that their social development benefits greatly and lastingly from having a high quality of social attachment with their mothers and suffers correspondingly from having only a poor quality of attachment with them (Bowlby, 1958). Observations of children who have experienced long periods of serious social deprivation or isolation in early life make it appear that a poor social environment can be at least as devastating to human development as it is to that of young monkeys (Guyot, 1998).

Song Development in Birds

Singing is one of the most prominent features of social behavior among many bird species. This is particularly true among the order of birds known as the Passeriformes.

The order Passeriformes contains more than half of the world's avian species. Most of these species belong to the suborder Oscines—the songbirds—rather than to the alternative suborder of Suboscines. The two suborders were separated originally on the basis of structural differences in the syrinx, which is the organ of vocal production in birds. In North America, eighteen of the nineteen passerine orders are Oscines and one is Suboscine (Ehrlich, Dobkin, & Wheye, 1988). Much evidence exists that song development among a great many (if not nearly all) Oscine species is molded by developmental experiences with the species song (Ball & Hulse, 1998; Kroodsma, 1988). That is to say, that it is in part a product of **song learning.** Song learning has been described in nearly three hundred species of the suborder of songbirds and in at least two of the twenty-three other avian orders.

Song learning is subject to a variety of constraints across numerous species, such as being limited to an important degree to a particular period in the developmental sequence or showing sensitivity only toward a limited range of stimulation centered about usual variations of species-typical songs (Ball & Hulse, 1998; Petrinovich, 1998). Often an early stage in the learning of birdsong involves neither any distinctive behavioral reaction by the subject nor any activity resembling practice of a song, yet the experience of hearing the species song at that early stage is necessary to normal development of singing at a later time (e.g., Marler, 1970). Song development across numerous species may be seen as representing a continuum of processes showing varying degrees of dependence on specific auditory stimulation and singing experience. In the following paragraphs, we will examine a number of different patterns of song development that may be viewed as representing several stages along such a continuum.

Development of the relatively simple calls or songs that are typical in pigeons and doves, and in chickens, turkeys, and quail, appears to be independent of particular auditory experiences; these calls develop normally even in individuals experimentally deafened at an early age (Ball & Hulse, 1998; Petrinovich, 1998). Many—perhaps all—Suboscine species of passerines also are able to develop their relatively simple songs independently of auditory experience (Kroodsma, 1988; Kroodsma & Konishi, 1991). Among Oscine species, however, several patterns of dependence upon auditory stimulation and song learning are seen. Song sparrows (*Melospiza melodia*) show a pattern of song learning in which normal development of their rather complex species song requires stimulus feedback from their own song performance but does not require hearing the songs of any other members of their species (Petrinovich, 1998). In this species, then, hearing the feedback stimulation from one's own singing is sufficient. Oregon juncos—now considered a race of the dark-eyed junco, *Junco hyemalis*—develop highly individualized songs that show considerable consistency within each individual. Normal development of these songs requires both feedback from individual practice as well as opportunity to hear siblings or other young juncos practicing their songs. But exposure to the tutorial experience of hearing the song performance of a mature adult is not necessary to normal development. The white-crowned sparrow requires critical experiences at two separate developmental stages for the acquisition of its normal, complex song (Marler, 1970). In the first stage, which should occur within a sensitive period between the ages of ten and one hundred days, young birds must hear the song performance of a mature adult. They do not practice any singing at this age but somehow store an internal representation, or memory, of the adult song that appears to guide the shaping of their own singing when it begins to occur for the first time near the end of the first year of life. Individuals that have been isolated from the song performance of an adult model in early life, or that have been deafened prior to the emergence of their own singing behavior—denying them an opportunity to match the feedback of their own singing to the memory of song performance by the adult model—fail to develop normal songs. Marler (1970) termed these two stages of song learning the **sensory stage,** which involves sensory reception but not action, and the **sensorimotor stage,** which involves both sensation and action.

The sensitive period of up to one hundred days of age for hearing an adult model can be extended appreciably beyond one hundred days if the providing model is a live tutor but not if it is merely a recorded song (Petrinovich, 1990). White-crowned sparrows studied in nature were found to perform the normal song of their species almost without exception. The songs of young birds settling in a region were found to reflect the particular dialects widely practiced in that region, and regional dialects were seen to change slowly over a number of years (Petrinovich, 1988).

Mockingbirds (*Mimus polyglottis*) are famous for mimicking the songs of other species heard in their vicinity. Despite their impressive skill as mimics, however, mockingbirds add typical mockingbird features to their mimicry by changing the timing of some syllables and changing some frequency modulations. These changes allow human observers—and undoubtedly other birds—to distinguish the mockingbird's song from that of the species it is mimicking (Petrinovich, 1998). Most nonmimicking species are not very flexible in the auditory inputs that affect their song development; they do not readily acquire the songs of alien species that may reside in their areas. However, under appropriate conditions of live tutoring, individuals of some nonmimicking species have shown an ability to acquire alien songs.

The brown-headed cowbird (*Molothrus ater*) is a parasitic nester whose eggs are deposited in the nests of other birds and whose young are raised by hosts of numerous other species. Under such circumstances, if young cowbirds were to acquire the songs most frequently heard during their early development, there would be little possibility that a distinct and species-typical cowbird song could exist. Instead, however, brown-headed cowbirds develop their songs according to experiences that occur during their first and later breeding seasons. One of the potentially important features of this experience is the opportunity to hear the songs of many mature brown-headed cowbirds. But what has now been shown to be particularly important to the shaping of singing in male cowbirds are the reactions of female cowbirds to a male's song (West & King, 1988, 1996). Females perform a display behavior called *wing stroking* in response to some male songs but not to others. This female display—related to the effectiveness of male song as an inducement to copulation—shapes male singing. Male songs that are successful at inducing female wing stroking are selected for more frequent performance; those that are unsuccessful at inducing female response are discarded. This sensitivity of male song to female response allows adult males to change their songs such as to adopt locally effective dialects when they are placed with females from different sections of the country. Brown-headed cowbird singing does show truly impressive plasticity. Still, we should not overlook the fact that this flexibility rests on an initial appearance of basic male songs that are then available for adjustment on the basis of the consequences they produce in female reaction.

Summary: Principles Introduced in This Chapter

We speak of communication whenever one animal's behavior has a predictable effect on the behavior of another animal, particularly another of its species. Communication may be transmitted by all sensory channels, and many intricate developments of communicative channels are illustrated by different species across the animal series. Communication may be seen as a basic process increasing the efficiency of all of the social relations and social functions discussed in this summary section as well as throughout this entire chapter.

Like all behavioral development, social development at any point may be viewed as an interaction among existing behaviors, physical maturation and emerging behaviors, and current stimulation. Much social development is importantly dependent on specific features of experience often referred to as critical experiences. Ordinary learning processes may be operating throughout the achievement of social development, but some of the behavioral adjustments that constitute this development display characteristics that separate them from ordinary examples of learning. For one thing, the experiences that prompt these adjustments may be maximally effective in that function only within a limited time span during development—that is, during a so-called sensitive period. If not encountered during the usual sensitive time span, these experiences will be relatively ineffective, whether given too early or too late. This fact probably is closely related to a second distinguishing feature of developmental adjustments; they tend to be rather more permanent than ordinary learned adjustments in that they are relatively unaffected by the imposition of later learning experiences.

Outstanding examples of the importance of critical experiences to social development are illustrated in the development of social attachment among birds and mammals and in the development of songs among the Oscine birds—the songbirds—through the process of song learning. Harlow's famous work on the development of social attachment in young rhesus monkeys not only revealed much about the nature of social attachment and related social behaviors but also provided clear demonstration of the importance of social stimulation—independently of associations with food—as a basic source of motivation.

KEY TERMS

Communication   a behavioral interaction between two animals in which the responses of one animal have a predictable effect on the actions of the other animal.

Contact comfort   Harlow's informal term used to summarize the type of social stimulation a young mammal normally receives from contact with its mother.

Courtship   the behaviors by which a male and a female locate and accommodate to one another in association with mating and sexual reproduction.

Critical experience   an experience that has been shown to be of critical importance to normal behavior development in a species and without which development will be rendered abnormal in some predictable feature.

Dawn solos (of gibbons)   territory-holding males of most gibbon species perform extended sessions of vocal, or singing, behavior very early in the day; each male sings alone from his own territory but often sings in turn with one or more adjoining males singing from their territories nearby.

Duets (of gibbons)   mated pairs of most species of gibbons perform elaborate and extended sessions of vocal behavior known as singing, in which both males and females have their own predictable and distinctive contributions to the song.

Great-call sequence   the third of three distinctive patterns displayed in territorial singing by mated pairs in most species of gibbons; this pattern typically is repeated many times in alternation with the organizing sequence in each extended session of song performance.

Honeybee dancing   a predictable pattern of behavior performed by a forager upon its arrival back at the hive and proposed, by von Frisch, to communicate information about the location of a food source just visited by the dancing bee.

Imprinting   rapid attachment to social stimuli encountered early in the life span, particularly by birds.

Introductory sequence   the first of three distinctive patterns displayed in territorial singing by mated pairs in most species of gibbons; this pattern typically occurs only at the beginning of an extended session, or bout, of song performance by the pair.

Organizing sequence   the second of three distinctive patterns displayed in territorial singing by mated pairs in most species of gibbons; this pattern typically is repeated many times in alternation with the great-call sequence during each session of song performance.

Pheromone   a hormone released by one organism that functions as a source of sexual attraction to conspecifics of the opposite sex, or gender.

Precocial   displaying certain adult-like capabilities at a very early point in the life span.

School (of fish)   a large group of fish that displays closely coordinated locomotor movement among the individuals comprising the group.

Sensitive periods   limited time in the life span during which a particular critical experience will have its greatest effects on development.

Sensorimotor stage (of song learning)   a period of time in the development of young birds during which the critical experiences necessary for normal song learning involve both the reception of stimulation and the practice of certain movements or behaviors.

Sensory stage (of song learning)   a period of time in the development of young birds during which the critical experiences necessary for normal song learning are limited to the reception of stimulation from the environment.

Sexual imprinting   the long-term determination of sexual orientation upon stimuli encountered in early social experience.

Shoal   a general term that refers to any large group of fish and that may be applied across a wide range of behaviors by members of the group.

Song learning (of birds)   the interactive process of experience and development by which songs are acquired in many species of birds.

REVIEW QUESTIONS

1. What events must take place to illustrate an occurrence of communication?

2. Briefly explain how honeybee dancing can be taken to illustrate communication.

3. Give an example of communication involved in the courtship behavior of some nonhuman animal.

4. Give an example of vocal communication among crows.

5. Discuss the vocal communication of gibbons in some detail in connection with their duets and their solos.

6. Briefly characterize the interactive nature of the performance of the great-call sequence in siamang gibbons.

7. Suggest one or two functions of chorus howling among wolves.

8. Give an example that can be taken as the communication of specific information among vervets.

9. Give an example of vocal communication among chimpanzees or bonobos.

10. Distinguish between *shoal* and *school* as technical terms used to designate behavior patterns of fish.

11. Suggest one or two functional advantages of schooling in fish.

12. Give an example of imprinting and suggest what its functional importance may be.

13. What sort of stimulus or experience is the critical experience for imprinting?

14. What is meant by the term *sensitive period?*

15. Briefly describe one or two important findings of Harlow's extensive study of the development of social attachment in young monkeys.

16. To what did Harlow refer by the term *contact comfort?*

17. Suggest how Harlow's findings can be applied to human social development.

18. Briefly describe how both the sensory and sensorimotor phases of song learning can be illustrated by the development of singing in the white-crowned sparrow.

19. Describe an example that illustrates flexibility in the song development of brown-headed cowbirds.

20. Describe features of both mimicry and species identity illustrated in the singing behavior of the mockingbird.

REFERENCES

Aronson, L. R., Tobach, E., Rosenblatt, J. S., & Lehrman, D. S. (1972). *Selected writings of T. C. Schneirla.* San Francisco: W. H. Freeman.

Ball, G. F., & Hulse, S. H. (1998). Birdsong. *American Psychologist, 53,* 37–58.

Boughey, M. J., & Thompson, N. S. (1981). Song variety in the brown thrasher (*Toxostoma rufum*). *Zeitschrift fur Tierpsychologie, 56,* 47–58.

Bowlby, J. (1958). The nature of the child's tie to his mother. *International Journal of Psycho-Analysis, 39,* 350–373.

Bramblett, C. (1980). A model for development of social behavior in vervet monkeys. *Developmental Psychobiology, 13,* 205–223.

Carpenter, C. R. (1940). A field study of the behavior and social relations of the gibbon (*Hylobates lar*). *Comparative Psychology Monographs, 16,* 1–212.

Chamberlain, D. R., & Cornwell, G. W. (1971). Selected vocalizations of the common crow. *Auk, 88,* 613–634.

Clark, C. W., & Clark, J. M. (1980). Sound playback experiments with southern right whales (*Eubalaena australis*). *Science, 207,* 663–665.

Crowder, L. B. (1985). Optimal foraging and feeding mode shifts in fishes. *Environmental Biology of Fishes, 12,* 57–62.

Dudzinski, K. M. (1996). Communication and behavior in the Atlantic spotted dolphins (*Stenella frontalis*): Relationships between vocal and behavioral activities. Unpublished doctoral dissertation, Texas A & M University.

Ehrlich, P. R., Dobkin, D. S., & Wheye, D. (1988). *The birder's handbook.* New York: Simon and Schuster.

Fitzgerald, G. J., & van Havre, N. (1985). Flight, fright and shoaling in sticklebacks (*Gasterosteidae*). *Biology of Behaviour, 10,* 321–331.

Gittens, S. P. (1984). Territorial advertisment and defense in gibbons. In H. Preuschoft, D. J. Chivers, W. U. Brockelman, & N. Creel (Eds.), *The lesser apes: Evolutionary and behavioural biology* (pp. 420–424). Edinburgh: Edinburgh University Press.

Godin, J.-G. J. (1986). Risk of predation and foraging behaviour in shoaling banded killifish (*Fundulus diaphanus*). *Canadian Journal of Zoology, 64,* 1675–1678.

Goodall, J. (1968). The behavior of free-ranging chimpanzees in the Gombe Stream Reserve. *Animal Behavior Monographs, 1,* 165–311.

Goodwin, D. (1976). *Crows of the world.* Ithaca, NY: Cornell University Press.

Grier, J. W., & Burk, T. (1992). *Biology of animal behavior.* St. Louis: Mosby-Year.

Guyot, G. (1998). Attachment in mammals. In G. Greenberg & M. M. Haraway (Eds.), *Comparative psychology: A handbook* (pp. 509–516). New York: Garland.

Haimoff, E. (1981). Video analysis of siamang songs. *Behaviour, 76,* 128–151.

Haimoff, E. (1984). Acoustic and organizational features of gibbon songs. In H. Preuschoft, D. J. Chivers, W. J. Brockelman, and N. Creel (Eds.), *The lesser apes: Evolutionary and behavioural biology* (pp. 333–353). Edinburgh: Edinburgh University Press.

Haraway, M. M., & Maples, E. G. (1998). Flexibility in the species-typical songs of gibbons. *Primates, 39,* 1–12.

Harlow, H. F. (1971). *Learning to love.* New York: Ballantine.

Herman, L. M., Kuczaj, S. A., & Holder, M. D. (1993). Responses to anomalous gestural sequences by a language-trained dolphin: Evidence of processing of semantic relations and syntactic information. *Journal of Experimental Psychology: General, 122,* 184–194.

Herzing, D. L. (1996). Dolphins in the wild: An eight year field study on dolphin communication and interspecies interaction. Unpublished doctoral dissertation, the Union Institute, Cincinnati, OH.

Johnsgard, P. A. (1983). *Cranes of the world.* Bloomington, IN: Indiana University Press.

Klinghammer, E. (1998). Wolves. In G. Greenberg & M. M. Haraway (Eds.), *Comparative psychology: A handbook* (pp. 499–506). New York: Garland.

Kroodsma, D. E. (1988). Contrasting styles of song development and their consequences among passerine birds. In R. C. Bolles & M. D. Beecher (Eds.), *Ecology and evolution of acoustic communication in birds* (pp. 157–184). Hillsdale, NJ: Lawrence Erlbaum.

Kroodsma, D. E., & Konishi, M. (1991). A *suboscine* bird (eastern phoebe *Sayoornis phoebe*) develops normal song without auditory feedback. *Animal Behaviour, 42,* 477–487.

Lindauer, M. (1961). *Communication among social bees.* Cambridge: Harvard University Press.

Lorenz, K. (1937). Imprinting. *Auk, 54,* 245–273.

Magurran, A. E., Oulton, W., & Pitcher, T. J. (1985). Vigilant behaviour and shoal size in minnows. *Zeitschrift fur Tierpsychologie, 67,* 167–178.

Maples, E. G., Haraway, M. M., & Hutto, C. W. (1989). Development of coordinated singing in a newly formed siamang pair (*Hylobates syndactylus*). *Zoo Biology, 8,* 367–378.

Marler, P. (1970). A comparative approach to vocal learning: Song development in white-crowned sparrows. *Journal of Comparative Psychology Monographs, 71,* 1–25.

Marshall, J., & Sugardjito, J. (1986). Gibbon systematics. In D. Swindler and J. Erwin (Eds.), *Comparative primate biology: Systematics, evolution, and anatomy,* Vol. I (pp. 137–185). New York: Alan R. Liss.

Mech, L. D. (1966). *The wolves of Isle Royale.* Washington, DC: U.S. Government Printing Office.

Nishida, N., & Hiraiwa-Hasegawa, M. (1987). Chimpanzees and bonobos: Cooperative relationships among males. In B. B. Smuts, D. L. Cheney, R. M. Seyfarth, R. W. Wrangham, & T. T. Struhsaker (Eds.), *Primate societies* (pp. 165–178). Chicago: University of Chicago Press.

Owren, M. J., & Bernacki, R. H. (1988). The acoustic features of vervet monkey alarm calls. *Journal of the Acoustical Society of America, 83,* 1927–1935.

Peterjohn, B. G., Sauer, J. R., & Link, W. A. (1994). The 1992 and 1993 summary of the North American breeding bird survey. *Bird Populations, 2,* 46–61.

Petrinovich, L. (1988). The role of social factors in white-crowned song development. In Zentall, T., & B. G. Galef (Eds.), *Social learning: Psychological and biological approaches* (pp. 255–278). Hillsdale, NJ: Lawrence Erlbaum.

Petrinovich, L. (1990). Avian song development: Methodological and conceptual issues. In D. A. Dewsbury (Ed.), *Contemporary issues in comparative psychology* (pp. 340–359). Sunderland, MA: Sinauer Associates.

Petrinovich, L. (1998). Bird song development. In G. Greenberg & M. M. Haraway (Eds.) *Comparative psychology: A handbook* (pp. 517–522). New York: Garland.

Pitcher, T. J. (1998). Shoaling and schooling behavior of fishes. In G. Greenberg & M. M. Haraway (Eds.), *Comparative psychology: A handbook* (pp. 748–760). New York: Garland.

Pitcher, T. J., Magurran, A. E., & Winfield, I. (1982). Fish in larger shoals find food faster. *Behavioral Ecology and Sociobiology, 10,* 149–151.

Rosenblatt, J. S., Turkewitz, G., & Schneirla, T. C. (1972) Development of home orientation in newly born kittens. In L. R. Aronson, E. Tobach, J. S. Rosenblatt, & D. S. Lehrman (Eds.), *Selected writings of T. C. Schneirla* (pp. 689–711). San Francisco: W. H. Freeman.

Salzen, E. A. (1998). Imprinting. In G. Greenberg & M. M. Haraway (Eds.), *Comparative psychology: A handbook* (pp. 566–575). New York: Garland.

Savage-Rumbaugh, E. S., & Wilkerson, B. J. (1978). Sociosexual behavior in *Pan paniscus* and *Pan troglodytes:* A comparative study. *Journal of Human Evolution, 7,* 327–344.

Searcy, W. A., Search, M. H., & Marler, P. (1982). The response of swamp sparrows to acoustically distinct song types. *Behaviour, 80,* 70–83.

Seyforth, R. M., & Cheney, D. L. (1980). The ontogeny of vervet monkey alarm calling behavior: A preliminary report. *Zeitschrift fuer Tierpsychologie, 54,* 37–56.

Seyforth, R. M., & Cheney, D. L. (1990). The assessment by vervet monkeys of their own and another species' alarm calls. *Animal Behaviour, 40,* 754–764.

Turner, G. F., & Pitcher, T. J. (1986). Attack abatement: A model for group protection by combined avoidance and dilution. *American Naturalist, 128,* 228–240.

Wenner, A. (1998). The honey bee "dance language" controversy. In G. Greenberg & M. M. Haraway (Eds.), *Comparative Psychology: A handbook* (pp. 823–836). New York: Garland.

West, M. J., & King, A. P. (1988). Female visual displays affect the development of male song in the cowbird. *Nature, 334,* 244–246.

West, M. J., King, A. P. (1996). Eco-gen-actics: A systems approach to ontogeny of avian communication. In D. E. Kroodsma & E. H. Miller (Eds.), *Ecology and evolution of acoustic communication in birds* (pp. 20–38). Ithaca, NY: Cornell University Press.

Yasukawa, K. (1981). Male quality and female choice of a mate in the red-winged blackbird (*Agelaius phoeniceus*): A test of the Beau Geste hypothesis. *Animal Behaviour, 29,* 114–125.

Yasukawa, K., Blank, J. L., & Patterson, C. B. (1980). Song repertoire and sexual selection in the red-winged blackbird. *Behavioral Ecology and Sociobiology, 7,* 233–238.

7 Reproduction

Birds do it, bees do it, people do it—in fact the vast majority of organisms do it—but sexual reproduction often seems more trouble than it's worth. For organisms, sex often means spending huge amounts of energy finding and wooing desirable partners. Within the cell, male and female genomes must recombine without major mistakes. Gametes must promote compatible fusions while upholding barriers between species. And, at each step, the conflicting interests of each sex must be delicately negotiated in order to benefit the species as a whole. (Hines & Culotta, 1998)

Whenever the male and female of a species join together in performance of the behaviors that result in the reproduction of their species, they have engaged in sexual behavior. **Sexual reproduction** is ubiquitous among living organisms, being seen among protocells and viruses, plants, single-celled animals, and multicellular animals. Of course, our focus in this chapter will be on the reproductive activities of animals. Reproduction is a very complicated process; and mating systems are comprised of numerous elements, including courtship, pair formation, copulation, insemination, intercopulatory and postcopulatory events, fertilization, cooperative parental care, and offspring–parent bonding (Alexander, Marshall, & Cooley, 1997).

Much of what is known about mechanisms underlying reproduction in vertebrates comes from studies of laboratory rodents. Nevertheless, researchers have identified some generalities that apply widely. These include the following: (1) Male and female sexual behaviors involve different neural areas, different gonadal steroids, and different anatomical structures (i.e., genitalia); (2) the same hormonal mechanisms operate in all the vertebrates; (3) similar brain regions appear to be involved in a diverse section of species; and (4) masculine and feminine behaviors are plastic during two different developmental stages: once, early in differentiation, and again later, when hormones become active (Moore, 1998).

Asexual Reproduction and the Evolution of Sex

Before proceeding to further discussion of sexual reproduction, we wish to raise an important question: Is sex necessary? The answer is No! Many species successfully reproduce asexually in a variety of ways. Among protozoa, the paramecium reproduces by **asexual reproduction** in a process called **binary fission.** The animal's body elongates, the genetic material doubles and divides, and the animal splits into two new organisms, each with an identical genetic makeup. If all paramecia reproduced this way, they would all be very nearly exact clones of each other. In this event, there would be very little variation available in the gene pool to enable the species to adapt to significant environmental changes. But on some occasions, for example, during dry conditions when ponds dry up and food is scarce, two paramecia join together at their oral cavities and their internal contents completely join. This sexual-like process is known as **conjugation** (Figure 7.1). Each then divides by binary fission. There are now four new cells where there once were two, and each contains a combination of genetic material from the two original paramecia.

More complex animals also reproduce asexually. The hydra does so by a process of **budding,** in which new animals form from buds at an area of the body called the budding region. Under some circumstances, however, budding stops and the animals reproduce sexually, some developing sperm-producing cells, others egg-producing cells, and still others both sperm- and egg-producing cells. In all cases, however, sperm and eggs are released into the surrounding area and fertilization occurs. This form of reproduction arises when food becomes scarce or when the level of carbon dioxide surrounding the animal reaches a critical level. Carbon dioxide concentrations are raised under crowded conditions. This process, then, reflects a biotaxic way of controlling reproduction in the hydra (Figure 7.2).

We have seen that sex is not necessary for reproduction. It is also trouble. It is costly, exposing partners to aggression, potential predation, disease vectors, and other dangers. So why is there sex? Why did sexual behavior evolve? The mainstay of explanations has been that sexual reproduction provided for a greater degree of phenotypic variability. Recall from our discussions of evolution in Chapters 1 and 2 that the three essential premises of evolution by natural selection are that species reproduce in greater numbers than can survive, that these large numbers of offspring represent a wide distribution of traits, and that nature selects from these variable traits those that confer adaptive advantages in particular ecological niches. Thus, in desert species,

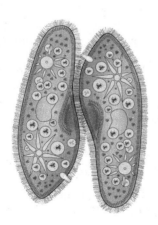

FIGURE 7.1   Conjugal Reproduction in the Paramecium

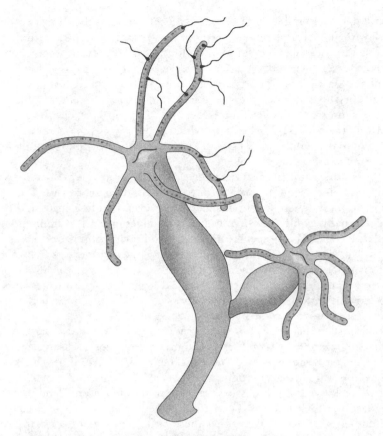

FIGURE 7.2   Reproduction by Budding in the Hydra

temperature tolerance is an adaptive trait. Those species members able to tolerate high temperatures survive to reproduce; those not able to tolerate such temperatures do not survive. Sexual reproduction involves recombining chromosomes and genes from a male parent and a female parent. This recombination of genetic material into many different possible arrangements provides great variability in traits, from which natural selection can choose. Sexual reproduction is thus seen as an adaptive phenomenon from an evolutionary perspective. It must be considered as well, however, that all this reshuffling may be as likely to break up good combinations of genes as to create them (Wuethrich, 1998).

For many years, the sort of analysis given above often was the only explanation offered for the evolution of sexual reproduction. Recently, however, a second hypothesis for the evolution of sexual reproduction has gained favor. It too is based on the recombination phenomenon that occurs as a result of male and female genetic contributions to offspring. But the **DNA Repair Hypothesis** (Bernstein, Hopf, & Michod,

1989) focuses on naturally occurring DNA damage and mutations (replication errors) that frequently lead to deleterious genetic combinations. According to this hypothesis, recombination of genetic material leads to the repair of replication errors and of damaged DNA. What is the best explanation for the evolution of sex? Many workers still understand this to be a major unsolved problem in evolutionary biology.

Sexual Reproduction

Species and Sexual Identification

In order for male and female **gametes** to join, several fundamental behavioral requirements have to be met. Males and females must get physically close to one another. (Sessile species solve this problem by using water and wind currents.) Movements must be guided or directed by stimuli from a potential reproductive partner; random movements of individuals are not likely to accomplish breeding in many species. Mates may be located via a wide variety of communication channels (Ehrman & Kim, 1998). Silk moth males respond neurally to as little as a single molecule of the female sex **pheromone;** drosophila, too, depend on pheromones during **courtship** and **mating;** crickets identify and attract partners by the sounds produced when they rub their hind limbs together; fiddler crabs attract mates by waving their chelae; firefly flashes are species-specific sexual advertisements, as are drosophila vibratory songs; frogs use species-typical vocal calls; crocodiles use roars; chameleons expose their dewlaps and also engage in head bobbing. Some mammals depend on olfactory cues to attract mates. For example, we often see dogs engaging in anogenital sniffing. Among many primates, both visual and chemical cues occurring in association with ovulation provide stimulation for sexual attraction of males toward a female. (Chapter 6 contains further discussion of stimulus channels of communication.)

Most animals cannot engage in sexual behavior until they have identified a potential mate. Species and sexual identification in many species are assured by the process of **sexual imprinting** (Chapter 5) and may be further facilitated by **sexual learning** (Chapter 9). Thus, many animals acquire their species identities early, as a result of the imprinting process, and may add to their sexual identification skills by later learning experiences. When the time comes for mating, they are able to respond differentially to appropriate members of their own species. But being responsive to sexually related stimuli solves only one of many problems. Gaining the acceptance of a mate is also problematic. In many cases, this process is aided by the display of courtship behavior.

Courtship

Partners usually must signal their intentions to mate, because both partners must be ready to mate at the same time. And both must perform their complementary sexual roles with competence (Figure 7.3). Courtship really is an attempt at social problem solving. Mates first have to find each other and then have to decide on and establish a social relationship. In the category of sexual behaviors, we often see very clearly the

FIGURE 7.3   Courtship Dance of Western Grebes

interrelationships of biological and psychosocial factors in behavior determination. Mating takes place only when mates are in a reproductive state, and this is very much a function of biological (e.g., hormonal) conditions. But these states are in turn much influenced by environmental factors such as day length, temperature, the presence of rain, and, of course, the presence of a potential mate.

Courtship is difficult. Besides being in the appropriate physiological condition, partners must find a potential mate and must coordinate their activities with those of the potential mate in ways that avoid conflicts. After all, the individual they have just sought out and chosen as a mating partner is likely to be a complete stranger. Perhaps for this reason, courtship often appears to arouse three response tendencies at once: to fight with a strange territorial intruder, to flee from a stranger, and to mate. The initial responses of males to females are often indistinguishable from typical aggressive displays of one male to another male. The "bowing coo" of the male ring dove is performed to both males and females. Thus, depending upon social circumstances, the display signals either aggression or courtship. The "fluffed feather posture" of the male chaffinch is likewise displayed to both males and females entering his territory. In general, attack postures are more likely to occur in those species characterized by minimal degrees of sexual dimorphism. The easier it is to tell a female from a male, the less likely are there to be threat displays by males toward females.

The interplay of conflicting motives occasioned by courtship is nicely illustrated by the well-known **zig-zag display** of courting three-spined stickleback fish (*Gasterosteus aculeatus*). This behavior appears to incorporate the conflict between competing response tendencies of approach (toward a potential mate) and withdrawal (away from a stranger) into a single pattern of movement. Other similar examples include the zig-zag display of courting chaffinches and the alternating postures of pointing toward and then away from the potential mate by courting gulls. Many species incorporate components of attack or aggressive responses into their copulatory sequences. Among cats, minks, and ferrets, for example, the male typically bites the female about the back of the neck during copulation. Other species reverse this process, incorporating sexual gestures into their aggressive encounters. For example, both primate females and males of subordinate status often express submission by displaying their hindquarters to a dominant male, who then may briefly mount and thrust either the male or the female.

Breeding Seasons

Mating is not a random event. It takes place at predictable times during the year. Each species has a regular mating or breeding season. Of course, this leads to a question— why do these mating periods occur when they do? For many species, the reason is the location of the breeding season. For example, the young of many species residing in the temperate zones of the earth are born during the spring and summer when the weather is mild and food is plentiful (Adsell, 1964).

As we see in Table 7.1, the **breeding seasons** and the gestation periods for many mammals are coordinated to ensure birth during a favorable period. There are, of course, obvious exceptions to the rule—bears that hibernate give birth in midwinter! The young do not emerge from the protection of the den, however, until the mother leaves it in early spring.

How do these animals know when to breed to fit this timetable? Of course, the animals are not aware of mathematical relations associating breeding seasons, gestation lengths, and environmental seasons. Rather, their behavior is stimulated by environmental conditions such as day length and temperature. The dark-eyed junco (*Junco hyemalis*), for example, winters in the United States and breeds in the spring in Canada. The **testes** of the males regress and become nonfunctional in the fall and grow again in the spring. Males that were captured in the fall and exposed to artificially increasing spring-like day lengths for six weeks showed almost normal spring growth of their testes, something not shown in control animals similarly caged but exposed to normal winter-season day lengths.

Illumination changes have four categories of effects. Systematic increases in illumination increase the activity of the anterior pituitary gland and this, in turn, leads to the development of **gonads** (**ovaries** of females, testes of males); increased anterior pituitary gland activity also leads to ovulation; increased illumination induces **ova**, or **egg**, placement and **sperm** emission in spawning species; and increased illumination has direct effects on the neural mechanisms associated with courtship and mating. Thus, day length functions as a signal that animals interpret physiologically and respond to behaviorally. The interpretation of the signal involves the entire set of physiological processes that transforms information about changing illumination conditions and mediates their effects on reproductive processes. Yet, other environmental conditions influence reproductive behavior as well. Temperature affects the reproductive behavior of ground

TABLE 7.1 **Breeding Seasons, Gestation Periods, and Birth Seasons for Several Mammalian Species**

Species	Breeding Season	Gestation Period	Births
Fallow deer	October–November	8 months	June–July
Wapiti (elk)	September-October	8 months	May–June
Hanglu	October	6 months	April
Japanese deer	September–November	8 months	May–June
Mule deer	November–December	6 months	May–June
Moose	September–October	8 months	May–June
Reindeer	September–October (Siberia)	8 months	May–June
Roe deer	July–August	10 months	May–June
European wildcat	March–May	2+ months	May–July
Bobcat	February–April	1.5–2 months	May–June
Puma	March–June	3 months	June–September
Northern coyote	February–April	2 months	April–June
Wolf	Late January–March	2 months	Late March–May
Arctic fox	April–May	2 months	June–July
Alaska fur seal	July–August	12 months	July–August
California sea lion	June 15–July 15	11.5 months	June
Steller's sea lion	May–June	12 months	May–June
Walrus	June	11 months	May

Source: Bermant & Davidson (1974), p. 57.

squirrels, which show a cycle of testicular activity independent of illumination. And rainfall may exert an effect on breeding behavior such that in some species, such as desert dwelling frogs and toads, reproductive activities follow the first rains of the season.

Female mammals that are sexually receptive in connection with ovulation are said to be "in heat," or in **estrus.** Estrus is a cyclic phenomenon, but the cycle may be interrupted by copulation, which normally results in pregnancy. Species in which the female cycles throughout the year (e.g., rats, mice, and most primates) are said to be *totally* **polyestrous;** those that cycle repeatedly during particular breeding seasons (e.g., horses, sheep, goats) are said to be **seasonally polyestrous;** and those species that cycle only once during their breeding season (e.g., bears) are referred to as **monestrous.** There may be differences within a species. Among dogs, for example, basenji females come into estrus annually close to the time of the autumnal equinox. Most other breeds have estrus cycles at any season of the year and about six months apart (Ehrman & Kim, 1998).

During these cycles, female **receptivity** is tied closely to ovulation. The evolutionary advantage of this arrangement is that females are maximally receptive at the time of maximum opportunity for pregnancy. Many animals show **spontaneous ovulation,** independent of their behavior during estrus—this is true of laboratory rodents, cattle, and dogs, among others. Cats and rabbits, however, do not ovulate unless they copulate. Although there are numerous physiological factors associated with estrus, its defining characteristics are behavioral—a female must be receptive to a male and must accept him for copulation.

As with other aspects of sexual behavior, the estrous cycle is under the control of environmental stimuli. A crucial factor again is light. Among many laboratory rodents, the timing of the four-day cycle is dependent on lighting conditions such that the cycle begins in the early evening. Experimentally manipulated shifts in evening onset result in corresponding shifts in the timing of female receptivity. Another crucial factor appears to be the social environment and the odors produced by conspecifics. The presence of a male shortens the cycle in female mice and also results in the synchronization of the cycles of several females housed together with males. These effects do not occur in anosmic females (which have been rendered unresponsive to odor stimulation).

These olfactory effects are mediated by compounds in male urine. One set of findings, labeled the **Bruce effect** (Bermant & Davidson, 1974; Parkes & Bruce, 1961), shows that male mouse urine interferes with successful pregnancy. If a female copulates and is then exposed to vapor from the urine of a second male, she is less likely to become pregnant than if she remains unexposed to these compounds. A related phenomenon, labeled the **Coolidge effect** (Bermant & Davidson, 1974), shows effects on male mating behavior. Males of many species usually copulate once and then require a period of time to recover before additional copulations can occur. In the presence of strange females, however, these recovery periods become much abbreviated. The Coolidge effect takes its name from an amusing story about remarks attributed to President and Mrs. Calvin Coolidge on the occasion of a visit to a chicken farm. Mrs. Coolidge remarked on the impressive attentiveness of a flock rooster to his hens and said that someone should point this out to Mr. Coolidge. President Coolidge retorted by remarking on the large number of hens that were available to the rooster and said that someone should point this out to Mrs. Coolidge. Like other behavior, estrous behavior results from a complex interplay of behavioral, hormonal, and nervous system processes (Moore, 1998).

To some degree there has been a shift from the biological to the psychological control of mating behavior among the primates. This shift is seen most obviously among humans but also extends to many other primate species. Nevertheless, there is evidence showing that primates respond to olfactory cues associated with reproduction. Thus, during estrus the vaginal tracts of rhesus and other monkeys contain volatile compounds to which males respond with sexual interest and arousal. Nevertheless, anosmic male monkeys copulate as frequently as normals throughout the female menstrual cycle, showing that sexual activity is not nearly as dependent on olfactory control as it appears to be in many nonprimate species (Goldfoot, Essock-Vitale, Asa, Thornton, & Leshner, 1978). Indeed, differential responsiveness of humans to odors collected at varying times during the menstrual cycle has recently been confirmed (Cutler, 1999; Stern & McClintock, 1998; Weller, 1998).

Mating Systems and Sexual Selection

A mating system is that aspect of a species' social organization that illustrates the ways in which males and females get together for the purpose of breeding. Outstanding among the varieties of mating systems are monogamy, polygamy, and promiscuity. There are several important questions to be considered in connection with mating systems: Why are some species monogamous and some polygamous? Why do males of some species fight over females? And what factors influence the choice of a mate?

Monogamy.   **Monogamous** animals are those in which breeding adults mate with only one individual. This pattern obviously resolves the problem of access to mates (Zilman, 1998). Monogamous breeding was long thought to be rather common in many species and rare only in mammals. However, biologists using new genetic techniques for determining paternity now report studies of organisms from birds to gibbons to rodents, which have revealed that some offspring raised by seemingly monogamous parents were in fact fathered by different males (Angier, 1995; Morell, 1998). There are variations of **monogamy.** Those species that are *perennially monogamous* mate for life or at least for periods of several years. This arrangement occurs in swans and some species of geese and cranes, among wolves and some other canids, and among the primates is typical in several species of small New World monkeys, in gibbons, and, to a considerable extent, in humans. Some species are *seasonally monogamous*, meaning that pairs get together for mating purposes but live apart out of their breeding seasons. This is the case among most migratory songbirds in which it is extremely difficult for pairs to remain together for long migratory flights. Among migratory songbirds, however, there is a tendency to return to the same breeding areas season after season. Thus, some individuals may remate in successive breeding seasons only to part again during the fall migration.

Monogamy tends to occur when the sex ratio is biased toward males and when the occurrence of receptive females is unpredictable (Preston-Mafham & Preston-Mafham, 1993). Among invertebrates, two forms of monogamy occur: *female guarding*, in which the male mates once and subsequently protects his mate from other males, thereby protecting his parentage of her offspring; and *male assistance*, in which the male stays with the female after mating and assists her in the care of the offspring, thereby increasing the probability of offspring survival.

Polygamy.   **Polygamous** animals are those in which an individual may have two or more mates that, in their turn, do not mate with others. In **polygamy,** some form of pair bond exists among the mates. Such pair bonds can be either simultaneous, in which the single individual maintains bonds with a number of mates at the same time, or they can be successive. In what is known as *serial polygamy*, an individual has a series of mates in succession, although only one mate at any time. This arrangement also is known as *serial monogamy*.

In **polygyny,** a single male mates with two or more females. This system is found in many mammalian species but only in about 2 percent of avian species. In **polyandry,** it is the female that takes more than one mate. Polyandrous species at least partially reverse some of the differences in gender characteristics seen in many species. Thus, it is common for the female to be the more territorial, dominant, and colorful member of the pair. This arrangement is nicely illustrated in the phalaropes, a family of shorebirds breeding primarily in the Arctic Circle and migrating to the south for the winter. In the courtship of such species, females actively seek out and court males, and it is typically the male that incubates the clutch of eggs while the female seeks and courts another male for additional mating. Polyandry is seen also in many quails and pheasants.

In insects polygyny is the norm, perhaps because there are many chances to achieve multiple matings. Female and resource defense by males often occurs among insects as it does in many other groups of species. A form of polygyny referred to as scramble competition occurs in swarming insects such as gnats and mosquitoes. As the term implies, this typically is a free-for-all mating system in which males race to reach each receptive female first (Preston-Mafham & Preston-Mafham, 1993). In these mating systems, females typically mate only once and, therefore, only with a single male. Many males, however, succeed in mating numerous times.

A number of species focus breeding activities in the location of a traditional breeding ground on which individual males establish small **breeding territories,** which they must defend aggressively against all competitors. This type of breeding ground is known as a **lek,** and the species that breed in this way are known as lek breeders. An example of lek breeding is shown by the North American sage grouse (*Centrocercus urophasianus*). Several weeks prior to the breeding season, males begin to gather and compete for territories on the lek. After a number of days of competition, a few superdominant males have gained stable possession of the choice locations in the lek and the remaining males begin to compete for positions along the edges of these territories. Often the situation at each territory becomes stable once males of second-order dominance establish their subterritories, about equidistant from one another, around the edges of a dominant bird's territory. These second-order birds now protect the superbird from further challenges by other males, as well as protecting their own positions at the edges of his territory. Most of the male population are unable to establish places either at the center or around the immediate edges of a choice territory and must content themselves with parading around the edges of the lek.

Although there are large numbers of animals present in leks, females choose the males in such arrangements, and there is no scramble by males to reach females. Females that are ready to mate are drawn toward the center of the large group of parading males at the lek. They are met by a dominant male at the edge of his territory and are escorted to its center, where further courtship and copulation occurs. Occasionally it happens that more than one female comes forward to breed at the same time, and one of the second-order birds will have an opportunity to breed while the territory owner is occupied. In a large field study of breeding behavior among sage grouse (Wiley, 1978), it was estimated that the relatively small number of dominant territory owners accounted for a large majority of breeding, the somewhat more numerous second-order birds for most of the remaining breeding, and the great number of lesser dominant males, together, for very little breeding.

Promiscuity.   Another type of mating system may be considered a form of polygamy except that no pair bonds are formed and both males and females may copulate with multiple partners during a single period of breeding. This type of breeding arrangement is known as **promiscuity.** The ancestral mating system among fish was very likely a form of promiscuity in which external fertilization occurred involving many males and females simultaneously (Berglund, 1997). This system is seen today among cod (*Gadus morhua*) and herring (*Clupea harangus*). Some nesting or brooding fish also may be promiscuous, as in the mouth brooder Lake Malawi cichlid (*Cyrtocara eucinostomous*), the brooding pipefish (*Sygnathus typhle*), and the nest-building garibaldi (*Hypsypops rubicundus*). Promiscuity leaves few options for exercising mate choice, and this may account for the lack of **sexual dimorphism** in such species. (Sexual dimorphism is the possession of identifying male and female physical features.)

Some degree of promiscuity is characteristic of mating among most nonhuman primates (Zilman, 1998). It is a mating strategy that has some obvious adaptive advantages. Not only does it curtail sexually based aggression by providing broad access to mates, but it also provides for a great degree of genetic recombination. Among bonnet macaques, for example, all males mate with estrous females. Little fighting occurs and social rank is of no importance. Among chimpanzees, social rank appears more important for mate access. Although males of widely ranging social status have a fair degree of access to sexually receptive females, high-ranking males may assert priority in courting females at the height of their estrus. Different chimpanzee groups differ with respect to the prevalence of female solicitation of mates. In the Gombe reserve of Tanganyika, only 15 percent of copulations are female solicited, whereas in the Budongo Forest of Uganda, most copulations are female solicited. Among howler monkeys, females solicit freely until copulation is achieved, and the males of a group appear to participate sexually on an equal basis.

Additional Varieties of Mating Systems.   Because mating systems can be influenced by many different factors, many species display a mixture of the various mating systems just described. Different populations within a single species, and even different individuals within a single population, may adopt different mating systems. This situation is illustrated rather obviously in our own species. Humans of different cultures and even different individuals within the same culture may be either perennially or serially monogamous, polygynous, polyandrous, or promiscuous.

Most mating systems are polygynous; although polyandry, once widely thought to be rare, is now understood to occur with considerable frequency (Angier, 1995). Monogamy appears to occur in cases in which two-parent care of offspring is highly desirable or necessary, in which mutual defense by both parents is important, or in which population density is low. Relaxation of any of these conditions may result in a change from monogamy toward polygamy (Berglund, 1997).

The mating systems we have discussed are characteristic of normal two-sex species. Other systems are possible in other species. Aplysia, or sea slugs, for example, are

hermaphrodites: A single animal may self-fertilize its own eggs. Cleaner fish show a mating system referred to as *protogynous hermaphroditism*, in which a single individual first acts as a female, then as a male—structurally and behaviorally! Among this species, a single male dominates a harem of three to six mature females, which maintains a linear dominance hierarchy. When the male dies, the largest and most dominant female transforms itself into a male within a span of only several hours. A similar situation is true for the coral reef fish (*Anthias squamipinnis*), which mature as females and are kept from becoming male by inhibitory stimulation associated with the presence of resident males. Reducing the numbers of males present in a population results in the occurrence of female changes into males (Moore, 1998). Individual sexual characteristics in many species of fish depend on a complex relationship of genetic and environmental factors including water pressure and temperature as well as local social conditions (Elia, 1988).

Competition for and among Mates

We have alluded to the costs and risks of mating. One of these is the potential for fighting to occur among strangers. Fighting may occur not only between rival males and rival females but also between the potential mating pair itself (Preston-Mafham & Preston-Mafham, 1993). Most often really damaging fights are avoided; the costs of injurious battles outweigh the benefits. Even so, however—and contrary to popular belief—there are many instances in which such fighting leads to death (Zilman, 1998). When fighting does occur, contests may be ritualized, and there may be a precombat display that allows the contestants to assess their chances of winning. This "risk assessment" involves the display of body parts showing the relative size of each potential combatant.

Male bighorn sheep engage in jousting matches in which the size and structure of their massive curved horns play an important role in the outcome (Figure 7.4A). The size of a ram's horns increase with each year of his life and signify not only his skill at surviving but also his adeptness at finding excellent pasturage (Geist, 1998). Only males that are somewhat evenly matched are likely to engage in a jousting match. Potential rivals go through an extended mutual visual inspection of one another prior to the onset of any combat. Small-horned males usually defer readily to a much larger-horned rival. When two well-matched males meet for the first time, however, an extended joust is likely to occur. After sizing each other up sufficiently, the combatants face each other from several meters apart and stare each other in the eyes. Then both charge forward at once, rise onto their hind legs for the final few steps, then drop forward and lunge, crashing their heads together, each receiving the blow near the base of the horns. Repeated charges may be made over long periods of time, until one of the combatants quits and retires, leaving the field and the victory to his rival. These combatants will recognize one another, at least for the length of the current breeding season. The question of dominance between them having been settled, it need not be contested further, at least for a while.

Somewhat similar contests occur among male white-tailed deer, which receive one another's charges on their tined antlers (Figure 7.4B). Then with antlers engaged,

FIGURE 7.4A   Jousting of Bighorn Rams—before Contact

FIGURE 7.4B   Sparring of White-Tailed Deer

they churn forward with their feet in a vigorous effort to gain enough purchase to force the rival backward and, perhaps, to throw him off of his feet. The tines, or "points," of the antlers are functional in fending off a rival's antlers and keeping them at a distance from one's own head and eyes. Again, once the issue has been settled between a given pair of bucks, one will have dominance over the other for the remainder of the breeding season—a definite advantage for the dominant buck in the event that both should attempt courtship of the same doe at the same time. Unlike the situation with the horns of the bighorn sheep, the antlers of the buck deer are features of sexual dimorphism that are shed at the end of each breeding season and grown anew prior to the beginning of the next. Thus, the buck's antlers do not necessarily get bigger year after year but, instead, reflect both his maturity and the state of his physiological condition each year.

Males frequently fight longer and harder for high-value resources such as the prime spot in a lek or a female that is ready to breed. Two different systems of fighting have been identified as occurring across a broad range of species. One of these is a "war of attrition" in which costs associated with fighting escalate with the duration of the conflict. In such contests success is measured by persistence, and the outcome may rest partly with the winner's nutritional status; the better-fed animal is likely to have the greater amount of stamina. The other form of fighting is the "hawk–dove" system shown by species equipped with weapons such as the "stabbing legs" of some thirps. Such weapons may be capable of ending a contest rather quickly.

Male competition for mates is likely to be high among polygynous mammals such as antelopes, buffalo, camels, deer, goats, horses, hippopotamuses, pigs, sea lions, sheep, sperm whales, and zebras, among other species (Zilman, 1998). The development of a polygynous mating system in these species may have been related to the greater physical strength of males over females. Thus, a powerful male may have been able readily to dominate a number of females. When access to females is controlled by intermale fighting, the mating system can be a costly one; males may be injured, and even killed, in male-to-male competition. Rarely, males may also fight with females to the extent of conveying injury.

In many cases, there are outstanding aspects of cooperation, as well as competition, in the breeding behavior of males (Zilman, 1998). Cooperation is seen in species that maintain communal breeding grounds such as many frogs and grouse. Among long-tailed manakin, a species of birds, two males cooperate in an elaborate song and dance to court a single female. Successful courting results in copulation by only one of the males, most often the same male of this pair, with the second male, or "helper," rarely gaining a chance to mate. Why then does the helper cooperate in this behavior? What advantage does this system afford to him? It may be that this arrangement gives the helper access to a territory that, when vacated by the successful mating male, provides the helper with prime access to a new female. Or it may sometimes occur that more than one receptive female is attracted to the area at the same time, and the helper may be able to achieve copulation with the second female while the dominant male is occupied with the first. Observations of such occurrences have been reported for the sage grouse, a lek-breeding species of North America (Gibson & Bradbury, 1987). Potential advantages to subordinate males in such cooperative systems, however, are a subject that requires further empirical study (Hayes, 1994).

A Phylogenetic Perspective on the Evolution of Reproductive Behavior

Invertebrates. Sexual reproduction first appeared in water-dwelling animals, this environment providing no obstacle to reproducing among animals that conjugate, or fuse. But with the appearance of gametes, water hazards such as currents resulted in the appearance of new reproductive strategies (Maxwell, 1994). Two distinct reproductive strategies have evolved, the *r* and the **K reproductive strategies.** The *r* strategy works toward ensuring adequate survival rates through the production of vast numbers of eggs and offspring at one time. Among *r* strategists, some individual females produce millions of eggs, only a small proportion of which will survive. The *r* strategy is widespread among sea animals and insects. Individual oysters, for example, produce between 500,000 and 1,000,000 eggs. Some of these are fertilized externally by sperm that have also been released into the surrounding water. The *r* strategy requires only a small parental investment per individual offspring. More intense parental care is impossible when there are so many eggs and offspring.

In the alternate, or *K* strategy, females produce few eggs and either gestate them or otherwise tend to them with diligence. The female octopus, for example, receives a sperm packet, internally, from the male. Fertilized eggs are then deposited in a sheltered place protected by the female (Elia, 1988; Maxwell, 1994). Whereas oysters produce hundreds of thousands of eggs, birds produce relatively few, with clutch sizes rarely exceeding ten. Parental investment among birds is intense, with numerous daily episodes of feeding and other parental behaviors. Multiple births among mammals are also quite limited in numbers. Rarely do numbers of young exceed the numbers of teats possessed by females. Nursing is extremely intense, forming the basis of social attachment in primates and perhaps in other mammals as well (Harlow, 1962).

Mating in some species of insects and spiders is deadly for the males, which are killed by the females following fertilization. This is the case with the black widow spider (*Latrodectus mactans*), the male of which is useless after fertilizing eggs (Maxwell, 1994). Much invertebrate sexual behavior is organized at the taxic and biotaxic levels of complexity. These levels of organization are not surprising given the relative lack of opportunities in these species to engage in learning experiences with parents—opportunities that are common to virtually all young mammals and birds (Alexander, Marshall, & Cooley, 1997). It often may be the case that the adult parents of young insects are dead before the infants hatch. Indeed, in a large number of species, individuals may never encounter another member of their own species prior to mating. Even when adults are present, parent–infant interactions are nonexistent among insects. Evidence from some insect species shows that individuals raised in total isolation show no mating deficits.

Although courtship and mating behaviors are varied and may be quite complex, they are organized rather simply by taxic and biotaxic factors such as tactual and pheromonal contact. Practices vary widely, as does anatomy, and can be quite complex, sometimes involving sperm deposits into which the female crawls and subsequently ingests, as in centipedes, such as *Scutigera colepatra*. Mating in Pulmonata (slugs, snails) seems to involve biotaxic factors, in that the process involves much mutual body contact as well as responsiveness to mucous secretions. The great grey slug (*Limax maximus*) performs an elaborate mating activity while suspended in midair from a long string of mucous. Among millipedes (Diplopoda), the male beats his front legs against the body of the female prior to transferring sperm to her via these same, specially modified, front legs. In the millipede species *Chordeuma silvestre*, males and females make contact by using acoustic stimulation. Once contact is established, tactual stimulation from the male keeps the female from withdrawing. As courtship continues, the female licks a gland of the male, and he secretes a pheromone that elicits the performance of copulatory postures by the female. Pheromonal communication plays an important role in almost all millipede courtship (Preston-Mafham & Preston-Mafham, 1993).

It is interesting that although reproduction is necessary for species survival, it sometimes proves deleterious to individual animals. Thus, longevity among female *Drosophila* is reduced when they are kept together with males (Partridge, 1988). The reasons for this may involve energy loss as a result of excessive egg laying or harm from males. Other examples are seen in the black widow spider and the praying mantis, in which mating proves fatal to the male.

Vertebrates

Fish. Given the enormous range in size of fish, from the pygmy goby at 0.00002 ounces and 0.33 inches to the whale shark at 12 tons and 70 feet, it is remarkable that they almost universally evolved **gonochorism,** or two distinct sexes (Elia, 1988). Sexual maturity in fish is closely linked to size, which in turn is linked to longevity. Small tropical species such as the dwarf perch (*Micrometrus minimus*) are sexually mature shortly after birth, whereas larger species of one foot or more may mature sexually only after two to five years of growth. Sturgeon, reaching a length of up to ten feet, mature later, at around fifteen years of age.

The three major groups of fish—cyclostomes, elasmobranchs, and bony fish— each show different reproductive methods. The cyclostomes, jawless roundmouths, are true hermaphrodites. Eggs and sperm may pass from any individual's gonads to be united and to develop externally. Elasmobranchs (sharks, skates, rays) show internal fertilization; young may be born live or may be hatched from eggs, depending on the species. Bony fish (such as aquarium and common food types) display a wide array of reproductive behaviors: sexually dimorphic species with internal or external fertilization, hermaphroditic species showing internal and external fertilization, and all-female species with internal fertilization (Elia, 1988).

Sexual selection in fish is not as pronounced as in land vertebrates probably because they do not have difficulty in locating mates, do not depend on physical contact for fertilization, and usually do not show a pattern of complex parental care. There is, however, a downside to this lack of sexual selection: Not all species are easily capable of distinguishing male from female conspecifics. Problems of gender discrimination are seen in zebrafish, some angelfish species, and herring. Among the cues that attract a female to a male fish are the chemistry of his secretions, the vibrations of his swimming, and perhaps properties of the nest he has built. Sometimes attractants bring more than one female and male together at the same time (Elia, 1988).

In many small freshwater fish, egg laying is synchronized with sunrise. In the presence of a male who courts successfully, a female expels her eggs from her oviducts. In the absence of a courting male, the female retains her eggs. This system reflects a complex interplay of stimulation combining daily and seasonal changes with social factors. Stimulation important to the reproductive process reaches the female via water currents and visual cues. As we have indicated elsewhere, sexuality in fish is under environmental as well as gonadal and genetic control. Crowding, starvation, social stress, and temperature influence gender in fish. "There is no natural law that demands that there be just two sexes in every species or that individuals retain one sex identity for life" (Elia, 1988, p. 49).

Among the most interesting reproductive patterns of fish is that of salmon, noted for their remarkable upstream swimming to return to their natal streams for spawning. Once considered an instinct under genetic control, this behavior can now be seen from the more parsimonious perspective of behavioral development taken throughout this book. The results of numerous experiments from a variety of scientific disciplines can be pooled to account for the salmon's spectacular but understandable behavior. It is now known that these fish early in life become imprinted to the chemical signature of waters from their home streams and later, as adults, recognize and respond preferentially to those waters (Schulz, Horall, Cooper, & Hasler, 1976). As adults nearing the time for spawning (Figure 7.5), they travel up and down a seacoast in response to changing water temperatures as the seasons change (Jonsson, Jonsson, & Hansen, 1990). As they swim through the dispersed effluent from upstream rivers—such currents can now be seen in images taken aboard the space shuttle—these fish cannot help but pass through water that is familiar to them. They initially orient to home waters as a result of taste and olfactory cues, then continue orienting on the basis of concentration gradients of home water elements within the stream. Maintenance of an orientation toward the elements of the home stream thus enables salmon to make correct choices at forks within the rivers and streams that lead to their natal waters (Elia, 1988). Once they have arrived at their natal streams, males pair with females and become aggressive to other males (Maxwell, 1994). The female lays eggs in a trench she has fashioned with her fins, and her mate then sheds his sperm over these eggs.

Sharks, and other cartilaginous fish, are capable of internal fertilization. The male fertilizes eggs via an organ that is part of his pelvic fins. This organ becomes

FIGURE 7.5   Male Salmon Ready to Spawn

erect under the influence of the hormone epinephrine during courtship of the female. Some sharks give birth to live young. These developments appear to anticipate reproductive arrangements that become common among more recently evolved vertebrates, chiefly among reptiles and mammals.

Finally, we have seen earlier that many fish display something of a reversal of the sex roles most often seen among more recently evolved vertebrates. It is quite common among fish for the male to receive a female's eggs in a nest he has prepared long before her appearance and for him to guard the eggs after fertilization and to guard the fry after hatching. An outstanding variation on this pattern is seen among sea horses. After fertilizing the eggs deposited by a female, the male tucks the fertilized eggs into a special receptacle and holds them within his body after until they are ready for hatching.

Amphibians and Reptiles. "Because we believe animals evolved from water to land habitats, we believe that reproductive trends proceed from minimal courtship, external fertilization, egg laying in large clutches, water spawning, and parental indifference toward the opposite situation in each case" (Elia, 1988, p. 70). The move to land was accompanied by a shift from *r* strategy to *K* strategy reproduction, from large egg clutches to small, and from simple courtship to complex. Coming out of the water was a giant evolutionary step, though amphibians took it only partially. They still must return to water for reproduction.

Frogs form **breeding congresses,** the males in great numbers calling loudly. Although it was once believed that the females simply followed these calls to the males, it now seems likely that they also are attracted to breeding areas by the odors of the algae growing in the breeding pools (Elia, 1988). These breeding areas contain thousands of reproducing pairs. Males mount females, clasping them by means of their forelegs. The male holds on tightly—in some species for days or even weeks—without releasing the female. Indeed, "even when the female is twice the size of the male, as in the African clawed toad, she can be squeezed so energetically that she faints, the male pressing out her eggs after she has lost consciousness" (Elia, 1988, p. 96). The female releases eggs in response to the tactual stimulation of the male's clasp. Lacking a penis, he releases sperm on top of the eggs. Except in three species—the bell toad (*Ascaphus truei*), the African frog (*Nectophrynoides*), and the frog *Ascaphus*—there usually is no contact between male and female reproductive organs.

Although many male frogs attract females by means of their loud calls, some individual males are notably silent. These males sometimes ambush a female as she makes her way toward a calling male, thereby achieving their own successful copulations by subterfuge, so to speak. Aggressive territory owners often chase these free-loading males away, however (Maxwell, 1994). The number of progeny produced by frogs varies widely, from a single egg laid by the Cuban frog, *Sminthillus*, to as many as 25,000 laid by the giant frog, *Rana goliath*.

Among lizards, the visual cues that attract females to males include a species-specific pattern of head bobbing, dramatic expansion of the throat sac, mouth opening, and tongue showing. It is of interest to note that head bobbing is also a component of threat display in these animals. Already present among these relatively primitive vertebrates, then, we may discern a close relationship between sexual and aggressive behavior. The reptiles also reveal the development of widespread and elaborate courtship, as well as being the first vertebrate group to engage in widespread copulation and the first to develop widespread and extensive female care of the young (Elia, 1988).

Reproductive activity in amphibians and reptiles is much influenced by light. It plays an important role in egg ripening, migration to breeding places, and sexual readiness (Elia, 1988). In frogs, reptiles, and birds, light is detected not only by the eyes but also by the pineal gland in the brain. With these species we see the evolutionary emergence as strong trends of nest building, incubation, and gestation accompanied by posthatching or postbirth care of the young.

Birds. Sexual dimorphism among birds is varied. It is well defined in some species and not clear at all in others. In some species males and females differ in appearance only during the mating season. Birds generally copulate by pressing together their cloacae as the male stands on the female's back. The cloacae are of both males and females and serve at once as the point of egress of all bodily wastes as well as the organ of transfer of sexual material from male to female. These organs are similar in males and females, except that the cloacae of males contain papillae, through which sperm are transferred to the female. A slight exception to this arrangement is seen in ducks, swans, and flightless birds such as ostriches and emus. In these species the male's papilla has achieved the status of a penis, which is inserted into the female's cloaca at copulation.

Internal fertilization of eggs in birds is a big evolutionary advance over the external techniques used by most amphibians. Successful courtship among birds relies on the songs and plumage of the males to gain and maintain possession of a desirable breeding territory as well as to attract a female. Pair bonding and social cooperation of the breeding pair are further aided by the performance of numerous species-typical displays of movement and dance that make use of a wide range of auditory, visual, and tactual stimulation (Figure 7.6).

Mammals/Primates. The primates display a wide variety of breeding behavior that encompasses nearly the entire range of breeding behavior among mammals. We noted earlier that most primates display a large degree of promiscuity in their sexual behavior (Zilman, 1998). In rhesus monkeys, a receptive female consorts with one dominant male for a period of many hours, then leaves the first to form a temporary association with another and then, perhaps, with still another. Males of lesser dominance often achieve matings either before or after a female has reached the height of her estrus. A similar pattern is seen among chimpanzees, except that couples don't remain in extended consort with one another after copulating. Many primate species display what are known as one-male groups, in which several mature females live more or less permanently in a social group in which there is a single dominant male. The dominant male in these groups has the opportunity to reserve most breeding opportunities with the group's females to himself. Thus, there is a strong element of polygamy illustrated in these groups. Often, however, other mature males within the group, and sometimes males from outside the group, are able to achieve copulations with group females. Dominant male gorillas often allow other mature males within the group to copulate with a female

FIGURE 7.6 Displaying Male Prairie Chicken

of the group without interference (Schaller, 1963). Patas monkeys live in one-male groups with high female-to-male ratios. The group male retains exclusive access to his sexually receptive females as well as he can, but nongroup males often succeed in "stealing" copulations despite his best efforts. Interestingly, nongroup males of this species also join group males in providing defensive behavior when young and females of a group are threatened by a predator. A more exclusively polygamous mating system exists among hamadryas baboons, in which several mature females are bonded to a single dominant male for long periods of time and breed almost exclusively with him.

Monogamous mating systems are seen among many small New World monkeys, the marmosets, tamarins, and titis, as well as among gibbons, the small apes of Southeast Asia. All of these species live on their own territories in single male–single female groups, and all establish and maintain possession of their territories by singing species-typical songs. Humans also display a strong tendency to form monogamous pair bonds on the basis of sexual behavior, as we shall address at greater length, but human mating behavior also is quite varied and, in one situation or another, may illustrate any of the various mating systems we have described. More information on sexual behavior, in relation to the characteristics of social groups, can be found in Chapter 5.

Within the group we may call the *higher primates*, comprised of the gibbons, orangutans, gorillas, chimpanzees, and ourselves, an inverse relationship has been suggested to exist between degree of sexual dimorphism and tendency toward monogamy (Maxwell, 1994). That is to say, the more greatly dimorphous species will tend less toward monogamy, and the more slightly dimorphous species will tend more toward monogamy. Indeed, the two members of this group that show the greatest degrees of sexual dimorphism—the gorilla and the orangutan—also display strongly polygamous mating tendencies; and the members of the group showing the least degrees of sexual dimorphism—the gibbons—display very strong monogamous mating tendencies.

However, both chimpanzees and humans show moderate degrees of sexual dimorphism but are dissimilar in their tendencies to form monogamous pair bonds. Chimpanzees seem to be almost totally promiscuous in mating and display no tendency toward monogamous bonds. Humans, on the other hand, display a wide variety of mating styles ranging from promiscuity and polygamy to monogamy. Notwithstanding this variation, there is unquestionably a strong tendency of humans to form monogamous pair bonds in association with sexual behavior. Simply consider the dominant occurrence of the pair-bonding theme of love stories and of falling into and out of love that pervades the popular literature, music, and drama of cultures throughout the world and as far back into human history as we can look (e.g., Cahill, 1998). Human pair bonds very frequently are long-lasting and often lifelong, as characterized by many of the marriage ceremonies that have been inaugurated throughout the world's different human cultures.

Maxwell (1994) also proposed the existence of a positive relationship between the size of the penis in a species and a tendency toward monogamy. This relationship appears less demonstrated by fact than the previous one. It is true that human males possess by far the largest penis found among the higher primates and that our species also displays strong tendencies toward monogamous pair bonds. However, the chimpanzee, with the second-largest penis in the group, displays complete promiscuity in mating, and the gibbons, with rather small penises, display probably the greatest degree of monogamy encountered in the higher primates.

Even so, the evolution of a large penis in our species may be seen to complement the development of a number of other outstanding sexual characteristics that, together, may be viewed as adaptations for the provision of heightened sexual experiences. These heightened sexual experiences, it may then be suggested, have functioned to strengthen the development of monogamous pair bonds between mates, and these bonds have resulted in increased survival rates of our very slowly maturing offspring—the slowest to mature of any animal species. What are these other outstanding sexual characteristics of our species? Actually, they make quite an impressive list.

First, unlike breeding behavior in other mammals and all other primates, breeding behavior in humans is virtually free of dependence upon estrous cycles. We have seen earlier that estrus is limited to a distinct breeding season in numerous animals and that breeding behavior is largely confined to the breeding season. In animals that breed throughout the year, breeding behavior still is largely restricted to the estrous season of an individual female. Neither males nor females appear much interested in sexual behavior outside the context of female estrus. The outstanding exception to this rule is the human species. Depending upon social circumstances, humans display fairly uniform sexual motivation and sexual activity throughout the life span from puberty into very old age.

Second, not only is there no restriction of sexual interest to the period of a female's estrus, but the condition of estrus itself is almost undetectable in human females, who display what has been termed **silent ovulation.** Thus, a woman intent upon achieving pregnancy, and expressly wishing to engage in sexual activity at the time of ovulation, must resort to methods such as monitoring her internal temperature in an effort to determine just when the time of ovulation occurs. Otherwise, its occurrence is unnoticeable to both her and her partner. This silent ovulation stands in marked contrast to estrus in other primate species, in which the event is marked by obvious changes of coloration and swelling of the genitalia and the production of chemical stimulation that arouses the sexual interest of males. In humans, then, sexual behavior is freed from a strict adherence to reproductive function and achieves increased importance as a pervasive source of motivation.

Third, humans are capable of great variation in the durations of single episodes of sexual behavior. Human sexual behavior passes through four distinct phases known as *arousal, plateau, orgasm,* and *recovery* (Masters & Johnson, 1966). The plateau phase of human sexual behavior is extremely flexible and capable of reaching completion within a period of a few seconds or of being extended across a period of many minutes. This flexibility affords considerable expansion in the amount of sexual experience that may be encountered in a single episode of sexual behavior.

Fourth, female **orgasm** is a distinct phase of human sexual behavior and one that is experienced routinely by human females (Masters & Johnson, 1966). Indeed, human females are capable of experiencing multiple orgasms before entering into a recovery phase in their sexual arousal, whereas males must go through a period of recovery following orgasm before further sexual arousal is possible. Female orgasm is exceedingly rare in the animal kingdom; its presence among human sexual characteristics is readily seen as providing an increase in the density or richness of sexual experience available to members of our species.

Fifth, in addition to the flexibility shown in the durations of individual episodes of sexual behavior, the degree of variation present in other behavioral parameters such as postures, positions, and specific forms of action in human sexual behavior stands in marked contrast to the rather limited range of variation observed in other animals in the performance of these highly species-typical and functionally critical behaviors. These features of human sexual behavior, taken together as a constellation of characteristics, are unique, and seem to justify their description as adaptations that have heightened the quality and intensity of human sexual experience. As unique as these sexual characteristics are to our own species, similar developments may have occurred, to a very limited degree, in the evolution of sexual behavior among bonobos, the smaller cousins of the chimpanzees (de Waal, 1995).

The Evolution of Parental Behavior

Across the animal kingdom parental behavior is as varied as any of the other behaviors discussed in this book. **Parental behavior** is usually defined by its function, as behavior that assures the normal growth and development of offspring up to the point of functional independence. Much of the following discussion is summarized from Rosenblatt (1998).

Insects

Little parental behavior is seen among species of more ancient origins than the insects. Very often, insect parents die, or are otherwise long absent, by the time their offspring hatch. Thus, much of the parental behavior seen among insects concerns preparations left by the parents that will provide for the feeding and or protection of their developing offspring once they hatch. Insect nervous systems are far less complex than those of vertebrates. Nevertheless, a number of species provide full-scale paternal care such as the building of brood chambers, active feeding of offspring, and active defense of the brood from predators. These patterns of behavior are illustrated best in the social insects such as social wasps, bees, ants, and termites. (See Chapter 6 for a description of parental behavior among honeybees.)

Fish

Parental behavior among fish can be arranged in a hierarchy of behavioral grades. The lowest grade includes species that scatter eggs for external fertilization and among which no parental care is provided. In species at the next higher grade, one or both parents select nest sites for egg laying and fertilization, and nest guarding and fanning of the eggs may occur. Mouthbreeding fish represent a still higher grade of parental care. In these species the male or female incubate the eggs in their mouths and, in some cases, provide protection to offspring for a few days following hatching.

Amphibia

The need to adapt to a more complex environment resulted in the evolution of more complex parental behaviors among these species, although quite a wide range of variation in degree of parental care is illustrated here. Aquatic and semiterrestrial species lay eggs in the water and provide no additional care. But terrestrial species must seek out aquatic environments for egg laying. Suitable locations may include tree holes or plant leaves. Even a more advanced pattern of parental care occurs in some frogs, in which the male guards eggs and continues to guard newly hatched tadpoles. Some amphibians even retain their eggs internally, providing, perhaps, a precursor to the well-established pattern defined by mammals. In these species, the female gives birth to live young and goes on to provide them with at least some nutrition. The Surinam toad, *Pipa pipa*, incubates her eggs in pits formed on the surface of her back. More interesting still is the practice of the Australian frog, *Rheobacrachus silus*, which swallows her fertilized eggs and carries them in her stomach until they become fully formed juveniles (Maxwell, 1994).

Reptiles

These species have evolved the most complex parental behaviors among the lower vertebrates—not surprising, considering the evolutionary pathway from reptiles to birds to mammals. The simplest parental behaviors among this group are exhibited by turtles and tortoises, which lay eggs in nests but then abandon them to their fate. The hatchlings find their way to the sea by orienting on polarized light, in addition to other sensory cues. Crocodile and alligator females make elaborate nests and provide protection to the nest and some degree of care to the hatchlings, even helping them through the hatching process. Recent studies have shown some reptiles to provide brood care similar to that shown by domestic farm birds. There is even an evolutionary argument for this behavior (Horner, 2000).

Birds

Among the birds we encounter the development of very complex and comprehensive patterns of parental care. Many birds display monogamous breeding relations throughout a breeding season. Often both parents cooperate in building a nest, brooding the eggs, feeding the hatchlings, and serving as guides and continual providers of food as their fledglings leave the nest and for days thereafter. Many birds display gender specialization in the **brooding** phase of parental behavior and in the early care of the hatched offspring. Females remain at the nest during most of the day, and the male forages both for himself and for the female, to which he brings food throughout the day. In many species, females are more cryptically marked or colored than are the males—an apparent adaptation to their specialized role in brooding and brood defense. In many species of hawks—birds possessing more intimidating weapons for the provision of brood defense than seen in most birds—adult females are systematically larger than adult males. Here, again, is an apparent adaptation to the specialized female role in parental behavior.

Mated pairs of the elegant trogon (*Trogon elegans*) of the American Southwest and Mexico alternate in brooding eggs and young. The nonbrooding member of the pair returns to the nest tree after enjoying a predictable period of freedom and gives a loud and distinctive call, whereupon its mate emerges from the nest hole, to be replaced there by the newly arrived pair-member. Sometimes the brooding member of the pair initiates a changing of the guard by appearing at the mouth of the nest hole and giving its own loud call, which is effective in summoning its absent mate back to the nest. It is interesting that both males and females of this rather large and powerful cavity-nesting species—whose nest is well hidden deep within a hole in a tree—are brightly colored, although the two sexes are differently colored and readily discernible from each other.

In some avian species, such as crows and geese, young birds remain with the parental social group throughout the first year of life. Prolonged interaction with the parents after leaving the nest clearly affords young birds an opportunity to learn much about surviving in their chosen environments as their own activities are guided to a large extent by the behavior of their parents. The long apprenticeships served by these young birds during their first year of development are surpassed only by some members of the mammals.

Mammals

Mammals display the most complex forms of parental behavior. While in many species parental care is provided by both parents, among mammals it is mostly limited to the female parent. This arrangement may be seen as the joint result of three major evolutionary developments (Rosenblatt, 1998):

1. Internal fertilization. Often, the male is not necessary, and may not even be present, when the young are born and thereafter. Among some vertebrates in which fertilization is external, care of the young can be provided by both male and female parents, and there is a greater tendency for the male to assume this role, as often occurs among fish.

2. Prolonged gestation. The extended period of gestation common among mammals requires suppression of estrous cycling to free the female from mating behaviors. Gestation ends with significant changes in the female's production of hormones, including ovarian hormones (**estrogen** and **progesterone**), pituitary hormones (**prolactin** and **gonadotropic hormones**), and perhaps others. These hormones exert an organizing effect for the synchronization of the crucial maternal events of **parturition, lactation,** and the onset of **maternal behavior.**

3. Lactation. This, of course, is the defining characteristic of the mammals, among which only the female can feed her young. This arrangement places a major burden of infant care directly upon the mother.

Among mammals we can distinguish three basic forms of parental behavior: a nesting pattern, a leading–following pattern, and a clinging–carrying pattern. The nesting pattern is the most prominent form of parental care among mammals. It is found from the rodents to the primates and is most common among species giving birth to altricial young. The pattern requires nursing, which, as we see most significantly in the primates, forms an important foundation for social affiliation and the coordination of social behavior. Prominent among instances of social affiliation, of course, is the establishment of mother–infant bonds. Nesting mothers display anogenital licking of offspring soon after the birth of their young. This behavior is critical in providing the stimulation needed to arouse functioning of the waste elimination system of the infant and, in addition, provides warmth to the infant. Nesting mothers also retrieve their young as they wander from the nest and provide for defense of the nest and of the young.

There is wide variation in nesting behavior. Some mothers, such as rodents and carnivores, nurse frequently, whereas others do so infrequently. Rabbits, for example, nurse only once a day. Their young are hidden in ground-level burrows covered with fur and field hay. These nests are so well concealed, and the young so well adapted to remain unnoticeable in this environment, that even a moderately alert, suburban-dwelling human can run his lawn mower over a nest before he discovers the young rabbits (personal anecdote of author GG)!

The leading–following pattern of parental behavior is common among species that give birth to precocial young, which have most of their senses and many of their movement capabilities functioning at a competent level either at birth or immediately thereafter. We see this pattern among domestic animals and other species in which the young from an early age are typically seen in company with the mother as she forages for food. In these species, the mother is able to recognize her own offspring on the basis of their smells and tastes. Accordingly, these mothers usually will consent to nurse only their own young and will reject others.

The clinging–carrying pattern is the primate pattern of parental care. Primates are born both semiprecocial and semi-altricial. Some of their senses are fully developed, yet they are incapable of independent locomotion. The young are born with crucially important reflexes that insure the maintenance of close contact between themselves and their mother. A **grasping reflex** and a *clinging reflex* allow them to hold on to the mother's fur even as she swings through the branches of trees. A **rooting reflex** allows them to find her nipple, and a *sucking reflex* allows them to feed. As Harlow (1962) pointed out in his now classic research, these first taxic and biotaxic responses form the foundations of later social behavior among primates.

As we have seen with all behaviors discussed in this book, parental behavior is regulated by a complex system of psychobiological factors. The control of mammalian parental behavior, however, still has not been well researched, and we have data from only a few species. Among the primates, parental responsiveness is controlled by a combination of hormonal and sensory factors during pregnancy and parturition. The female's initial aversive responses are overcome as she is subsequently attracted to her offspring, providing them with crucial interactions that will lay the foundation for the development of a strong social bond between them.

Summary: Principles Introduced in This Chapter

Evolution has provided for both asexual and sexual reproduction. The asexually re-producing paramecium, for example, reproduces by a process known as binary fission, and the hydra reproduces by budding. A limitation of asexual reproduction is that it produces little variation among offspring or between offspring and parent. In sexual reproduction, by contrast, there is a mixing of genes between males and females that provides for a great increase in phenotypic variability. An additional proposed advan-tage of sexual reproduction is that it provides an opportunity for correcting genetic mistakes. This proposal is known as the DNA Repair Hypothesis.

In connection with sexual reproduction, animals identify potential mates by means of imprinting as well as sexual learning. Courtship is a process by which repro-ductive partners signal their intentions to mate. Mating activity typically is located within predictable breeding seasons for each species. The timing of these breeding seasons, in combination with the gestation period of each species, results in the birth of offspring under environmental conditions that maximize survivability.

A number of different mating systems have evolved. A mating system is a type of social organization in the context of which breeding is accomplished. The mating system of each species should maximize breeding success. Mating systems include mo-nogamy, polygamy, and promiscuity. Many species display aspects of more than one of these systems.

Competition for mates is part of the selective process involved in sexual reproduc-tion and underscores the risks often incurred in mating. Fighting most often occurs be-tween competing males but also occurs between females and even within a mating pair.

Phylogenetic consideration reveals a progressive development in the complexity of all reproductive behaviors, including courtship, mating, and parental behavior. These behaviors are likely to be increasingly complex as one moves from invertebrates to fish, amphibians, reptiles, birds, and mammals. Two distinct reproductive strategies have evolved, *r* and *K*. In the *r* strategy, adequate survival numbers are assured by the produc-tion of vast numbers of offspring but a very limited degree of parental investment in any one offspring. In the *K* strategy, few offspring are produced but those few receive intense parental investment.

KEY TERMS

Asexual reproduction   reproduction accomplished by an organism's duplication of its chromosomes and genes and then division to form two or more "daughter" organisms.

Binary fission   a means of asexual reproduction seen among paramecia.

Breeding congress   the gathering together of a number of different males and females in a limited area in association with breeding behavior.

Breeding season   a limited portion of the year during which most of the mating behavior of a species occurs.

Breeding territory   a territory held during breeding season, the possession of which may enhance breeding opportunities for the territory owner.

Brooding   protective behavior addressed to the eggs or young, particularly among birds and fish.

Bruce effect   an interference to the occurrence of pregnancy in a female mouse that has been fertilized by a first male if she is later exposed to the odor of urine from a second male.

Budding   an asexual reproductive process demonstrated by hydra, for example, in which new animals form as buds in an area of the parent animal referred to as the budding area.

Conjugation   a sexual-like reproduction process in which two protozoa such as paramecia combine their genetic material.

Coolidge effect   an enhancement of sexual vigor in a male that results from the presence of a large number of different females as potential mates.

Courtship   the behaviors by which a male and a female locate and accommodate to one another in association with mating and sexual reproduction.

DNA Repair Hypothesis   the idea that recombination of genetic material leads to the repair of replication errors and of damaged DNA.

Estrogen   one of the primary female hormones and a regulating factor of female reproductive cycles.

Estrus   the physiological condition that is distinctly associated with sexual receptivity of females in many species; the term also may be applied to patterns of behavior that may be uniquely associated with this condition.

Gametes   reproductive cells such as sperm and ova, each of which possesses half of the chromosomes and genes of a parent organism; gametes combine to produce an offspring.

Gonadotropic hormone   a hormone of the pituitary gland that affects reproductive cycles.

Gonads   the ovaries of females and the testes of males.

Gonochorism   the evolution and development of two distinct sexes.

Grasping reflex   reflexive, or elicited, closing of the fingers of the hand in response to tactile stimulation to the palm of the hand, seen normally among newborn primates.

Hermaphrodite   a single individual that possesses both male and female sexual organs.

Internal fertilization   fertilization of an ovum by a sperm taking place within the body of the female.

K reproductive strategy   the reproductive strategy that stresses the provision of high survival rates among a small number of offspring over the production of a great number of offspring.

Lactation   the production of milk by a female mammal.

Lek   a well-defined area within which a number of male birds maintain individual breeding territories.

Maternal behavior   the parental behavior of a female.

Mating   the sexual union of two organisms, usually a male and a female, often resulting in the production of offspring.

Monestrous   the physical condition in which estrous behavior occurs only once during an animal's breeding season. This is typical of bears and dogs, for example.

Monogamy   a restriction of mating behavior of a single male and a single female such that they mate only with each other.

Monogamous   a mating system in which a single male and a single female mate exclusively with each other.

Orgasm   the occurrence of sexual climax in copulation, associated in males with the release of sperm.

Ova, eggs   the gametes, or reproductive cells, of females.

Ovaries   the female reproductive organs responsible for the production of ova and certain female hormones.

Parental behavior   behavior of a parent toward its offspring or in relation to its offspring.

Parturition   the process of giving birth.

Pheromone   a hormone released by one organism that functions as a source of sexual attraction to conspecifics of the opposite sex, or gender.

Polyestrous   the physiological condition in which estrous behavior occurs repeatedly throughout the year rather than in a specific breeding season. This is typical of mice, rats, and most primates, for example.

Polyandry   a polygamous system in which a single female mates with a number of different males.

Polygamy, Polygamous   a mating system in which a single individual mates with a number of other individuals.

Polygyny   a polygamous system in which a single male mates with a number of different females.

Progesterone   a female hormone and a regulating factor of female reproductive cycles.

Prolactin   a hormone of the pituitary gland associated with milk production in female mammals.

Promiscuity   the situation in which mating behavior is relatively unrestricted with respect to which individuals mate with which other individuals.

***r* reproductive strategy**   the reproductive strategy that stresses the production of a great number of offspring over the provision of high survival rates among a small number of offspring.

Receptivity   in sexual behavior, usually the state of responsiveness in which a female will accept courtship from a male that may lead to mating.

Rooting reflex   reflexive movements of the head in response to tactile stimulation to the face and lips in newborn primates; these movements tend to bring the young primate's mouth into contact with the stimulus-object being applied.

Seasonally polyestrous   the physiological condition in which estrous behavior occurs repeatedly in a specific breeding season. This is typical of horses, sheep, and goats, for example.

Sperm   the gametes, or reproductive cells, of males.

Spontaneous ovulation   ovulation during the estrous cycle that is not dependent upon the occurrence of any particular behavior, such as copulation.

Sexual dimorphism   the possession of widely different bodily characteristics by the males and females of a species, particularly in regard to the relative size of males and females.

Sexual imprinting   the long-term determination of sexual orientation upon stimuli encountered in early social experience.

Sexual learning   the modification of sexual behavior on the basis of learning experiences.

Sexual reproduction   reproduction that is accomplished by the combining of chromosomes and genes from two different organisms.

Sexual selection   the evolutionary selection of characteristics that have functioned to enhance reproductive fitness by benefiting success in courtship and/or breeding.

Silent ovulation   an occurrence of ovulation that is not heralded by any obvious physiological or behavioral signals.

Testes   the male reproductive organs responsible for the production of sperm and certain male hormones.

Zig-zag display   a pattern of courtship behavior seen in male sticklebacks.

REVIEW QUESTIONS

1. How is sexual behavior defined (for application across the animal series)?

2. What is the extent of occurrence of sexual reproduction across the animal series—that is, just how common is it?

3. Name a potential advantage of sexual as opposed to asexual reproduction.

4. What is a potential disadvantage of sexual reproduction?

5. Describe an early form of sexual-like behavior seen in paramecia.

6. What is the idea of the DNA Repair Hypothesis and how is this idea related to the functional significance of sexual behavior?

7. What is meant by courtship?

8. Describe a courtship behavior of male stickleback fish.

9. What is considered the main function of the concentration of breeding behavior in a definite breeding season, as is seen in numerous species?

10. What is meant by estrus?

11. What is the Coolidge effect? The Bruce effect?

12. What do we mean when we say a species is monogamous?

13. What is the difference between polygyny and polyandry?

14. Describe some of the main features of breeding behavior among sage grouse.

15. What is meant by promiscuity, and how is it related to breeding behavior among many primate species?

16. Briefly describe male competition among either bighorn sheep or whitetail deer.

17. What is the advantage of a male's maintaining high dominance status throughout the breeding season?

18. Contrast the *r* strategy and the *K* strategy as reproductive systems.

19. Briefly describe an example of a breeding congress.

20. Describe breeding arrangements among hamadryas baboons.

21. Contrast the relative degree of sexual dimorphism seen among gibbons, gorillas, and humans, and tell how this variation has been related to the occurrence of monogamy among these groups.

22. List three or four outstanding features of human sexual behavior as compared to that of most other primates.

23. Either give an example to illustrate or a description to characterize parental behavior among insects, fish, birds, and mammals. (This is quite an extensive assignment. You may consider it to be several questions rather than one.)

24. Comment on the role of hormones in the regulation of parental behavior in mammals.

25. Describe two reflexes of newborn primates that may be considered to contribute to the success of parental behavior.

REFERENCES

Adsell, S. A, (1964). *Patterns of mammalian reproduction,* 2nd ed. Ithaca, NY: Comstock Publishing Associates.

Alexander, R. D., Marshall, D. C., & Cooley, J. R. (1997). Evolutionary perspectives on insect mating. In J. C. Choe & B. J. Crespi (Eds.), *Mating systems in insects and arachnids* (pp. 4–31). Cambridge, England: Cambridge University Press.

Angier, N. (1995). *The beauty of the beastly: New views on the nature of life.* Boston: Houghton Mifflin.

Berglund, A. (1997). Mating systems and sex allocation. In J.-G. J. Godin (Ed.), *Behavioural ecology of teleost fishes* (pp. 237–265). Oxford, England: Oxford University Press.

Bermant, G., & Davidson, J. M. (1974). *Biological basis of sexual behavior.* New York: Harper & Row.

Bernstein, H., Hopf, F. A., & Michod, R. E. (1989). The evolution of sex: DNA repair hypothesis. In A. E. Rasa, C. Vogel, & E. Voland (Eds.), *The sociobiology of sexual and reproductive strategies* (pp. 3–18). London: Chapman & Hall.

Cahill, T. (1998). *The gifts of the Jews.* New York: Doubleday.

Cutler, W. B. (1999). Human sex–attractant hormones: Discovery, research, development, and application in sex therapy. *Psychiatric Annals, 29,* 54–59.

de Waal, F. (1995). Sex as an alternative to aggression in the bonobo. In P. R. Abramson & S. D. Pinkerton (Eds.), *Sexual nature, sexual culture. Chicago series on sexuality, history and society* (pp. 37–56). Chicago: University of Chicago Press.

Ehrman, L., & Kim, Y.-K. (1998). Courtship. In G. Greenberg & M. M. Haraway (Eds.), *Comparative psychology: A handbook* (pp. 637–648). New York: Garland.

Elia, I. (1988). *The female animal.* New York: Holt.

Geist, V. (1998). Mountain sheep. In G. Greenberg & M. M. Haraway (Eds.), *Comparative psychology: A handbook* (pp. 441–445). New York: Garland.

Gibson, R. M., & Bradbury, J. W. (1987). Lek organization in sage grouse: Variations on a central theme. *Auk, 104,* 77–84.

Goldfoot, D. A., Essock-Vitale, S. M., Asa, C. A., Thornton, J. E., & Leshner, A. I. (1978). Anosmia in male rhesus monkeys does not alter copulatory activity with cycling females. *Science, 199,* 1095–1096.

Harlow, H. (1962). Development of affection in primates. In E. L. Bliss (Ed.), *Roots of behavior.* New York: Harper & Row.

Hayes, N. (1994). *Principles of comparative psychology.* Hove, UK: Lawrence Erlbaum.

Hines, P., & Culotta, E. (1998). The evolution of sex. *Science, 281,* 1979.

Horner, J. R. (2000). Dinosaur reproduction and parenting. *Annual Review of Earth and Planetary Science, 28,* 19–45.

Jonsson, B., Jonsson, N., & Hansen, L. P. (1990). Does juvenile experience affect migration and spawning of adult Atlantic salmon? *Behavioral Ecology and Sociobiology, 26,* 225–230.

Masters, W., & Johnson, V. (1966). *Human sexual response.* New York: Lippincott, Williams, & Wilkins.

Maxwell, K. (1994). *The sex imperative: An evolutionary tale of sexual survival.* New York: Plenum.

Moore, C. (1998). Vertebrate sexual behavior. In G. Greenberg & M. M. Haraway (Eds.), *Comparative psychology: A handbook* (pp. 783–792). New York: Garland.

Morell, V. (1998). A new look at monogamy. *Science, 281,* 1982–1983.

Parkes, A., & Bruce, H. (1961). Olfactory stimuli in mammalian reproduction. *Science, 134,* 1049–1054.

Partridge, L. (1988). Lifetime reproductive success in *Drosophila.* In T. H. Clutton-Brock (Ed.), *Reproductive success: Studies of individual variation in contrasting breeding systems* (pp. 11–23). Chicago: University of Chicago Press.

Preston-Mafham, R., & Preston-Mafham, K. (1993). *The encyclopedia of land invertebrate behaviour.* Cambridge, MA: MIT Press.

Rosenblatt, J. (1998). Psychology of parental behavior in mammals. In G. Greenberg & M. M. Haraway (Eds.), *Comparative psychology: A handbook* (pp. 736–747). New York: Garland.

Schaller, G. B. (1963). *The mountain gorilla.* Chicago: University of Chicago Press.

Schulz, A. T., Horrall, R. M., Cooper, J. C., & Hasler, A. D. (1976). Imprinting to chemical cues: The basis for home stream selection in salmon. *Science, 192,* 1247–1249.

Stern, K., & McClintock, M. (1998). Regulation of ovulation by human pheromones. *Nature, 293,* 177–179.

Weller, A. (1998). Communication through body odor. *Nature, 392*, 126–127.

Welles, R. E., & Welles, F. B. (1961). *The bighorn of Death Valley.* Washington, DC: U.S. Government Printing Office.

Wiley, R. H. (1978). The lek mating system of the sage grouse. *Scientific American, 238*, 114–125.

Wuethrich, B. (1998). Why sex? Putting theory to the test. *Science, 281*, 1980–1982.

Zilman, D. (1998). *Connections between sexuality and aggression*, 2nd ed. Mahwah, NJ: Erlbaum.

CHAPTER

8 Predator Defense and Protective Behaviors

Most animals are potential prey for other larger or more powerful animals, sometimes even other individuals of their own species. They may even be threatened by competitor species for which they do not constitute food items. Many face possible death by predator attack on nearly a constant basis. Fallow deer, impala, wildebeest, zebra, and many other African hoofed mammals live within the hunting domain of the lion, the leopard, the hyena, and the hunting dog. Every day of their lives they are likely to experience being part of a group whose members are stalked, attacked, tested, and killed by these predators. Here is evolutionary selection at its clearest and most dramatic. Fanselow and De Oca (1998) pointed out that the consequences of a failed feeding attempt may be as innocuous as going hungry for a brief time, but the consequences of a failed attempt at predator defense may well be immediate death. Defensive behavior literally is a matter of life or death. Individuals unable to defend themselves against predator attack are unlikely to reach breeding age. Parents unable to defend their young are unlikely to achieve successful reproduction.

Defensive Behaviors

Defensive behaviors are of such importance that they usually override other motivational concerns such as hunger, thirst, courtship, and so on. Bolles (1970) suggested that once an animal is faced with a situation that is fearful enough or dangerous enough, its responses become limited to what he termed **species-specific defensive reactions** (SSDRs), which form the core of each species' defensive behaviors. The particular components of the SSDRs differ with each species, as do the stimuli effective to elicit these behaviors. Even so, we are able to discern general patterns across many species.

We stated earlier that approach and withdrawal behaviors are practically universal features of animal life. In the most ancient animal species, defensive behavior is limited to a circumspect withdrawal from dangerous stimulation. The escape behavior of the protozoan, *Amoeba proteus*, is a direct derivative of its tendency to withdraw from any intense stimulation. The same basic reaction tendency accomplishes escape behavior for the paramecium, but in this instance the escape is more quickly accomplished by a reversal in the direction of beating cilia when contact is made with intense stimulation. Adults of the multicelled sponges usually attach themselves to the ocean floor for life. After that, their only means of withdrawal—and their only protective reaction—is to close the osculum at the end of each of their chimneys, thus stopping the inflow of outside water into their bodies. Such a reaction is elicited by intense stimulation of the cells of the osculum.

The flatworms and the earthworms add more elaborate defensive responses to the basic reaction of withdrawal from intense stimulation. An intense stimulus applied to the surface of these animals elicits a vigorous writhing and whipping of the body, wherein the ends of the body are brought quickly close together on first one side, then on the other. These whipping responses may separate the animal from contact with a harmful stimulus. The animal then can withdraw by moving in a direction away from the area of contact. These species not only possess specific and elaborate forms of escape behavior, but they are also capable of learning to respond with escape behavior to low-intensity stimuli that have repeatedly preceded a high-intensity stimulus, and that thus serve as signals for the imminent onset of the intense stimulus. This capability for psychotaxic organization—widely demonstrated in the laboratory—very likely plays a role in defensive behavior in the natural habitats of these species.

Bats are among the most deadly predators encountered by nocturnal moths. Many moths have evolved sensitivity to the sound waves by which a hunting bat locates its prey. They also are able to distinguish the relative distance between a hunting bat and themselves on the basis of these sounds. When a moth detects a bat's "sonar" at relatively great distance, it changes its line of flight in a direction away from the bat's line of flight. Such a maneuver may allow the moth to avoid being detected by the bat. If the bat's sonar is detected from a small distance away, on the other hand, the moth immediately begins a swerving, diving flight that may cause the bat to miss in its attack (Grier & Burk, 1992; Roeder, 1962). In observing the pursuit flights of flycatchers such as the eastern kingbird or the eastern wood pewee, one often sees them veer rapidly in one direction after another as they track the evasive escape flights of the flying insects they are chasing (Figure 8.1).

An ordered pattern of response to predator threat is first seen at least as early in the animal series as the spiders and occurs widely across many more recently evolved species. The pattern may be represented as a series of progressively more hazardous steps, each of which is a response to increasingly higher degrees of predatory danger. A pattern similar to this was presented by Fanselow and De Oca (1998), who presented the illustration replicated in Figure 8.2.

The first step in the series—encountering the least exposure to risk—is to hide quietly or to remain still and hidden. With any luck on the hider's part, the predator will pass and leave the vicinity without detecting its presence. The second step—if the hider is detected or, seemingly, is about to be detected—is to flee the scene at maximum speed. This step may be preceded by an attempt to leave quietly or to slip away unnoticed, a reaction particularly likely in animals that possess strong means of inducing avoidance by a predator: species such as rattlesnakes, skunks, or porcupines. Flight also may be preceded by behaviors seemingly designed to achieve information about the precise location of a predator, as in the case of fallow deer that detect the odor of a nearby leopard on a dark night but hesitate to take an escape direction until the location of the threat can be more precisely fixed.

FIGURE 8.1   An Eastern Kingbird Attacks as an Insect Takes Evasive Flight.

In many instances there is no stage beyond running or fleeing, and this pattern continues until the runner either escapes—perhaps by arriving at a safe haven—or is killed. In many other cases, however, when an animal is cornered or hard pressed, it will turn and confront its pursuer. This reaction occurs readily in species such as skunks and porcupines, which rarely engage in rapid escape behavior but, instead, offer to use their powerful "weapons" if pursued as they attempt retreat from an area. First, the cornered animal will threaten or bluff its pursuer and then, if the pursuer continues its attack, the prey will loose its weapon or fight back. The defensive pattern, at this point, has reached quite a desperate stage. Death may be close at hand for the defending animal. Still, as its last-ditch defense appears about to fail, there may be a final tactic that has a chance of succeeding. The defender can *appear* to die.

Predators usually break off their attacks once they have killed their prey, and this cessation can also be produced by a feigning of death (Fox, 1969). If the prey can appear realistically to die while remaining alive, it may have a chance to slip away later. The opossum of North America is well known as an expert at this defense, which is popularly called "playing 'possum." There are numerous examples of death feigning, also called **tonic immobility** (Gallup, 1998), throughout the animal series from spiders to mammals (Fanselow & De Oca, 1998). Animals engaging in this behavior may be sensitive to escape possibilities in the surrounding environment. Crabs placed on loose

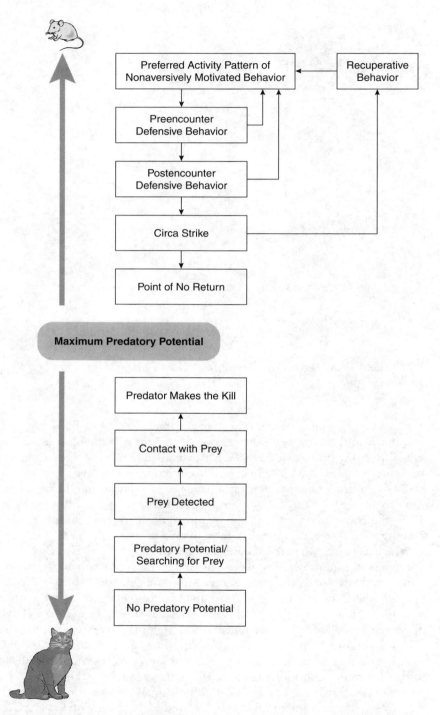

FIGURE 8.2 A Predatory Imminence Continuum

sand (Henning, Dunlap, & Gallup, 1976) and lizards placed near thick foliage (O'Brien & Dunlap, 1975) displayed briefer periods of tonic immobility than they showed in other circumstances in which the prospects of successful hiding were less favorable. The effectiveness of this defensive reaction is the reason for common advice given to humans traveling on foot in grizzly-bear country: If attacked and overcome by a bear, go suddenly limp and cease to move; this may induce the bear to stop its attack.

An interesting variation on the death feigning theme is engaged in by lizards such as the green anole. The intense stimulation of being grasped or struck by a predator causes the lizard to become immobilized for a moment as a section of its tail snaps off and begins a frantic, writhing motion. Predators often turn their attention toward the vigorously active tail section while the "business" section of the lizard is able to slip away and escape. It can then rejuvenate its missing appendage at leisure.

Escape for a moose challenged by gray wolves can take two forms (Mech, 1966). An adult moose is a very large and powerful animal. As such, a healthy adult is capable of successfully standing up to a wolf pack. A challenged moose may back up to a steep bank or a dense growth of brush and wait alertly, ready to counter wolf charges with jabs of its forefeet. Even a cow with a young calf often is able to ward off a wolf attack, provided the calf is adept at keeping in a protected location beneath the cow's belly as she shifts her position to keep the wolves in front of her. Wolves often break off attacks on moose that take a bold stand after only a few minutes. The second form of escape for a moose is to make a good run. Wolves often follow along behind a running moose for only one hundred meters or so before breaking off the chase. They appear able to make early judgments of strength and weakness of their prospective prey. Wolves break off their attacks quickly on twelve of each thirteen moose they challenge. When they do continue an attack for longer than a brief time, however, Mech observed that they nearly always make a kill of the individual being pursued, even if many hours are necessary to complete the task.

For the much smaller caribou, speed is its main edge against its chief predator, the gray wolf. A single wolf often is able to kill a caribou, and there is very little question of the outcome when two or more wolves get close enough to a caribou to obtain a tooth hold. But the wolf's top speed is no match for the caribou's. Unless wolves are able to catch and injure a caribou before it reaches its top speed—or unless they detect preexisting weakness in a challenged animal—the caribou can leave its attackers behind, gasping in the wind, and forced to await another feeding opportunity.

A rapid getaway also is the main protection of the herd animals of Africa from their consummate predator, the African lion. The lion excels at stealth and at waiting in ambush—two tactics that often bring it close enough to its prey to make an explosive charge. The lion is astonishingly fast in a short sprint, and so large and powerful that it can bring down a large antelope with a single blow of its forepaw. If a prey animal can escape the initial lion attack and reach its top speed, however, the danger can be left behind for a time. Lions seldom continue chases beyond a few dozen meters (Schaller, 1972). The same escape tactics serve well in encounters with the leopard, another superb stalker of African hoofed mammals. A rapid sprint can remove a threatened animal from danger. But when a leopard stealthily approaches its prey on dark nights, the problem for the prey is to detect its exact location. The threatened animals mince about on bunched leg muscles, nervously vocalizing back and forth, ready to break at the first strong indication of the leopard's location. Too hasty an escape may take them almost literally into the leopard's jaws; too long a hesitation, and the leopard may creep close enough for a successful lunge.

An additional escape capability certainly useful in meeting attacks of lion and leopard is absolutely necessary in surviving attack by another superb African predator, the cheetah. Speed alone is no protection against the cheetah. As the world's fastest land animal, it can outrun any antelope. Survival for the prey here depends on an ability to make quick turns and changes of direction followed by rapid acceleration on the new course heading. If an individual can make enough of these successful escape maneuvers, the cheetah may tire or protective cover may be reached, and life may continue.

Leopards are also a major predator of many African primates, including baboons and vervet monkeys. We have seen earlier (Chapter 5) that the defensive strategy developed in the baboons' social structures is considered an important factor in enabling them to become the world's most widely spread terrestrial primate group other than ourselves (Bramblett, 1976; Fobes & King, 1982). Among savanna baboons, social groups revolve around several dominant males. These individuals are found near the center of the social group as it rests or moves about foraging. Subdominant males, in the meantime, patrol the edges of the group. At the first sign of predatory threat, the group's dominant males quickly converge on the point of attack and present a united defensive challenge to the threatening predator. Even a predator as large and powerful as a leopard must respect the baboons' challenge. Certainly a leopard may attack and kill an adult male baboon—and sometimes leopards do—but the leopard itself may be injured in the exchange. The greater the number of defending male baboons, the greater the risk of an attack to the leopard. A standoff may often be the best adjustment of the situation on both sides.

The relatively sparse environment of the hamadryas baboon has dictated the evolution of primary social groups containing a single dominant male and several adult females. These primary groups are maintained during foraging expeditions through the sparse environment. However, as soon as foraging is accomplished for the time being, as when the animals are nooning at a water hole or going into rest at night quarters, several primary groups join together into bands and groups of bands. Social cooperation among the males of these bands in meeting predatory challenges then provides a formidable alliance of predatory defense.

Like baboons, vervet monkeys also spend a great deal of their time on the ground, especially when foraging (Seyfarth & Cheney, 1980). They face predatory threat from leopards, snakes, and eagles. In Chapter 5, we saw that vervet monkeys have developed a system of vocal communication that helps them to react in specific and appropriate ways to warnings related to each of these different threats. Adult vervet monkeys make acoustically distinctive alarm calls when they spot a snake, a leopard, or an eagle. Other monkeys respond to the snake alarm by looking down at the ground, to the leopard alarm by running toward trees, and to the eagle alarm by looking up at the sky. Very young members of the vervet troop react to these calls in a more general way, merely becoming more aroused and alert. As they grow and encounter numerous learning experiences within the social group, their reactions to the alarm calls become more specifically appropriate.

A few decades ago many sports hunters across the eastern half of the United States were ardent pursuers of the bobwhite quail (*Colinus virginianus*). Hunters maintained highly trained dogs year-round for the pleasure of taking them afield for a few weeks each autumn and winter to find and "point" the quail, which, at that season of the year, keep together in groups of twelve or fifteen birds, called coveys. The disappearance of many small farms over recent decades has greatly limited both the amount of habitat available for bobwhites and the number of sites open to quail hunting. But anyone who has experienced the escape flight of a large covey of quail will not soon forget the sensation.

The quail crouch and "freeze" at the near approach of the dog, whose job is to creep near enough to hold the birds motionless—but not to flush them. In doing this, the dog will slowly assume a pose with its muzzle pointed directly at the hiding quail and its tail held out rigidly behind it, hence the term *pointing*. When the quail are flushed—perhaps by the arrival of the hunters—their combined wing beats make a loud and startling flapping sound as the covey explodes in all directions. Many of the birds fan out in front of the hunter and dog. But many a hunter—confused by the sound and fury of the quails' escape flight—fails to get off a shot or, if managing to shoot, fails to focus his attention on any single bird and so simply shoots into the covey as a whole, hitting only air. There is reason to believe that the swirling confusion of a covey's escape flight makes the harvesting of quail more difficult not only for human hunters but also for other predators.

The same source of confusion serves many other groups of animals as they are attacked by predators. Ducks and shorebirds scatter in all directions when approached by a peregrine falcon in flight. Groups of songbirds at a feeder do the same when attacked by a sharp-shinned hawk or a Cooper's hawk—bird hawks that hunt the woods and thickets rather than the open marshes, fields, and shores frequented by falcons. Against the sharp-shinned hawk, the songbirds must scatter into thick foliage as rapidly as possible and take cover. African herds of hoofed mammals also scatter in all directions when attacked by lions (Schaller, 1972).

We have already mentioned that the rapid, coordinated movements of shoals of fish pose sensory challenges to the successful attacks of their many predators. Pitcher (1998) describes a number of different reactions of fish shoals to predatory threats. A rapid movement of shoaling fish outward from the center of the shoal is called **flash expansion.** Following such an expansion, members of the shoal either rapidly reassemble or go into hiding within the substrate, thus avoiding being isolated as a single target of the predator. Other defensive movements observed in shoaling fish are *skitters* and *compactions*. Skitters are rapid boomerang movements that provide both predator warnings for other shoal members as well as confusing visual stimulation to the predator. Compactions are rapid movements of shoal members toward the center of the shoal that greatly reduce the distance between neighbors. Such movements promote coordination of further escape maneuvers and may also contribute to predator confusion. The compacted group may glide slowly out of range of the predator and into hiding, or a narrow column of fish may extend into an adjoining subschool and a continued movement of individuals along this pseudopodium may result in the more threatened subschool being gradually absorbed into the more distant subschool.

As just alluded to, rapid coordinated movements of individuals within schools of fish can have a communicative effect that is quickly transmitted throughout the school at large. This phenomenon has been termed the *Trafalgar effect*—named in reference to the rapid transfer of information across a fleet of ships by the use of signal flags. Information signaled by coordinated movements among tightly assembled, polarized schools of fish travels up to seven times faster than the approach of a predator (Pitcher, 1998; Godin & Morgan, 1985; Foster & Treherne, 1981). The evasion tactics of schooling fish appear to be effective. Experiments have shown that success of attacks by a wide variety of predators decreases as school size increases and that fish that become separated from a school encounter an increased chance of being eaten by a predator (Pitcher, 1998).

We have seen previously that many species have evolved communicative actions that serve as warning signals of predatory threat to other members of their groups. Several further examples of such signals deserve consideration in the present context. Family groups of crows, and larger groupings containing many different families, warn of predatory threats by vocalizations that are responded to with flight by other crows not in a position to have seen the predator themselves. Similar vocal warnings are made by prairie dogs and serve to warn not only the communicator's own family group but also members of surrounding family groups. The white-tailed deer of eastern North America is named for the white flag presented by the underside of its tail, which is raised in flight, providing a warning to others of its feeding group, several of which may be its close kin.

Many warning signals appear clearly to impose an increased risk of attack upon the communicator of the warning. Members of shoals of fish sometimes separate briefly from the shoal and move toward a potential predator, then return to the shoal. This behavior has been termed *predator inspection*, and its apparent dangers have made it a matter of interest how such a behavior pattern evolved (Pitcher, 1998). Several potential advantages of the behavior are that the inspector may gain information whose value in evading an oncoming attack exceeds the risk of temporarily placing itself in a vulnerable position, or that the inspection behavior may serve to inhibit predator attack. Furthermore, experiments with one-way mirrors have demonstrated that the returning inspector somehow communicates predator information to other shoal members, raising the possibility that evolution of inspection behavior may have been based at least in part upon kin selection. At present, the nature of kinship relations among members of fish shoals is unclear.

The appropriateness of applying the idea of kin selection in such situations may be suggested by recent findings among Gunnison's prairie dogs (*Cynomys gunnisoni*), which frequently perform warning calls at the appearance of a predator (Hoogland, 1996). Hoogland showed that females with kin in the home area—and particularly females with young offspring nearby—were more likely to give warning calls to the presentation of a stuffed badger than were females without kin in the home area.

One of the most intriguing phenomena to be considered within the context of predator inspection is the widespread practice of predator **mobbing** by birds, directed particularly toward hawks and owls by some of their potential victims (Ehrlich, Dobkin, & Wheye, 1988). A useful and well-known trick used by experienced birders to bring birds out of hiding and into close view is a technique called "spishing." The technique consists of passing air through the lips to make a prolonged and rather loud hissing or shushing noise while repeatedly closing the lips as though pronunciating the letter *p*. This action produces a continuous sound something like "shhh-pshhh-pshhh-pshhh-pshhh." The spishing evidently sounds to birds like one bird scolding another—or perhaps like several birds scolding a predator. The technique is often spectacularly successful at calling curious birds into the vicinity from dozens of meters away.

We have mentioned earlier (Chapter 5) how the raucous sound of crows mobbing a hawk or an owl sometimes attracts hundreds of crows from far distances to the scene of the mobbing. This characteristic of crows has often been used by human crow hunters to bring dozens of crows within range of their guns. The hunters place an owl decoy on prominent display and then hide nearby as they use crow calls to simulate the excited sounds of crows mobbing the owl. On several occasions in the fall, one of the authors has imitated the distinctive call of the barred owl within a quiet afternoon woods and watched as numerous blue jays slipped into the area, apparently looking about avidly in search of the owl.

The sudden appearance of a sharp-shinned hawk on the wing will send a group of feeding songbirds such as cardinals, sparrows, kinglets, and chickadees scurrying into cover for their lives. Yet the same birds will gather all about a perching sharp-shinned hawk, flitting close to its head, shoulders, and back and scolding vocally with great energy. This is apparently risky behavior on the part of the mobbers. But perhaps the success of a sharp-shinned hawk depends importantly upon stealth, and the opportunity to burst upon an unsuspecting victim while already in full flight itself. Mobbers often succeed in driving a harried hawk from the vicinity, but one sees nothing to prevent the hawk from shortly making a stealthy return. At least all the mobbers in the area will have been well and recently reminded of the imminent danger of hawks.

In addition to the preceding acts of inspecting or mobbing a predator whose presence has already been detected, overt acts of wariness or watchfulness are widely observed among prey species. Anyone who has watched white-tailed deer feeding in the open will have been impressed at the frequency with which they interrupt their feeding at seemingly random intervals to lift their heads and hold their ears erect in a watchful pose. Their legs and trunks remain motionless at these times until, at an unpredictable moment, they suddenly switch their tails back-and-forth several times and lower their heads again to resume feeding. Similar actions of monitoring can be observed in the feeding behavior of white-throated sparrows and many other ground-feeding birds. In these species, the acts of watchfulness appear less as interruptions of feeding than as interwoven components of the feeding behavior itself. As the sparrows scratch through leaves and search the ground about their feet for food, they continually lift their heads briefly between bites and other feeding movements to look about the general area and, presumably, to listen. Feeding flocks of white-throated sparrows repeatedly emit soft peeping vocalizations. The sight or sound of a potential predator—such as a creeping person—instantly quiets the peeps and stops all other movement as well. Further stimulation from the intruder results in immediate flight and at least a temporary dispersal of the group.

Inducing Predator Avoidance

Next we will consider some of the weapons different species have evolved that induce potential predators to avoid contact with them. We are all familiar with bees, hornets, and wasps. Many of these species can inflict painful and even dangerous stings upon intruders into the area of their nests. And, of course, they may make no distinctions between the innocent bungler and the would-be predator. Numerous species of ants possess similar weapons.

As is so often the case with species possessing outstanding capability to inflict aversive stimulation on others, the capability is rendered even more functional by clear behavioral advertisement. Consider the riveting visual stimuli provided by a swirling cloud of wasps or honeybees disturbed at their nests or by an undulating swarm of thousands of ants surrounding a disturbed anthill. Many predators having experience with these outstanding signals respond to them with precipitate avoidance behavior, obviating the need for the prey to advance their defensive reaction to its highest level—actual use of their weapons.

A similar pattern is seen in behavioral reactions of both rattlesnakes and cottonmouth moccasins, each named for the character of the warning stimuli presented in the bluffing phase of their defensive behavior. Members of the cobra tribe perform similarly impressive threat displays. Any predator that fails to withdraw at these warning signals may receive a painful bite accompanied by a sickening, and perhaps fatal, dose of venom.

The vivid contrast of the black-and-white coloration of North American skunks is well known and widely recognized. It serves as a visual marker advertising the powerful chemical weapon possessed by these species. If threatened, they lift their tails high and orient their rear ends toward the threat in a showy display that, if not heeded by the intruding predator, will be followed by a stream of blinding and nauseating spray from a gland beneath the skunks' tails, aimed at the face and eyes of the offender. Porcupines have a distinctly prickly appearance even when relaxed. If threatened, their display of erecting their quills and turning their backs and heavily quilled tails toward the enemy makes their weapons all the more noticeable. A quick swipe of a porcupine's tail can impale the mouth and head area of a predator with numerous quills, each of which inflicts a persistent and painful injury—in some cases, eventually, a fatal injury.

The skunks' and porcupines' distinct visual appearances are characteristics that they possess at all times, no matter what behaviors they are occupied with at a particular time. Such permanent features, which afford predator protection on a constant basis, were termed **primary defenses** by Edmunds (1974). Other examples of primary defenses are the bright coloration of the venomous coral snake and the shells of turtles. As we have seen in the preceding examples, the effectiveness of these primary defenses often is enhanced by complementary behavioral reactions. These, and other, defensive behavioral reactions were termed as **secondary defenses** by Edmunds. They are not constantly present as permanent characteristics, although they may always be available as reactions to meet specific threats.

As other secondary defenses, consider the reactions of threatened lions and other large cats such as tigers and leopards. They display aggressive disposition, with growls and roars and with baring of canines. These warnings can be backed up by dangerous attacks if the warnings fail to remove the threat. Often in the animal series, however, we may observe vivid warning signals presented by animals that possess scant additional resources with which to back up the warnings, as we will see in the next section.

Mimicry

The evolution of many species appears to have taken advantage of the showy stimuli by which animals with potent weapons advertise their presence—and the avoidance of those stimuli by predators. Many innocuous species have evolved similar stimulus properties to those presented by noxious species, although these mimics lack the weapons with which to back their advertisements. Various forms of **mimicry** have been given different names according to the nature of the stimulus being copied and the identity of the scientist who first described that mimicry. These include Batesian mimicry, Mullerian mimicry, and others (Grier & Burk, 1992).

In company with its bright and distinctive orange-and-black color pattern, the monarch butterfly evolved a noxious taste and a capability to induce violent nausea in predators that consume its flesh. A very similar color pattern appears to have been mimicked in the evolution of the viceroy butterfly, an otherwise innocuous species. In many parts of the eastern United States there occur both the deadly poisonous coral snake and the relatively harmless scarlet snake. Both species have evolved distinctive visual patterns of bright, horizontal rings of contrasting colors. Country people living in the habitat of these species devised a quaint homily that has been handed down through the generations to teach a distinction between the two species: "Red on yellow will kill a fellow; red on black is a friend to Jack."

The distinctive buzz of a disturbed rattlesnake is so famous among country people in the United States that—given appropriate context cues—its recognition might even be guessed by people hearing it for the first time. Rattlesnakes of numerous species occur throughout the country. Numerous other serpents residing there, and lacking the venomous weapon of the rattlesnake, have evolved a similar habit of rapidly vibrating their tails when disturbed. If this action occurs while these serpents are among dry leaves or other vegetation, as they often are, it produces a buzzing sound that is very difficult to approach, even if one is almost certain that the sound—in this instance—is merely mimicry.

The success of mimicry—as well as the value of possession of outstanding stimulus markers by noxious species—seems to depend importantly on a widespread capability of predators quickly to learn to avoid distinctive but otherwise innocuous stimuli that have been associated in their experience with a noxious or aversive stimulus. Of course, the effectiveness of such outstanding—and, in that sense, intense—stimuli to evoke avoidance may also benefit from a widespread tendency of animals (discussed in detail in Chapter 2) to withdraw from intense stimulation.

Noxious defensive systems that are importantly dependent on learning require that each predator must acquire, for itself, the experiences on which to base its avoidance of innocuous stimuli that signal the presence of a noxious agent. Many individuals of the noxious species, then, may be injured in the provision of these experiences to naive predators. Some of these injuries, such as in the case of a monarch butterfly eaten by a blue jay, may be fatal. Thus it appears likely that kin selection (Chapter 5) has been an important factor in the evolution of these defensive systems.

Defense of the Young

In the late summer of a year not long ago, a garden spider constructed her web across the frame of a window at the home of one of the authors. She built a large, rather open web of widely separated but very strong strands. It functioned well to ensnare large insects such as katydids and moths, which she raced from her position at the center of the web to fall upon and twirl into a cocoon of silk that she rapidly spun out. In the early weeks of her web hunting, she hid behind a thick, vertically oriented gauze of silk she had woven into the center of her web.

As the summer waned she eventually constructed two large egg sacs that she secured, one each, just off the upper corners of her web. As fall came on, she allowed the gauze of silk that had obscured her presence at the center of the web to deteriorate. By the time of late fall she stood out, stark and obvious on the web. She never captured prey anymore, yet she remained starkly on guard at her web, an ominous predator to many potential intruders. Eventually the first frost of winter came, and her body sagged a little, in death. But it remained at the center of the web, where it hung for two weeks more, a lifeless but still threatening emblem of protection for the developing spiderlings within her egg sacs.

Defense of the brood is extremely important. On it depends the successful individual reproduction on which evolution is based. We can readily understand why evolution has produced numerous variations on the theme of parental defense across the animal series.

Both parents of the largemouth bass remain with the fertilized eggs, protecting the nest against predation by bluegill bream and other small species of fish. These will, in turn, become the prey of the young bass within the eggs, provided they manage to develop and achieve adult status. After a day or so, the female bass departs, but the male remains at his task for many days, until after the eggs have hatched and the fry have had some time to mature. The vigor of his parental defense is a large factor in determining how many of his offspring survive to reach the fingerling stage.

The bobwhite quail and the killdeer are among the many avian species that illustrate variations of the broken-wing display, a pattern of parental defense. The young of these species leave the nest at an early age and travel about on the ground in the company of their mothers as the group forages. Being unable as yet to fly, these young birds are particularly vulnerable to predation. If a predator threatens the group, however, the mother moves away from her brood and begins flapping her wings wildly in partial and convulsive-like strokes. She slowly spins around in a circular motion, apparently in great distress to escape, but unable to fly away. Upon the outset of their mother's noisy and visually dramatic display, her young offspring crouch and remain motionless. Their **cryptic** coloration makes them difficult to spot among the leaves and grass. The mother continues her helpless gyrations until the predator charges near. Just as she appears about to be caught, she suddenly recovers enough to fly a short distance away, where she resumes the broken-wing display. This cycle of events is repeated several times as the predator is led farther and farther away from the hiding brood. Eventually, the mother "recovers" from her difficulty and flies completely away from the predator, making a wide semicircle back to the spot where her young await.

Many years ago the great pioneer of ornithology, A. C. Bent (1927), made a fascinating observation about the parental defensive reaction of the killdeer. He noticed that if a killdeer mother and brood were approached by a riderless horse, the mother killdeer made the sort of defense seen in many avian species whose young remain for an extended time in the relative safety of a nest in a tree. She flew repeatedly at the horse's head and eyes, performing loud, scolding vocalization all the while. If the horse had a *human rider*, however, with the forward-facing eyes that are a common hallmark of the predator, the bird went into its broken-wing display.

Showy escapes that may distract a predator's attention from vulnerable offspring are seen in a far-ranging variety of mammals including rabbits, racoons, and patas monkeys. We learned earlier (Chapter 5) about the protection of young animals that is afforded by large social groups ranging from colonial nesting birds through prairie dogs, gray wolves, and primates.

Other Protective Behaviors

Numerous behaviors we may not consider entirely or even primarily as predator defenses may be equally deserving consideration under the broader term of protective behaviors. These behaviors may afford protection from predators but also afford protection from a wide array of aversive conditions such as temperature extremes, weather, food shortage, or simply the presence in the environment of an aversive stimulus object.

Defensive Burying

A number of mammalian species that readily dig and use tunnels and burrows, will use their digging skills vigorously to cover up or bury an aversive stimulus object discovered within their tunnels or other frequented areas of their regular daily environment. The phenomenon is called **defensive burying,** and it has been widely studied in rats and mice. It occurs also among many hamsters, but apparently not among gerbils (Arnaut & Shettleworth, 1981; Fanselow & De Oca, 1998; Treit, Terlecki, & Pinel, 1980). Ground squirrels sometimes spray sand into the face of an approaching snake and cover their entrances to their burrow if driven out of them by a snake. Such actions impede the snake's pursuit and could result in trapping the snake within the burrow (Owings & Coss, 1977).

Defensive burying is often considered in relation to individual variations in behavior within the category of emotional characteristics. Rats that had been bred to produce distinct populations of high- and low-emotional individuals were tested for defensive burying by receiving shock from a shock prod. High-emotional rats showed both more defensive burying and more immobility following shock than did low-emotional rats (Wada & Makino, 1997). A similar study compared groups of wild house mice selected on the basis of aggressive tendencies. Aggressive individuals, or those characterized as having short attack latencies, showed more defensive burying in one test than did non-aggressive or long-attack-latency animals (Sluyter et al., 1996). The two groups performed comparable amounts of defensive burying when the agent for burying was sawdust from the home cage rather than fresh sawdust. Under that condition, both aggressive and nonaggressive animals displayed strong tendencies for defensive burying.

In keeping with its relation to the emotional dimension of behavior, defensive burying is viewed as an aggressive alternative to simple flight or to freezing. Also in keeping with this view, and with the results of Sluyter (1996) just mentioned, defensive burying is also seen as a form of nest or home area maintenance (Fanselow & De Oca, 1998). In cases involving shock prods, bad-tasting foods, and the bodies of dead conspecifics—all of which have been placed and left within the nest or home area, and all of which have been targets for defensive burying (Parker, 1988; Sei, Skolnick, & Arora, 1992; Wilkie, MacLennan, & Pinel, 1979)—an aversive stimulus object "invades" the nest and stays there. Defensive burying provides a means of closing off further contact with the offensive object while retaining possession and use of the nest.

Sleep and Hibernation

Current theoretical models of sleep view it as a process adapted to various ecological demands imposed by the environment in which particular species evolved (Webb, 1998). One of the chief ecological demands indicated as a factor in the evolution of sleep characteristics of prey species is predator protection. For example, numerous species are dependent upon daylight for the accomplishment of many of the environmental interactions on which their lives depend. Like the baboons, they may depend heavily on the visual sense and may function abroad at a considerable handicap during the night as opposed to during the day. At the same time, many of the most dangerous predators of these animals, such as the leopard, may be more active, and may hunt more efficiently, by night than by day. Baboons, then, might be well served to quit the field as daylight wanes and repair for the night to a safer location.

Thus, sleep can serve to keep the animals occupied and relatively out of harm's way during the hours of darkness. It also, of course, provides a quiet period during which bodily tissues can recover from fatigue brought on by daytime activities. The placement of these restorative quiet times, however, and the amount of indulgence in resting daily appear strongly related to ecological demands beyond the restorative function of sleep.

Webb (1998) points out that grazing animals such as horses, cattle, and sheep engage in comparatively small amounts of sleeping daily (about three to four hours). And their sleep is divided into brief naps scattered throughout the entire day, although concentrated more heavily during times of darkness. Historically, these prey species lived in open grasslands affording few safe havens for sleeping hoofed mammals. Their safety depended on being constantly alert and ready to use their speed to run away from predatory dangers, whenever they occurred. Furthermore, these grazers could continue to feed effectively as they remained alert, by night or by day. Their amounts of sleeping daily, as well as their patterns of sleep distribution, appear suited to these considerations. (More coverage of the topic of sleep is to be found in Chapter 2.)

One of the primary functions of sleep, as Webb (1975) stated, is to "aid and maintain periods of nonresponding" that "are necessary for survival" (p. 13). **Hibernation** is another adaptive process that imposes periods of nonresponding that may be imperative for survival. In this case, however, the degree of change from normal waking functioning is even more profound than in sleep and usually is maintained for much longer periods of time—for weeks or months rather than for hours. Like migration, which was discussed in Chapter 3, hibernation provides a means of bridging the gap across a period of time within an environment when life for the hibernating species is untenable because of excessive cold, drought, lack of food, or possibly other reasons. Hibernation occurs widely in numerous insects, amphibians, reptiles, and mammals, including deer mice, bats, ground squirrels, marmots, and bears (e.g., Dahbi & Lenoir, 1998; Ignat'ev, Vorob'ev, & Ziganshin, 1998; Hartman & Crews, 1996).

Numerous birds—maintaining internal temperatures in the neighborhood of 104°F—have such high rates of metabolism that the period of nonfeeding imposed by a night's sleep might be too long a time over which to sustain life unless the life processes can be slowed and reduced in the manner of hibernation. Such conditions of **torpor,** as it is called, occur on nights when recent feeding opportunities have been insufficient to sustain the individual at its normal rate of metabolism until dawn. The ability to become torpid at these times constitutes an important adaptation for survival. Torpor is most well known among hummingbirds, but occurs also in swallows, swifts, and poorwills (Ehrlich, Dobkin, & Wheye, 1988; Calder & King, 1974; Kayser, 1961).

Sheltering Behavior

In most cases, animals going into a period of hibernation must do so within some protected location, just as many animals retiring for a period of sleeping must do as well. Thus, **sheltering** behavior is a final topic of interest in our consideration of protective behaviors. Selection or seeking out of a protected location in which to sleep or rest is seen among octopuses, many species of fish, numerous birds, and mammals, including primates. Some degree of manufacturing one's own shelter is seen among prairie dogs, squirrels and chipmunks, marmots, picas, gerbils, beavers, and chimpanzees. Manufacture of shelter in keeping with parental behavior is also seen in insects, fish, alligators, birds, rabbits, gray wolves, and many other groups of species.

Summary: Principles Introduced in This Chapter

Because the consequences of a failure of defensive behavior may be immediate death, defensive behaviors override other motivational concerns. In defensive situations, an organism's responses become limited to species-specific defensive reactions and complementary behavior patterns. These patterns are subject to variation across species. Nevertheless, a number of generalities in defensive behavior may be discerned.

Withdrawal behavior is almost a universal aspect of defense. An ordered pattern of response to predator threat is seen widely across the full range of species complexity. The pattern may be viewed as a progressive reaction to increasing predatory danger. The pattern advances from hiding or remaining hidden to slipping or running away, to aggressive bluffing, to actual fighting, to perhaps feigning death. In addition to these responses to the actual presence of a predator, numerous species display patterns of wariness or watchfulness that seem designed to provide early detection of and/or information about potential predator threats.

In many species, a number of defensive advantages accrue to members of social groups, including the following:

1. Group members have an advantage in respect to early detection of predator threats.
2. Numerous species have evolved signals that communicate warning of predatory threat to other members of their social group.
3. Numerous species display patterns of predator inspection and group communication of predator information.
4. Group members encounter a reduced probability of being the focus of predator attack as compared to members of the same species that are alone.
5. Members of a group engage in a variety of group movements that hinder the success of predator attack upon the group. Widespread scattering of a group attacked by a predator is nearly universal.
6. Group members often cooperate to induce predator avoidance of the group.

Many species have evolved impressive means of imposing aversive stimulation upon potential predators. These "weapons," and warning stimuli associated with them, are often effective to induce predator avoidance.

Similar species living in the same vicinity as a species that possesses an outstanding weapon or weapons sometimes evolve similar stimulus characteristics to those that function as warning stimuli in the similar, and more noxious, species. This is known as mimicry.

Defense of offspring often is critical to the achievement of reproductive success; species have evolved a wide variety of behaviors that accomplish that function.

Other than direct predator defenses, additional protective behaviors include defensive burying, sleep, hibernation, and sheltering.

KEY TERMS

Cryptic   difficult to see or discern; an animal possessing cryptic coloration has an increased chance of escaping the notice of a predator.

Defensive burying   the covering up or burying of aversive stimulus objects, particularly in areas that are inhabited or frequently visited by the animal undertaking the burying.

Flash expansion   a rapid movement of closely grouped fish outward away from the center of the group; similar movements are seen in many closely grouping animals upon the occasion of a predator attack.

Hibernation a state of profound and prolonged sleep-like inactivity in which there is a general decrease in basic physiological processes such as heart rate and breathing rate.

Mimicry in respect to defensive behavior, the possession of characteristics that resemble those of another species in which the characteristics are associated with strong sources of predatory defense that are *not* possessed by the mimicking species.

Mobbing the harassing attack of members of a prey species, often in large numbers, against a potential predator, seen particularly among avian species.

Primary defenses permanent physical features, present at all times, that are considered to function in defending an animal against predation.

Secondary defenses behavioral reactions that come into play only when an animal encounters a predator attack or other aversive stimulation.

Sheltering selection or creation of a protected location in which to sleep or rest.

Species-specific defensive reactions a group of species-typical behaviors that occur in reaction to predator attack and other sources of strong aversive stimulation throughout an entire species.

Tonic immobility a state of profound unresponsiveness to stimulation that may function as an emergency defensive reaction, as in death feigning.

Torpor a state of profound inactivity and decreased physiological functioning similar to hibernation, but often not as long-lasting as usual episodes of hibernation.

REVIEW QUESTIONS

1. Briefly explain the critical importance of predator defense in evolutionary selection.

2. Natural selection has provided animals with an array of species-typical behaviors that function in emergency conditions of predatory attack. What are these emergency behaviors called?

3. Briefly cite evidence of psychotaxic organization of defensive behavior in flatworms.

4. Describe what is known as the "continuum of defensive reactions."

5. Tell one or two ways how a moose can successfully defend against attack by wolves.

6. Describe the behavior of dominant male baboons at times when the troop is threatened by predator attack.

7. What vocal behavior of vervets aids in their defense against predators such as leopards and eagles?

8. African wildebeests and bobwhite quail show a similar reaction that helps protect them when attacked by a predator. What is it?

9. What term is given to similar reactions among shoals of fish?

10. Describe an example of mobbing behavior of crows.

11. Describe the wariness of feeding deer or sparrows.

12. Describe an example of defensive behavior of ants or wasps.

13. Give an example of what is considered a primary defense.

14. What is the distinction of what is called a secondary defense?

15. Give an example of defense of the young among fish.

16. What is the "broken-wing" display?

17. Describe an example of defensive burying.

18. Explain how sleep can be viewed within the context of defensive behavior.

19. Distinguish between sleep and hibernation.

20. What is meant by the term *sheltering?*

REFERENCES

Arnaut, L., & Shettleworth, S. J. (1981). The role of spatial and temporal contiguity in defensive burying in rats. *Animal Learning and Behavior, 9*, 275–280.

Bent, A. C. (1927). *Life histories of North American birds. Shore birds* (Part 1). Washington, DC: Smithsonian Institution, United States National Museum.

Bolles, R. C. (1970). Species-specific defense reactions and avoidance learning. *Psychological Review, 77*, 32–46.

Bramblett, C. A. (1976). *Patterns of primate behavior.* Palo Alto, CA: Mayfield Publishing Co.

Calder, W. A., & King, J. R. (1974). Thermal and caloric relations in birds. In D. S. Farner, J. R. King, & K. C. Parkes (Eds.), *Avian Biology* (Vol. 4, pp. 259–413). New York: Academic Press.

Dahbi, A., & Lenoir, A. (1998). Nest separation and the dynamics of the gestalt odor in the polydomous ant *Cataglyphis iberica* (*Hymenoptera, Formicidae*). *Behavioral Ecology and Sociobiology, 42*, 349–355.

Edmunds, M. (1974). *Defense in animals.* Essex: Longmans Press.

Ehrlich, P. R., Dobkin, D. S., & Wheye, D. (1988). *The birder's handbook.* New York: Simon & Schuster.

Fanselow, M. S., & De Oca, B. M. (1998). Defensive behaviors. In G. Greenberg & M. M. Haraway (Eds.), *Comparative psychology: A handbook* (pp. 653–665). New York: Garland.

Fobes, J. L., & King, J. E. (Eds.). (1982). *Primate behavior.* New York: Academic Press.

Foster, W. A., & Treherne, J. E. (1981). Evidence for the dilution effect in the shellfish herd from fish predation on a marine insect. *Nature, 293*, 466–467.

Fox, M. W. (1969). Ontogeny of pre-killing behavior of *canidae. Behaviour, 35*, 259–272.

Gallup, G. G., Jr. (1998). Tonic immobility. In G. Greenberg & M. M. Hathaway (Eds.), *Comparative psychology: A handbook* (pp. 777–782). New York: Garland.

Godin, J.-G. J., & Morgan, M. J. (1985). Predator avoidance and school size in a cyprinodontid fish, the banded killifish (*Fundulus diaphanus Lesueur*). *Behavioral Ecology and Sociobiology, 16*, 105–110.

Grier, J. D., & Burk, T. (1992). *Biology of animal behavior.* St. Louis: Mosby-Year.

Hartman, V., & Crews, D. (1996). Sociosexual stimuli affect ER- and PR-mRNA abundance in the hypothalamus of all-female whiptail lizards. *Brain Research, 741*, 344–347.

Henning, C. W., Dunlap, W. P., & Gallup, G. G., Jr. (1976). Effect of distance and opportunity to escape on tonic immobility in *Anolis carolinensis. Psychological Record, 26*, 313–320.

Hoogland, J. L. (1996). Why do Gunnison's prairie dogs give anti-predator calls? *Animal Behaviour, 51*, 871–880.

Ignat'ev, D. A., Vorob'ev, V. V., & Ziganshin, R. Kh. (1998). Effects of a number of short peptides isolated from the brain of the hibernating ground squirrel on the EEG and behavior in rats. *Neuroscience and Behavioral Physiology, 28*, 158–166.

Kayser, C. (1961). *The physiology of natural hibernation.* New York: Pergamon.

Mech, L. D. (1966). *The wolves of Isle Royale.* Washington, DC: U.S. Government Printing Office.

O'Brien, T. J., & Dunlap, W. P. (1975). Tonic immobility in the blue crab (*Callinectes sapidus*, Rathbun): Its relation to threat of predation. *Journal of Comparative and Physiological Psychology, 89*, 86–94.

Owings, D. H., & Coss, R. G. (1977). Snake mobbing by California ground squirrels: Adaptive variation and ontogeny. *Behaviour, 62*, 50–69.

Parker, L. A. (1988). Defensive burying of flavors paired with lithium but not amphetamine. *Psychopharmacology, 96*, 250–252.

Pitcher, T. J. (1998). Shoaling and schooling behavior of fishes. In G. Greenberg & M. M. Hathaway (Eds.), *Comparative psychology: A handbook* (pp. 748–760). New York: Garland.

Roeder, K. D. (1962). The behavior of free flying moths in the presence of artificial ultrasonic pulses. *Animal Behaviour, 10,* 300–304.

Schaller, G. (1972). *The Serengeti lion.* Chicago: University of Chicago Press.

Sei, Y., Skolnick, P., & Arora, P. K. (1992). Strain variation in immune response and behavior following the death of cage cohorts. *International Journal of Neuroscience, 65,* 247–258.

Seyfarth, R. M., & Cheney, D. L. (1980). The ontogeny of Vervet monkey alarm calling: A preliminary report. *Zeitschrift für Tierpsychologie, 54,* 37–56.

Sluyter, F., Korte, S. M., Bohus, B., & Van Oortmerssen, G. P. (1996). Behavioral stress response of genetically selected aggressive and nonaggressive wild house mice in the shock-probe/defensive burying test. *Pharmacology, Biochemistry and Behavior, 54,* 113–116.

Treit, D., Terlecki, L. J., & Pinel, J. P. (1980). Conditioned defensive burying in rodents: Organismic variables. *Bulletin of the Psychonomic Society, 16,* 451–454.

Wada, Y., & Makino, J. (1997). Defensive burying in two strains of rats selected for emotional reactivity. *Behavioral Processes, 41,* 281–289.

Webb, W. B. (1975). The adaptive functions of sleep patterns. In P. Levin & W. P. Koella (Eds.), *Sleep 1974* (pp. 13–19). Basel, Switzerland: Karger.

Webb, W. B. (1998). Sleep. In G. Greenberg & M.M. Hathaway (Eds.), *Comparative psychology: A handbook* (pp. 327–331). New York: Garland.

Wilkie, D. M., MacLennan, J., & Pinel, J. P. (1979). Rat defensive behavior: Burying noxious food. *Journal of the Experimental Analysis of Behavior, 31,* 299–306.

CHAPTER

9 Learning as a Process of Development

The concept of learning remains one of the cornerstones of a psychological perspective on animal behavior and one of the key processes of behavior development. In this chapter, we will view learning as both a process that figures in the initial development of many species-typical behaviors as well as one that can modify many species-typical behaviors long after their initial development. Recall that the *development* of behavior appeared earlier as one of the three elements specified in our definition of comparative psychology, along with *evolution* of behavior and *species-typical behavior*. As a major factor in the development and modification of species-typical behavior, learning is a concept of central importance in comparative psychology.

A simple example will illustrate the power of learning as a dynamic influence of behavior development. Genetically, we are very little different today from people of the Stone Age of 12,000 years ago. Our diets and the controlled environments of our homes are among many living conditions that are different from theirs, and those differences undoubtedly have impacted our development. The greatest differences between ourselves and Stone Age people, however, are products of learning experiences, shared by all of us, which are vastly different from those encountered in earlier ages—experiences with automobiles, television, airplanes, shopping malls, computers, written language, formal education, mathematics, national political identities, and so on. Today the great grandchildren of New Guinea tribesmen—among the latest groups to represent Stone Age people in the modern age—may be found piloting jetliners around a globe that their ancestors hardly knew existed. The appearance of such feats results almost entirely from individual learning experiences that separate today's people from their forebears.

Review of the Concept

Again, by the term **learning,** we refer to a process whereby behavior is modified in a lasting way as a result of experience. Specifically, we are most interested in learning experiences in which two or more separate elements are associated with one another in their occurrence. The learning that results from such experiences is known as **associative learning.** In Chapter 1 we saw that two basic model types, or paradigms, of learning experience have proven particularly useful in the analysis of associative learning. They are known as classical and instrumental conditioning.

To review briefly, the protocol for classical conditioning calls for two stimulus events to occur together in sequence, one shortly before the other. The process works best if the second of the two stimuli is an outstanding or dominant event—one we might think worthy of having a signal to announce its occurrence in the future. Learning under this protocol is demonstrated when the first of the two associated stimuli begins to act as a signal for the second. That is, it begins to provoke behaviors that anticipate the imminent occurrence of the second event. In everyday life, this learning process can provide animals with signals for many of the dominant events on which their survival may turn. Having received a signal, animals can be ready for the occurrence of the important event. That event may be a danger, and readiness may provide protection. Or the event may represent opportunity, and readiness may allow taking advantage of it.

The protocol for instrumental conditioning calls for a particular act or response of the learner to produce important consequences in the environment. These consequences should have **motivational** importance, in that they are either notably attractive or notably aversive—notably rewarding (reinforcing) or notably punishing. Learning under this protocol usually is demonstrated when the learner begins to repeat the performance of **rewarded** responses with increased frequency, perhaps modifying their performance in the direction of improved efficiency of producing the reward. In the case of **punished** responses, the opposite occurs: The learner begins to omit or to avoid performance of responses that were previously punished. Notice that in the instrumental learning experience, the learner's behavior is controlling important aspects of its own environment; its responses are *instrumental* in this way. Through this learning process, an individual can learn how to bring about environmental events or circumstances that are important to its survival and reproductive success and to avoid the provocation of events or circumstances that threaten survival.

Levels of Learning

Of course, it is possible to recognize many more categories of learning than the two basic types stressed above. Razran (1971), for example, identified eleven levels of learning complexity ranging from nonassociative habituation through complex symbolic learning. A listing and brief description of these levels appears in Table 9.1. Razran's ordering of learning according to levels of complexity fits well with the idea of levels of behavioral complexity, one of the cornerstone ideas of this book.

The simpler forms of learning recognized in Razran's list occur across a wide range of species from the complexity level of the flatworms onward. However, learning plays an increasingly important role in development among more recently evolved species, and the more complex forms of learning in Razran's list are observed only among birds and mammals. In respect to levels of learning, we see once again a close relationship between complexity of nervous system development and complexity of behavior. Many of the more complex forms of learning correlate strongly with increases in brain size and complexity (Masterson & Berkley, 1974; Masterson & Skeen, 1972; Rumbaugh & Pate, 1984). Fobes and King (1982) reported a high correlation (0.72) between performance on discrimination-reversal learning tasks and degree of

TABLE 9.1   Razran's Levels (Grades) of Learning Representing an Evolutionary Hierarchy

Grade I. Reactive Learning (Nonassociative)

1. Habituation: waning or weakening of a response as a result of responding
2. Sensitization: enhancing or strengthening of a response as a result of responding

Grade II. Connective Learning (Associative)

3. Inhibitory conditioning: weakening of a response as a result of punishment
4. Classical conditioning: eliciting a response as a result of its association with another stimulus
5. Instrumental conditioning: strengthening a response as a result of its association with reinforcement (positive or negative)

Grade III. Integrative Learning (Learning to Perceive)

6. Sensory preconditioning: association of two stimuli in which one then becomes a conditioned stimulus for the other
7. Configuring learning: conditioning with compound stimuli in which the pattern or configuration of elements is important in response elicitation
8. Educative learning: perceptual learning or learning without awareness

Grade IV. Symbolic Learning

9. Symbosemic: the formation and use of symbols to represent categories
10. Sememic: symbols conveying a higher level of abstract meaning as in language
11. Logimemic: the emergence and use of logic in conveying meaning

neocortical-telencephalon development across species. Deacon (1990) identified three levels of complex learning with different degrees of nervous system complexity. According to Deacon, the use of language becomes possible only at the highest level of symbolic learning, in which symbols are freed from having reference only to one object or event and take meaning, as well, from context and relationships between and among symbols. Still another formulation of the levels concept applied to learning is Rumbaugh's (Rumbaugh, Washburn, & Hillix, 1996) triarchic organization of behavior to which he adds to classical and instrumental conditioned responses a more complex level of learned behavior, "emergents." Included in this category of learned behaviors are learning set, concept learning, representational use of symbols, numerical organization, and the like. Rumbaugh attributes "emergent behaviors" to increasingly complex nervous systems. This idea is highly compatible with our understanding of the relationship between nervous system evolution and complexity and the resulting increase in cognitive sophistication.

Theoretical Perspectives and Comparative Psychology

From the beginning of the modern history of learning theory, students of learning have stressed its adaptive significance for the success of the learning individual. Pavlov (1927), the first student of classical, or Pavlovian, conditioning, remarked how animals could learn to react to even the least outstanding or impressive stimulus if its presence indicated the proximity of an event of critical importance to survival. Thorndike (1911), the first student of what is now called instrumental conditioning, noted how his **Law of Effect** nearly always served to bring an animal into efficient adjustment with its environment: Actions that led to success were directly strengthened by that success, whereas those that led to failure or punishment were directly weakened by that outcome. (Many years later, in the late 1930s, Thorndike altered his Law of Effect to omit the role of punishment, restricting the law to a statement of how reward strengthens responses that precede it. Later work, however [e.g., Boe & Church, 1967], demonstrated clearly that punishment is quite capable of producing marked and lasting suppression of punished responses, as specified in Thorndike's original statement.)

Clark Hull (1943) proposed perhaps the most influential theory of learning yet stated—and one of the several most influential theories yet constructed by a psychologist. A major strength of Hull's theory was that it tied learning directly to biological success and the theory of evolution. According to Hull, animals learned those responses—and only those responses—that contributed directly to the preservation of life and reproductive success through the mechanism of **drive reduction.** Hull imported the concept of **drive** from the field of physiology (Cannon, 1932) to make it a major factor in the learning process. As Hull used the concept, drive was aroused as a reaction to physiological need and became stronger in reaction to increasing urgency of need. Needs were defined as conditions that threatened either individual or species survival. Because drives represented threats to survival, and learning required drive reduction, the only responses learned, in Hull's system, would be those that had a life-saving or life-preserving function. At the time when Hull's theory was stated, one would have been hard pressed to conceive of a system of learning more suitable to the theory of evolution.

Unfortunately for Hull's theory, it eventually became clear that learning often occurs outside of the immediate context of drive reduction and sometimes occurs even within a context of *increase* in drive (e.g., Sheffield, 1967; Spence, 1956). Although it is no longer considered a necessary component of *all* learning situations, drive reduction continues to appear, at the least, a circumstance that is very favorable to the occurrence of learning, and Hull's concept of learning through drive reduction remains a powerful idea.

R. W. White (1959) offered a theory of motivation that envisioned the experience of **competence** as a basic source of reinforcement in instrumental conditioning. White's conception of motivation, like Hull's, also fits elegantly with the theory of evolution. Competence is a synonym of fitness. It is demonstrated by any action that contributes to survival and reproductive success. Logically, competence includes any actions that reduce drive but is not restricted to those actions alone. It extends also to any practice or development of behavior that may contribute to drive reduction at a later time or that, indeed, is clearly associated with an increase in capability or efficiency.

A theoretical proposition by Glickman and Schiff (1967) makes many of the same predictions as White's theory while also suggesting a physiological mechanism to underlie these predictions, particularly with respect to the development of species-typical behavior. Glickman and Schiff proposed the very phenomenon of reinforcement itself developed originally as a means of ensuring appropriate development and lifelong performance of species-typical behaviors, the proper occurrence of which, they emphasized, is vital to survival. According to their theory, activation of neural substrates associated with the occurrence of species-typical behaviors is appetitive and conveys a strengthening or reinforcing effect upon responses that provide that activation. Glickman and Schiff considered such activation to derive primarily from feedback stimulation resulting directly from the performance of species-typical behaviors. A recent application of Glickman and Schiff's view (Haraway & Maples, 1998b) emphasized the investment of reinforcing capabilities not only in direct feedback stimulation but also in environmental consequences provoked by species-typical behaviors throughout the evolutionary history of the species being considered. We will see later in this chapter how this system of reinforcement provides for both the initial development and the lifelong adjustability of species-typical behaviors.

Thus far in this section we have explored conceptions of learning and motivation that forge explicit ties to the theory of evolution. Some students of behavior, however, have preferred to treat the issue of reinforcement without reference to physiological ideas such as drive reduction or behavioral substrates. One can always take the approach recommended by B. F. Skinner (1938): that certain events should be recognized as **reinforcers** entirely on the basis of their effectiveness at strengthening responses that precede their occurrence. In light of the foregoing discussion, we suggest, with Glickman and Schiff (1967), that species-typical behaviors and their usual stimulus consequences are likely candidates for inclusion within Skinner's category of reinforcing events.

Learning and Functional Utility across the Animal Series

We have seen in our previous discussions of feeding and other categories of functional behavior that learning is a factor in behavioral organization among species from the complexity level of the flatworms onward across the animal series. Straightforward evidence of associative learning below the complexity level of the flatworms is lacking, although there is good evidence of habituation learning (see Chapter 1) in starfish, phylum Echinodermata, and, indeed, even within the phylum Protozoa. Long-standing claims of associative learning demonstrated within the phylum Protozoa (Gelber, 1952, 1965) appear to have been successfully contested, at least for the present (Dewsbury, 1978).

Most observations of learning have been made in controlled laboratory conditions, and often the responses that were the focus of learning have been selected more on a basis of observational convenience than of **functional importance.** Neverthe-less, a number of studies have examined learning within a context of functional impor-tance to the fitness of the learner within its natural environment.

Males and females of blue guorami fish, *Trichogaster trichopterus*, were more suc-cessful in their breeding behavior when provided with Pavlovian conditioned stimuli that signaled the nearby presence of a conspecific than when not provided such sig-nals. An initial study (Hollis, Cadieux, & Colbert, 1989) demonstrated that a red light signaling visual presentation of an opposite-sex conspecific became an effective condi-tioned stimulus to elicit frontal displays of fin spreading as well as reduced aggression and more ready social accommodation in both males and females. In a later study (Hollis, Pharr, Dumas, Britton, & Field, 1997), similarly prepared pairs of male and female subjects were presented a red-light signal for a brief time just prior to their being allowed access to one another for a five-day period for possible breeding. Exper-imental subjects produced approximately 1,000 offspring per pair, while control sub-jects, for whom earlier presentations of the CS (the red light) and the US (visual presentation of an opposite-sex conspecific) had been made in an unpaired fashion, were largely unsuccessful at reproduction. This latter study, then, provides clear evi-dence of a direct increase in fitness resulting from classical conditioning.

Two experiments by Domjan and colleagues also provide outstanding evidence of the functional importance of sexual conditioning. Ejaculation was elicited in male Japanese quail following exposure to a probe stimulus resembling a female quail (Domjan, Blesbois, & Williams, 1998). Just prior to their exposure to the probe, the males were placed in a distinctive holding cage with which all were equally familiar. For experimental subjects, however, the cage had been established as a Pavlovian CS that had preceded copulation with a female quail. Control subjects had received simi-lar copulatory experiences but in a different context. Experimental subjects released greater volumes of semen and greater numbers of sperm in the ejaculation test than did the control subjects. Amounts of semen and numbers of sperm released may be viewed as attributes of reproductive fitness. The experiment demonstrates a benefit to these attributes as a consequence of Pavlovian conditioning. Similar benefits were demonstrated in a different way in another experiment with Japanese quail (Gutierrez & Domjan, 1996). Two conditioned stimuli were presented to each subject in the ex-periment. One stimulus (CS+) consistently signaled an opportunity for copulation with a female; the other stimulus (CS–) did not. In the test of reproductive fitness, a receptive female was released into a cage containing two males. Just prior to the fe-male's appearance, a stimulus was presented to the males. This stimulus had been es-tablished as CS+ for one of the subjects but had been established as CS– for the other subject. During most of the tests, the male for whom the pretest stimulus was a CS+ achieved copulation with the female before the male for whom the pretest stimulus was a CS– (see Figure 9.1).

A series of investigations into the learning abilities of honeybees by Bitterman and associates (Bitterman, 1988; Buchanan & Bitterman, 1989) succeeded in demon-strating a wide variety of basic learning phenomena (Papini, 1998). Many of these ex-periments were carried out within a context of natural foraging behavior, and the learning observed can be described as embodying an increase in the efficiency of

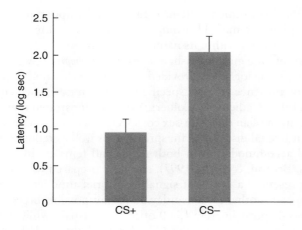

FIGURE 9.1 Sexual Conditioning in Japanese Quail
Source: Gutierrez & Domjan (1996), p. 173.

foraging behavior with experience. For example, bees readily learned to distinguish colors and other stimulus characteristics previously associated with large amounts of food and to select those stimuli for future approaches and landings in preference to stimuli previously found associated with smaller amounts of food. Bitterman's formal demonstrations of learning by honeybees are complemented by the observations of Dukas and Visscher (1994) that individual honeybees increase greatly in their foraging efficiency over the course of their first week's experience at foraging. Maldanado (1964) reported similar improvements in the efficiency of attack behavior of the common octopus over the course of foraging experiences with natural prey. The changes observed included the octopuses' launching their jet-assisted leaps onto prey from greater distances with increasing experience as well as their achievement of an improved success rate in their capture attempts.

Animals quickly learn to recognize stimulus changes that are associated with opportunities to feed. This phenomenon came to be known as the **caretaker effect** because Sheffield (Sheffield & Campbell, 1954) first noticed it as a reaction of laboratory rats to the arrival of the caretaker prior to his delivery of their daily food supply (Figure 9.2). Species in which similar reactions have been observed include fish, frogs, chickens, rats, cattle, horses, dogs, cats, and several species of primates. The advantage of learning to respond quickly to feeding opportunities in the natural environment seems obvious enough, even though lacking of formal demonstration. At a lake in a city park near the home of one of the authors, park visitors often throw chunks of bread into the water from a high pier at the lake's edge, where they are eaten avidly by the fish and turtles of the lake. If anyone walks out to the edge of this pier at almost any time of the day and simply stands for a minute or two, he or she will soon see turtles swimming toward him or her from all over the lake, making maximum turtle speed for the site of previous bread distribution.

Jill and Lynn Devenport (1994, 1998) have conducted innovative experiments on the foraging and learning of chipmunks in the natural settings provided by forest campgrounds in the western United States. These experimenters introduced chip-

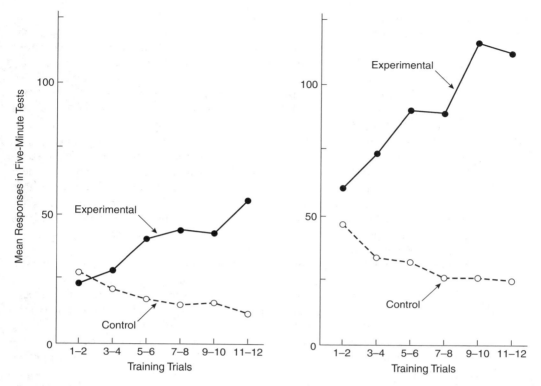

FIGURE 9.2   Conditioning of Locomotor Activity to a CS Paired with Feeding
Source: Sheffield & Campbell (1954), p. 98.

munk feeding stations into the habitat and allowed chipmunks plenty of opportunity to learn about them. The stations were platforms located atop posts that the chipmunks could climb, except when access to the upper post was blocked by a barrier imposed by the experimental regime. One of two feeding posts was provided a history as a rich food patch while a second feeding post was given a history as a relatively poor food patch. The chipmunks, of course, established a strong preference for visiting the richer of the two feeding posts. Once this preference was well established, the experimenters reversed the two food patches in relative richness. The formerly rich patch became poor and the formerly poor one became rich. The experimenters ensured that both patches were sampled by imposing barriers first on one patch and then the other. After the chipmunks had encountered experience with both patches in their new conditions of richness, barriers were placed on both feeding posts for a period of time before a preference test was run.

Not only were the chipmunks able to reverse their former preference in light of their most recent experience with the two patches, but their new preference now depended on the timing of the preference test. If the test were run within a short time of their last sampling of the two food patches, the chipmunks chose in favor of the patch that was most recently the richer of the two. If the test were run many hours after their last sampling, however, the chipmunks chose in favor of the patch with the long history of being the richer of the two. Thus it appeared that the chipmunks were capable not only of learning about the foraging opportunities afforded by the two patches but also of reacting differently to the same information on the basis of its recency (Figure 9.3).

Other members of the *sciurid* family, most notably various species of squirrels and ground squirrels, have displayed impressive capacities of spatial learning and spatial memory (Devenport & Devenport, 1998). Survival through the winter in these species depends upon their caching of hundreds of nuts or other food items in widely distributed locations throughout their home ranges. Their subsequent retrieval of these cached items many weeks later appears greatly facilitated by learning. Observations both of the high percentage of hidden items retrieved and of the directness and efficiency with which each retrieval is conducted make it appear that the squirrels have learned and remembered the locations of most cached items. Similarly impressive abilities of spatial learning and memory have been reported for the corvids, a family of birds (*Corvidae*) in which survival of individuals in many species depends upon the caching and successful retrieving of food items (Balda & Kamil, 1989; Kamil, Balda, & Olsuh, 1994).

Earlier in this book (Chapter 4) we discussed the complex adjustments of foraging behaviors observed in captive rats as they encountered a variety of foraging conditions in a closed economy designed to simulate nature (Collier & Johnson, 1998). The findings of Collier and his colleagues suggest that rats learn to adjust numerous aspects of their feeding behavior in such a way as to take efficient advantage of opportunities afforded by the environmental variations they encounter.

There is much evidence that choices of food objects in foraging behavior are greatly influenced by learning in a wide variety of species. Human infants, for example, display preferences only for sweet flavors and for salty flavors and display aversion to bitter and to sour flavors (Capaldi, 1998). All other taste preferences and aversions

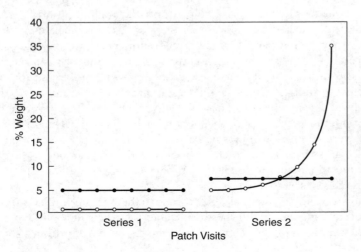

FIGURE 9.3 The Effect of Time Since Last Sampling on the Choice Between Two Feeding Stations with Different Histories of Richness

Source: Devenport & Devenport (1994), p. 788.

are at least partly products of experience. Taste preferences are established on the basis of experiences in which a new flavor is associated with a flavor that is already attractive, a new flavor is associated with the ingestion of a highly caloric substance, or a flavor is simply ingested several times in a neutral situation. With respect to flavor–calorie associations, the strength of the preference established for a flavor is a positive function of the amount of caloric content with which it has been associated (Capaldi, Campbell, Sheffer, & Bradford, 1987).

Taste aversions are established when a flavor is experienced in association with physical illness or sickness, particularly intestinal sickness involving nausea (Garcia & Koelling, 1966). Two obvious functions of taste learning are that it permits animals to form preferences for the tastes of foods that are readily digestible and that convey caloric benefits, and to form aversions for the tastes of foods that induce physical illness. The learning of taste aversions displays some interesting and unusual characteristics that we will explore in detail later in this chapter.

A considerable amount of work has addressed learning in relation to the critically important functional area of sexual behavior. This work has been reviewed by Domjan and Holloway (1998). Conditioning studies have revealed an impressive degree of plasticity in the sexual behavior of male fruit flies (genus *Drosophila*). Recently mated female fruit flies produce a distinctive pheromone that markedly reduces male sexual responsiveness. This suppression of sexual responsiveness has been shown conditionable to other stimulus characteristics of female fruit flies besides the pheromone (Siegel & Hall, 1979). Experience with recently mated females reduces male responses to virgin females, which share numerous stimulus characteristics with recently mated females, but which lack the pheromone originally responsible for the lack of male responsiveness. In the analysis of this conditioning, the pheromone functions as the unconditioned stimulus—suppressing male responsiveness—and other female characteristics common to both mated and virgin females function as conditioned stimuli (Domjan & Holloway, 1998). Similar conditioning of courtship suppression has been accomplished with more arbitrarily chosen conditioned stimuli of quinine (Ackerman & Siegel, 1986) and of acetate (Zawistowsik, 1988), each of which was paired with the suppressive pheromone as an unconditioned stimulus for experimental subjects but not for controls.

Sevenster (1973) used the sight of a gravid, or egg-laden, female apparently ready for reproductive behavior, as an effective reinforcing stimulus for increasing the frequency of occurrence of a response of swimming through a metal ring by a male stickleback. The same reinforcer, however, was unsuccessful when presented as a reward for the more aggressive response of biting a rod by a male stickleback. Responsiveness to the female reinforcer evidently was incompatible with the rod-biting response, and this poor "fit" between the instrumental response and its reinforcer prevented the instrumental strengthening effects otherwise to be expected. We will discuss other examples of good and poor fits between the elements of associative learning shortly.

Beyond the two experiments considered earlier in this chapter, Domjan and associates (e.g., Crawford & Domjan, 1993; Domjan, Akins, & Vandergriff, 1992; Domjan, Huber-McDonald, & Holloway, 1992; Domjan, Lyons, North, & Bruell, 1986; Domjan, O'Vary, & Green, 1988; Holloway & Domjan, 1993; Koksal, Domjan, &

Weisman, 1994) have conducted a wide-ranging series of investigations of classical conditioning of sexual behavior in Japanese quail, *Coturnix japonica*. Both visual presentation of and actual copulation with a female quail were found effective as unconditioned stimuli for the conditioning of courtship responses. Not surprisingly, actual copulation produced stronger conditioning than mere visual presentation of a female. A wide variety of stimuli, ranging from colored lights to a woodblock and a stuffed toy, were used effectively as conditioned stimuli in numerous studies. Where CS–US intervals were short and the CS presented an object that afforded physical support for the copulatory responses of grabbing, mounting, and so on, the conditioned response observed included actual copulation. The presence of a neck, a head, and some amount of plumage appeared to be a necessary component of the CS in these instances, however. In other circumstances, with a brief CS–US interval and a localized CS, the conditioned response included locomotor approach and sexual arousal. Use of the lengthy CS–US interval of twenty minutes produced conditioned responses of general locomotor arousal rather than locomotor approach to the CS.

Conditioned sexual arousal of males was also observed as a reaction to context cues provided by distinctive environments in which females had been encountered (Domjan, Akins, & Vandergriff, 1992). We may easily imagine that the physical readiness for mating demonstrated here should serve a male quail well in taking advantage of mating opportunities in a natural environment. Increased likelihood of taking advantage of mating opportunities also should result from the increased ability of experienced males—having both copulatory experience with females and noncopulatory experience with males—to discriminate between male and female conspecifics (Domjan & Nash, 1988; Nash, Domjan, & Askins, 1989). The sensitivity of quail sexual behavior to adjustment on the basis of associative learning experiences that is demonstrated so well in these experiments suggests strongly that such learning plays a functional role in sexual behavior in the natural environments of these and many similar species, and that it has done so for a very long time.

Domjan & Holloway's (1998) review also describes numerous demonstrations of sexual learning in mammals, including hamsters, mice, rats, and humans. The greatest number of studies has been done with rats. In numerous instances, opportunity to copulate has been used successfully as a reinforcer of instrumental behavior of both male and female rats. Intromission alone, without copulation, was shown to be an effective reinforcer, but intromission proceeding to ejaculation was shown even more effective, both for males (Kagan, 1955) and for females (Hill & Thomas, 1973). Components of the copulatory responses themselves have been found to be modifiable by instrumental contingencies (Kagan, 1955; Peters, 1983; Whalen, 1961). Both facilitative and suppressive effects have been shown. Silberberg and Adler (1974) found that males that were restricted in the number of intromissions permitted before being separated from females made the adjustment of achieving ejaculation with fewer intromissions as compared to males that were not so restricted in their access to females. In a further demonstration of alteration of sexual behavior, sexual conditioning was shown to improve the sexual performance of males with established sexual dysfunctions (Cutmore & Zamble, 1988). Classical conditioning has been shown effective in establishing conditioned responses of sexual arousal in male rats (Zamble, Hadad,

Mitchell, & Cutmore, 1985) and in human males (e.g., Rachman, 1966). Although studies of sexual learning in humans have been restricted by ethical considerations, sufficient results exist to suggest that human sexual responding is modifiable to a considerable degree by conditioning contingencies (Domjan & Holloway, 1998).

A series of studies by Maples, Haraway, and associates (Haraway, Maples, & Tolson, 1981, 1988; Maples & Haraway, 1982; Maples, Haraway, & Collie, 1988; Maples, Haraway, & Hutto, 1989) demonstrated the flexibility of species-typical vocalizations in adjustment to varying environmental stimulation in four species of gibbons, lesser apes of the genus *Hylobates*. In several of these experiments, individual gibbons increased the durations of their episodes of singing in response to receiving contingent reinforcement for singing in the form of audio playback of accompanying vocalization by a simulated family member, mate, or neighbor. Another study documented a series of adjustments that occurred as a newly mated pair of siamangs accommodated their duet singing to one another to achieve a coordinated duet. In still another study, to be considered in more detail later in this chapter, a male Mueller's gibbon actively adjusted the pacing of his dawn solo such as to accommodate changes in the pacing of solo singing by a simulated neighbor, whose singing, of course, was manipulated by the experimenters. The adjustments of behavior observed in each of these studies are readily interpreted as instances of learning, and each of the adjustments can be seen as being directly contributory to functions widely supposed to be served by gibbon vocal behavior in the natural environment (Haraway & Maples, 1998c).

General Laws and Species Variations

The grand theories of learning offered by Thorndike (1911), Hull (1943), and others focused on general principles of learning that were supposed to apply more or less equally across a broad range of animal species—at least across all vertebrate species, for example. Studies of learning during the first half of this century and beyond most often were addressed to a few species that, it was believed, could be considered as representatives, or models, for many species in respect to demonstration of general principles of learning. The Norway rat and the domestic pigeon were the most popular choices for this work. A small number of studies were done as well with chickens, dogs, cats, monkeys, and human children. The overwhelming interest in these studies was in the similarity of the learning process across various species; little interest was addressed toward the description of any differences in learning from one species to another.

Numerous attempts to describe systematic differences in learning capability among vertebrates focused on *quantitative* comparisons of the efficiency with which different species learned a wide variety of tasks, but these efforts found little evidence that permitted clear interpretation (Brookshire, 1970; Dewsbury, 1978; Warren, 1965). Such differences as did exist often appeared rather arbitrary: Goldfish might perform as well as chimpanzees; skunks might perform better than squirrel monkeys. Results often appeared to depend importantly on the selection of one type of learning task rather than another. For example, rats learned **discriminations** in a Y-maze more rapidly than did either squirrel monkeys or rhesus monkeys (Rumbaugh, 1968). It was difficult—or impossible—to determine to what extent observed differences between species represented differences in learning capacity and to what extent they merely represented differences in sensory systems, locomotor capabilities, motivational systems, or excellence of fit between the learning task and the evolutionary niche of the learner.

In an effort to overcome such obstacles, Bitterman (1960) devised a strategy of looking to see how different learning capabilities might be revealed by the occurrence of *qualitative* differences in the manner in which learning was related to a number of causal variables in different species. One important series of comparisons (Bitterman, 1965a, 1965b; Bitterman, Wodinsky, & Candland, 1958) looked for differences in the performance of rats, pigeons, turtles, and fish in learning to reverse experimentally established preferences in discrimination learning tasks. The tasks presented two prominent stimuli to the learners. Responses to one of the stimuli were reinforced while responses to the alternate stimulus were not reinforced. After this procedure had established a strong preference for responding to the reinforced stimulus, the reinforcement contingencies for the two stimuli were reversed, requiring the learners to reverse their previously established response preferences if they were to earn reinforcement under the new protocol. Particular interest turned on the question of whether learners would improve in the efficiency of their **reversal learning** when given repeated exposure to reversal problems. This work succeeded in illustrating several patterns of performance associated with the different classes of species examined.

The birds and mammals illustrated systematic improvement in reversal learning as a function of increased exposure to reversal problems. The fish failed to show such improvement. Turtles showed improvements in reversal learning under some conditions but not under others. Thus, Bitterman succeeded in demonstrating three patterns of learning among different classes of vertebrates: one associated with birds and mammals, one associated with fish, and an intermediate pattern associated with reptiles (turtles). Later study decreased the absolute appearance of differences among these vertebrate groups in reversal learning (Bitterman, 1975). Fish were shown capable of improving their reversal learning with extended training in some instances. Nevertheless, clear differences continued to be evident between their capabilities of reversal leaning as compared to those of birds and mammals.

A similar pattern of results emerged from Bitterman's (1965a) studies of **probability learning** among these groups of species. Animals experienced two response alternatives with different probabilities of reinforcement associated with each. Trials were arranged such that only one of the two response alternatives was to be reinforced for any single choice. That is, if reinforcement probabilities for the two alternatives were 30 percent and 70 percent, reward was obtainable only for response 1 on 30 percent of the trials and was obtainable only for response 2 on 70 percent of the trials. In this situation, animals choosing the high-probability alternative on every trial will maximize the number of their responses that earn a reward. Patterns of responding that describe that sort of response strategy are called **maximizing.** An alternative response strategy is one in which response choices approximate a **matching** of response choices to the probabilities of reinforcement for each choice. The matching strategy pays off systematically less than the maximizing strategy. In this type of learning situation, Bitterman again found a qualitative difference between the learning of fish, which usually followed a matching rather than a maximizing pattern in their responding, and mammals, which usually followed a maximizing pattern. Again, these differences did not provide for an absolute separation of fish and mammals, but they were found in most of the situations studied (Bitterman, 1965b).

Despite the success of Bitterman's work—now widely appreciated—interest in the field turned away from attempts to describe species differences in general learning capability and toward the demonstration of specific constraints and special preparedness of different species for learning particular types of associations. Current thinking on the issue of species comparisons in general learning capability is well represented by the recent conclusion of Timberlake and Hoffman (1998): "What is difficult to reconcile with evolution is the assumption that there exists a coherent continuum of learning stretching across phyla and culminating in an ideal type, the learning of humans" (p. 537). As Domjan (1998) maintained, along with general principles of learning, we must appreciate highly differentiated learning capabilities that are distinctive to the different evolutionary niches of different species of learners.

Constraints and Special Preparedness

During the first five or six decades of this century, the principles of learning were usually considered to apply equally to all modifiable behaviors, to all combinations of conditioned and unconditioned stimuli, and to all combinations of instrumental responses and reinforcing events. Thorndike (1911) understood that some behaviors are not very open to adjustment and had stated his Law of Effect in application only to **modifiable** connections of stimuli and responses. He also recognized that certain modifiable responses were particularly amenable to reward by reinforcing stimuli that seemed to **belong** in association with those responses in the world in which the ancestors of the subject of the learning had evolved. Nevertheless, little attention was paid to variations in the application of learning principles across many different responses, stimuli, motivational systems, and reinforcing stimuli (e.g., Skinner, 1938). The results of a considerable body of work done in the past few decades have given us an explicit appreciation that the characteristics of learning—like other characteristics of behavior—have been shaped in some detail by the evolutionary history of each different species. As we shall see, learning characteristics are capable of varying not only from one species to another, but within each species, from one response system to another, from one stimulus–stimulus association to another, and from one response-consequence association to another. The work that has demonstrated this remarkable variability in learning characteristics is often discussed under terms such as **constraints on learning, preparedness** and **contrapreparedness,** and **belongingness.**

Breland and Breland (1961) inadvertently discovered some surprising limits on the degree to which certain behaviors could be adjusted by learning in a number of species whose members they intended to use as trained acts in their entertaining animal shows. Raccoons were to be trained to take large tokens, or coins, and deposit them in a piggy bank, for which they would receive a food reward. As the raccoons proceeded with their training, they became progressively unable to handle the coins without going through extended episodes of rubbing the coins together. That sort of behavior pattern is species-typical for raccoons in handling food objects, and it seemed they could not refrain from treating the food-associated coins in the same manner, even though that behavior interfered with and delayed their attainment of real food. Domestic chickens, given the same training with smaller coins, seemed unable to drop the coins into a bank without first scratching them around on the floor, a species-typical pattern of behavior in their foraging for food in a natural environment. Pigs had similar difficulties in the task. They seemed unable to insert their coins into a piggy bank without first rooting them back and forth across the floor, even though, again, this behavior interfered with their obtaining real food. Breland and Breland coined the term *the* misbehavior *of organisms* in the title of a paper describing these limitations. What the Brelands had demonstrated were surprising inabilities of their subjects to adjust locomotor and manipulatory behaviors on the basis of their instrumental consequences. At the time, these inabilities were unexpected by the Brelands—and by practically everyone else—hence their humorous designation as "misbehavior."

The idea of species preparedness for certain types of learning experiences was also incorporated within Kuo's (1967) concept of **behavior potentials**—that each species has its own unique set of potentials to behave in particular ways. These specific potentials are a result of species genetics and evolutionary history and are not equally open to other species with other histories of evolution. Kuo's ideas were intended as an alternative to the explanation of behavior by instinct and are complementary to our current concept of species-typical behavior.

The Brelands' observations of "misbehavior" remind us of another finding related to a later-studied phenomenon of classical conditioning called **sign tracking.** In the protocol for sign tracking, a highly localized conditioned stimulus is presented on each trial a few seconds before presentation of food or some other attractive reinforcing stimulus. No responses of the learners are required to ensure delivery of the reinforcing stimulus. It occurs on schedule every trial, regardless of what the learners do. The basic finding of sign tracking is that learners come to approach the food-associated CS, approaching it from some distance away as though it were food (Brown & Jenkins, 1968; Domjan, 1998). An even more surprising finding, however, is that subjects in these studies persist in approaching the food-associated CS even when that behavior delays—or prevents entirely—their approaching and obtaining food, itself. The subjects appear unable to omit these classically conditioned approach responses, even though the instrumental consequences of those responses are to delay or prevent the acquisition of food that otherwise could be readily obtained (Hearst & Jenkins, 1974).

Both the Brelands' findings and the similar observations from sign tracking fit well with expectations of **behavior systems** theory (Timberlake, 1983), which holds that conditioned stimuli generally come to activate not merely a single, discrete response but rather an entire system of responses that have been associated with a particular unconditioned stimulus throughout the evolutionary history of the species being addressed. Thus, well-localized and discrete stimuli that have been associated with food evoke a whole host of responses that, historically, have been evoked by food itself. Again, the outstanding point of these studies as concerns limitations on learning is that—at least under some circumstances—animals have been unable to adjust loco-motor and manipulatory responses that, under general conditions, have been quite susceptible to modification in keeping with their instrumental consequences.

Similar limitations on learning have been described in relation to the relative ease or difficulty with which certain types of CS and US events may be associated in classical conditioning and with which certain types of response–consequence events may be associated in instrumental conditioning (Domjan, 1998). These variations in ability to learn associations on the basis of different pairings of stimuli and responses have been described by application of the concept of preparedness. When conditioned associations occur with outstanding ease, we speak of preparedness; when such associations occur only with outstanding difficulty, or not at all, we speak of contra-preparedness.

An early demonstration of these ideas came from a well-known study by Garcia and Koelling (1966). The experimenters allowed rats to drink distinctively flavored water, and each lick of this water was accompanied by the flash of a light and the click of an electrical relay. Following their drinking of the water, different groups of rats either received electric shock or were made sick by either radiation or injection of a nauseating chemical. The rats were tested later for the degree of suppression of drinking produced by each of the two categories of conditioned stimulus. During the test for conditioned aversion, the water either possessed the same distinctive flavor as it had during conditioning, or the animal's drinking of the water was accompanied by the same light flashes and clicks presented during conditioning. The results showed that animals that had encountered sickness as the unconditioned stimulus during conditioning acquired much greater aversion to the taste CS than to the light–sound CS, whereas those that had encountered electric shock as the unconditioned stimulus acquired much greater aversion to the light–sound CS than to the taste CS (see Figure 9.4).

These findings show that the rats were well prepared to learn the association of an auditory-visual cue with an attack from the outer environment but were not prepared to learn the association of a taste cue with such an attack. On the other hand, the rats were well prepared to learn the association of a taste cue with internal sickness but were not prepared to learn the association of an audiovisual cue with sickness. It seems likely that the association of taste and nausea is one that would have occurred numerous times, and with important consequences for survival, during the evolutionary history of rats. In language associated with the concept of *belongingness*, we might say that these types of stimuli "belong" together in respect to their relevant historical association with one another. The same can be said of the association between visual and auditory stimuli and the impending attack of a predator. But taste would seldom or never have provided a signal of predator attack, and noises and variations in visual stimulation would seldom or never have provided a signal of impending sickness. Such stimulus events do not "belong" together in a historical context.

Later work by Gemberling and Domjan (1982) found similar results in one-day-old rats, indicating that this stimulus-relevancy effect does not require the support of extensive previous experiences. Conditioned taste aversions are seen across a wide range of species, from crustaceans and insects through fish, amphibians, reptiles, birds, and mammals (Garcia & Riley, 1998). Demonstrations of the effects of CS–US relevancy in classical conditioning also have been reported for pigeons, which more

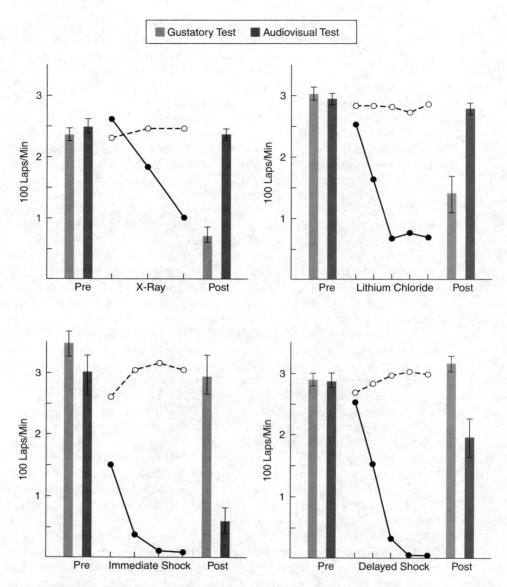

FIGURE 9.4   Effectiveness of Classical Conditioning of Taste Aversion as a Function of the Match-Up Between CS-Type and US-Type

Source: Garcia & Koelling (1966), p. 124.

readily learn visual cues than auditory cues for a food US (LoLordo, Jacobs, & Foree, 1982), for Japanese quail (Cusato & Domjan, 1998), and for rhesus monkeys (Cook & Mineka, 1990).

Shettleworth (1975) investigated the related issue of the relevance of associations between response type and type of reinforcer in instrumental conditioning. She found that responses that must have functioned many times in the foraging behavior of the wild ancestors of hamsters—responses such as digging and scratching at a wall—were easily strengthened by association with food reinforcement. On the other hand, responses that were unlikely functional components of foraging behavior, such as grooming of the face or scratching of the body, were not readily modifiable by food reinforcement (see Figure 9.5). Once again, these results are in line with predictions of behavior systems theory (Domjan, 1998; Timberlake, 1983). Shettleworth (1975) found that digging and scratching at a wall were increased in frequency of occurrence by food deprivation, but grooming responses were unaffected by it. The sensitivity of the digging and scratching responses to food deprivation is an indication that they are elements of a behavior system historically associated with feeding and, therefore, may be predicted to be readily amenable to food reinforcement, which they are. Similar observations were used to confirm predictions of response–reinforcer relevance and

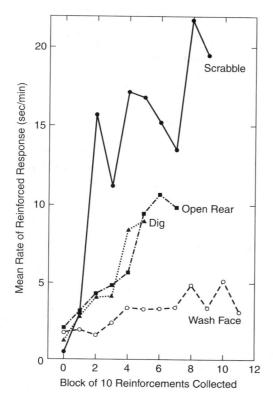

FIGURE 9.5 Effectiveness of Instrumental Reinforcement as a Function of the Match-Up of Response-Type and Type of Reinforcer

Source: Shettleworth (1975), p. 78.

corresponding reinforcer effectiveness for conditioning selected responses of carnivorous versus herbivorous mice (Timberlake & Washburne, 1989).

Besides revealing preparedness with respect to sensitivity to historically relevant cue stimuli, the conditioning of taste aversions also is remarkable with respect to another dimension of preparedness: It is capable of taking place across very long delay periods between CS occurrence and the onset of the US. The effectiveness of conditioning trials usually decreases markedly as the delay interval between CS and US presentations is increased beyond a length of eight seconds or so. The findings of a study of **conditioned taste aversion** by Smith and Roll (1967) illustrate how the conditioning of a taste aversion continues to be remarkably effective across delay intervals of at least six hours.

This remarkable feature of the taste-aversion conditioning may be viewed as being uniquely suited to the solution of evolutionary problems involving an animal's selection of food. In considering the outstanding temporal characteristics of taste-aversion conditioning, Garcia and Riley (1998) suggested the operation of two defensive systems in the learning of aversions—one system associated with defense of the skin and one associated with defense of the gut. If they were to be of maximum functional value, skin defenses, such as defenses against predator attack, would have needed to operate over the short time intervals that often must have separated reception of visual or auditory signals of the approach of a predator from the occurrence of an actual predator attack. Gut defenses, on the other hand, would have needed to operate across the long intervals that often would have separated reception of the taste of a food item from the onset of an illness that might result from ingestion of that food item. Furthermore, the skin defensive system could have been most beneficial by becoming especially sensitive to associations with visual and auditory stimulation, which often may have preceded predator attack; whereas the gut defense system could have been most beneficial by becoming especially sensitive to associations with taste stimulation, which often would have preceded food-induced illness. Garcia and Riley (1998) also stressed that conditioned taste aversions operate independently of cognition, in that humans preserve strong conditioned aversions to "innocent" foods they happened to eat prior to the onset of a physical illness, even though they are well aware that the now-detested food actually bore no responsibility for causing the illness.

The Shaping of Behavior by Experience

One of the major effects of instrumental conditioning is that of changing the **topography** of responses, modifying their form such that response variations that are among the most effective at provoking reinforcement come to be performed with greater frequency of occurrence. Numerous observations have shown that if a precisely defined form of response is required for delivery of reinforcement, that form of response often can be conditioned for frequent performance (e.g., Skinner, 1953; Weiss & Greenberg, 1998). Through means of a conditioning technique called the **method of successive approximations,** or **shaping,** responses can be honed by the changing requirements of reinforcement into improbable variations that might never have occurred without this special training. At the beginning of training, any rough approximation of the final desired form of response is accepted for reinforcement. Later, the requirements for reinforcement are refined systematically as occurrences of rough approximations of the response become frequent. At each step in the process, successively closer and closer approximations of the final response form are required until, in due time, the response form that was originally desired is achieved.

The method of successive approximations is based partly on the fact of response variation. No response is performed exactly the same way from one occurrence to another—there is always variation. This being the case, some of these response variations will be in the desired direction and others will not. By limiting reinforcement to suitable variations in the desirable direction, the animal trainer can shape behavior in impressive ways.

In the natural environment of many animals, differential reinforcing effects of varying forms of response can shape behavior in a similar fashion. Some response forms pay off more than others, or produce more attractive outcomes. The particular form that is most effective may vary from one circumstance to another. Response variability and a capacity to track differential reinforcement conditions in their performance of instrumental behaviors enable animals to discover and maximize the occurrence of precise forms of response in adjustment to the differing reinforcement demands of many different situations.

Limits of Behavioral Variation

Despite the great adjustability of instrumental behavior, it is important to realize that all responses are limited in their range of variability. Sometimes the range of variation is so great that we may fail to notice its limits. Even so, the limits are always there. Let us consider the case of rats being taught to run a six-foot straight runway to receive a food reward in the goal box at the runway's end. On each training trial, a rat is held in the start box at one end of the runway until the beginning of the trial, then the start box door is opened, and the way is clear for the rat to move down the six-foot alleyway to reach the goal box and obtain the food. The faster the rat starts to run and the faster it moves in running, the sooner it will obtain the food. Rats typically move slowly and with hesitation in the early trials of training but come to run faster and faster as training continues. Eventually they learn to crouch in the start box and to spring forward as soon as the door opens, running at high speed into the goal box, which they reach in running times ranging from slightly less to slightly more than one second. This is as fast as rats can run. At this point, they have reached the upper speed limits of their running behavior.

If we wished to observe the lower speed limits of their running behavior, we could employ the shaping techniques described earlier to make the rats run progressively slower and slower if they are to receive the reward. In carrying out this procedure, we require that the rats maintain a continuous flow of running from the start box all the way to the goal box on each trial that is to be reinforced. After a while we will reach a limit as to how slowly rats can continue their running before having to change over to a slower gait of forward movement (Vogel, 1998). Even if we are willing to allow the rats to move downward through progressively slower gaits in their forward movement, and continue to accept this performance for reinforcement, we still will reach a lower limit as to how far we can shape their behavior in the direction of slower and slower, but continuously maintained, forward movement.

We all are familiar with athletic contests that regularly probe the upper limits of various human behavior patterns. These limits are displayed most clearly in contests of individual performance such as seen in Olympic competition. One unique and highly cognitive feature of human social behavior is that we have established formal rules for the demonstration of numerous athletic skills and formal meetings for contesting their performance. These contests are attended by athletes and audiences from around the world. Permanent records are kept of the best performances yet achieved by humans in each category of competition. Similar meetings are held for the demonstration of outstanding achievements in music, dance, chess, billiards, and so on.

An experiment in which one of the authors was a participant (Maples, Haraway, & Collie, 1988; Haraway & Maples, 1998c) explored the limits of variation of one feature of the dawn singing of a male gibbon (see Figure 9.6). We designed the experiment, particularly, to demonstrate whether a male Mueller's gibbon would engage in **countersinging** with a simulated neighbor in the performance of his **dawn solo**. The dawn solos of male gibbons are composed of brief episodes of singing separated by quiet pauses during which a neighbor's song may occur and be heard. The demonstration of countersinging we sought required that the subject of our experiment perform his discrete song phrases in something of a "conversational" exchange with the songs of his neighbor, singing only in the pauses between his neighbor's vocalizations and

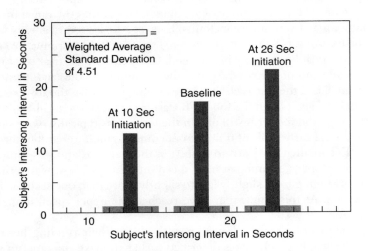

FIGURE 9.6   Adjustments in the Countersinging of a Male Mueller's Gibbon as a Function of Variations in the Singing Behavior of a Simulated Neighbor

Source: Haraway & Maples (1998c), p. 4.

maintaining that part–counterpart relationship across variations in the pacing of the neighbor's singing.

At the beginning of the experiment (baseline), we simply observed the subject's performance for several mornings as he sang his dawn song alone, without accompaniment. We determined that he initiated a song about once every eighteen seconds, with a standard deviation of about four seconds. Each episode of song lasted from two to four seconds, there was a pause of fourteen to sixteen seconds, then another song was performed. This behavior pattern often continued in progress for twenty to thirty minutes or more.

When we began to sing along with our subject, we programmed the neighbor's song—which was tape-recorded—to have an initiation rate of one song each eighteen seconds, with slight random variation built in to alleviate monotony. Our subject sang for long periods with the simulated neighbor, pacing his own singing slightly faster now at one song every seventeen seconds. His songs were performed almost exclusively in the pauses between his neighbor's songs.

After a number of dawn singing sessions, we increased the pace of the neighbor's singing to one song each fourteen seconds. This was an increase of one standard deviation of our subject's unaccompanied pace of singing. He responded by increasing the pace of his singing such as to match almost exactly his neighbor's new pace. He continued this pace of performance for a number of sessions; then we increased the neighbor's pace by another standard deviation, to one song each ten seconds. Our subject again increased his pace of singing, but only up to a rate of one song each twelve seconds. During our experimental variation thus far, the subject had increased his singing pace by 1.5 standard deviations, and it appeared that he had reached the limits of his adjustment capability in respect to faster pacing of his singing behavior.

Next, we slowed the pace of the neighbor's singing. With the simulated neighbor again singing at one song each eighteen seconds, our subject returned readily to the approximate level of his original pace, yet remained at a slightly faster singing pace than his neighbor's, perhaps as a carryover of his recent fast singing. He appeared reluctant to match further decreases in the neighbor's singing pace as, over numerous sessions, we slowed the pace by one, then by two standard deviations. Eventually, however, he slowed to a rate of one song each twenty-four seconds over a number of sessions when the neighbor's pace was programmed at one song each twenty-six seconds. At this time, we had slowed the subject's pace of singing by 1.5 standard deviations. Over the course of the experiment, then, our subject adjusted his pace of singing by 1.5 standard deviations in each direction, faster and slower. Throughout the range of his adjustment, he consistently sang in the pauses between his neighbor's songs, "interrupting" his neighbor at less than one-sixth the rate of occurrence expected by chance.

West and King (1988) similarly observed a wide range of adjustable variation in the phrasing of male brown-headed blackbird songs in response to reactions of females from various geographic areas. Males quickly center on the performance of song variations that succeed in eliciting a rapid wing flick from females and perform those variations to the relative exclusion of others. Although West and King made no attempt to test the extremes of adjustment of singing in these observations, they described flexible adjustments of male songs across a range of variations occurring naturally in the performance of species-typical songs across the wide geographical distribution of the species.

The functional value of such variations as these is apparent. They allow individuals to adjust to the range of naturally occurring variations of their species-typical behavior patterns across varying circumstances that may be frequently encountered by members of their species. These may well include variations across different circumstances encountered time and again even within their own individual lifetimes. In the case of dawn singing among male gibbons, for example, an individual may increase the pace of its singing to match that of a fast-paced neighboring competitor or decrease the pace of singing to accommodate a countersinging arrangement among at least three neighbors that are singing together over the same period of time—a circumstance that arises frequently in the natural environment (Marshall & Marshall, 1976).

In the course of the preceding discussion we have seen that learning is not a unitary process applying equally across all response systems and all associations of stimuli and responses. Rather, it is a process that has been honed by the evolution of each species and honed separately in respect to different response systems, different stimulus–stimulus associations, and different response–consequence outcomes. General principles of learning apply across all of the wide variety of instances of learning, but these principles must be adjusted to particular circumstances of species, stimulus classes, and response systems.

The study of constraints on learning is an ongoing field of investigation, yet sufficient work has been done for the illustration of several general themes. Indeed, in the course of this work, illustrations of these themes often have been successfully predicted by investigators on the basis of evolutionary principles. Stimulus–stimulus associations and response–consequence associations of a sort that may reasonably be considered to have been important across the evolutionary history of a species will be relatively easily formed in learning experience, whereas those of a sort that may be considered to have been irrelevant in species history will be difficult to form. Similarly, response systems that may reasonably be considered to have had a wide range of functional variation across species history—particularly those for which the point of highest functional effectiveness might vary with other circumstances—will demonstrate a wide range of flexible adjustment with learning experience. But those that have had a narrowly focused range of functional effectiveness will demonstrate little flexibility.

The study of constraints on learning also lends credence to a perspective of learning that dovetails nicely with the centrally important concept of species-typical behavior, defined in Chapter 1, and discussed and illustrated throughout this book. Furthermore, it is possible to see the coordination of these two concepts as a resolution of a long-standing opposition between the concepts of learning and instinct.

The Resolution of Learning and Instinct

We have discussed earlier in this book that the term **instinct** has been largely replaced in comparative psychology by the concept of *species-typical behavior* (Haraway & Maples, 1998a), a concept that has the advantages of being more flexible and inclusive while also being free of associations with ideas of invariability, single-factor genetic causation, and innate internal causes of behavior. The coordination of learning and species-typical behavior we have in mind views species-typical behavior as the basic raw material for learning and learned behavior as an adjustment of species-typical behavior brought about primarily by the experiences of the sort identified with procedures of classical and instrumental conditioning. In this view, learning proceeds from the interaction of species-typical behavior with the environment. Some behavior patterns are capable of wide-ranging adjustment whereas others are subject only to a narrow range of variation. When a form of behavior remains within the central portion of a range of variation commonly seen throughout the species of the behaving individual, we speak of species-typical behavior. When a form of behavior is far removed from its **modal** characteristics, and there is evidence that this variation results from learning experiences, we speak of learned behavior. Because there are many instances in which particular learning experiences are critically important to the normal development of species-typical behavior patterns, many examples of behavior may be taken to illustrate both species-typical behavior and learned behavior at one and the same time. But we shall see more about that eventuality shortly.

First, let us apply these ideas to the behavior of rats given reward training at running a runway, as described in the preceding section. Clearly, the running of rats is species-typical behavior. It may be expected to occur in nearly all mature and healthy rats under numerous appropriate circumstances and may be observed readily among populations of wild rats in their natural environments. However, precipitate performance of high-speed running as a reaction to the opening of a start-box door in a runway apparatus occurs with very few rats in their initial encounters with the apparatus and is predictable only in rats that have been given sufficient training in running down the runway and receiving a reward in the goal-box section of that runway. In this example, running is species-typical behavior. But fast and precipitate running in a particular runway apparatus is learned behavior.

It is important to understand that the rapid running seen in the runway apparatus has not generally displaced the learners' species-typical capabilities of locomotor movement in any way. These individuals continue to possess their full range of species-typical locomotor behaviors. Rather, their rapid and precipitate running in the runway has been added to the usual compliment of behaviors possessed by members of their species, and the performance of this behavioral skill has been keyed for occurrence to the particular runway encountered in their learning experience.

Learning and the Development of Behavior

By the term **development** we refer to the continual progression of behavioral change that accompanies physical growth and maturation from the birth of an organism to the attainment of adult status. In the course of this progression each individual acquires the typical behaviors that characterize its species. The process was envisioned by Schneirla (e.g., Schneirla & Rosenblatt, 1963) as a dynamic interaction of three basic elements: current stimulation, already existing or previously developed behavior patterns, and new behavior patterns currently emerging at a given point in the

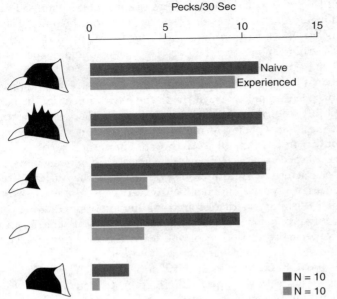

Pecks/30 Sec

Naive
Experienced

N = 10
N = 10

FIGURE 9.7
Development of the Configural Preference for the Parent's General Outline (Head Shape). The "standard" model that most closely resembles the actual parent comes to receive the greatest proportion of pecks in experienced chicks. Lengths of bars indicate mean pecking rates. (See text for explanation.)
Source: Hailman (1967), p. 89.

progression of physical growth. These three interacting elements may be seen in one instance or another as bearing the impact of each of the basic influences of development discussed in Chapter 1: the phylogenetic, individual, ontogenetic, experiential, and cultural influences.

Because current stimulation is one of the three interacting elements giving rise to development, it follows that the presence of certain stimuli can be critical to the occurrence of normal development. We have seen examples of the effects of critical social stimuli in the developmental processes of imprinting and social attachment (Chapter 7). The critical stimulation involved in development, in some cases, may be readily described as a learning experience resembling either classical or instrumental conditioning.

Hailman's (1967) classic analysis of the ontogeny of pecking in young laughing gulls (*Larus atricilla*) showed that the pecking of young birds improved steadily as a function of practice and that their pecking behavior was sensitive to differing circumstances of practice (see Figure 9.7). Hailman used models of adult heads representing several related gull species to elicit pecking responses in young chicks. He found that a number of different models were effective to elicit pecking in naive chicks and that several different models were approximately equally effective. With continued learning experiences the pecking behavior of the chicks became progressively more well controlled and more accurate as well as becoming more selectively directed toward adult models that had been associated with feeding. Chicks became selectively responsive to whatever adult models were associated with feeding, whether the models were replicas of the chicks' own species or were replicas of other gulls. Several features of the experiences involved in Hailman's study may be readily interpreted as instances of classical and instrumental conditioning.

Stimulus–stimulus association of certain models with food and with feeding provides for enhanced arousal of food responses to those models by means of classical conditioning. Response–consequence association between pecking responses and the presentation of food provides for strengthening of pecking responses by means of instrumental conditioning. Strengthened responding is differentially keyed to stimulus configurations of models associated with feeding, whereas the differentially successful consequences of well-directed and well-coordinated pecking responses provide for selective strengthening of those forms of response.

By imposing systematic differences of experience upon young laughing gulls, Hailman produced corresponding differences in the development of their pecking behavior. Under normal conditions, however, a young gull's feeding experiences occur only in association with the presence and actions of its own parents, and these uniform experiences contribute to a corresponding uniformity in the development of pecking behavior.

Often, environmental events involved in the progress of normal development may be well described simply as necessary stimulation. This will be the case whenever it appears that the mere *occurrence* of a certain stimulus rather than the *association* of stimulus–stimulus or response–stimulus events provides the critical circumstance for normal development. In either situation, the occurrence of the critical stimulus or critical learning experience must be ubiquitously available during the ontogeny of a species. Otherwise, it could not function as a factor in the development of species behavior characteristics.

It also follows from Schneirla's view of development that critical stimuli or experiences must be available at appropriate periods in the physical growth process, when new forms of behavior are emerging or are ready to emerge. Similarly, in respect to any instance of development, it can be important that behavior patterns scheduled for acquisition earlier in the normal schedule are present in the repertoire and available to interact with the emerging behavior in the normal fashion.

In their biological theory of reinforcement, introduced earlier in this chapter, Glickman and Schiff (1967) outlined a process by which feedback stimulation engendered directly by the occurrence of species-typical behaviors actively facilitates their development and differentially strengthens the more effective forms of these behaviors throughout the lifetime of the individual animal. This process can be seen as working like an internally established regime of successive approximations training based upon the reinforcing power of direct feedback stimulation and consequent environmental stimulation resulting from the occurrence of species-typical behaviors. The parameters of the reinforcement system associated with the development of each different pattern of species-typical behavior are seen as having been tailored by the unique evolutionary history of each species. The developmental system envisioned here provides each species not with a set of rigid behaviors but, instead, with a set of adjustable behavior patterns sensitive to variations of the environment for which the species is evolved. This arrangement has the great theoretical advantage not only of permitting and actually guiding the behavioral flexibility that logic tells us is necessary for maximum functionality but also of accounting for the wide range of variability of species-typical behavior that we commonly observe.

The usefulness of Glickman and Schiff's (1967) theory may be illustrated by applying it to the analysis of development and adjustment of several species-typical behavior patterns. Consider again the complex development of singing in male white-crowned sparrows (Chapter 7). The young male must hear the adult male's song during the first few weeks of life, although it does no singing at that age—only listening. In the Glickman and Schiff view, this hearing of the adult song activates discrete portions of the listener's sensory brain, differentiating those areas as reinforcement areas for activation, later in life, by stimulus feedback from a bird's own singing. We may view this differentiation to be critical to later reinforcement because we know that without this early "listening" phase of their song development, young birds will fail to acquire the song in later life (Marler, 1970).

Singing begins to emerge as a behavior in the tenth month of a young bird's life; it occurs at that time even in deafened birds and birds that never have heard the adult song. Acquisition of a normal song, however, occurs only in normally hearing birds that have heard the adult song in early life. Developing singers practice their songs for several weeks, gradually molding them into close approximations of the songs they heard as fledglings. In the Glickman and Schiff view, stimulus feedback from the practice of singing activates neural structures established as reinforcement areas in the early, "listening," phase of song development. Activation of these areas then differentially reinforces the performance of song pattern that resembles those heard early in life, gradually shaping the singer's performance into closer and closer approximations of those early songs.

This system of song development might permit a young sparrow to adjust his song in the direction of the songs of neighboring males in situations in which its own father's song is not the most commonly performed song type in the neighborhood. Such flexibility could be an important breeding advantage among male white-crowned sparrows, a species that displays notable geographical song dialects.

It should be instructive to consider instances of constraints and preparedness encountered in the preceding analysis. The listening phase of song learning is limited to the early portion of the life span, a time when the young bird is residing in the nest and its vicinity as its father and other male sparrows in the nesting habitat perform their territorial songs. The performing phase of song learning also occurs at a predictable time in the life span. Singing emerges near the end of the first year of life, several weeks before the beginning of the next breeding season. Young sparrows also may be considered highly prepared to listen particularly to the adult songs of their own species, and to learn those songs in preference to other noises and the songs of other species that may be common in the area. Instances of constraints and special preparedness such as these are seen commonly in the ontogeny of species-typical behaviors, regardless of whether the stimulus events involved are more readily viewed as simple stimulus effects or as associative learning.

Application of the Glickman and Schiff theory to the countersinging of male gibbons would suppose that a male's placement of his songs within the pauses between a neighbor's songs supplies the maximum reinforcement to be obtained by the performance of this species-typical behavior. In addition, the theory must suppose that maintenance of roughly a one-to-one correspondence between the occurrence of his own songs and his neighbor's song approximates an ideal circumstance with respect to the reinforcing effects attendant upon this type of behavior. Specific verification of these predictions independently of the data on which they are based is not available at this time; but it has been shown in other studies that singing with another gibbon is more reinforcing than singing alone (Haraway, Maples, & Tolson, 1981; Maples & Haraway, 1982) and that singing with the accompaniment of one's own species is more reinforcing than singing with the accompaniment of a different but related species (Haraway, Maples, & Tolson, 1988).

The progressive achievement of a well-coordinated duet by a newly formed pair of siamang gibbons (Maples, Haraway, & Hutto, 1989; Haraway & Maples, 1998b) provides another instance of behavioral variation that conforms well with expectations of Glickman and Schiff's views. In this instance, one would propose that the performance of a coordinated duet provides numerous points of dense reinforcement as compared to the performance of a poorly coordinated duet. The differential availability of this reinforcement for the performance of coordinated singing would be expected to shape a pair's song performance with practice, providing closer and closer approximations to the species standard of coordinated singing. Figure 9.8 shows the

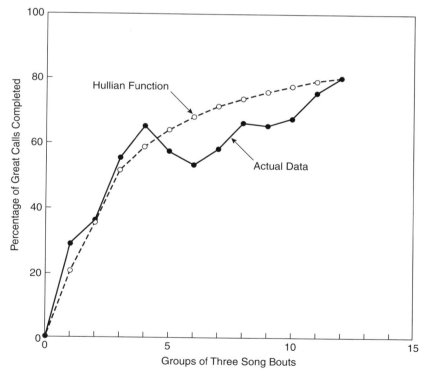

FIGURE 9.8   Progressive Achievement of Song Coordination of a Siamang Pair with Practice at Singing Together, Shown in Comparison to an Ideal Learning Function

Source: Haraway & Maples (1998c), p. 5.

progress of song coordination actually observed by Maples and colleagues and compares it to an ideal learning function generated from Hull's (1943) theory through the same asymptotic value actually observed. The strong resemblance between the two functions is impressive.

The preceding examples illustrate how Glickman and Schiff's theory provides one way by which the process of learning can play a lifelong role in the development and flexible adjustment of species-typical behaviors. As Haraway and Maples (1998c) said, this theory offers a process through which "a pattern of species-typical behavior remains adjustable for life to the consequent events that have defined the effectiveness of that pattern in the history of the species" (p. 9).

Summary: Principles Introduced in This Chapter

Learning is one of the major influences of behavior development. Its influences become prominent in the mollusks and are seen across the animal series at all higher levels of behavioral complexity. Associative learning through experiences approximated by classical and instrumental conditioning procedures accomplishes adjustments of behavior that can benefit survival. Classical conditioning primarily concerns associations between stimulus events over which the learner has no control. Such experiences provide signals for the recurrence of important events in the future. Instrumental conditioning primarily concerns associations between a learner's behavior and stimulus consequences of that behavior. It leads to the repetition of responses that provoke attractive consequences and avoidance of responses that provoke aversive consequences.

The functional value of learning is shown directly or is strongly suggested by a large and widespread volume of evidence. This evidence embraces animal species ranging from octopuses, flies, and honeybees throughout all classes of vertebrates, and categories of functional behavior including feeding, food preferences and aversions, sexual reproduction, territorial and sexual communication, and predator avoidance.

General principles of learning require adjustment in their application to different species and different types of experiences in relation to the historical relevance of those experiences to the survival of each species within its particular environmental niche. The necessity for such adjustment has been widely demonstrated by a body of experimental work concerning the ideas of constraints on learning, preparedness and contrapreparedness for particular instances of learning, and belongingness of the fit between elements that are to be associated in a learning experience.

The topography, or total form, of many behaviors is capable of being shaped and molded by instrumental conditioning experiences approximated by training procedures known as "shaping" and the "method of approximations." Much shaping of behavior undoubtedly occurs as animals experience the consequences of their actions in a natural environment. The range of variation across which a particular response may be capable of adjustment must be considered in relation to the range of its effective occurrence within the history of its species.

The concepts of instinct (species-typical behavior) and learning may be resolved to each other by the proposition that species-typical behavior supplies the raw material for all learning and that learned behavior results from the interaction of species-typical behavior with experience. It is not helpful to envision an absolute separation, or dichotomy of behavior, in relation to these two concepts. Rather, when a behavior pattern remains near the central portion of its range of variation in a species, it provides a clear example of species-typical behavior; but when a behavior pattern is far removed from its modal characteristics, and learning experiences can be invoked as the cause of variation, then that pattern provides a clear example of learned behavior. In many instances, a pattern of behavior illustrates both species-typical behavior and learned behavior at one and the same time. Examples such as this are seen in cases in which learning experiences are critical to the normal development of an instance of species-typical behavior.

Behavior development from birth to the attainment of adult status may be conceived as the product of a dynamic interaction of three elements: current stimulation, already existing or previously developed behavior patterns, and new behavior patterns currently emerging with physical growth. The presence of any and all of these elements at the appropriate moment in the normal developmental schedule may figure as a critically important circumstance to the development of a particular behavior pattern.

Within the category of current stimulation, many critically important stimuli may play their full role in development merely by being experienced, in and of themselves, without the necessity of being systematically associated with other stimuli or other responses beyond those directly evoked by the stimuli themselves. Other critically important stimuli, however, may play their role only by occurring in systematic association with another particular stimulus or response. In these instances, the required experience qualifies also as a learning experience.

Long after its initial development, a pattern of behavior may remain flexible and adjustable on the basis of learning experience. The theory of reinforcement offered by Glickman and Schiff provides for the lifelong adjustment of species-typical behavior patterns through a process similar to instrumental training procedures of shaping, or the method of approximations.

KEY TERMS

Associative learning   learning that is understood as involving associations of events that have occurred together or in sequence, as do the events in classical conditioning and instrumental conditioning procedures.

Behavior potentials   characteristics of behavior that are likely to develop in an individual as a normal representative of its species; *behavioral potential* was a term introduced by the comparative psychologist Kuo as a way of addressing species-typical behavior.

Behavior systems   groups of responses that often occur together in the same situations and that vary together as a function of a learning procedure that has been addressed to any member of the group; this concept applies particularly to groups of responses that occur commonly in reaction to a given unconditioned stimulus used in classical conditioning.

Belong, belongingness   in application to possible associations among stimuli and responses, the elements being associated are said to belong together, or to illustrate belongingness, if they often occurred together or were associated in the world inhabited by early ancestors of the species under study.

Caretaker effect   a marked increase in locomotor behavior or locomotor excitement provoked by a stimulus that has signaled past opportunities for feeding.

Competence   fitness, capability; competence is demonstrated by actions that contribute to survival and reproductive success.

Conditioned taste aversion   a learned aversion to a formerly neutral taste that results from encountering that taste prior to the onset of a strongly aversive stimulus or condition.

Constraints on learning   actually, constraints on the universal application of general *laws* of learning equally across all species and all stimuli and responses.

Contrapreparedness   an animal's being unprepared to learn a particular response or associations of particular stimuli or of particular stimuli and responses because of the unique evolutionary history of its species. (See also *belongingness* and *preparedness*.)

Countersinging   the performance of vocalizations by two or more animals in counterpoint to one another; particularly applied to the behavior of individuals of different groups as each sings from its own territory.

Dawn solo   Territory-holding males of most gibbon species perform extended sessions of vocal, or singing, behavior very early in the day; each male sings alone from his own territory but often sings in turn with one or more adjoining males singing from their territories nearby.

Development   in the context of behavior, development refers to a process of emergence and adjustment of behavior patterns that accompanies physical maturation, physical growth, and experience.

Discriminations   responding differently to closely similar stimuli; that is, differentiating between these similar stimuli.

Drive   an intervening variable associated with changes in motivation and thought of as resembling a state of behavioral tension resulting from physiological deficits or needs.

Drive reduction   a reduction of drive associated with the satisfaction of a motivational need.

Functional importance   importance to survival or to reproductive fitness.

Instinct   a term now largely outdated in psychology, instinct referred to built-in, innate, and fixed behavior patterns that were common throughout an entire species; old usages of the term often appeared to refer to unobserved and vaguely animistic internal causes of such fixed behavior.

Law of Effect   the principle introduced by Thorndike to deal with the basic facts of what is now known as instrumental conditioning; in today's terminology, that the occurrence of reinforcement strengthens the preceding response (or S–R connection) whereas the occurrence of punishment weakens the preceding response (or S–R connection).

Learning   a process by which behavior changes according to the individual experience of the learner. Learning is defined by lasting changes in behavior such as those seen in conditioning.

Matching   when responses to two different stimuli have different probabilities of being reinforced, matching is illustrated if the numbers of responses to each of the stimuli are roughly proportional to the probabilities of reinforcement associated with the two stimuli.

Maximizing   when responses to two different stimuli have different probabilities of being reinforced, maximizing is illustrated if nearly all responses are made to the stimulus associated with the higher probability of reinforcement; animals behaving in this way will maximize the number of reinforcements they receive.

Method of successive approximations   same as *shaping*, a technique of instrumental or operant conditioning in which the attainment of reinforcement is progressively made dependent on the performance of successively closer approximations of some highly defined response that may never have occurred without the use of this technique. The same sort of shaping can occur when reinforcement is differentially dependent upon more "skillful" and effective forms of response in the natural environment.

Modal   most frequently occurring, as in the most frequently occurring form of a response.

Modifiable   changeable or adjustable, particularly as a result of experience.

Motivational   having to do with motivation; that is, having to do with attractions and aversions, with approach behavior and withdrawal behavior, with reinforcement and punishment.

Preparedness   an animal's being prepared to learn a particular response or associations of particular stimuli or of particular stimuli and responses because of the unique evolutionary history of its species.

Probability learning   learning to respond at different rates to stimuli associated with different probabilities of reinforcement, that is, different probabilities that a response will be reinforced. (See also *maximizing* and *matching*.)

Punished, punishment   the occurrence of an aversive outcome as the result of a response. (See also *positive punishment* and *negative punishment*.)

Reinforcers   in Skinner's definition, stimuli that can be manipulated to strengthen a preceding response, through either onset of the stimulus (positive reinforcement) or offset of the stimulus (negative reinforcement).

Reversal learning (discrimination reversal)   learning to adjust quickly to reversals in a discrimination task in which the stimulus formerly associated with reinforcement of a response and the stimulus formerly associated with nonreinforcement of the response are reversed in their roles.

Rewarded, reward, reinforcement   the occurrence of an appetitive outcome as the result of a response.

Shaping   (See *method of successive approximations*.)

Sign tracking   an animal's learning to approach a particular stimulus merely on the basis of its having been presented as a signal for the presentation of food or some other strongly appetitive stimulus.

Species-typical behavior   behavior that is characteristic of an entire species and that develops at a predictable time in the life span in nearly all members of a species.

Topography (of a response)   the overall form and appearance of a response; the overall detail of movements that comprise a response.

REVIEW QUESTIONS

1. Very briefly tell what learning has to do with development.

2. What is the significance of the word *associative* in the designation of associative learning? Give an example to indicate what things are viewed as being associated here.

3. What is meant by the term *motivational importance*?

4. Name or identify one or two of the "higher" levels of learning listed by Razran.

5. Briefly tell what competence has to do with motivation according to the thinking of R. H. White.

6. How is species-typical behavior related to motivation in the theory of Glickman and Schiff?

7. Give an example of evidence that indicates how learning is related to the functional effectiveness of behaviors that are important to the "real" lives of animals in the "real" world.

8. What is the caretaker effect?

9. State one unusual characteristic of the conditioning seen in the case of conditioned taste aversions.

10. Briefly tell how the technique known as discrimination reversal has been used in the comparative study of learning.

11. How does an animal behave that is maximizing in a probability learning task?

12. What is meant by the term *belongingness*? Give an example to illustrate your answer.

13. Give an example from the work of Garcia and Koelling to illustrate the idea of preparedness.

14. What is a main idea of behavior systems theory?

15. Describe the method of successive approximations and tell how it can be related to the behavior of animals in their natural environment.

16. Tell how the idea of limits of behavioral variation relates to possibilities of shaping behavior through the method of successive approximations.

17. Give an example to illustrate flexible adjustment of the species-typical vocal behavior of gibbons.

18. Write a sentence or two to indicate the importance of species-typical behavior as a factor in learning. (There are several good answers to this question.)

19. What is meant by the modal form of a behavior pattern?

20. Briefly describe how Hailman demonstrated the role of learning in the development of a species-typical behavior pattern.

21. What three elements interact with each other to produce normal behavior development according to Schneirla's analysis?

22. Tell what sorts of experiences serve to reinforce coordinated singing of siamang duets according to an application of the ideas of Glickman and Schiff.

REFERENCES

Ackerman, S. L., & Siegel, R. W. (1986). Chemically reinforced conditioned courtship in *Drosophila*: Responses of wild-type and the *dunce, amnesiac,* and *Don Giovanni* mutants. *Journal of Neurogenetics, 3,* 111–123.

Balda, R. P., & Kamil A. C., (1989). A comparative study of cache recovery by three corvid species. *Animal Behaviour, 38,* 486–495.

Bitterman, M. E. (1960). Toward a comparative psychology of learning. *American Psychologist, 15,* 704–712.

Bitterman, M. E. (1965a). Phyletic differences in learning. *American Psychologist, 20,* 396–410.

Bitterman, M. E. (1965b). The evolution of intelligence. *Scientific American, 212,* 92–100.

Bitterman, M. E. (1975). The comparative analysis of learning. *Science, 188,* 699–709.

Bitterman, M. E. (1988). Vertebrate–invertebrate comparisons. In H. J. Jerison & I. Jerison (Eds.), *Intelligence and evolutionary biology* (pp. 251–275). Berlin: Springer-Verlag.

Bitterman, M. E., Wodinsky, J., & Candland, D. K. (1958). Some comparative psychology. *American Journal of Psychology, 71,* 94–110.

Boe, E. E., & Church, R. M. (1967) Permanent effect of punishment during extinction. *Journal of Comparative and Physiological Psychology, 63,* 486–492.

Breland, K., & Breland, M. (1961). The misbehavior of organisms. *American Psychologist, 16,* 681–684.

Brookshire, K. H. (1970). Comparative psychology of learning. In M. H. Marx (Ed.), *Learning: Interactions* (pp. 291–364). New York: Macmillan.

Brown, P. L., & Jenkins, H. M. (1968). Auto-shaping the pigeon's key peck. *Journal of the Experimental Analysis of Behavior, 11,* 1–8.

Buchanan, G. M., & Bitterman, M. E. (1989). Learning in honeybees as a function of amount of reward: Tests of the equal-asymptote assumption. *Animal Learning and Behavior, 17,* 475–480.

Cannon, W. B. (1932). *The wisdom of the body.* New York: W. W. Norton.

Capaldi, E. D. (1998). Conditioned preferences. In G. Greenberg & M. M. Haraway (Eds.), *Comparative psychology: A handbook* (pp. 543–548). New York: Garland.

Capaldi, E. D., Campbell, D. H., Sheffer, J., & Bradford, J. P. (1987). Conditioned flavor preferences based on delayed caloric consequences. *Journal of Experimental Psychology: Animal Behavior Processes, 13,* 150–155.

Collier, G., & Johnson, D. F. (1998). Laboratory simulations of foraging. In G. Greenberg & M. M. Haraway (Eds.), *Comparative psychology: A handbook* (pp. 646–712). New York: Garland.

Cook, M., & Mineka, S. (1990). Selective associations in the observational conditioning of fear in rhesus monkeys. *Journal of Experimental Psychology: Animal Behavior Processes, 16,* 372–389.

Crawford, L. L., & Domjan, M. (1993). Sexual approach conditioning: Omission contingency tests. *Animal Learning and Behavior, 21,* 42–50.

Cusato, B., & Domjan, M. (1998). Special efficacy of female species typical cues in sexual conditioning: Tests with a CS preexposure design. *Learning and Motivation, 29,* 152–157.

Cutmore, T. R., & Zamble, E. (1988). A Pavlovian procedure for improving sexual performance of noncopulating male rats. *Archives of Sexual Behavior, 17,* 371–380.

Deacon, T. W. (1990) Rethinking primate brain evolution. *American Zoologist, 30,* 629–705.

Devenport, J., & Devenport, L. (1998). Squirrel foraging behavior. In G. Greenberg & M. M. Haraway (Eds.), *Comparative psychology: A handbook* (pp. 492–498). New York: Garland.

Devenport, L. C., & Devenport, J. A. (1994). Time-dependent averaging of foraging information in least chipmunks and golden-mantled ground squirrels. *Animal Behaviour, 47,* 787–802.

Dewsbury, D. A. (1978). *Comparative animal behavior.* New York: McGraw-Hill.

Domjan, M. (1998). *The principles of learning and behavior.* Pacific Grove, CA: Brooks/Cole.

Domjan, M., Akins, C., & Vandergriff, D. H. (1992). Increased responding to female stimuli as a result of sexual experience: Tests of mechanisms of learning. *Quarterly Journal of Experimental Psychology, 45B,* 139–157.

Domjan, M., Blesbois, E., & Williams, J. (1998). The adaptive significance of sexual conditioning: Pavlovian control of sperm release. *Psychological Science, 9,* 411–415.

Domjan, M., & Holloway, K. S. (1998). Sexual learning. In G. Greenberg & M. M. Haraway (Eds.), *Comparative psychology: A handbook* (pp. 602–613) New York: Garland.

Domjan, M., Huber-McDonald, M., & Holloway, K. S. (1992). Conditioning copulatory behavior to an artificial object: Efficacy of stimulus fading. *Animal Learning and Behavior, 20,* 350–362.

Domjan, M., Lyons, R., North, N. C., & Bruell, J. (1986). Sexual Pavlovian conditioned approach behavior in male Japanese quail (*Coturnix coturnix japonica*). *Journal of Comparative Psychology, 100,* 413–421.

Domjan, M., & Nash, S. (1988). Stimulus control of social behavior in male Japanese quail, *Coturnix coturnix japonica. Animal Behaviour, 36,* 1006–1015.

Domjan, M., O'Vary, D., & Greene, P. (1988). Conditioning of appetitive and consummatory sexual behavior in male Japanese quail. *Journal of the Experimental Analysis of Behavior, 50,* 505–519.

Dukas, R., & Visscher, P. K. (1994). Lifetime learning by foraging honey bees. *Animal Behaviour, 48,* 1007–1012.

Fobes, J. L., & King, J. E. (1982). Measuring primate learning abilities. In J. L. Fobes & J. E. King (eds.), *Primate behavior* (pp. 289–326). New York: Academic Press.

Garcia, J., & Koelling, R. A. (1966). Relation of cue to consequence in avoidance learning. *Psychonomic Science, 4,* 123–124.

Garcia, J., & Riley, A. L. (1998). Conditioned taste aversions. In G. Greenberg & M. M. Haraway (Eds.), *Comparative psychology: A handbook* (pp. 549–661). New York: Garland.

Gelber, B. (1952). Investigation of the behavior of *Paramecium aurelia*: I. Modifications of behavior after training with reinforcement. *Journal of Comparative and Physiological Psychology, 45,* 58–65.

Gelber, B. (1965). Studies of the behavior of *Paramecium aurelia. Animal Behavior, 13,* 21–29.

Gemberling, G. A., & Domjan, M. (1982). Selective association in one-day-old rats: Taste–toxicosis and texture–shock aversion learning. *Journal of Comparative and Physiological Psychology, 96,* 105–113.

Glickman, S., & Schiff, B. (1967). A biological theory of reinforcement. *Psychological Review, 74,* 81–109.

Gutierrez, G., & Domjan, M. (1996). Learning and male–male sexual competition in Japanese quail (*Coturnix japonica*). *Journal of Comparative Psychology, 110*, 170–175.

Hailman, J. P. (1967). The ontogeny of an instinct. *Behaviour Supplements, 15*, 1–159.

Haraway, M. M., & Maples, E. G., Jr. (1998a). Species-typical behavior. In G. Greenberg & M. M. Haraway (Eds.), *Comparative psychology: A handbook* (pp. 191–198). New York: Garland.

Haraway, M. M., & Maples, E. G., Jr. (1998b). Gibbons: The singing ape. In G. Greenberg & M. M. Haraway (Eds.), *Comparative psychology: A handbook* (pp. 422–430). New York: Garland.

Haraway, M. M., & Maples, E. G., Jr. (1998c). Flexibility in the species-typical songs of gibbons. *Primates, 39*, 1–12.

Haraway, M. M., Maples, E. G., & Tolson, J. S. (1981). Taped vocalization as a reinforcer of vocal behavior of a siamang gibbon *(Symphalangus syndactylus)*. *Psychological Reports, 49*, 995–999.

Haraway, M M., Maples, E. G., & Tolson, J. S. (1988). Responsiveness of a male Mueller's gibbon to his own species-song, that of a *lar* gibbon, and a synthetic song of similar frequency. *Zoo Biology, 7*, 35–46.

Hearst, E., & Jenkins, H. M. (1974). *Sign-tracking: The stimulus-reinforcer relation and directed action.* Austin, TX: Psychonomic Society.

Hill, T. E., & Thomas, T. R. (1973). The role of reinforcement in the sexual behavior of the female rat. *Physiology and Behavior, 11*, 911–913.

Hollis, K. L., Cadieux, E. L., & Colbert, M. M. (1989). The biological function of Pavlovian conditioning: A mechanism for mating success in the blue gourami (*Trichogaster trichopterus*). *Journal of Comparative Psychology, 103*, 115–121.

Hollis, K. L., Pharr, V. L., Dumas, M. J., Britton, G. B., & Field, J. (1997). Classical conditioning provides paternity advantage for territorial blue gouramies (*Trichogaster trichopterus*). *Journal of Comparative Psychology, 111*, 219–225.

Holloway, K. S., & Domjan, M. (1993). Sexual approach conditioning: Unconditioned stimulus factors. *Journal of Experimental Psychology: Animal Behavior Processes, 19*, 38–46.

Hull, C. L. (1943). *Principles of behavior.* New York: Appleton-Century-Crofts.

Kagan, J. (1955). Differential reward value of incomplete and complete sexual behavior. *Journal of Comparative and Physiological Psychology, 48*, 59–64.

Kamil, A. C., Bulda, R. P., & Olsuh, D. J. (1994). Performance of four seed caching corvid species in the radial-arm maze analog. *Journal of Comparative Psychology, 108*, 385–393.

Koksal, F., Domjan, M., & Weisman, G. (1994). Blocking of the sexual conditioning of differentially effective conditioned stimulus objects. *Animal Learning and Behavior, 22*, 103–111.

Kuo, Z.-Y. (1967). *The dynamics of behavior development.* New York: Random House.

LoLordo, V. M., Jacobs, W. J., & Foree, D. D. (1982). Failure to block control by a relevant stimulus. *Animal Learning and Behavior, 10*, 183–193.

Maldanado, H. (1964). The control of a attack by *Octopus*. *Zeitschriftfür Vergleichindl Physiologie, 47*, 656–674.

Maples, E. G., & Haraway, M. M. (1982). Taped vocalization as a reinforcer of vocal behavior in a female agile gibbon (*Hylobates agilis*). *Psychological Reports, 51*, 1–18.

Maples, E. G., Haraway, M. M., & Collie, L. (1988). Interactive singing of a male Mueller's gibbon with a simulated neighbor. *Zoo Biology, 7*, 115–122.

Maples, E. G., Haraway, M. M., & Hutto, C. W. (1989). Development of coordinated singing in a newly formed siamang pair. *Zoo Biology, 8*, 367–378.

Marler, P. (1970). A comparative approach to vocal learning: Song development in white-crowned sparrows. *Journal of Comparative and Physiological Psychology Monograph, 71*, 1–25.

Marshall, J. T., & Marshall, E. R. (1976). Gibbons and their territorial songs. *Science, 193*, 235–237.

Masterson, R. B., & Berkley, M. A. (1974). Brain functions: Changing ideas in the role of sensory, motor, and association cortex in behavior. *Annual Review of Psychology, 25*, 277–312.

Masterson, R. B., & Skeen, L. C. (1972). Origins of anthropoid intelligence: Prefrontal system and delayed alternative in hedge hog, tree shrew, and bush baby. *Journal of Comparative and Physiological Psychology, 81*, 423–433.

Nash, S., Domjan, M., & Askins, M. (1989). Sexual discrimination learning in male Japanese quail (*Coturnix coturnix japonica*). *Journal of Comparative Psychology, 103*, 347–358.

Papini, M. R. (1998). Classical conditioning. In G. Greenberg & M. M. Haraway (Eds.), *Comparative psychology: A handbook* (pp. 523–530). New York: Garland.

Pavlov, I. P. (1927). *Conditioned reflexes.* (Translated by G. V. Anrep). London: Oxford University Press.

Peters, R. H. (1983). Learned aversions to copulatory behaviors in male rats. *Behavioral Neuroscience, 97,* 140–145.

Rachman, S. (1966). Sexual fetishism: An experimental analog. *Psychological Record, 16,* 293–296.

Razran, G. (1971). *Mind in evolution: An East–West synthesis of learned behavior and cognition.* New York: Houghton Mifflin.

Rumbaugh, D. (1968). The learning and sensory capacities of the squirrel monkey in phylogenetic perspective. In L. A. Rosenblum & R. W. Cooper (Eds.), *The squirrel monkey* (pp. 255–317). New York: Academic Press.

Rumbaugh, D. M., & Pate, J. L. (1984). Primates' learning by levels. In G. Greenberg & T. Sach (Eds.), *Behavioral evolution and integrative levels* (pp. 221–240). Hillsdale, NJ: Erlbaum.

Rumbaugh, D. M., Washburn, D. A., & Hillix, W. A. (1996). Respondents, operants, and emergents: Toward an integrated perspective on behavior. In K. Pribram & J. King (Eds.), *Learning as a self-organizing process* (pp. 57–73). Hillsdale, NJ: Erlbaum.

Schneirla, T. C., & Rosenblatt, J. S. (1963). "Critical periods" in the development of behavior. *Science, 139,* 1110–1115.

Sevenster, P. (1973). Incompatibility of response and reward. In R. A. Hinde & J. Stevenson-Hinde (Eds.), *Constraints on learning.* London: Academic Press.

Sheffield, F. D. (1967). A drive induction theory of learning. In R. N. Haber (Ed.), *Current research in motivation* (pp. 98–110). New York: Holt, Rinehart and Winston.

Sheffield, F. D., & Campbell, B. A. (1954). The role of experience in the "spontaneous" activity of hungry rats. *Journal of Comparative and Physiological Psychology, 47,* 97–100.

Shettleworth, S. J. (1975). Reinforcement and the organization of behavior in golden hamsters: Hunger, environment, and food reinforcement. *Journal of Experimental Psychology: Animal Behavior Processes, 1,* 56–87.

Siegel, R. W., & Hall, J. C. (1979). Conditioned responses in courtship behavior of normal and mutant *Drosophila. Proceedings of the National Academy of Sciences, USA, 76,* 3430–3434.

Silberberg, A., & Adler, N. (1974). Modulation of the copulatory sequence of the male rat by a schedule of reinforcement. *Science, 185,* 374–376.

Skinner, B. F. (1938). *The behavior of organisms.* New York: Appleton-Century-Crofts.

Skinner, B. F. (1953). *Science and human behavior.* New York: Macmillan.

Smith, J. C., & Roll, D. L. (1967). Trace conditioning with X-rays as an aversive stimulus. *Psychonomic Science, 9,* 11–12.

Spence, K. W. (1956). *Behavior theory and conditioning.* New Haven, CT: Yale University Press.

Thorndike, E. L. (1911). *Animal intelligence.* New York: Macmillan.

Timberlake, W. (1983). The functional organization of appetitive behavior: Behavior systems and learning. In M. D. Zeiler & P. Harzem (Eds.), *Advances in analysis of behavior,* Vol. 3. *Biological factors in learning* (pp. 177–221). Chichester, England: John Wiley.

Timberlake, W., & Hoffman, C. W. (1998). Comparative analyses of learning. In G. Greenberg & M. M. Haraway (Eds.), *Comparative psychology: A handbook* (pp. 531–542). New York: Garland.

Timberlake, W., & Washburne, D. L. (1989). Feeding ecology and laboratory predatory behavior toward live and artificial moving prey in seven rodent species. *Animal Learning and Behavior, 17,* 2–11.

Vogel, S. (1998). Cats' paws and catapults: Mechanical worlds of nature and people. New York: W. W. Norton.

Warren, J. M. (1965). Comparative psychology of learning. *Annual Review of Psychology, 16,* 95–118.

Weiss, E., & Greenberg, G. (1998). Operant conditioning of compliant behaviors in zoo animals. Paper presented at the spring meeting of the Southwestern Comparative Psychology Association, New Orleans.

West, M. J., & King, A. P. (1988). Female visual displays affect the development of male song in the cowbird. *Nature, 334,* 244–246.

Whalen, R. E. (1961). Effects of mounting without intromission and intromission without ejaculation on sexual behavior and maze learning. *Journal of Comparative and Physiological Psychology, 54,* 409–415.

White, R. W. (1959). Motivation reconsidered: The concept of competence. *Psychological Review, 66,* 297–333.

Zamble, E., Hadad, G. M., Mitchell, J. B., & Cutmore, T. R. (1985). Pavlovian conditioning of sexual arousal: First- and second-order effects. *Journal of Experimental Psychology: Animal Behavior Processes, 11,* 598–610.

Zawistowski, S. (1988). A replication demonstrating reduced courtship of *Drosophila melanogaster* by associative learning. *Journal of Comparative Psychology, 102,* 174–176.

CHAPTER

10 Animal Cognition and the Evolution of Language

Animals do some pretty amazing things. Many of the things they do make it look to us as if they had insightful and understanding minds. Some of their accomplishments seem almost as impressive as our own. In speaking of our own behavior, we do not hesitate to attribute complex actions to the operation of our minds. Are we equally ready to extend similar mental capacities to other animals? Historically, laymen have been quite ready to do so, and sometimes the same assertion has been made by careful students of animal behavior. But what do we mean by animal mind? That is one of the questions we must address in the following section.

First, let us consider what we mean by saying that our own behavior is a function of our minds. Perhaps we mean that we are aware of what we are doing "now" and what we are about to do next. We can say what it is we intend to do, then do it. Sometimes we can give convincing answers about why we are acting as we are and what we hope to accomplish by our actions. Sometimes we are aware of what information we are depending upon to guide our action. By no means are we always aware of reasons for our behavior or of features of the environment that are guiding our actions, but sometimes we are. Even when we are aware of reasons and guides for our behavior, we can never be sure how much of the full story of our behavior control is represented in our awareness. Many famous philosophers, and psychologists covering the range from Sigmund Freud to John Watson, have believed we have only a limited understanding of what controls our own behavior.

Yet consider how much more fortunate we are in contemplating the conscious understanding of behavior in our own species as compared to our position in contemplating a similar understanding of behavior in another species. At least we humans can testify to one another concerning mental experiences. We can investigate directly whether particular features of awareness exist in connection with causes, environmental cues, and goals in the behavior of our fellow human beings. With all other species, we must judge these matters entirely by observation of *nonverbal* behaviors. An exception to this restriction may be achieved soon in relation to the possession of language skills by a few individual great apes; if so, that will be the single exception.

Because we are unable to obtain direct testimony about mental features of behavior in nonhuman species, the only way that we can address such features scientifically is by means of a theoretical interpretation of behavior. The respected theoretical device of the **intervening variable** (Chapter 1) can invoke mental features as mediating factors permitting the summarization of numerous observed cause-and-effect relationships.

Two terms often employed to address mental features and operations involved in the mediation of behavior are **cognition** and **cognitive behavior.** It is through the use of these terms that present-day psychologists engage the issue of the animal mind.

Many authors have seen cognition as a convenient summarizing concept to apply to complex instances of learning and sensation/perception, to behaviors that accomplish timing and counting of events, to complex foraging behaviors, complex communication, and language. In this book, we adopt the definition advanced by Shettleworth (1998): "Cognition refers to the mechanisms by which animals acquire, process, store, and act on information from the environment" (p. 5). Shettleworth's definition focuses on how animals handle **information**—that is, on how animals behave in the face of the objects and events that continually impinge upon them, representing the current state of the environment and the animal's situation within it. The term *cognitive behavior* provides another way to refer to cognition; it is simply behavior that offers an opportunity for applying the idea of cognition.

One of the cardinal implications of evolutionary theory for behavior is that widely established behavior characteristics should have functional value. If cognition is a widely established characteristic of behavior, then what are its functions? Included among possible functions of cognition are maintenance of attention on cues critical to the performance of behavior-in-progress, maintenance of attention on behavioral consequences relevant to current motivational needs, maintenance of attention on attractive and aversive outcomes likely to result from current behavior, and anticipation of upcoming events in an ongoing sequence. In these ways, and doubtless in many others, cognition is easily conceived as having functional relevance. "Whatever consciousness is, we appear to have it in large measure, implying that it must have evolved gradually from small beginnings in simpler animals because it has adaptive advantages" (Thompson, 1993, p. 410).

If cognitive events are to be invoked as mediators of behavior, what sorts of intervening variables will be required? Consider the following three generic examples created by the current authors for illustrative purposes. Each example follows the same format: Any member of a class of observable causes is viewed as producing a change in an intervening variable, and that change in the intervening variable is viewed as being reflected equally well by any member of a class of observable effects. This is how the causal sequence of each intervening variable is viewed:

Causes → Intervening Process → Effects

1. **Anticipation of Forthcoming Events (as in Classical Conditioning)**
   Causes: Repeated experience of a sequence of environmental events: A—B
   Intervening Process: Cognitive anticipation of event B, given occurrence of event A
   Effects: Performance of anticipatory responses appropriate to event B, upon occurrence of event A
2. **Arousal of Food Motivation**
   Causes: Occurrence of food deprivation or other means of increasing the body's need for food
   Intervening Process: Activation of cognitive processes representing "food ideas," including attention to and attraction to food and to food-related stimuli and responses

Effects: Increased responsiveness to food and food-related stimuli; increased performance of food-related responses

3. **Activation of Goal-Directed Behavior**

Causes: (a) Experience of a sequence of events such that R→delivery of food from the environment; (b) occurrence of food deprivation or other means of arousing food motivation; (c) encounter with stimulus conditions in which food reinforcement of R has occurred

Intervening Process: Attention to some cognitive representation of the past sequence of events wherein R→food; cognitive attraction to food

Effects: Businesslike or purposive-appearing performance of the response pattern associated with past food reinforcement

Note that in each of these examples the causes and effects are observable events, whereas the intervening process is never directly observed but is included as a means of interpreting the observations and of summarizing perhaps a great number of similar observations. It is appropriate to be conservative in our use of this sort of theoretical interpretation. We should require that the observations at hand clearly compel the chosen interpretation and that no simpler interpretation is equally plausible. As Blumberg and Wasserman (1995) have said, "many…bold conclusions about conscious mental processes are rash and will not stand close scrutiny…" (p. 142). Remember that Morgan's canon (Chapter 1) requires us to accept the simplest interpretation possible in respect to psychological abilities assigned to the organisms being addressed.

Numerous casual observations had been made of American crows dropping nuts onto hard-surfaced roads in front of oncoming cars. Whenever a car ran over a nut and crushed it, a crow was enabled to get at the meat within the shell that, until then, had been unobtainable. It was readily assumed that these crows were quite clever, able to appreciate the advantage of dropping nuts into the path of oncoming cars in order to have the nuts crushed for eating. When more careful observations were made, however, it was discovered that the crows were equally as likely to drop nuts when no cars were approaching as when cars were near (Shettleworth, 1998). They did not appear to have any understanding of the role of cars in crushing nuts. The crows no longer appeared as clever as they once had, yet some indication of cleverness remained. After all, the crows still were dropping nuts onto a hard surface, and repeated occurrences of this behavior often resulted in breaking open the shell and exposing the meat. Such behavior can be viewed as an instance of instrumental conditioning, perhaps enhanced by the social environment of crows (Chapter 4). Even so, many of us may consider it likely that the crows have some awareness of the relationship between dropping a nut onto a particular sort of stimulus array and exposure of the meat for eating. We may wish to adopt a cognitive interpretation of this behavior by use of an intervening variable.

Learning

As we have indicated earlier in the book, behavior becomes increasingly more complex as we ascend through the behavioral levels. We have for the most part attributed this to increasing complexity of nervous systems, although other processes are involved as well. This idea is perhaps clearest for the broad topic of learning, discussed at length in an earlier chapter. The simplest forms of learning appear across many phyla and do not correlate well with increases in nervous system complexity. One reason for accounts that purport to discern no differences in learning speed across species (Pearce, 1997) is a failure to take this important fact into account. On the other hand, several forms of complex learning do show this important correlation (Masterson & Berkley, 1974; Masterson & Skeen, 1972; Rumbaugh & Pate, 1984a, 1984b). The absence of this relationship may at first appear to contradict the rule of progressive complexity; it is, in fact, precisely what the concept of levels of organization predicts. Behaviors organized at lower levels are not replaced by higher forms of those behaviors; rather they are subsumed at the higher levels. Referring to Table 10.1, animals functioning at the highest levels will be expected to display all learning below that which is characteristic of their level, although not higher forms of learning. Thus, we expect animals at many levels of neural complexity to display simple stimulus–response learning. Organisms with simple neural organization are limited to these simpler forms of learning, whereas for animals with more complex neural organization, such learning represents only a base level of learning capability.

Related to Razran's (1971) formulation of eleven levels of learning (see Table 9.1 on p. 220) is that of Deacon (1990), who identified only three levels of complex learning correlated highly with nervous system complexity. The least complex form is characterized by an ability to reference objects in the environment to symbols that represent those objects only, in a one-to-one manner. One token or symbol can represent only one object. This level of learning permits simple and inefficient communication only. To be able to reference twenty objects, the organism needs twenty separate symbols. At the next level of learning complexity, objects and events can be represented by patterns of symbols, allowing a relatively large number of objects or events to be represented by a relatively small number of symbols arranged in different combinations. A good example is the Arabic numeral system in which only ten symbols can be combined and recombined to represent an infinite number of events. But it is only at the highest level of learning complexity that symbolic learning becomes possible. Symbols here are not restricted to object referencing, and meaning can be extracted from relationships between and among symbols. This is exemplified by algebraic concepts in contrast to a static numbering system. Deacon (1990) suggests that these learning levels represent levels of cognitive complexity, language becoming possible only when the highest level is achieved. We have adopted this formulation and see it as an important correlate of the three highest psychosocial behavioral grades we have postulated in this book.

Of course, complex learning can be measured in several ways. It is possible to identify measures of learning that correlate learning complexity to measures of nervous system advance. Early comparative approaches to learning made use of a procedure studied first by Harlow (1949), the learning set, or the "learning to learn" paradigm. In this technique animals were taught successive discrimination tasks, and if their performances were shown to improve over the series, they were getting better; they were **learning to learn.** This approach proved popular to psychologists studying species differences in learning ability. It was a simple procedure and appeared to demonstrate species differences in acquisition speed of successive discrimination tasks.

TABLE 10.1 Proposed new stages of awareness, with examples

Stage	Basis of assessment	Purpose	Examples
	Sensation/perception/cognition		
(1)	Sensation	Detection	Reflexive Absolute threshold Simple reaction time Motion Sensory memory, color vision Brightness Contrast Sensitivity Motion parallax
(2)	Sensation/Perception	Discrimination	Acuity Complex reaction time Optic flow Difference threshold Imagery
		Depth	Binocular Monocular Size constancy (perceptual) Perspective (perceptual)
(3)	Perception/Cognition; perceptions (Gregory (1980)) as hypotheses	Recognition Organization	Gestalts Pattern Form Object Short-term, working memory Events Location (Ego centrality) Hallucination Mental rotation
(4)	Cognition Executive	Evaluation	Imagery Long-term memory and stored knowledge Experience Problem solving (e.g., tool use) Decision making Stroop effect
		Meaning Purely "Intrinsic"	Mental representation Volition, intent Self-awareness and that of others Mental states Creativity

Source: Piggins & Phillips (1998), p. 195.

However, the procedure made no allowances for the diversity of various animal forms, for their sizes, manual dexterity, food preferences, or sensory systems. An improvement was made in the procedure, such that the correct choices are switched from always being "A" at the conclusion of a series of problems to now being "B" (Rumbaugh & Pate, 1984a, 1984b; Rumbaugh, Washburn, & Pate, 1998). That is, we were now testing the animals' ability to reverse what they just learned. Rumbaugh (1969) labeled this procedure the **Transfer Index** (TI), because it offered some measure of animals' ability to transfer what they had just learned to some new tasks.

The TI is a measure of the subject's ability to transfer small amounts of learning. It is a ratio based on percentage of choices correct on transfer test trials relative to the criterional learning level used in training. Criterional training procedures establish the subject's performance at a specific level (i.e., 67 percent and 84 percent responses correct) on each of a series of two-choice visual discrimination problems, at which point a per problem transfer-of-training test is given. To the degree that transfer testing yields accuracy of choice levels higher than the prior criterional training level, positive transfer is indicated and vice versa (TI > 1.00 or TI < 1.00, respectively). Within the primate order, there is a high and positive correlation between brain size/complexity and ability to transfer learning positively rather than negatively. Additionally, an increase in the criterional training level (i.e., from 67 percent to 84 percent responses) enhances transfer testing for the primates with the larger and more complex brains, whereas it deters transfer for primates with the smaller and less complex brains.

Since its introduction, the TI has been taken as a suitable measure of learning complexity. The TI is widely understood to provide a measure of the animal's ability to abstract symbolic relationships from reference-index relationships. Fobes and King (1982) reported a correlation of 0.72 between neocortex–telencephalon size and TI scores. Thus, as neocortex and telencephalon size increased, fewer trials were required for animals to reach reversal learning performance criteria. The relationship between prereversal performance criterion and the number of trials required to reach postreversal criterion is also of interest. Rumbaugh and Pate (1984a) have shown that as the prereversal criterion is increased from 67 percent to 84 percent correct responses, performance is improved for chimpanzees, gorillas, and orangutans, whereas it did not change, or worsened, in **prosimians** and monkeys.

Shown in Figure 10.1 is the relationship between the encephalization quotient and learning set (TI) performance. The anagenetic trend in learning capability is apparent in the figure.

Cognitive Aspects of Foraging

In Chapter 4 of this book we described some remarkable findings concerning foraging feats accomplished by squirrels and chipmunks, rats, and corvids, a family of birds that includes the jays and crows. Many squirrels, chipmunks, and corvids inhabit an environment in which cold and snow-filled winters place a premium on their ability to store away large quantities of food during summer and fall for use as a food supply

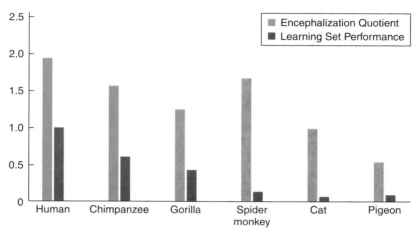

FIGURE 10.1   Cross-Species Comparison of Learning Set and Encephalization Quotient

during the scarcities of winter. These food caches must be well hidden as a hedge against their being found and eaten by a competitor, and many squirrels and corvids spread their caches across a great many locations, which prevents the discovery of any one cache by a competitor from threatening the entire food supply. These widely scattered food caches would be of little use, however, if the cache owners couldn't relocate them months later in times of food scarcity. Recent careful studies have confirmed that these animals are successful in relocating and using a high percentage of the food caches they make, and that their success at this task appears to rely on memory of the cache sites. Thus, squirrels and corvids appear to have evolved outstanding spatial memories that enable them to survive in the environmental niches they occupy. Their accomplishments in the relocation of food caches provide a good focal point for the application of concepts of information storage and usage.

Likewise, behavioral feats of chipmunks recently described by Lynn and Jill Devenport (1998) seem well suited to interpretation on the basis of information storage and usage. Foraging choices of these animals appear to depend not only on the storage of information about recently visited feeding stations but also on the relative recency of the information. When recent changes reversed a long-standing difference between the relative richness of two feeding stations, chipmunks chose the station that was the richer of the two on their *last* visit, provided their next choice was close to the time of their last visit. If their next choice between the two stations was delayed for more than a few hours, however, they chose in favor of the station with the greater *history* as a rich station.

Foraging behavior of rats and gerbils on radial mazes (Chapter 4) also seems open to interpretation as information storage and use. In foraging tests in which these subjects are allowed a period of free access to foraging environments offering eight or more separately located feeding stations, they seldom make the mistake of revisiting a station they have already depleted. (Depleted stations are not replenished during a given foraging period.) These animals, then, appear to remember where they have already been during a given period, enabling them to avoid fruitless revisits.

Instances of correspondence often found between predictions of optimal foraging theory and actual foraging decisions of animals also are open to interpretation as information use, as are variations in foraging behaviors of search and consumption in reaction to varying economic conditions of need, difficulty of locating food, and difficulty of consuming food once it has been located (see Chapter 4). Complex feeding behaviors described among crows and complex social cooperation observed among social predators such as wolves and African lions are further candidates for the application of ideas about information use. It is true that many of these behaviors are open to explanation as examples of instrumental conditioning. But we may ask whether an explanation by instrumental conditioning alone, with all notions of information use and cognition omitted, is equally as plausible as explanations that include such ideas as part of their understanding not only of these complex behaviors, but of instrumental conditioning itself. A second remaining question is whether explanations that incorporate information use and cognition gain thereby in their range of application and in their summarization power. These are open questions. But the popularity of cognitive interpretations of such complex behaviors among current psychologists is undeniable.

Navigation by Migrating Animals

We have seen in Chapter 3 that students of animal migration—particularly the long-distance migrations accomplished by many fish, reptiles, and birds—often have invoked the role of cognitive capabilities in interpreting these feats. Even given the use of these cognitive interpretations, many of us may find that current accounts of these phenomena still are not sufficiently complete to permit satisfaction. We find ourselves wishing for further explanation of behavioral accomplishments that continue to provoke our wonder and imagination. Animal migration remains an area in which we continue to look for quantum improvements in our understanding as additional description and study of the subject goes forward in the future.

One of the things that often happens as complex problems continue to be scrutinized by careful observation now seems to be occurring in relation to one instance of animal navigation about which many students of behavior wondered for years. The return of monarch butterflies from northern locations in Canada all the way back to Mexico, from whence their ancestors of several generations began a northern migration years before, has intrigued laymen and scientists alike (see Figure 10.2). How do these butterflies find their way back to a place they have never been? How do they recognize landmarks in country they have never seen? Without landmark recognition, how do they navigate successfully across such vast distances? Many had assumed some type of cognitive process must be involved in the production of this impressive behavior.

FIGURE 10.2   Monarch Butterfly Swarm

Recent observations (Marriott, 1999; Wenner & Harris, 1993) suggest the matter may have an explanation considerably simpler than anyone had previously imagined. Appraisal of all data available on monarch migration suggests to Wenner that the monarchs that manage a return to Mexico may simply have been carried there by prevailing winds. Passive flying under the influence of prevailing winds would be sufficient to deliver quite a number of migrating monarchs back to Mexico. After all, only a small proportion of the migrating population of monarchs actually accomplishes the return to Mexico. It is true that more monarchs tagged in the United States and Canada have been found in Mexico following migration than have been found in other directions, but almost no one has been looking for them in any other location. It's also true that monarchs in migration are often seen flying in the wrong direction, heading north rather than south.

Our understanding of behavior always benefits from more complete observation of the phenomena we aim to understand. In the case of monarch migration, we may soon conclude that the full complement of observations on the subject permits the simple explanation proposed by Wenner. Navigational ability may not be required by monarchs for the accomplishment of the migration they actually achieve. In that case, cognitive processes of navigation will not be required, and Morgan's canon will be served.

Self-Recognition in Nonhuman Primates

Information storage and use do not necessarily imply a self-conscious awareness that one possesses such information and has the choice of whether to use it. In other words, we may recognize a difference between "knowing something" and having the ability to ponder and speculate about what we know and about our own existence as a thinking entity within an environment external to our selves. Self-consciousness is a further quality of mind, beyond the mere possession and use of information. Human beings have self-consciousness and self-awareness. We are not sure whether there is another species anywhere that shares with us this quality. Much recent interest has been devoted to investigating this question in relation to our closest relative among living species, the chimpanzee (and the bonobo), as well as among others of the apes and higher primates.

Beginning with an interesting and surprising experiment (Gallup, 1970) that found chimpanzees seemed able to recognize their own self-images in a mirror, a series of reports appeared offering evidence that chimpanzees and orangutans, but not other primates, are capable of such self-recognition. Briefly, the procedure used by Gallup involved equipping chimpanzees with a mirror for several weeks prior to the critical experimental test so as to allow them to gain mirror experiences. For the experimental test, animals were anesthetized for a time during which a yellow spot was painted over one eye and on the opposite ear with an odorless and nonirritating dye. The yellow marks were located so that they could be seen by the animals only when they looked into the mirror. Following their recovery form anesthesia, subjects were observed first with no mirror present and second with a mirror present. (One benefit of this procedure may have been to draw the animal's attention to the mirror as it was reintroduced into the cage.)

Experimenters noted an increase in mark-directed responses by chimpanzees during the mirror-present condition. The interpretation of the findings was that the animals recognize themselves in the mirror, and that they reveal this recognition by responses that have reference to the marks on their faces. After his original publication of these findings, Gallup (1982) expanded his interpretation to indicate that chimpanzees and orangutans, which also display mirror self-recognition, have a concept of self, are self-aware or self-conscious, and have minds that are capable of attribution, empathy, and deception (Swartz, 1998). These latter capabilities make sense only if the attributing, empathizing, and deceiving individual realizes that other individuals also have minds with capabilities of intention (for attribution), suffering (for empathy), and accepting false information (for deception). Thus, some interpretations of the degree of self-awareness present in chimpanzees and orangutans have now extended this far.

A number of critics of these interpretations have appeared (e.g., Heyes, 1994; Swartz, 1998), suggesting that the findings of mirror tests are open to explanations other than self-awareness in the subjects. Because subjects in these mirror tests experienced the mirror-absent portion of the test first and the mirror-present portion second, they may have been more fully recovered from the effects of general anesthesia during the second portion. Thus, they may have been more active, generally, during that portion of the test. Increased general activity could include increased numbers of face-touching and face-referencing responses. Perhaps there is nothing more indicated by these findings than increased general activity. Species differences in spontaneous touching of the face may account for the "success" of chimpanzees and orangutans in these tests as compared to gorillas and monkeys.

Both Heyes (1998) and Swartz (1998) point out that the frequency of occurrence of mirror-guided touching of the face is surprisingly low, given the momentous conclusions that derive from those findings. As Heyes reports, the 1988 study by Calhoun and Thompson found that only two of four chimpanzee subjects they tested exhibited any face touching, and those two subjects only made two responses each. Povinelli and colleagues (1993) tested thirty chimpanzees and observed an average 2.5 face touches prior to spot painting followed by only 3.9 face touches afterward. One may find that such a small increase in face touching fails to impress. Swartz found wide individual differences in face touching rates in her studies. In one of her studies only four of eleven chimpanzee subjects displayed any face-touching at all; only one of these eleven subjects made enough such responses to be said to have "passed" the mirror test.

A further challenge to the self-awareness interpretation of mirror-guided face touching is provided by findings of Epstein, Lanza, and Skinner (1981) showing that pigeons were readily trained to direct pecking responses to a blue dot on their bodies that could be seen only in a mirror. Their finding that such responses were easily established in pigeons through the use of ordinary techniques of instrumental conditioning suggests that similar response patterns may have been established unintentionally in a few chimpanzee subjects through the same ordinary process.

Povinelli (1993; Povinelli, Rulf, Landau, & Bierschwale, 1993) has conducted a series of ingenious tests that have presented chimpanzees a variety of opportunities to demonstrate their awareness that their human caretakers have minds. If chimpanzees have the sort of complete self-awareness that enables them to engage in attribution, empathy, and deception, then they should suspect that their caretakers have the same sort of knowledge and awareness that the chimpanzees have themselves. Therefore, if placed in a situation in which a human caretaker must be expected to have possession of information that a chimpanzee needs to solve a problem, the chimpanzee should show no reluctance in asking for that information. Povinelli's tests—carefully designed to prohibit success based on simple instrumental conditioning—have failed to provide indications that chimpanzees are aware of human minds.

The Evolution of Language

We have seen that communication is a common and important adaptive feature of social behavior across the animal kingdom. But communication in humans is obviously different from what we have described in any other species. It is much more elaborate and much more symbolic. It is, in a word, *language*. There are many ways to define language. Some definitions seem designed to preserve the special status of our species as the sole possessor of language. In choosing the definition we will use, we want to avoid adopting one that appears on its face to exclude all nonhuman species. Yet, as we shall see, the use of language in humans is unique in several respects. Let us adopt the widely accepted definition proposed by Tobach (1987, p. 258): "Language is a socialized means of communication of thinking, using arbitrarily socialized rules of symbolism, referential systems, and expressive of spatial-temporal relationships among individuals, categories, and events." More simply, **language** is a system of communication based in the use of words according to rules of **grammar** and **syntax,** and that displays **generativity.** That is, language involves the use of a systematic body of words according to regular patterns or rules (grammar), put together in regular ways to make sentences (syntax), and displaying capability for the production of new words and sentences (generativity). A central question about language—one that is endlessly intriguing—is the following: How did it happen that only one species among millions developed the ability to use language? We address this question in the remaining portion of this chapter.

In this book we are attempting to present a unified theoretical way of examining animal behavior. Details of our perspective were presented in earlier chapters in which we introduced basic concepts and analyzed feeding behavior from an anagenetic point of view, and in terms of the idea of behavioral grades. Recall that the behavioral grades proposed by Tobach and Schneirla (1968) extend from the taxic level through the biotaxic, biosocial, and psychotaxic levels to the psychosocial. When we come to the topic of language we are at the highest level of the highest behavioral grade, the psychosocial. Because of the great range of communicative sophistication among the primates, we earlier proposed the recognition of three behavioral grades at the psychosocial level:

- **Psychosocial I,** which includes numerous nonprimate species and the vast majority of communicating, but not language-using, primates
- **Psychosocial II,** to which belong species that have mastered at least a crude level of language—chimpanzees and bonobos, and perhaps gorillas and orangutans
- **Psychosocial III,** which includes only one species, *Homo sapiens*—a species in which the use of language has reached an unprecedented degree of complexity and the only species for which the use of language is species-typical behavior

The definition of language we have adopted clearly allows us to classify the complex linguistic skills demonstrated by some chimpanzees and bonobos as language-like behavior, although at a level far less complex and extensive than seen in humans (Figure 10.3). We refer to this as **proto-language.** Even the researchers involved in work that documents this proto-language liken the language skills of their animals to those of an average human child of no more than 1.5 to 2.5 years of age (Rumbaugh, 1997; Savage-Rumbaugh & Sevcik, 1984).

In attempting to achieve an understanding of the origins of language, we have an opportunity to elaborate an application of our idea of dynamic systems theory to a real problem. Recall from discussions in Chapters 1 and 2 that the nervous system increases in complexity from the lowest to the highest behavioral grades. We believe that the high degree of neural complexity—as measured by the encephalization quotient—achieved in the evolution of the primates is highly related to their sophisticated degree of communication and other cognitive capabilities (Greenberg, Partridge, Weiss, & Haraway, 1999). The **encephalization quotient** (Jerison, 1994; Plotkin, 1983) (*log* brain weight/*log* body weight) for monkeys is smaller than for chimpanzees, which, in turn, is smaller than for humans.

If we examine the evolution of cultural complexity among primates, we see that it is easily related to the factors of nervous system complexity and the evolution of com-

FIGURE 10.3   Lana at the Lexigram Keyboard

municative capabilities. We may define **culture** as the transmission of social knowledge within and between generations. We favor formulations of levels of increasing cultural sophistication, such as that proposed by Parker and Russon (1996). Thus, among **pre-cultural** monkeys and other social mammals, culture is primitive and its transmission is based upon biological processes and straightforward and simple conditioning mechanisms that do not depend upon either imitation or teaching. The communication system of vervet monkeys, in which different calls represent threats from different predators, is an example of this primitive level of culture, as is the transmission of new food choices and uses among Japanese macaques. A higher level of complexity is achieved in **proto-culture,** in which the transmission of knowledge is based on true imitation and simple forms of teaching, as seen in chimpanzees. An illustration of this process is the way in which West African chimpanzees teach their young to construct stone hammer and anvil tools to use in cracking nuts (Matsuzawa, 1998).

The anthropologist Robin Dunbar (1993, 1996) has shown that the size of primate groups also correlates highly with the neocortical ratio—the size of the cortex relative to the entire brain. We saw earlier that an important cohesive force among primates is social grooming. To some extent, time spent grooming is a linear function of group size. The more animals there are in one's group, the more separate opportunities there are to spend time in grooming. There must come a point, however, at which the group becomes so large that no single individual can find the time to maintain grooming relationships with all other group members. Dunbar reasons that the development of spoken language could have functioned to bolster and to partially replace the cohesive force of social grooming among early humans. Such a development would have been an important contributor to the social strength of large groups of perhaps 150 individuals.

In human evolution, neural evolution was accompanied by the evolution of other structures and processes such as **bipedalism** and the vocal tract. Bipedalism made the world of **hominids** very different from that of the great apes by freeing the hands for new uses, by affecting the senses, and by putting new gravitational demands on the muscular and skeletal systems.

To the extent that behavior is a driving force behind evolutionary change, these developments not only opened new niches to be occupied, but these niches in turn provided ecological pressures that contributed to further evolutionary change. Thus, bipedalism freed the hands to be used in new ways, eventually making possible sophisticated cultural inventions such as toolmaking, writing, and pictorial representations. However, before those cultural changes could occur, new uses of the hands contributed to enhanced development of motor areas of the brain, enhancing fine motor coordination of the fingers and hands. Indeed, the new gravitational forces experienced by bipedal hominids contributed to the overall wiring of the nervous system, which in turn contributed to changes in the behavioral potentials of those species. Recall from our discussion in Chapter 2 that, while the general structure of the nervous system is regulated by genes, the precise circuitry of individual nervous systems is very much under experiential (e.g., trophic) control. And, the vocal apparatus was evolving as well, which exerted evolutionary pressures on the accompanying tongue and mouth musculature, in turn contributing to neural patterning.

Thus, at least four sets of factors converged and interacted dynamically to yield the development of spoken language: nervous system evolution, evolution of structures of the vocal tract, evolution of fine muscular coordination of the hands and fingers and of the tongue and lips, and evolution of complex cognitive behavior and culture. From our perspective of **dynamic systems theory,** once a sufficient or critical number of significant factors are in place, new and unprecedented developments are likely to emerge out of the dynamic interplay of those factors. We believe that is the case with respect to the appearance of language in apes and humans.

The emergence of language occurred during a time of impressive environmental, neurological, and cultural changes. In conjunction with the expansion of cortical development illustrated among the great apes, only hominids underwent the evolutionary pressures of immigration into a new way of life in a grassland environment. Only they developed true bipedalism, widespread and complex stone toolmaking, massive exploitation of meat as a food source, and establishment and use of semipermanent **home bases.** The demands of life in this complex and unprecedented biological niche placed unprecedented importance on effective communication among individuals within a cooperative social group. Only among the hominids did the complexity of culture reach the level to spark the dynamic interaction of factors that led to the emergence of language.

Middle Pleistoscene hominids displayed **ur-culture,** which involved the transmission of knowledge through symbolism. Perhaps the cave paintings of Neanderthals is an example of this level of cultural development. Finally, our own species is characterized by *eu-culture*, the highest cultural development. The transmission of knowledge among our species involves propositional language and declarative planning. Humans can think into the future and can represent those not-yet-occurring events with language. The transition from *neanderthalis* to *Homo sapiens* was accompanied by the transition from gesturing and picture drawing on cave walls to the universal use of spoken language and, in not so long a time, to the use of alphabets and books.

If our analysis is correct, one would not expect to find anything remotely close to complex language skills below the level of apes, and certainly not below the primates. We have proposed that the highest behavioral level, the psychosocial, can be divided into three sublevels, reflecting communication complexity. Non-language-using animals belong at psychosocial level I, individual apes using proto-language would be at psychosocial level II, and *Homo sapiens*, the only true language users, would be at psychosocial level III. As we discussed in another chapter, although some interpret the communications of some honeybees as language, alternative explanations (e.g., Wenner, 1998; see Chapter 4) preserve Morgan's canon and are consistent with our proposal.

Cognition and Behavioral Levels

Throughout this book we have referred repeatedly to the trend toward increasing behavioral complexity with increasing recency of evolutionary emergence of species across the animal series. We have seen in this chapter that cognitive interpretations of behavior are increasingly likely to be applied as the behaviors to be explained become more complex. It should come as no surprise, then, that there is a clear trend across the animal series in respect to the application of cognitive interpretations of behavior. Cognitive explanations of behavior are hardly encountered in application to species of more ancient origin than the arthropods, and their application to arthropod behavior has been slight. More cognitive interpretation is encountered in the explanation of behavior of fish and reptiles, and much more is encountered as we reach the level of the birds and mammals. Among the birds and mammals, we find even greater use of cognitive explanations as we reach the primates, and among the primates, much greater use of cognitive explanations as we reach the great apes.

Recently it has been suggested that there is measurable physiological evidence for levels of cognition, more specifically, for one measure of cognitive capability, that of awareness (Piggins & Phillips, 1998). It has been suggested that retinal ganglion cells that process amounts of light and single cells that respond to lines of specific orientation are awareness processors. These processes have been identified as feature detectors. The first feature detectors were discovered in frogs (Lettvin, Maturana, McCulloch, & Pitts, 1959) and were quite simple. The frog's eye allowed it to detect moving edges, the turning on and off of lights, and moving spots of light, that is, "bug detectors." More recently, it has been discovered that monkeys possess very specific face and body movement detectors at high levels of the brain, in the cerebral cortex (Perrett, Rolls, & Caan, 1982; Perrett, Smith, Mistlin et al., 1984; Perrett, Smith, Potter et al., 1985). Could the brain function somehow as a social organ?

Work of this sort has led some to identify levels of awareness from simple sensation, to more complex perception, and to even more complex cognition. At the sensory level, all information is purely biological and sensory; at the perceptual level, the organism interprets stimulation; at the cognitive level the dimension of learning is added (Piggins & Phillips, 1998). This matches quite well with our own postulated levels of behavioral complexity. Their formulation is presented in Table 10.1.

Piggins and Phillips (1998) argue that greater differences in brain capacity and brain connections are reflected in differences in cognitive capabilities. As one would expect from our own position, the more complex the organism, and thus the more information it is capable of processing, the more advanced, or the higher, will be the degree of cognitive capabilities. That their ideas mirror our own is apparent in this statement:

> We suggest that higher levels of thought patterns are almost entirely the domain of humans. The degree to which tools have been invented is one example. The existence of humour…is another. Rudiments of these two examples are present in higher primates, and perhaps even domesticated animals. (p. 186)

Summary: Principles Introduced in This Chapter

Cognition is the means by which animals acquire, store, and act on information. As with all other behaviors, it may be considered as having functional value in allowing animals to focus on critical events. Cognition implies consciousness, or awareness, of the environment. Across the animal spectrum, degree or complexity of consciousness correlates with the behavioral levels we have proposed in this book. Even more than with most topics, Morgan's canon and the principle of parsimony must be adhered to when discussing cognitive behaviors. Lacking satisfactory means to examine the mental states of animals, we find it all too easy to attribute human-like interpretations to their behavior. Monarch butterflies—thought by many to display complex navigational skills—actually may be passively carried by prevailing wind currents to overwintering sites in Mexico. Self-recognition studies with chimpanzees are interpreted by many as evidence of a concept of self, and of mind. But, again, far less complex and more parsimonious explanations for that behavior can be offered.

Learning increases in complexity as we ascend the behavioral grades. Various investigators have proposed levels of learning, as many as eleven and as few as three. The Transfer Index, a measure of complex learning, correlates highly with nervous system complexity.

KEY TERMS

Bipedalism   walking on two feet as a primary means of locomotion.
Cognition   an intervening variable associated with cognitive behavior and thought of as resembling the possession of conscious awareness and the use of information by the behaving animal.
Cognitive behavior   behavior that suggests the operation of mental activity and mental faculties.

Culture   basically, a complex of behavior patterns or customs transmitted from one generation to another on the basis of social learning experiences; however, customary usage of the term *culture* has emphasized transmission that involves imitation, teaching, and symbolic knowledge.

Dynamic systems theory   a theoretical perspective that views its subject matter, such as behavior, for example, as being the product of an interaction of a number of different causal factors; alteration in any one of the causal factors usually present may change the mix sufficiently to produce quite a different outcome from that usually expected.

Encephalization quotient   the ratio of brain weight to body weight (*log* brain weight divided by *log* body weight) used as a rough measure of the relative degree of encephalization illustrated by different species.

Generativity   with respect to language, the capability to generate new words, phrases, and sentences.

Grammar   rules of language concerning which word forms are used in combination together.

Home base   a location where an animal spends much of its time and to which it returns repeatedly after forays or journeys into the surrounding environment; specific to the hunter–gatherer society of early humans, the home base was a place where very young, very old, and ill or indisposed members of the social group could remain protected while other members of the group went out on hunting-and-gathering ventures.

Hominids   human-like animals; perhaps direct ancestors of the human species.

Information   we may say that the substance of information consists in the relationships that exist among particular objects and events. Information can be considered scientifically by inspecting relationships that hold true among *observable* objects and events. Responding on the basis of such relationships may be described as responding to information.

Intervening variable   a form of theoretical statement in which it is supposed that an unobserved hypothetical process intervenes between observed causes and their observed effects *as though* the observed causes influence the intervening process that, in its turn, produces the observed effects; to remain within the realm of scientific interpretation, the intervening variable must be firmly tied to observed causes and observed effects in all cases.

Language   a system of communication based in the use of words according to rules of grammar and syntax and displaying the capability to generate new words and phrases.

Learning to learn   when animals are given repeated training with the same type of learning problem, they often require progressively less training to achieve proficiency as they acquire more experience in dealing with that type of problem. This increase in learning proficiency is called learning to learn.

Precultural, preculture   a primitive form of culture in which the transmission of customs is based primarily in biological processes and straightforward and simple learning experiences.

Prosimian   primates whose origins preceded the appearance of modern monkeys.

Proto-culture   a midlevel of cultural complexity in which the transmission of customs is based importantly on imitation and simple examples of what might be called teaching.

Proto-language   language-like behavior such as seen among certain chimpanzees and bonobos that is far less extensive and complex than the language behavior of humans.

Syntax   rules of language concerning the pattern in which different word forms are arranged to form sentences.

Transfer Index   a species-fair measure of the ability to transfer operationally defined levels of learning to novel test situations (e.g., where the cue values have been changed).

Ur-culture   an advanced form of culture in which the transmission of knowledge is based importantly upon the use of communicative symbols such as picture drawings or words.

REVIEW QUESTIONS

1. Comment on the proposition that our own behavior is under the control of our own mind. Include considerations that argue for both the positive and the negative sides of this proposition.

2. What is the great advantage of studying conscious awareness in humans as compared to other animals?

3. Tell what is meant by the term *cognitive behavior.*

4. Suggest one or two functions that might be served by cognition.

5. Make your own sketch to illustrate how cognition or cognitive processes can be represented as an intervening variable that mediates the occurrence of some instance of behavior.

6. Comment on how the higher levels of learning suggested by Razran or by Deacon can be related to considerations of cognitive behavior.

7. Give an example of the sort of evidence used to illustrate the phenomenon called learning to learn.

8. Comment on the use of the Transfer Index as a means of evaluating cognitive behavior in learning.

9. Give an example of foraging behavior that can be interpreted as an illustration of cognitive behavior.

10. Mention one of the criticisms raised by Wenner to the interpretation that butterflies are capable of navigation across long distances.

11. Draw a distinction between *information usage* and *self-consciousness.*

12. Briefly describe the technique and the idea behind the use of mirrors to look for evidence of self-recognition in chimpanzees.

13. Briefly characterize the outcome thus far of Povinelli's search for evidence of self-consciousness among chimpanzees.

14. Indicate how the illustration of rules in communication helps us to define language.

15. What is meant by saying that language includes the quality of generativity?

16. Compare the language skills developed by well-trained chimpanzees to those of a human child.

17. What sorts of observations provide the basic foundation of concepts of culture, that is, observations of what sort of behavioral events?

18. Give an example of what is considered as proto-culture.

19. Comment on how the advent of bipedalism may have functioned as a factor in the development of language.

20. Name two other factors that may have interacted with bipedalism to produce the evolution of language.

21. Briefly tell how the use of cognitive interpretations varies in keeping with recency of species origin.

REFERENCES

Blumberg, M. S., & Wasserman, E. A. (1995). Animal mind and the argument from design. *American Psychologist, 50,* 133–144.

Cheney, D. L., & Seyfarth, R. M. (Eds.). (1990). *How monkeys see the world.* Chicago: University of Chicago Press.

Deacon, T. W. (1990). Rethinking mammalian brain evolution. *American Zoologist, 30,* 229–305.

Devenport, J., & Devenport, L. (1998). Squirrel foraging behavior. In G. Greenberg & M. M. Haraway (Eds.), *Comparative psychology: A handbook* (pp. 492–498). New York: Garland.

Dunbar, R. I. (1993). Coevolution of neocortical size, group size and language in humans. *Behavioral and Brain Sciences, 16,* 681–735.

Dunbar, R. (1996). *Grooming, gossip, and the evolution of language.* Cambridge, MA: Harvard University Press.

Epstein, R., Lanza, R. P., & Skinner, B. F. (1981). "Self-awareness" in the pigeon. *Science, 212,* 695–696.

Fobes, J. L., & King, J. E. (1982). Measuring primate learning abilities. In J. L. Fobes & J. E. King (Eds.), *Primate behavior* (pp. 289–321). New York: Academic Press.

Gallup, G. G. (1970). Chimpanzees: Self-recognition. *Science, 167,* 86–87.

Gallup, G. G. (1982). Self-awareness and the emergence of mind in primates. *American Journal of Primatology, 2,* 237–248.

Greenberg, G., Partridge, T., Weiss, E., & Haraway, M. M. (1998). Integrative levels, the brain and the emergence of complex behavior. *Review of General Psychology, 3,* 168–187.

Harlow, H. F. (1949). The formation of learning sets. *Psychological Review, 56,* 51–65.

Heyes, C. M. (1994). Reflections on self-awareness in primates. *Animal Behaviour, 47,* 909–919.

Heyes, C. M. (1998). Theory of mind in nonhuman primates. *Behavioral and Brain Sciences, 21,* 101–134.

Jerison, H. J. (1994). Evolution of the brain. In D. W. Zeidel (Ed.), *Neuropsychology* (pp. 53–82). San Diego: Academic Press.

Lettvin, J. Y., Maturana, H. R., McCulloch, W. S., & Pitts, W. H. (1959). What the frog's eye tells the frog's brain. *Proceedings of the Institute for Radio Engineering, 47,* 1940–1951.

Marriott, D. F. (1999). Catching an autumn wind: Do monarchs use the Santa Anas? *Monarch News, 9*(11), 1, 6–7.

Masterson, R. B., & Berkley, M. A. (1974). Brain functions: Changing ideas in the role of sensory, motor, and association cortex. *Annual Review of Psychology, 25,* 277–312.

Masterson, R. B., & Skeen, L. C. (1972). Origins of anthropoid intelligence: Preferred system and delayed alternative in hedge hog, tree shrew, and bush baby. *Journal of Comparative and Physiological Psychology, 81,* 423–433.

Matsuzawa, T. (1998). Chimpanzee behavior: A comparative cognitive perspective. In G. Greenberg & M. M. Haraway (Eds.), *Comparative psychology: A handbook* (pp. 360–375). New York: Garland.

Pearce, J. M. (1997). *Animal learning and cognition: An introduction,* 2nd ed. East Sussex, UK: Psychology Press.

Parker, S. T., & Russon, A. E. (1996). On the wild side of culture and cognition in the great apes. In A. E. Russon, K. A. Bard, & S. T. Parker (Eds.), *Reaching into thought: The minds of the great apes* (pp. 430–450). Cambridge, England: Cambridge University Press.

Perrett, D. I., Rolls, E. T., & Caan, W. (1982). Visual neurones responsive to faces in the monkey temporal cortex. *Experimental Brain Research, 47,* 329–342.

Perrett, D. I., Smith, P. A. J., Mistlin, A. J., Chitty, A. J., Head, A. S., Potter, D. D., Broennimann, R., Milner, A. D., & Jeeves, M. A. 1984. Visual analysis of body movements by neurones in the temporal cortex of the macaque monkey: A preliminary report. *Behavioural Brain Research, 16,* 153–170.

Perrett, D. I., Smith, P. A. J., Mistlin, A. J., Head, A. S., Milner, A. D., & Jeeves, M. A. (1985). Visual cells in the temporal cortex sensitive to face view and gaze direction. *Proceedings of the Royal Society, London [B], 223,* 293–317.

Piggins, D., & Phillips, C. J. C. (1998). Awareness in domesticated animals—Concepts and definitions. *Applied Animal Behaviour Science, 57,* 181–200.

Plotkin, H. C. (1983). The functions of learning and cross-species comparisons. In G. C. L. Davey (Ed.), *Animal models of human behavior* (pp. 117–134). New York: Wiley.

Povinelli, D. J. (1987). Monkeys, apes, mirrors and minds: The evolution of self-awareness in primates. *Human Evolution, 2,* 493–509.

Povinelli, D. J. (1993). Reconstructing the evolution of mind. *American Psychologist, 48,* 493–509.

Povinelli, D. J., Rulf, A. B., Landau, K. R., & Bierschwale, D. T. (1993). Self-recognition in chimpanzees: Distribution, ontogeny, and patterns of emergence. *Journal of Comparative Psychology, 107,* 347–372.

Razran, G. (1971). *Mind in evolution.* New York: Houghton Mifflin.

Rumbaugh, D. M. (1969). The transfer index: An alternative measure of learning set. In C. R. Carpenter (Ed.), *Proceedings of the Second International Congress of Primatology* (pp. 267–272). Basel, Switzerland: Karger.

Rumbaugh, D. M. (1997). Competence, cortex, and primate models: A comparative perspective. In N. Krasnegor, R. Lyon, & P. Goldman-Rakic (Eds.), *Development of the prefrontal cortex: Evolution, neurobiology, and behavior* (pp. 117–139). Baltimore, MD: Paul H. Brookes.

Rumbaugh, D. M., & Pate, J. L. (1984a). The evolution of cognition in primates: A comparative perspective. In H. L. Roitblatt, T. G. Bever, & H. S. Terrace (Eds.), *Animal cognition* (pp. 569–587). Hillsdale, NJ: Lawrence Erlbaum.

Rumbaugh, D. M., & Pate, J. L. (1984b). Primates' learning by levels. In G. Greenberg & E. Tobach (Eds.), *Behavioral evolution and integrative levels* (pp. 221–240). Hillsdale, NJ: Lawrence Erlbaum.

Rumbaugh, D. M., Washburn, D. A., & Pate, J. L. (1998). Discrimination learning set and transfer. In G. Greenberg & M. M. Haraway (Eds.), *Comparative psychology: A handbook* (pp. 562–565). New York: Garland.

Savage-Rumbaugh, E. S., & Sevcik, R. A. (1984). Levels of communicative competency in the chimpanzee: Pre-representational and representational. In G. Greenberg & E. Tobach (Eds.), *Behavioral evolution and integrative levels* (pp. 197–219). Hillsdale, NJ: Erlbaum.

Shettleworth, S. J. (1998). *Cognition, evolution, and behavior.* New York: Oxford University Press.

Swartz, K. B. (1998). Self-recognition in primates. In G. Greenberg & M. M. Haraway (Eds.), *Comparative psychology: A handbook* (pp. 849–855). New York: Garland.

Thompson, R. F. (1993). *The brain: A neuroscience primer,* 2nd ed. New York: W. H. Freeman.

Tobach, E. (1987). Integrative levels in the comparative psychology of cognition, language, and consciousness. In G. Greenberg & E. Tobach (Eds.), *Cognition, language, and consciousness: Integrative levels* (pp. 239–267). Hillsdale, NJ: Erlbaum.

Tobach, E., & Schneirla, T. C. (1968). The biopsychology of social behavior of animals. In R. E. Cook & J. Levin (Eds.), *The biological basis of pediatric practice* (pp. 68–82). New York: McGraw-Hill.

Wenner, A. M. (1998). Honey bee "dance language" controversy. In G. Greenberg & M. M. Haraway (Eds.), *Comparative psychology: A handbook* (pp. 823–836). New York: Garland.

Wenner, A. M., & Harris, A. M. (1993). Do California Monarchs undergo long distance directed migration? In S. B. Malcolm & M. P. Zalucki (Eds.), *Biology and conservation of the Monarch butterfly* (pp. 209–218). Science Series Contribution #38. Natural History Museum of Los Angeles County.

CHAPTER

11 Overall Summary: Principles of Comparative Psychology

In this concluding chapter we present an overall summary of the principles introduced throughout previous chapters of the book. We have attempted to organize this statement in such a manner as to construct the outline of a theory of comparative psychology. Such a theory must serve not only as a summary of the principles and facts presented in this book but also as a basis upon which new facts may be predicted. There are three important tests of a scientific theory: How well does it summarize current facts within its scope of operation? How well does it stimulate new research? How well does it predict new facts that will be added to its field in the future?

We begin the chapter with an informal and descriptive statement of the basic principles of the field. Then we proceed to a more formal set of theoretical statements together with a number of examples of how both currently established facts and new facts may be deduced from these statements. These examples should serve to illustrate how the theoretical statements formulated here might function in relation to the three tests of a scientific theory.

Foundational Principles: Postulates

We have defined the focus of comparative psychology as the evolution and development of behavior throughout the range of the animal kingdom. An account of the operation of evolution and development to produce the characteristics of animal behavior, then, must constitute the foundational principles of comparative psychology.

The Principle of Evolution

Comparative psychology grew out of application of the theory of evolution to the field of animal mind, psychology, and behavior. Thus we begin our statement of a theory of comparative psychology by borrowing the theory of evolution, intact, from the field of biology. Comparative psychology assumes, with present-day biology, that the genetic characteristics of modern species have resulted from a process of evolution as described by current versions of Darwin's theory of evolution by natural selection. Evolution provides the genetic influence, certainly a major influence of both biological and behavioral development.

Correspondence of Biological and Psychological Variation

Psychology rests upon a biological basis and, in turn, upon a chemical and a physical basis. We expect strong correspondence between biological and psychological events. Particularly relevant among biological correlates of behavior have been variations in neural and hormonal conditions. Psychology can never violate the laws of biology, nor those of chemistry and physics. But just as the laws of chemistry are not anticipated in detail by the laws of physics, and the laws of biology are not anticipated in detail by the laws of chemistry, so also the laws of psychology extend beyond those of biology. Psychological law must in all cases be consistent with biological law, but it need not be confined to it.

The Principle of Multiple Causation

The characteristics of animal behavior, without exception, are products of multiple causation. Elements of genetic causation and other factors impacting the developmental process combine in a dynamic interaction to produce each behavior characteristic. By describing the developmental process as a "dynamic interaction," we mean to imply that the whole outcome of development is a function of numerous factors working in combination. Single factors working alone produce nothing.

We human beings often like to simplify complex processes by assigning separate and absolute roles to each of a number of causal factors thought to be involved. For example, we may wish to attribute a certain percentage of overall behavior determination to genetic causation versus environmental causation. We may even indulge in the convenience of speaking as though some behavioral characteristic is determined entirely by one causal factor, merely because that is the causal factor we are interested in at the moment.

Fortunately for the science of psychology, often it *is* possible to account for a definite amount of the observed *variation* in certain behavioral measures by the operation of a single causal variable. Such accounts are achieved by comparing what happens when a single causal factor is varied while all others are held constant. Thus, one cause is allowed to vary between two groups of subjects while numerous other causes are shared in common by both groups. This arrangement permits us to say, not that overall behavior in either group resulted from a single cause, but that the *difference* in behavior between the two groups resulted from a single cause.

We may compare a number of children of different genetic background and find that 80 percent of the observed variation in measured intelligence within the group is accounted for by their different genetics. In making this comparison, we assume that environmental conditions, which are uncontrolled, are similar for both groups. On the other hand, we may hold genetic background constant and vary environmental conditions during the development of two groups of rats and find that 80 percent of an observed variation in their performance on several measures of learning is accounted for by the difference in their developmental environments. Thus, one study finds that 80 percent of an observed variation in behavior is accounted for by a genetic cause whereas the other finds that 80 percent of an observed variation in a similar behavior is accounted for by an environmental cause. Both studies can be correct. When one factor is varied and the other held constant, great differences in behavior can be produced, regardless of which factor is varied and which is held constant. In neither case is it correct to make an assignment of the relative degree to which behavior can be influenced by genetic as compared to environmental factors.

Overall behavior, in all cases, remains dependent upon a totality of causal factors working together in combination. It simply is not possible to view the developmental results produced by a single causal factor working alone: Behavior is a phenomenon observed in an organism within a certain environment. Organisms do not exist outside of environments, and behavior does not occur without organisms to do the behaving.

We find it helpful to recognize five separate factors involved in the interaction from which behavior characteristics derive. These may be termed the *phylogenetic, individual, ontogenetic, experiential,* and *cultural* factors. Not all of these factors are involved in the establishment of behavior characteristics at all behavioral levels; the final two in the list—the experiential and cultural factors—become increasingly important at more complex behavioral levels.

The Phylogenetic Factor.   The phylogenetic factor includes all genetic influences associated directly with an animal's species identity, that is, its evolutionary standing as a species. These influences derive from genetic characteristics shared commonly among members of a species. Genetic characteristics are a major influence of both biological and behavioral development. We have defined comparative psychology in relation to the evolution and development of behavior. The entire influence of evolution is represented by the phylogenetic factor.

The Individual Factor.   This factor represents influences deriving from the particular version of its species genetics possessed by a given individual. One of the bases of evolutionary theory is that individuals of the same species vary greatly in genetic makeup. Individual variation in genetic makeup is assured by the process of sexual reproduction, in which the genetics of a new individual are comprised of a "random" selection of one-half of its father's genetics in combination with a random selection of one-half of its mother's genetics. The implications of the individual factor for behavior are that individuals should be expected to vary from one another in the precise nature of their behavior characteristics.

The Ontogenetic Factor.   This factor represents influences on behavior associated with an individual's current status in relation to the usual schedule of behavior development that occurs with physical growth and maturation in normal members of its species. Newborn or newly hatched members of a species often display different behavior characteristics from those seen in mature members of that species. Mature forms of behavior may be achieved only after a prolonged process of behavioral change accompanying physical growth. The ontogenetic factor is addressed to this process of behavioral change. A major predictor in the consideration of this factor is the current age of an individual. Another important predictor is the degree to which an individual has accomplished the development of behavior characteristics already expected to have occurred by the time of its current age.

The Experiential Factor. This factor represents stimulus influences of behavior development, including proprioceptive stimulation that may accompany the practice of movements and including all learning experiences, either within the maturational period of development or beyond. Also within the realm of this factor are other possible environmental influences of physical and behavioral functioning such as atmospheric temperature and pressure, gravitational force, relative content of oxygen and other gases in the atmosphere, characteristics of nutritional sustenance, and almost countless additional variables such as these. In relation to the experiential factor, we expect to see numerous instances in which variations of experience have a profound effect upon behavior characteristics.

The Cultural Factor. This factor might be considered as a subcategory of experiential influences. Nevertheless, we find it to be distinctive enough as a social influence and a medium of group dynamics to warrant separate consideration of its own. This category represents experiential influences derived from social stimulation encountered routinely by members of a given group or population and perhaps unique to that particular group as compared to other groups or populations of the same species. The operation of these influences probably always involves the process of learning, and such influences are to be expected increasingly at the higher levels of complexity among vertebrate species.

The Principle of Hierarchical Levels

A definite progression—that is, a continued variation of consistent direction—is observed as one moves from the most primitively established organisms toward the most recently established organisms. The direction of this change is toward greater complexity of both biology and behavior with increased recency of the initial appearance of species. Whether or not we find sufficient logical reasons for understanding the trend across continuing evolution from the simple toward the complex, we do observe it clearly, and we recognize it here as a basic principle of comparative psychology. It is important, once again, to realize that we are speaking of progress here only as an ongoing variation of consistent direction, from the simple to the complex. We intend no implication that more complex species are better or somehow more cosmically valuable than are simple species. That issue doesn't resolve into a scientific question and, as scientists, we have no concern with it one way or the other. And once again, we refer here to progressive change in respect to the establishment of *new* species. Numerous forms illustrating the simplest levels of behavioral complexity continue as highly successful species through the current moment.

Variation in levels of behavioral complexity across the animal kingdom may be described systematically by application of an adapted version of the scale proposed by Schneirla and Tobach (Chapter 1). This scale divides behavior into five major levels of complexity: the taxis, biotaxis, biosocial, psychotaxis, and psychosocial. Behavior at the taxic level is under the direct control of stimulus agents currently present in the environment, and no distinction is made between biological and nonbiological agents. Behavior at the biotaxic level is similar, except that distinctions are made between biological and nonbiological agents. At the biosocial level of complexity, behavior is influenced by stimulation provided by an organism's social group. At the psychotaxic level of complexity, behavior is influenced by past stimulation that is not present in the current stimulus array. It is at this level that we first encounter influences of learning, memory, and possibly cognitive behavior. At the psychosocial level, we encounter the first influences of histories of social experiences with distinct and recognized individuals such as parents, mates, offspring, and siblings. The psychosocial level may be further divided into sublevels I, II, and III, with the higher sublevels recognizing the use of proto-language by a few individual great apes and the far more complex and wide-ranging use of language by all cultures of human beings.

It is possible to obtain graphic representation of the progression of behavioral complexity with recency of species origin by evaluating the complexity of behavioral organization illustrated in different groups and species; then assigning behavioral complexity scores according to the degree of complexity illustrated in each group and plotting these scores against a scale of the age of species or group origin. Such a representation appears in Chapter 4, in Figure 4.9.

Derivative Principles: Corollaries

The following principles are of similar generality and importance to the postulates, but because they may be deduced from those postulates, they may be stated as corollaries.

Species-Typical Behavior

The principle of species-typical behavior may be derived from the fact of basic similarity of conditions shared by most species members with respect to phylogenetic, ontogenetic, and experiential factors in nearly all species, and with respect to cultural factors among the members of some other species as well. The principle recognizes the many similar forms of behavior that are shared in common by nearly all members of a given species and that serve to distinguish a particular species from all others. The entire complement of species-typical behaviors provides each species with its basic behavioral resources for the securement of survival and reproductive success.

Functionality of Behavior Characteristics

This principle recognizes the clear functional value of nearly all species-typical behaviors and behavior characteristics. The principle of evolution assumes that genetic foundations influencing the ontogenetic development of species-typical behaviors have been subjected to natural selection across vast numbers of generations. The functional value of behavior characteristics follows as a direct product of this selection, which has been made on the basis of survival and reproductive success.

Selective Orientation

Organisms are differentially responsive to certain particular stimulus sources that make up only a small fraction of the physical objects and energy variations within their environments. This selectivity results in part from the evolution of sensory mechanisms that are responsive to the most relevant potential stimulus sources in the environment, the most relevant, that is, to survival and reproductive success. Selective responsiveness also rests in part upon the evolution of mechanisms by which alterations in responsiveness to specific stimuli vary with an individual's current behavioral status (e.g., that the individual is water-deprived or food-deprived).

Motor and Locomotor Capacities

The functional value of motor behaviors to manipulate features of the environment and of locomotor behaviors to enable movement from place to place within the environment is obvious. Evolution occurs, of course, within the world of physics. Given the physical possibilities provided by Newton's Third Law, the presence within the environment of objects and substances that are helpful and others that are harmful, and the need of animals to obtain their food from ready-made sources outside their own bodies, then the evolution of means of locomotion exploiting Newton's Third Law is predictable.

A direct correspondence of locomotor change to sensory input, as described by the *perception-as-action* theory, provides a parsimonious alternative to the conception of perception as a hypothetical process intervening between sensory input and action. Evolution of direct locomotor responsiveness such as this is predictable for all frequently repeated locomotor sequences.

Approach and Withdrawal

As required by evolutionary theory, stimulus events that evoke approach generally are beneficial to survival and/or reproductive success and stimulus events that evoke withdrawal generally are harmful. Also predictable are the active maintenance of proximity to an approach stimulus and of distance from a withdrawal stimulus (avoidance).

Schneirla's approach/withdrawal theory recognized a widespread tendency of organisms to approach stimulus intensities occupying the mild portion of the intensity range over which differential responding is observed and to withdraw from stimulus intensities occupying the strong portion of the intensity range. These tendencies are lifelong among organisms at the simpler levels of behavior complexity but are modified by individual experience during maturational development among organisms at higher levels of behavior complexity.

Motivation

Differential orientation and approach/withdrawal behavior constitute rudimentary elements of a concept of motivation in two respects. First, if these differential responses vary in association with physiological conditions and/or with other behaviors in progress, such as food or water deprivation, then they provide the beginnings of motivational variation. The advantages of an organism's being selectively sensitive to food when food-deprived or to the stimuli provided by a sexual partner during breeding season are obvious. Second, if one identifies the tendency to approach with attraction and the tendency to withdraw with aversion, then one has the beginnings of concepts of reward (onset of the attractive) and punishment (onset of the aversive). In the present context, one need imply nothing more by attraction than a tendency to move toward or maintain, and by aversion, nothing more than a tendency to withdraw from or avoid.

Learning and Cognition

Learning represents a capability of behavior to be modified in lasting fashion on the basis of individual experience. The study of animal learning has stressed the association of events in experience, or *associative learning*. Individuals learn to respond differentially to stimuli that have preceded the occurrence of important events in past experience and to repeat actions that have led to reward and omit actions that have led to punishment. The functional value of such adjustments has long been stressed by classical theories of learning. Associative learning occurs from the level of the flatworms onward across the more complex behavioral levels of more recently evolved species. As we approach the higher reaches of behavioral complexity among the birds and mammals it becomes increasingly attractive to interpret learning, and the enactment of behavior that has resulted from learning, as the acquisition and use of information, that is to say, as cognition.

Proto-forms of learning known as sensitization and habituation occur in a number of species in which no evidence of associative learning exists. These results follow from the frequent recurrence of a single stimulus and involve an adjustment either upward (sensitization) of downward (habituation) in the strength of responses to the repeated stimulus.

In dealing with the subject of learning, comparative psychologists rely upon the continuing development of fact and theory within the related and venerable field of animal learning.

Formal Statement of Principles

Foundational Principles: Postulates

I. The Principle of Evolution

Genetic characteristics of all animal species are products of evolution by natural selection, or selection on the basis of differential success at survival and reproduction of past members of those species.

II. Correspondence of Biological and Psychological Variation
Behavioral variation corresponds closely with biological variation.

III. The Principle of Multiple Causation
The development of behavioral characteristics is the result of a dynamic inter-action of multiple causal factors that, depending upon the level of behavioral complexity illustrated, include the following.
A. The Phylogenetic Factor, species genetics
B. The Individual Factor, individual genetics
C. The Ontogenetic Factor, maturational status
D. The Experiential Factor, history of experience
E. The Cultural Factor, history of social experience in relation to group membership

IV. Hierarchical Organization of Levels
Behavioral characteristics across the animal kingdom describe a hierarchy of levels of complexity illustrating a progression of increasing complexity with recency of species origin. This hierarchical arrangement may be viewed as comprising five major levels of behavioral complexity.
A. Taxis, direct stimulus control of behavior
B. Biotaxis, behavioral distinction of biologic agents
C. Biosocial, influences of the social group
D. Psychotaxis, behavioral influences of past experience
E. Psychosocial I, behavioral influences of past social experiences with recog-nized individuals; II, use of proto-language by certain great apes; and III, complex and wide-ranging use of language among humans

Derivative Principles: Corollaries

I. Species-Typical Behavior
All species possess numerous forms of behavior that occur in a similar form and under similar circumstances in nearly all members of the species. Differ-ences in species-typical behavior distinguish each species from all others.

II. Functionality of Behavior Characteristics
Behavior characteristics shared in common by most members of a species have clear functional value to facilitate survival and reproductive success.

III. Selective Orientation
Behavior is focused on selective aspects of the environment that tend to be more relevant to survival and reproductive success than would be a random se-lection of all potential stimulus sources in the environment.

IV. Motor and Locomotor Capacities
The evolution of species-typical motor and locomotor capacities has been uni-versal across the animal kingdom. The evolution of much locomotor movement has taken advantage of physical prospects addressed by Newton's Third Law.

Locomotor sequences that are frequently repeated within a species are subject to direct control by corresponding changes in sensory input.

V. Approach and Withdrawal
Approach and withdrawal are comprised of the combination of orientation and locomotion and are universal features of animal life. Stimuli for approach generally are beneficial to survival and/or reproductive success; stimuli for withdrawal generally are harmful or dangerous.

Stimulation within the lower portion of the intensity range of differential responsiveness is likely to evoke approach whereas that in the higher portion of the intensity range is likely to evoke withdrawal. These tendencies are seen throughout life in organisms at lower levels of behavioral complexity but are increasingly modified by individual developmental experience in organisms at higher levels of behavioral complexity.

VI. Motivation
    A. Motivational variation is practically universal in animal life. It combines persistent tendencies for approach and withdrawal with systematic variation in the strengths of these tendencies—and in the degree of behavioral arousal associated with them—with variations in physiological conditions and other behaviors in progress.
    B. Motivation provides an important basis of reinforcement, or of reward and punishment, as described in treatments of instrumental learning.

VII. Learning and Cognition
Learning ability, or an ability of behavior characteristics to be modified by experience, is an important factor in behavior development across a wide range of species. Observations inviting interpretation in terms of the acquisition and use of information—that is, of cognition—occur increasingly among the more recent vertebrates.

Some Specific Deductions

Numerous deductions may be generated by application of these four postulates and seven corollaries to circumstances supposed to have existed during the development of various species of animal life. The intricacies of evolution and development, combined with an inability to gain precise information about the status of many factor loadings with respect to causal variables, makes precise predictions of evolutionary/developmental outcomes difficult. Often the best we can claim is to have generated deductions in broad outline that, nevertheless, may be limited enough to be judged according to their correspondence with actual facts of observation.

Other than the theory of evolution, the principles presented here may be considered as having been induced from the facts reported earlier in this book. The statements to follow are intended to demonstrate how one may proceed from these principles back to a deduction of the facts from which they were induced as well as to the prediction of similar facts yet to be observed. These deductions are grouped according to the arrangement of the chapters of this book.

1. Biological Bases of Behavior
    a. The basic correspondence of biological and psychological variations is well illustrated by the covariation of neural complexity and behavioral complexity seen across the animal kingdom from the earliest to the most recently evolved species. This covariation is in direct accord with Postulates I, II, and IV. Numerous similar instances of covariation between biological and behavioral events are addressed in later deductions.
    b. Numerous relationships observed to exist between physical size and various behavioral characteristics are described in Chapter 2 as examples of *allometry*. These comparisons illustrate Postulate II.
    c. Variation among individuals of the same species in virtually all physical and behavioral characteristics illustrates Postulate III, part B.
2. Orientation
    a. The close correspondence observed between sensory structure and behavioral responsiveness accords directly with Postulates I and II.
    b. The superb fit of sensory capacities to species ecology illustrates Postulate I and Corollaries II and III.
    c. Observed complexity of modifications of approach/withdrawal orientations with learning experience increases progressively with recency of species origin in direct accord with Postulate IV.
    d. Species-typical approach orientations are widely illustrated in the process of habitat selection across the animal kingdom and accord directly with Postulate I and with Corollaries I, II, and III. A clear prediction may be derived that animals placed and kept outside of the range of preferred habitat of their species must incur losses in rates of survival and reproductive success.
3. Locomotion
    a. The universal presence of locomotor capacity in animal life is deducible from Postulate I in combination with the characteristics of the physical world in which evolution must have occurred.
    b. The widespread use of Newton's Third Law by evolved systems of locomotor behavior across the animal kingdom is deducible from Postulate I, in combination with Corollary V, as are numerous other instances of correspondence between other principles of physics and evolved characteristics of structure and behavior affecting locomotion. Examples include the sleek, smooth-flowing bodily designs of species that move rapidly through either the airstream (birds) or the water stream (fish and marine mammals).
    c. The species-typical nature of locomotor behaviors across the animal kingdom illustrates Postulate I; Postulate III, part A; and Corollary I.
    d. Approach/withdrawal behaviors are virtually universal characteristics of animal life: Corollary V.
    e. Almost universally, objects and events that evoke approach are beneficial while those that evoke withdrawal are harmful: Corollaries II and V.
    f. Maturational development of locomotor behavior in many animal species illustrates Postulate III, part C.

g. The application of the perception-as-action hypothesis stated in Corollary IV is well illustrated by the locomotor control of gannets while diving on prey (Chapter 3). Similar demonstrations of locomotor control by the changing flow of sensory input throughout the progression of frequently repeated locomotor sequences are predictable across the entire range of animal species.

h. The combination of orientation and locomotor behavior yields approach/withdrawal: Corollary V; the addition of variation in arousal with variation in physiological and behavioral conditions yields the basic facts of motivation: Corollary VI.

i. Widespread observation of motivation as an important functional characteristic illustrates Corollary II.

j. The modification of species-typical forms of locomotor behavior through learning, seen only at the higher levels of behavioral complexity, is directly consistent with Postulate IV.

4. Feeding and Foraging

    a. Feeding behavior across the animal kingdom is comprised largely of species-typical behavior: Corollary I. The primary exception to this rule is the feeding behavior of present-day humans, in which cultural effects are a dominant factor: Postulate III, part E.

    b. Feeding behavior is superbly tailored to species and ecological conditions: Corollary II.

    c. Feeding behavior across the animal kingdom illustrates hierarchical progression in complexity with recency of species origin: Postulate IV. An outstanding exception to this rule, however, is seen in the phylum Echinodermata, which is thereby highlighted for study by the present perspective to the end of understanding why this discrepancy should exist.

    d. Maturational development of feeding behavior seen across the animal kingdom illustrates Postulate III, part C.

    e. Motivational variation in feeding behavior, illustrating increased attraction to food with increased food deprivation, is observed on nearly a universal basis: Corollary VI.

    f. An apparent role of learning in the development of feeding behavior in individuals at the more complex levels of behavior accords with Postulate III, part D, and with Corollary VII.

        (1) Specific examples of the role of learning in feeding include development of feeding behavior among octopuses, honeybees, and herons (Chapter 4). Similar examples are predictable in species from the behavioral complexity of octopuses across more complex forms.

        (2) The superb fitness of outstanding learning characteristics seen among corvids and sciurids (Chapter 4) illustrates Postulate I; Postulate IV, part D; and Corollaries II and VII. Similar instances of outstanding ecological fitness of learning characteristics are widely predictable across other species.

g. The role of learning is seen to be of increasing importance with increasing recency of species origin: Postulate III, part D; Postulate IV; Corollary VII.

h. An increasing parental role is seen in the development of feeding behavior of offspring as one moves forward across species at the more complex levels of behavior: Postulate III, parts D and E; Postulate IV; Corollary VII.

i. Cultural effects on feeding behavior are outstanding among northwestern crows, African lions, and gray wolves (Chapter 4): Postulate III, parts D and E; Corollary VII. Such effects also are seen widely among primates and are predictable among numerous other species in which offspring remain with parents in stable social groups during the first year or more of life. Outstanding candidates for the additional demonstration of such effects should be various species of whales and dolphins, as well as African wild dogs.

j. The numerous approximations of optimal foraging demonstrated by proponents of the Optimal Foraging Theory illustrate Postulate I; Postulate IV, part D; and Corollaries II and VII; as does the body of findings on the management of feeding behavior in relation to deprivation and economic conditions described by Collier and his colleagues (Chapter 4).

5. Social Behavior

a. The rule of increasing complexity of behavior with increasing recency of species origin is well illustrated by social behavior: Postulate IV. Social behavior that turns upon past experiences with recognized individuals becomes prominent among the birds and primates; individual influences among the earlier vertebrates and invertebrates are confined to the establishment of stable dominance orders such as those seen among crayfishes and breeding bullfrogs: Postulate III, parts D and E; Postulate IV; Corollary VII.

b. The development of stable dominance relations among individuals of a social group requires the ability of behavior to be modified by learning experience. The occurrence of stable dominance relations illustrates Postulate III, part D, and Corollary VII; the relative absence of such relationships below the level of the earlier vertebrates and their nearly ubiquitous occurrence among the more recent vertebrates illustrate Postulate IV.

c. The widespread occurrence of altruistic behavior within social groups of closely related individuals illustrates a strong genetic influence upon social behavior: Postulate III, part A.

d. The course of social development, particularly among birds and mammals, illustrates the importance of ontogenetic, experiential, and cultural factors in the determination of behavior characteristics: Postulate I; Postulate III, parts C, D, and E; and Corollary VII.

e. The role of learning experiences in the ontogenetic development of birdsong illustrates Postulate III, parts C and D; and Corollary VII.

6. Reproductive Behavior

a. Widespread individual variation in physical and behavioral characteristics provides a primary requirement for the theoretical operation of evolution: Postulate I and Postulate III, part B.

    b. Reproductive behavior is based in species-typical behavior across the animal kingdom: Corollary I.

    c. The pervasiveness and demanding nature of sexual motivation across a broad range of species accords with Corollaries II and VI.

    d. Widespread occurrence of definite breeding seasons assuring birth of offspring at a mild and benevolent season of the year accords with Corollary II.

    e. Parental roles in the development of offspring throughout the maturational period increases dramatically with recency of species origin: Postulate III, parts D and E; Postulate IV; Corollary VII.

7. Predator Defense

    a. The overriding influence of demands for predator defense over all other sources of motivation illustrates Corollary II, as does the hierarchy of defensive reactions widely seen across a broad range of species.

    b. Advantages in predator defense of membership in a social group illustrate advantages of social grouping in relation to Corollary II.

    c. Defensive behaviors are largely species-typical: Corollary I; the importance of learning experience to defensive behavior becomes increasingly obvious among the recent invertebrates and the vertebrates: Postulate III, part D; Postulate IV; Corollary VII.

8. Learning and Cognitive Behavior

    a. Widespread occurrence of learning across the animal kingdom accords with Corollary VII.

    b. Actual demonstrations of gains in fitness resulting from learning (Chapter 9) as well as persuasive interpretations of functionality provided by classic learning theories accord with Corollary II.

    c. The importance of learning in the development of species-typical behaviors across a broad range of species accords with Postulate III, part D, and with Corollaries II and VII.

    d. The increasing importance of learning with increased recency of species origin accords with Postulate IV.

    e. The basic role of motivation in instrumental learning accords with Corollaries V and VI.

    f. The widespread and widely demonstrated role of learning in modifying species-typical behaviors for the production of learned skills (Chapter 9) illustrates Postulate III, part D, and Corollary VII.

    g. Additional demonstrations of the role of learning in the development of species-typical behavior, as well as additional demonstrations of the direct value of learning to promote fitness, are predictable across a broad range of species: Postulate III, part D, and Corollaries II and VII. Demonstrations of the functional value of learning are limited only by our ability to obtain direct measures of increased fitness.

    h. Dramatic increases in the frequency of occasions for the application of cognitive interpretations of behaviors as species increase in recency of origin accords with Postulate IV.

Concluding Statement

That completes our outline of a theory of comparative psychology. We offer it as an early approximation of a comprehensive theory to encompass all aspects of our field. It describes a general psychology focused upon the evolution and development of behavior characteristics across the full range of animal life. It provides a framework within which numerous theories and ideas of more limited and finely drawn focus may be organized in an articulated conception of the entire field. We hope this outline will form the basis of many testable hypotheses across coming years and that it will be useful enough to require numerous corrective adjustments in the future.

GLOSSARY

Accipiters   a group of species of hawks with short, broad wings and long tails that are adept at chasing down other birds on the wing, often while flying through heavy cover in woods or brush; members of this group are largely responsible for use of the name *chicken hawk* by country people and farmers.

Afferent impulse   a neural impulse traveling in an incoming direction from the bodily extremities toward the brain.

Allometry   the statistical comparison of biological and behavioral characteristics, as in describing the relation between an animal's size or weight and its maximum running speed or its normal heart rate.

Altruistic behavior   behavior that benefits another animal at the expense of the behaving individual.

Anagenesis   the idea that there is a directional progression over time in evolution; this directional progression is seen most clearly in the evolutionary appearance of new species out of the base provided by the existence of older, or more anciently established, species.

Anecdotal evidence   in psychology, evidence drawn from casual and uncritical observations without concern for whether the observations have any generality or whether they are repeatable.

Animistic explanation   a type of false or pseudo-explanation in which we endow an animal or other active agent with an unobserved spirit or feelings and then take the spirit or feelings as the causes of its observed actions (for example, that wasp stung me because it was mad; instinct causes birds to fly south before winter).

Anthropomorphism   the practice of ascribing human qualities and abilities to nonhuman animals.

Appetitive response   generally, a response to an appetitive stimulus or approach stimulus; however, the term has specific application to a distinctive behavior pattern that occurs in the feeding behavior of aplysia.

Approach   locomotor movement toward a particular stimulus agent within the environment or, in some instances, actions that lead toward the occurrence of a particular outcome familiar to past experience.

Approach stimulus   a stimulus that elicits approach; an appetitive stimulus, one likely to be effective in the role of positive reinforcer.

Approach/withdrawal theory   the theory of T. C. Schneirla that animals at the lower behavioral levels, throughout the life span, and all animals, during the early portion of the life span, tend to approach stimuli of mild intensity and to withdraw from stimuli of strong intensity.

Arousal   the feature of behavior identified with an animal's level of activation, usually ranging from high activation and excitement to deep sleep.

Asexual reproduction   reproduction accomplished by an organism's duplication of its chromosomes and genes and then division to form two or more "daughter" organisms.

Associative learning   learning that is understood as involving associations of events that have occurred together or in sequence, as do the events in classical conditioning and instrumental conditioning procedures.

Axon   the transmitting end of a neuron that, by the flow of neurotransmitter chemicals, transfers the excitation of a neural impulse across a synapse to the dendrite of another neuron.

Behavior systems   groups of responses that often occur together in the same situations and that vary together as a function of a learning procedure that has been addressed to any member of the group; this concept applies particularly to groups of responses that occur commonly in reaction to a given unconditioned stimulus used in classical conditioning.

Behavioral ecology   a subfield of the biological science of ecology, emphasizing the matching of evolutionary adaptations to complex environmental or ecological systems; behavioral ecology focuses on the evolutionary adaptation of behavior to the complex of ecological conditions within which the evolution of particular species occurred.

Behavior levels   the idea that behavior across the animal series illustrates a succession of levels, within each of which behavior is organized somewhat differently than at other levels and across which behavior varies in complexity.

Behavior potentials   characteristics of behavior that are likely to develop in an individual as a normal representative of its species; *behavioral potential* was a term introduced by the comparative psychologist Kuo as a way of addressing species-typical behavior.

Behaviorism   the perspective on psychology urged by John B. Watson, in the early 1900s, that psychology should confine its study to *observable* behavior alone; Watson's attempt to establish psychology as a *science* based on the study of observable events had a great influence on the development of comparative psychology.

Belong, belongingness   in application to possible associations among stimuli and responses, the elements being associated are said to belong together, or to illustrate belongingness, if they often occurred together or were associated in the world inhabited by early ancestors of the species under study.

Bilateral symmetry   a symmetrical design of the body in which each side of the body is closely similar or identical to the other.

Binary fission   a means of asexual reproduction seen among paramecia.

Biological rhythms   regular patterns of alternating activity and inactivity; these patterns are regulated by both internal conditions and external stimuli.

Biosocial, biosocial level   biosocial organization represents the third behavioral level envisioned by Schneirla and Tobach, in which behavior is differentially influenced by groups of other organisms as social agents; the major behavioral levels include *taxis, biotaxis, biosocial, psychotaxis,* and *psychosocial*.

Biosocial science   by saying that psychology is a *biosocial science*, we mean to distinguish it from being merely a biological science, governed solely by *biological* principles; instead, we view psychology as not only subject to biological law but also influenced by factors at the higher organizational levels of psychological and sociological law.

Biotaxic, biotaxis   biotaxis represents the second level of behavioral organization, in which behavior is differentially influenced by the presence of biological agents outside the body of the behaving individual; across the major behavioral levels envisioned by Schneirla and Tobach, behavior is organized by *taxic, biotaxic, biosocial, psychotaxic,* and *psychosocial influences*.

Bipedalism   walking on two feet as a primary means of locomotion.

Brachiation   locomotor movement by means of swinging from hand to hand beneath a source of support such as a limb; an important locomotor behavior of all species of apes at some portion of the life span and the mainstay of locomotion in gibbons, the lesser apes, throughout the life span.

Breeding congress the gathering together of a number of different males and females in a limited area in association with breeding behavior.

Breeding season a limited portion of the year during which most of the mating behavior of a species occurs.

Breeding territory a territory held during breeding season, the possession of which may enhance breeding opportunities for the territory owner.

Brooding protective behavior addressed to the eggs or young, particularly among birds and fishes.

Bruce effect an interference to the occurrence of pregnancy in a female mouse that has been fertilized by a first male if she is later exposed to the odor of urine from a second male.

Budding an asexual reproductive process demonstrated by hydra, for example, in which new animals form as buds in an area of the parent animal referred to as the budding area.

Buteos a group of species of hawks with long, broad wings and broad tails that are particularly adept at soaring and that do much of their hunting while soaring, so much so that they are often called the soaring hawks (although all hawks are capable of soaring).

Caches supplies of some substance, usually food, that have been hidden away and that may be used at a later time by the animal that made the caches.

Caching food hiding of a supply of food, as in making a food cache.

Capturing behavior a basic component of feeding behavior, whereby an animal captures or takes hold of its food or prey.

Caretaker effect a marked increase in locomotor behavior or locomotor excitement provoked by a stimulus that has signaled past opportunities for feeding.

Caste a distinct class of individuals within a social group; members of a caste display certain characteristics that distinguish them from other members of the social group that are not members of the same caste.

Cell membrane the outer covering of each cell; like the skin of an organism, the cell membrane forms a cell's boundary and separates it from other cells.

Cilia movable, hair-like cells covering the skin surface or outer membrane surface of some animals; the movement of cilia aids in locomotion as well as in moving material along the length of the body and away from the animal.

Circadian activity cycles that are about the duration of a single day.

Circular explanations a form of false or pseudo-explanation in which an event to be explained is given a label, then the label is said to have caused the event (for example, the dog ate because it was hungry, and we know it was hungry because it ate).

Circulatory system the system that supplies the circulation of blood to all parts of the body.

Classical conditioning a model type of learning experience in which, in typical cases, a dominant stimulus event occurs in series with a signal event that precedes it; the learning that often results from this type of experience is demonstrated when the learner responds to the signal event in ways that appear to anticipate occurrence of the dominant stimulus with which it has been associated; in strict classical conditioning procedure, the learner's behavior has no effect either to bring about or to prevent the occurrence of the dominant stimulus in question; the study of classical conditioning was pioneered by Pavlov, and the procedure is often called *Pavlovian* conditioning.

Closed economies   this term is usually applied to an experimental design in which subjects of an experiment must obtain all of their food by the means specified by experimental procedure and are given no food outside of that procedure; closed economies represent attempts to approximate the situation faced by animals in nature.

Cognition   an intervening variable associated with cognitive behavior and thought of as resembling the possession of conscious awareness and the use of information by the behaving animal.

Cognitive behavior   behavior that is well understood by relating it to hypothetical mental, or cognitive, events that may be thought of as involving conscious awareness and active use of information; cognitive behaviors are usually associated with theoretical interpretations conceived as intervening variables.

Cognitive map   an intervening variable that envisions cognitive, mental, or informational representation of the environment as a map, or a representation of the sort of information that is available on a map.

Colonial nesting   the habit of many species of birds, particularly seabirds, of building their nests and rearing their young in close proximity to other nesting pairs of the same species in what are known as nesting colonies.

Communal behavior   actions undertaken together by several members of the same community of animals.

Communication   a behavioral interaction between two animals in which the responses of one animal have a predictable effect on the actions of the other animal.

Comparative psychology   a branch of psychology that studies the evolution and development of animal behavior, taking particular interest in species-typical behavior.

Competence   fitness, capability; competence is demonstrated by actions that contribute to survival and reproductive success.

Competition   two or more animals competing against one another for an attractive or appetitive outcome that may be available to only one of them.

Conditioned response   the name given by Pavlov to the response that an animal learns to make to the conditioned stimulus during the course of conditioning experience, so named because conditioning experience is required to ensure occurrence of this response to the conditioned stimulus.

Conditioned stimulus   the name given by Pavlov to the signal stimulus presented in classical conditioning procedure, so named because the response selected for study by the experimenter can be elicited by the conditioned stimulus only as a result of an animal's conditioning experience.

Conditioned taste aversion   a learned aversion to a formerly neutral taste that results from encountering that taste prior to the onset of a strongly aversive stimulus or condition.

Conjugation   a sexual-like reproduction process in which two protozoans such as paramecia combine their genetic material.

Conspecifics   two or more animals of the same species.

Constraints on learning   actually, constraints on the universal application of general *laws* of learning equally across all species and all stimuli and responses.

Consummatory behavior   a series of responses that culminates in bringing an animal into a state of adjustment.

Contact comfort   Harlow's informal term used to summarize the type of social stimulation a young mammal normally receives from contact with its mother.

Continuum of mind   Romanes's idea—and a cornerstone of comparative psychology—that there is a more or less continuous progression of mental capability and complexity as one looks across the animal series from the simplest animals toward the most complex.

Contrapreparedness   an animal's being unprepared to learn a particular response or associations of particular stimuli or of particular stimuli and responses because of the unique evolutionary history of its species. (See also *belongingness* and *preparedness*.)

Coolidge effect   an enhancement of sexual vigor in a male that results from the presence of a large number of different females as potential mates.

Cooperative, cooperation   two or more animals working together in a way that is likely to produce progress toward the attainment of an attractive or appetitive outcome.

Corvids   members of a group of avian species that includes jays, crows, nutcrackers, and others.

Countersinging   the performance of vocalizations by two or more animals in counterpoint to one another; particularly applied to the behavior of individuals of different groups as each sings from its own territory.

Course reversal   a hypothetical process whereby animals return to a previous location by reversing the compass heading they held on the outward journey from that place; ideally, such hypothetical processes should be given formal statement as intervening variables.

Courtship   the behaviors by which a male and a female locate and accommodate to one another in association with mating and sexual reproduction.

Crespuscular   active during the edges of the day, at twilight and at dawn.

Critical experience   an experience that has been shown to be of critical importance to normal behavior development in a species and without which development will be rendered abnormal in some predictable feature.

Cryptic   difficult to see or discern; an animal possessing cryptic coloration has an increased chance of escaping the notice of a predator.

Cultural set   one of five sets of factors viewed as joint determiners of behavior; the cultural factors may be seen as a particular class of experiential factors; they are experiential influences deriving from an individual's membership in its particular social, or cultural, group.

Culture   basically, a complex of behavior patterns or customs transmitted from one generation to another on the basis of social learning experiences; however, customary usage of the term *culture* has emphasized transmission that involves imitation, teaching, and symbolic knowledge.

Dance language   as proposed by ethologist Karl von Frisch, the predictable movements made by returning foragers among honeybees can be represented as a dance whose movements encode information about the location of the last food source visited by the forager before its return to the hive; these movements are seen as a "language" that communicates food locations to other foragers in the hive.

Dawn solos (of gibbons)   territory-holding males of most gibbon species perform extended sessions of vocal, or singing, behavior very early in the day; each male sings alone from his own territory but often sings in turn with one or more adjoining males singing from their territories nearby.

Defensive burying   the covering up or burying of aversive stimulus objects, particularly in areas that are inhabited or frequently visited by the animal undertaking the burying.

Dendrite   the receiving end of a neuron, sensitive to the flow of neurotransmitter chemicals such as acetylcholine and epinephrine.

Development   in the context of behavior, development refers to a process of emergence and adjustment of behavior patterns that accompanies physical maturation, physical growth, and experience.

Digestive system   the system that processes food into usable forms of energy for distribution through the circulatory system to all parts of the body.

Direction   the aspect of an animal's behavior that is identified with its orientation toward or away from particular stimulus agents within its environment.

Direct orientation   orientation involving heading for a target that affects sensory activity.

Discrimination learning   learning to distinguish between closely similar stimuli, usually on the basis that one of two similar stimuli signals that a particular response will be reinforced while the other stimulus signals that the same response will *not* be reinforced and, indeed, may even be punished.

Discriminations   responding differently to closely similar stimuli; that is, differentiating between these similar stimuli.

Discriminative stimulus   the stimulus in discrimination learning that is associated with reinforcement.

Diurnal   active during times of daylight.

DNA   (deoxyribonucleic acid) the extensive molecules, formed in the shape of a double helix, whose details of the construction comprise the genetic code.

DNA Repair Hypothesis   the idea that recombination of genetic material leads to the repair of replication errors and of damaged DNA.

Dominance   an individual's standing on the issue of "who defers to whom" among the members of a social group; the dominant individual often has first right of access to mates, food items, and other sources of attraction within the common environment of a social group.

Drive   an intervening variable associated with changes in motivation and thought of as resembling a state of behavioral tension resulting from physiological deficits or needs.

Drive reduction   a reduction of drive associated with the satisfaction of a motivational need.

Drive state   a state of behavioral tension induced by a deficit or deprivation of some substance or activity needed to maintain the physical health or well-being of an organism; this concept is closely associated with Hull's treatment of motivation.

Duets (of gibbons)   mated pairs of most species of gibbons perform elaborate and extended sessions of vocal behavior known as singing, in which both males and females have their own predictable and distinctive contributions to the song.

Dynamic systems theory   a theoretical perspective that views its subject matter, such as behavior, for example, as being the product of an interaction of a number of different causal factors; alteration in any one of the causal factors usually present may change the mix sufficiently to produce quite a different outcome from that usually expected.

Effective intensity   an idea associated with Schneirla's approach/withdrawal theory, that the relative intensity of a stimulus must be judged within the context of a species' sensitivity to that type of stimulus and that variations in sensitivity to particular stimuli may have resulted from selective forces in the evolution of each species.

Effectors   the muscles and the glands, the tissues and organs that allow us to behave.

Efferent impulse   a neural impulse traveling in an outgoing direction from the brain toward bodily extremities.

Encephalization   a concentration of the body's neural tissues inside the head; that is, a concentration of neural tissues in a brain.

Encephalization quotient   the ratio of brain weight to body weight used as a rough measure of the relative degree of encephalization illustrated by different species.

Endocrine, or hormonal, system   the system that supplies critical chemicals regulating physiological functioning, growth, and development.

Epigenetic processes, epigenesis   a process envisioned as an interaction of numerous active influences in the determination of behavior; epigenesis stands in opposition to ideas of behavior determination that emphasize genetic causes to the near exclusion of other influential factors.

Estrogen   one of the primary female hormones and a regulating factor of female reproductive cycles.

Estrus   the physiological condition that is distinctly associated with sexual receptivity of females in many species; the term also may be applied to patterns of behavior that may be uniquely associated with this condition.

Ethology   a branch of biology that focuses upon animal behavior.

Evolution   a process of change over time; the process of change envisioned in the theory of evolution is guided by the natural selection of plants and animals whose characteristics enable them to survive and reproduce themselves in a hazardous world, passing on versions of their own genetics to future generations.

Evolutionary psychology   a branch of psychology that focuses upon genetic bases of human social behavior.

Excretory system   the system that collects and removes waste products from the body.

Experiential set   one of the group of five sets of factors viewed as joint determiners of behavior; the experiential factors are influences deriving from an individual's unique history of experience; they include *all* stimulative effects on the organism, throughout its life history.

Explanations, scientific explanations   scientific explanations state the general rule of which the occurrence being explained is an instance; in doing so, they must state a relationship between two separate observable events; only if they do this can they be tested by observation, that is, by science.

Facts   in science, facts are matters of observation—events that are known to us by way of sensory experience.

Falcons   a group of species of hawks with long, pointed wings and swift and graceful flight; most species in the group prey upon other birds in open terrain.

Feeding behavior   the behavior by which an animal gains its food; feeding behavior is species-typical to a large degree in all species except our own; even so, we humans retain the behavioral capabilities to develop hunting-and-gathering skills that were mainstays of feeding behavior in the lives of our distant ancestors.

Figure eight dance   one of the types of dances proposed by von Frisch whereby honeybees communicate the location of food sources; the dance forms an approximation of a figure eight and includes a straight-line run that is repeated numerous times; characteristics of this straight run were thought by von Frisch to communicate specific information about the direction of and distance to a food location.

Fixed-action-pattern   a term that is rapidly becoming obsolete, along with the concept it sought to replace—*instinct*; like instinct, fixed-action-pattern referred to built-in, genetically determined, and fixed behavior patterns common throughout a species; an advantage of this term, as compared to instinct, was that it sought to avoid implication of animistic, internal causes that often seemed associated with the term *instinct*.

Flash expansion   a rapid movement of closely grouped fish outward away from the center of the group; similar movements are seen in many closely grouping animals upon the occasion of a predator attack.

Foot stirring   a behavior pattern employed in the feeding behavior of some herons and egrets wherein the wading bird moves its feet rapidly back and forth across an area of the bottom of a pool; the behavior probably serves to drive small aquatic animals to the surface, and feeding birds often make a succession of rapid captures just after engaging in foot-stirring behavior.

Foraging   behavior that usually serves to obtain or gather some needed substance such as food or water.

Functional importance   importance to survival or to reproductive fitness.

Gait   a particular pattern of locomotor behavior; animals often progress through several different patterns of locomotor behavior, or gaits, as their speed of travel increases.

Gametes   reproductive cells such as sperm and ova, each of which possesses half of the chromosomes and genes of a parent organism; gametes combine to produce an offspring.

Ganglion   a cluster of closely packed neural cells located outside the brain.

Gene pool   the genes represented by all the surviving members of a species, containing all existing gene variations.

Generativity   with respect to language, the capability to generate new words, phrases, and sentences.

Genetic code   the code built in to the details of construction of DNA molecules and considered the physical agent of inheritance.

Genotype   the actual genetic makeup of an individual, regardless of whether the potential represented by that genetic makeup is developed or how it is developed.

Goal-directed behavior   behavior that appears to be organized around the attainment of a particular outcome; the behavior in question must be recognizable independently of its usual outcome, and the outcome must be clearly specified in each case to which the term *goal-directed behavior* is applied.

Goal-object   the stimulus agent identified with the outcome of an instance of goal-directed behavior.

Gonadotropic hormone   a hormone of the pituitary gland that affects reproductive cycles.

Gonads   the ovaries of females and the testes of males.

Gonochorism   the evolution and development of two distinct sexes.

Grammar   rules of language concerning which word forms are used in combination together.

Grasping reflex   reflexive, or elicited, closing of the fingers of the hand in response to tactile stimulation to the palm of the hand, seen normally among newborn primates.

Great-call sequence   the third of three distinctive patterns displayed in territorial singing by mated pairs in most species of gibbons; this pattern typically is repeated many times in alteration with the organizing sequence in each extended session of song performance.

Habitat   a complex of environmental surroundings within which a particular species is usually found.

Habitat imprinting   an experiential effect in which young animals acquire an attraction to or affiliation with features of the environment present during their early development; this term makes allusion to a similar process known as social imprinting or, simply, imprinting.

Hermaphrodite   a single individual that possesses both male and female sexual organs.

Hibernation   a state of profound and prolonged sleep-like inactivity in which there is a general decrease in basic physiological processes such as heart rate and breathing rate.

Home base   a location where an animal spends much of its time and to which it returns repeatedly after forays or journeys into the surrounding environment; specific to the hunter–gatherer society of early humans, the home base was a place where very young, very old, and ill or indisposed members of the social group could remain protected while other members of the group went out on hunting-and-gathering ventures.

Home range   an area or location within which an individual remains and lives for an extended period of time.

Homeostasis   the idea that the physiological conditions characteristic of normal life within each species will be maintained within specifiable limits of variation; imbalances in these conditions usually induce reactions that tend to reestablish the normal balance; more specifically, in physiology, the ability of warm-blooded animals (homoiotherms) to regulate their internal environments such that bodily functions are maintained at acceptable limits.

Homing   the locomotor movement of an animal back to its home area from some distance away.

Homo erectus   the species considered the direct ancestor of our own, *Homo sapiens*.

Homoiotherms   warm-blooded animals.

Hominids   human-like animals; perhaps direct ancestors of the human species.

Honeybee dancing   a predictable pattern of behavior performed by a forager upon its arrival back at the hive and proposed, by von Frisch, to communicate information about the location of a food source just visited by the dancing bee.

Hunt from a watching post   one of two basic styles of hunting employed by most species of hawks—to remain at a perch while keeping alert to the appearance of their prey; the other basic style of hunting is to hunt while soaring.

Hunt while soaring   one of two basic styles of hunting employed by most species of hawks—to hunt on the wing; the other basic style of hunting is to hunt from a watching post.

Hunting and gathering   the descriptive name applied to basic foraging behaviors that appear to have been important in early human society from the time of *Homo erectus*; hunting for meat and gathering of vegetable foods.

Hypotheses   hypotheses represent an early stage in the achievement of theoretical explanation; they are reasonable interpretations of observable events, but interpretations that have not yet been tested by application to a very large set of observations; hence, as interpretations that have not been widely tested, they are interpretations about which we must remain somewhat skeptical.

Hypothetical interpretations a *reasonable* interpretation of a given set of observable events; the correctness and value of the hypothetical interpretation are judged by its agreement with the observed facts to which it is addressed and the degree of its simplicity as compared to competing interpretations of the same events.

Imprinting rapid attachment to social stimuli encountered early in the life span, particularly by birds.

Indirect orientation a hypothetical process whereby animals orient themselves with respect to places or locations that are outside their current range of sensory reception; ideally, such hypothetical process should be given formal statement as intervening variables.

Individual set one of the group of five sets of factors viewed as joint determiners of behavior; the individual factors are the influences proceeding from the particular version of its species' genetic endowment that a particular individual happens to receive.

Information we may say that the substance of information consists in the relationships that exist among particular objects and events. Information can be considered scientifically by inspecting relationships that hold true among *observable* objects and events. Responding on the basis of such relationships may be described as responding to information.

Infradian activity cycles that are of longer duration than a day.

Instinct a term now largely outdated in psychology, instinct referred to built-in, innate, and fixed behavior patterns that were common throughout an entire species; old usages of the term often appeared to refer to unobserved and vaguely animistic internal causes of such fixed behavior.

Instrumental conditioning (operant conditioning) a model type of learning experience in which a particular response by the learner controls the occurrence of an appetitive or an aversive stimulus (often known as positive and negative reinforcers); learning is demonstrated when the rate of the response in question is adjusted according to the consequences that the response has; the control of an important stimulus event by the learner's behavior in instrumental conditioning is in direct contrast to the situation presented by classical conditioning procedure, in which the learner's behavior has no such effects.

Integrative levels the idea that the universe is well viewed as a progression of increasingly higher, or more complex, levels of organization; laws operating at higher levels may be different from—but not contradictory to—laws operating at a lower level.

Integumental system (skin) the tissues covering the external surface of the body, providing a boundary between the body and the environment and functioning to protect the organism from infection.

Internal fertilization fertilization of an ovum by a sperm taking place within the body of the female.

Intervening variables a form of theoretical statement in which it is supposed that an unobserved hypothetical process intervenes between observed causes and their observed effects *as though* the observed causes influence the intervening process that, in its turn, produces the observed effects; to remain within the realm of scientific interpretation, the intervening variable must be firmly tied to observed causes and observed effects in all cases.

Introductory sequence the first of three distinctive patterns displayed in territorial singing by mated pairs in most species of gibbons; this pattern typically occurs only at the beginning of an extended session, or bout, of song performance by the pair.

***K* reproductive strategy**   the reproductive strategy that stresses the provision of high survival rates among a small number of offspring over the production of a great number of offspring.

Kin selection   the reproduction of an individual's genes by way of the selection of one of its relatives, who possesses some genes in common with the individual in question.

Lactation   the production of milk by a female mammal.

Language   a system of communication based in the use of symbols according to rules of grammar and syntax and displaying the capability to generate new words and phrases.

Law of Effect   the principle introduced by Thorndike to deal with the basic facts of what is now known as instrumental conditioning; in today's terminology, that the occurrence of reinforcement strengthens the preceding response (or S–R connection) whereas the occurrence of punishment weakens the preceding response (or S–R connection).

Laws   laws are statements that summarize and interpret a large number of observations; they are statements that have been verified many times in their application to observed facts and, therefore, are interpretations in which we have a higher degree of confidence than we have in hypotheses.

Learning   a process by which behavior changes according to the individual experience of the learner. Learning is defined by lasting changes in behavior such as those seen in conditioning.

Learning to learn   when animals are given repeated training with the same type of learning problem, they often require progressively less training to achieve proficiency as they acquire more experience in dealing with that type of problem. This increase in learning proficiency is called learning to learn.

Lek   a well-defined area within which a number of male birds maintain individual breeding territories.

Linear   in respect to dominance orders, a dominance order is said to be *linear* when members of the order can be ranked in dominance such that no exceptions in ranking occur; that is, if an individual ranks fourth, for example, it dominates every individual of a lower rank and submits to every individual of a higher rank, without exceptions. In dominance ranking, number one is the highest, most dominant rank, number two is the second most dominant, and so on.

Locomotion, locomotor behavior   behavior that moves or propels animals from one location to another within the environment.

Marginal Value Theorem   an early proposition of optimal foraging theory, that in an environment containing food patches of varying richness, there is an optimal time for an animal to leave one food patch and go in search of another; that time is when the success rate in the patch being foraged falls to the success rate that holds for the environment as a whole.

Matching   when responses to two different stimuli have different probabilities of being reinforced, matching is illustrated if the numbers of responses to each of the stimuli are roughly proportional to the probabilities of reinforcement associated with the two stimuli.

Maternal behavior   the parental behavior of a female.

Mating   the sexual union of two organisms, usually a male and a female, often resulting in the production of offspring.

Maximizing   when responses to two different stimuli have different probabilities of being reinforced, maximizing is illustrated if nearly all responses are made to the stimulus associated with the higher probability of reinforcement; animals behaving in this way will maximize the number of reinforcements they receive.

Method of successive approximations same as *shaping*, a technique of instrumental or operant conditioning in which the attainment of reinforcement is progressively made dependent on the performance of successively closer approximations of some highly defined response that may never have occurred without the use of this technique. The same sort of shaping can occur when reinforcement is differentially dependent upon more "skillful" and effective forms of response in the natural environment.

Migration movement of animals over distances much greater than those traveled on a frequent or daily basis within the home environment, particularly seasonal movements that may recur several times in the life of a single individual.

Mimicry in respect to defensive behavior, the possession of characteristics that resemble those of another species in whom the characteristics are associated with strong sources of predatory defense that are *not* possessed by the mimicking species.

Mobbing the harassing attack of members of a prey species, often in large numbers, against a potential predator, seen particularly among avian species.

Modal most frequently occurring, as in the most frequently occurring form of a response.

Modern Synthesis the synthesis of the ideas of *natural selection* and *genetics* to form the modern theory of evolution.

Modifiable changeable or adjustable, particularly as a result of experience.

Monestrous the physiological condition in which estrous behavior occurs only once during an animal's breeding season. This is typical of bears and dogs, for example.

Monogamous a mating system in which a single male and a single female mate exclusively with each other.

Monogamy a restriction of mating behavior of a single male and a single female such that they mate only with each other.

Morgan's canon a rule instituted by early comparative psychologist Lloyd Morgan that explanations should be based on the lowest degree of mental activity sufficient to account for the behavior observed; that is, it is improper to presume the presence of a high degree of mental functioning to explain instances of behavior that can be accounted for by simpler processes.

Motivation the attractions and aversions that typify a species or an individual; closely associated with the arousal level and the directional orientation of behavior.

Motivational having to do with motivation; that is, having to do with attractions and aversions, with approach behavior and withdrawal behavior, with reinforcement and punishment.

Motivational variation a variation in motivation, that is to say, in arousal, in the attractive value of an approach stimulus, or in the aversive value of a withdrawal stimulus.

Muscular system the primary system enabling an organism's movement and action.

Myelin a sheath of material covering the axons of many neurons, serving to increase the speed of transmission of neural impulses down the length of the axons.

Natural selection the differential representation of certain genetic variations across succeeding generations of plants and animals based on the differential reproductive success of individuals possessing those genetic variations; one requirement for reproductive success, of course, is survival to the age of reproductive maturity.

Navigation, true navigation a hypothetical process of complex orientation that envisions animals using a cognitive map of large portions of the environment and following compass courses in moving from one place to another within the area of the map; ideally, such hypothetical processes should be given formal statement as intervening variables.

Need reduction (also, **drive reduction**)   the reduction or satisfaction of a physical need and of the state of behavioral tension that accompanies such need, according to the treatment of motivation provided by psychologist Clark Hull.

Negative punishment   a procedure of instrumental conditioning in which the learner's response causes removal or loss of an appetitive stimulus, with the usual effect of weakening (decreasing the occurrence of) the response in question.

Negative reinforcement   a procedure of instrumental conditioning in which the learner's response serves to terminate or remove an aversive stimulus, with the usual effect of strengthening (increasing the occurrence of) the response in question.

Negative reinforcer   an aversive stimulus; a stimulus whose termination or removal following a particular response serves to increase the frequency of occurrence of that response.

Nematocysts   cells containing the barbed filaments that are the "weapons," or nettles, of members of the phylum *Cnidaria*, the nettle bearers.

Nervous system   the system that receives sensory input and integrates it with motor output.

Neural impulse   a wave of chemical/electrical action that travels along the cell membrane of a neuron from the dendrite to the axon and is transmitted by the release of chemicals across the synapse from the axon of one neuron to the dendrite of another neuron.

Neuroanatomical plasticity   the ability of the circuitry of the brain to change over the lifetime of an animal as a result of its experience.

Neurons   individual cells of the nervous system.

Neurotransmitters   the chemical agents that carry neural messages across the synapse between one neuron and the next.

Newton's Third Law   a basic law of physics—that for every action there is an equal and opposite reaction; this law established an important condition of the environment in respect to the evolution of locomotor behavior in various species.

Nocturnal   active during times of darkness.

Nurturance (Nurture)   these terms refer to environmental influences that impinge on an individual throughout its history.

Observation   one of the basic sources by which we human beings may obtain knowledge about the world and ourselves; other such sources recognized by early philosophers were reason and intuition; observation was chosen by science as its primary source of knowledge and its final arbiter of truth; observation relies on information deriving directly from sensory experiences such as seeing and hearing—information that is open to normal members of the public and can be attended to by several people at the same time, thus, *public* observation.

Ontogenetic set   one of the group of five sets of factors viewed as joint determiners of behavior; the ontogenetic factors are those deriving from an individual's age and its maturational status at its particular position in the life span normal to its species.

Optimal foraging theory   a theoretical perspective proceeding from the proposition that evolution should have made animals into approximations of ideal foragers; thus, if we can calculate how an ideal forager must behave under particular sets of conditions, we can generate many testable predictions as to how real animals should behave.

Organizing sequence   the second of three distinctive patterns displayed in territorial singing by mated pairs in most species of gibbons; this pattern typically is repeated many times in alteration with the great-call sequence during each session of song performance.

Orgasm   the occurrence of sexual climax in copulation, associated in males with the release of sperm.

Orientation   the directional focus of an animal's behavior on particular stimulus agents in its environment.

Osculum   the passageway to the interior of the body located at the tip of a sponge's ray or rays; opening and closing of this passageway coordinates the overall activity of the sponge.

Ova, eggs   the gametes, or reproductive cells, of females.

Ovaries   the female reproductive organs responsible for the production of ova and certain female hormones.

Pair bond   a lasting social bond of mutual attraction between mated individuals.

Parental behavior   behavior of a parent toward its offspring or in relation to its offspring.

Parsimony   the quality of simplicity by which theoretical explanations are judged; one of the principal functions of a theoretical explanation is to summarize its subject matter, and the explanation that accomplishes this job by use of the least number of separate principles or laws is judged the simplest and the best.

Parturition   the process of giving birth.

Path integration   a hypothetical process whereby animals appear to combine outward-bound experiences to achieve a more direct return to a place than that offered by the path followed in the outward journey; ideally, such hypothetical processes should be given formal statement as intervening variables.

Peacemaking   a term applied to certain recognizable behaviors that appear to function in resolving conflicts between individuals within a social group.

Pecking order   a term used to describe dominance order among chickens, referring to the issue of "who gets to peck whom" among the members of a flock; this term sometimes is used in a general way to refer to dominance orders among other animals besides chickens.

Perception and action   the theoretical perspective that perception consists of an animal's responses to information that is directly available within the environment it encounters.

Persistence until   a phrase used by psychologist E. C. Tolman to indicate a defining quality of *goal-directed* behavior—that such behavior may be expected to continue in progress until it achieves a predictable outcome.

Phenotype   the actual characteristics developed in the interaction of an individual's genetic makeup and the environment in which the individual develops.

Pheromone   a hormone released by one organism that functions as a source of sexual attraction to conspecifics of the opposite sex, or gender.

Phylogenetic set   one of the group of five sets of factors viewed as joint determiners of behavior, the phylogenetic factors are the genetic influences commonly encountered by nearly all members of an individual's species.

Pilotage   a hypothetical process whereby animals appear to orient, in turn, on a succession of different landmarks in returning to a given location; ideally, such hypothetical processes should be given formal statement as intervening variables.

Polyandry   a polygamous system in which a single female mates with a number of different males.

Polyestrous   the physiological condition in which estrous behavior occurs repeatedly throughout the year rather than in a specific breeding season. This is typical of mice, rats, and most primates, for example.

Polygamy   a mating system in which a single individual mates with a number of other individuals.

Polygyny   a polygamous system in which a single male mates with a number of different females.

Positive punishment   a procedure of instrumental conditioning in which the learner's response causes presentation of an aversive stimulus, with the usual effect of weakening (decreasing the occurrence of) the response in question.

Positive reinforcement   a procedure of instrumental conditioning in which the learner's response causes presentation of an appetitive stimulus, with the usual effect of strengthening (increasing the occurrence of) the response in question.

Positive reinforcer   an appetitive stimulus; a stimulus whose presentation following a particular response serves to increase the frequency of performance of that response.

Precocial   displaying certain adult-like capabilities at a very early point in the life span.

Precultural, preculture   actually, a primitive form of culture in which the transmission of customs is based primarily in biological processes and straightforward and simple learning experiences.

Predator   an animal that obtains its food by killing and eating other animals; an animal that preys upon others.

Predatory behavior   the behavior whereby one animals preys upon another, as in killing and eating it.

Preparedness   an animal's being prepared to learn a particular response or associations of particular stimuli or of particular stimuli and responses because of the unique evolutionary history of its species.

Prey   an animal that is subject to being killed and eaten by another animal.

Primary defenses   permanent physical features, present at all times, that are considered to function in defending an animal against predation.

Probability learning   learning to respond at different rates to stimuli associated with different probabilities of reinforcement, that is, different probabilities that a response will be reinforced. (See also *maximizing* and *matching*.)

Progesterone   a female hormone and a regulating factor of female reproductive cycles.

Prolactin   a hormone of the pituitary gland associated with milk production in female mammals.

Promiscuity   the situation in which mating behavior is relatively unrestricted with respect to which individuals mate with which other individuals.

Prosimian   primates whose origins preceded the appearance of modern monkeys.

Proto-culture   a midlevel of cultural complexity in which the transmission of customs is based importantly on imitation and simple examples of what might be called teaching.

Proto-language   language-like behavior such as seen among certain chimpanzees and bonobos that is far less extensive and complex than the language behavior of humans.

Proximal cause   an influence coming from the immediate internal condition or external environment of an animal.

Proximal mechanism   a system of cause–effect relationships guiding an animal's behavior during a particular time frame.

Pseudo-explanation   in science, explanations that name only one observable event rather than stating a relationship between at least two observable events are considered as false or pseudo-explanations.

Pseudopod   the leading portion of an amoeba's body in locomotion; it often forms a rather narrow, extended pouch that can be likened to a "false foot," or pseudopod.

Psychosocial   psychosocial organization represents the fifth behavioral level envisioned by Schneirla and Tobach, in which behavior is influenced by individual social agents according to past experiences of the behaving individual with those particular social agents; the major behavioral levels are *taxis, biotaxis, biosocial, psychotaxis,* and *psychosocial.*

Psychosocial I   the first and lowest level of psychosocial functioning, absent communication systems that approach the use of language.

Psychosocial II   the midlevel of psychosocial functioning, displaying language-like communication as seen in specially trained chimpanzees and bonobos.

Psychosocial III   the highest level of psychosocial functioning, displaying the full development of language as seen in human adults.

Psychotaxic, psychotaxis   psychotaxis represents the fourth level of behavioral organization envisioned by Schneirla and Tobach, in which behavior is influenced by stimulus agents according to the past experiences of the behaving individual with those stimulus agents; the major behavioral levels are *taxis, biotaxis, biosocial, psychotaxis,* and *psychosocial.*

Punished, punishment   the occurrence of an aversive outcome as the result of a response. (See also *positive punishment* and *negative punishment.*)

***r* reproductive strategy**   the reproductive strategy that stresses the production of a great number of offspring over the provision of high survival rates among a small number of offspring.

Radial maze   a maze consisting of a central starting area from which numerous narrow pathways (usually eight of them) lead outward from the center as radials of a circle; these mazes are often used to test animals' foraging efficiency.

Radial symmetry   an organization of the body in which cross sections of the body display structures that are symmetrically arranged on all sides.

Reactivity   the relative degree to which an animal is responsive to stimulation from one time or one condition to another.

Receptivity   in sexual behavior, usually the state of responsiveness in which a female will accept courtship from a male that may lead to mating.

Receptors, sensory receptors   neural cells that receive and transmit information about immediate conditions around them by means of their sensitivity to particular sources of energy from the environment.

Reductionistic thinking, reductionism   in psychology, an approach to the study of behavior that seeks to view behavior as a straightforward function of biological causes or factors; that is, an attempt to *reduce* psychology to a matter of biology.

Reinforced   to have received reinforcement; in *positive* reinforcement an individual's actions result in its attainment of an appetitive stimulus; in *negative* reinforcement an individual's actions result in its avoidance of or escape from an aversive stimulus; in either case of reinforcement, the reinforced behavior is likely to be increased in its future frequency of occurrence.

Reinforcers   in Skinner's definition, stimuli that can be manipulated to strengthen a preceding response, through either onset of the stimulus (positive reinforcement) or offset of the stimulus (negative reinforcement).

Reproductive system   the system that manufactures and delivers or receives the physiological elements that provide for continuation of the species beyond the life span of the individual organism.

Respiratory system   the system that absorbs oxygen from the environment and removes carbon dioxide from the body.

Reversal learning (discrimination reversal)   learning to adjust quickly to reversals in a discrimination task in which the stimulus formerly associated with reinforcement of a response and the stimulus formerly associated with nonreinforcement of the response are reversed in their roles.

Rewarded, reward, reinforcement   the occurrence of an appetitive outcome as the result of a response. (See also *positive reinforcement* and *negative reinforcement.*)

Rooting reflex   reflexive movements of the head in response to tactile stimulation to the face and lips in newborn primates; these movements tend to bring the young primate's mouth into contact with the stimulus-object being applied.

Route-based orientation   a hypothetical process whereby animals return to a place on the basis of stimuli laid down themselves, or on the basis of learning experiences along the route of their outward journey from that place; ideally, such hypothetical processes should be given formal statement as intervening variables.

School (of fish)   a large group of fish that displays closely coordinated locomotor movement among the individuals comprising the group.

Search image   a hypothetical process applied to the observation that certain "preferred" types of prey are taken at a greater proportion than would be expected on the basis of their relative presence within the overall population of potential prey within a given environment.

Seasonally polyestrous   the physiological condition in which estrous behavior occurs repeatedly in a specific breeding season. This is typical of horses, sheep, and goats, for example.

Secondary defenses   behavioral reactions that come into play only when an animal encounters a predator attack or other aversive stimulation.

Sensitive periods   limited time in the life span during which a particular critical experience will have its greatest effects on development.

Sensorimotor stage (of song learning)   a period of time in the development of young birds during which the critical experiences necessary for normal song learning involve both the reception of stimulation and the practice of certain movements or behaviors.

Sensory stage (of song learning)   a period of time in the development of young birds during which the critical experiences necessary for normal song learning are limited to the reception of stimulation from the environment.

Sexual dimorphism   the possession of widely different bodily characteristics by the males and females of a species, particularly in regard to the relative size of males and females.

Sexual imprinting   the long-term determination of sexual orientation upon stimuli encountered in early social experience.

Sexual learning   the modification of sexual behavior on the basis of learning experiences.

Sexual reproduction   reproduction that is accomplished by the combining of chromosomes and genes from two different organisms.

Sexual selection   the evolutionary selection of characteristics that have functioned to enhance reproductive fitness by benefiting success in courtship and/or breeding.

Shaping   (See *method of successive approximations.*)

Sheltering   selection or creation of a protected location in which to sleep or rest.

Shoal   a general term that refers to any large group of fish and that may be applied across a wide range of behaviors by members of the group.

Sign tracking   an animal's learning to approach a particular stimulus merely on the basis of its having been presented as a signal for the presentation of food or some other strongly appetitive stimulus.

Silent ovulation   an occurrence of ovulation that is not heralded by any obvious physiological or behavioral signals.

Skeletal system   an organism's internal system of structural support.

Sleep   a state of relative inactivity and decreased responsiveness to stimulation that recurs on a regular basis.

Social   having to do with groups of animals; that is, relations or interactions involving two or more individuals.

Social grooming   grooming refers to behavior that adjusts or cleans an animal's skin, hair, or feathers; in social grooming, one animal grooms the body of another member of its social group.

Social predators   predators that hunt together as a social group; good examples are wolves, African lions, and killer whales.

Sociobiology   a branch of biology that focuses upon genetic bases of social behavior.

Song learning (of birds)   the interactive process of experience and development by which songs are acquired in many species of birds.

Species-specific defensive reactions   a group of species-typical behaviors that occur in reaction to predator attack and other sources of strong aversive stimulation throughout an entire species.

Species-typical behavior   behavior that is characteristic of an entire species and that develops at a predictable time in the life span in nearly all members of a species.

Sperm   the gametes, or reproductive cells, of males.

Spontaneous ovulation   ovulation during the estrous cycle that is not dependent upon the occurrence of any particular behavior, such as copulation.

Stand and wait   one of two basic styles of feeding behavior employed by nearly all species of herons, egrets, and bitterns, in which an individual stands still within the habitat of its prey while remaining alert to feeding opportunities; the other basic style of feeding behavior is called *walk slowly.*

Status   status refers to an individual's social standing within its group; individuals of high status usually are dominant over individuals of lower status.

Step reflex   the rays of an echinoderm, such as a starfish, are served on their undersides by numerous muscular appendages called tube feet; a step reflex is a single cycle of movement in which a tube foot reaches outward, toward a source of stimulation, then back toward the center of the ray; step reflexes are important in locomotion and in the capture and ingestion of prey.

Stimulus gradients   the distribution within the environment of graded intensities of a particular stimulus such that an animal's locomotor movement may result in its encountering progressively stronger intensities of that stimulus, if approaching it, or progressively weaker intensities of the stimulus, if withdrawing from it.

Submissive, submission   to defer to another in respect to dominance.

Synapses   a space between two neurons, across which neural impulses are transmitted by the flow of neurotransmitter chemicals such as acetylcholine and epinephrine.

Syntax   rules of language concerning the pattern in which different word forms are arranged to form sentences.

Taxic, taxis   taxis represents the first level of behavioral organization, in which behavior is controlled by the direct action of stimulus agents without behavioral distinction between biologic and nonbiologic agents and without influence of past experience with the stimulus; the major behavioral levels envisioned by Schneirla and Tobach are *taxis, biotaxis, biosocial, psychotaxis,* and *psychosocial.*

Teleological explanation   often called explanation by purpose, a type of false or pseudo-explanation in which the outcome of a series of events is taken as the cause of the series (for example, we developed large ears and noses in order to support eyeglasses).

Territories, territory   an area that is defended against intrusion by other members of one's own species, particularly others of the same sex as the defender.

Testes   the male reproductive organs responsible for the production of sperm and certain male hormones.

Theories   a theory is a set of statements that, taken together, accounts for all observed facts within a given area of study or within the scope of the theory; theories essentially are statements of the laws that apply within an area and of the relationships that hold among those laws; a theory remains accountable for all of the facts that fall within its proper scope of application, both now and in the future, and remains open to competition from alternative theories that may provide a better account of the same facts.

Tonic immobility   a state of profound unresponsiveness to stimulation that may function as an emergency defensive reaction, as in death feigning.

Tool use   using an object from the environment to enable the performance of goal-directed behavior.

Topography (of a response)   the overall form and appearance of a response; the overall detail of movements that comprise a response.

Torpor   a state of profound inactivity and decreased physiological functioning similar to hibernation, but often not as long-lasting as usual episodes of hibernation.

Transfer Index   a measure of complex learning in which original rates of learning are compared to rates of learning new, reversed sets of discrimination problems.

Ultimate cause   in evolutionary theory, characteristics that convey reproductive fitness are naturally selected to continue in future generations of a species; this process is regarded as the ultimate cause of species characteristics.

Ultradian   activity cycles that are of shorter duration than a day.

Unconditioned response   the name given by Pavlov to the response elicited by an unconditioned stimulus, so named because the response could be elicited without prior benefit of conditioning experience.

Unconditioned stimulus   the name given by Pavlov to the dominant stimulus presented in classical conditioning procedure, so named because an animal required no conditioning experience to respond to this stimulus with the response selected for study by the experimenter (for example, salivation).

Ur-culture   an advanced form of culture in which the transmission of knowledge is based importantly upon the use of communicative symbols such as picture drawings or words.

Walk slowly   one of two basic styles of feeding behavior used by nearly all species of herons, egrets, and bitterns, in which an individual stalks slowly through the environment of its prey while remaining alert to feeding opportunities; the other basic style of feeding behavior is called *stand and wait*.

Withdrawal   locomotor movement away from a particular stimulus agent in the environment.

Withdrawal stimulus   a stimulus that elicits withdrawal, or movement away from the stimulus; an aversive stimulus, one likely to be effective in the role of negative reinforcer.

Zeitgebers   external influences of biological rhythms, from the German construction meaning "time givers."

Zig-zag display   a pattern of courtship behavior seen in male sticklebacks.

NAME INDEX

SUBJECT INDEX

Credits

Page 11, From the personal collection of Gilbert Gottlieb; pp. 8, 54, 202, Copyright © 1998 From *Comparative Psychology: A Handbook* by Gary Greenberg and Maury Haraway. Reproduced by permission of Taylor and Francis, Inc./Routledge, Inc., http://www.routledge-ny.com; p. 40, From *The Conscious Brain* by Steven Rose. Copyright © 1973 by Steven Rose. Reprinted by permission of Alfred A Knopf, a Division of Random House Inc; p. 43, © 1979 by Patricia J. Wynne; p. 49, Reprinted with permission of Allyn and Bacon; pp. 69 (bottom), 108, 128, © 1998 by Mark C. Reed; p. 68 (bottom), © Jennifer Mather; p. 68, © Sumio Harada; p. 69 (top), Michael Nichols/NGS Image Collection; p. 71, From *The Gannet*, by Bryan Nelson (1978); p. 73, Illustration from *A Field Guide to the Birds of Eastern and Central North America* by Roger Tory Peterson. Copyright © 1980 by Roger Tory Peterson. Reprinted by permission of Houghton Mifflin Company. All rights reserved; p. 95, Roy L. Caldwell, University of California, Berkeley; p. 102, © Konrad Wothe/Minden Pictures; p. 103, Robert Sisson/NGS Image Collection; p. 107, © Monty Sloan/Wolf Park; pp. 109, 133, Courtesy of George B. Schaller; pp. 122, 131, © Frans Lanting/Minden Pictures; p. 134, Robert Hynes © Cartographic Division, National Geographic; p. 149, Museum of Zoology, University of Michigan; p. 150, © David Crews; p. 153, © Jim Brandenburg/Minden Pictures; p. 160, © Mitsuaki Iwago/Minden Pictures; p. 172, Photo by Gary L. Nuechterlein; p. 174, Courtesy of Gordon Bermant; p. 180 (top), © Discovery Images/Jeff Foott; p. 180 (bottom), © Deb Henson/Lucid Images; p. 184, Natalie Fobes/NGS Image Collection; p. 187, © Tim Fitzharris/Minden Pictures; p. 202, Fanselow, M. S., & De Oca, B. M. (1998). Defensive Behaviors. In G. Greenberg and M. Haraway (Eds.), *Comparative Psychology: A Handbook*. New York: Garland Publishers. pp. 653–665; p. 224, Copyright © 1996 by the American Psychological Association. Reprinted with permission; p. 225, From Sheffield, F. D., & Campbell, B. A. (1954). The role of experience in the "spontaneous" activity of hungry rats. *Journal of Comparative and Physiological Psychology, 47,* 97–100; p. 226, Devenport, L. C., & Devenport, J. A. (1994). Time dependent averaging of foraging information in least chipmunks and golden-mantled ground squirrels. *Animal Behaviour, 47,* 787–802; p. 234, Garcia, J., & Koelling, R. A. (1966). Relation of cue consequence in avoidance learning. *Psychonomic Science, 4,* 123–124; p. 235, Copyright © 1975 by the American Pscychological Association. Reprinted with permission; pp. 239, 245, Interactive singing of a male Mueller's gibbon with a simulated neighbor, by M. M. Haraway and E. G. Maples, *Zoo Biology,* Copyright © 1988 Wiley–Liss, Inc. Reprinted by permission of Wiley–Liss, Inc, a Subsidiary of John Wiley & Sons, Inc; p. 243, Hailman, J. P. (1967). The ontogeny of an instinct. *Behaviour Supplements, 15,* 1–159 Fig. 32, p. 89; Fig. 43, p. 11; Fig. 44, p. 111, Brill Academic Publishers, Leiden/ Boston/Köln; p. 259, Reprinted from *Applied Animal Behaviour Science, 57,* Piggins, D., & Phillips, C. Awareness in domesticated animals—concepts and definitions, pp. 181–200, Copyright © (1998), with permission from Elsevier Science; p. 263, James Amos/NGS Image Collection; p. 267, © Duane Rumbaugh/Photographer Frank Kieman.